MEMOIRS O

WILLIAM GERHARDIE

MEMOIRS OF A POLYGLOT

WILLIAM GERHARDIE

Robin Clark
London

First published in paperback in 1990 by Robin Clark Ltd
A member of the Namara Group
27/29 Goodge Street, London W1P 1FD
First published in 1931 by Duckworth
Copyright © the Estate of William Gerhardie

British Library Cataloguing in Publication Data
Gerhardie, William 1895–1977
Memoirs of a polyglot.
I. Title
823'.912

ISBN 0-86072-111-6

Printed and bound in Great Britain by
BPCC Hazell Books
Aylesbury, Bucks, England
Member of BPCC Ltd.

CONTENTS

CHAPTER FIVE
FOR KING AND COUNTRY

CHAPTER SIX
WITH THE DIPLOMATISTS

CHAPTER SEVEN
ROUND THE WORLD ON A MISSION

PART III
LIFE: A VOCATION

CHAPTER EIGHT
OXFORD

CHAPTER NINE
THE CAREER OF LITERATURE

CHAPTER TEN
FATHER'S DEATH

PART IV
THE VISIBLE WORLD EXISTS?
CHAPTER ELEVEN
LONDON

CHAPTER TWELVE
THE COTTAGE AT TOULON

CHAPTER THIRTEEN
THE ARTIST AND THE WORLD

PART V
EAST AND WEST

CHAPTER FOURTEEN
THE ADVENTURE OF FAUST

CHAPTER FIFTEEN
HOW TO LECTURE IN AMERICA

PUBLISHER'S NOTE
In 1967 William Gerhardie changed the spelling of his surname, adding the final *e*. The present edition of *Memoirs of a Polyglot* is a reprint of the 1931 edition in which the author spelt his name without the extra *e* (Gerhardi).

THE AUTHOR'S SPEECH

READERS,—My relations with the Sitwells continue to be friendly. H. G. Wells approves of me unreservedly; Bernard Shaw in essentials. The attitude of the critics to me has been christian. No new work of mine has escaped commentary; always—"A new book by Mr. Gerhardi." Never a wrong word. True, I have not as yet, as the phrase is, "touched the imagination of the masses of the people" by distinguishing myself in a Test Match. An autobiography at thirty-five is not encouraged? Yet the idea that I should consecrate a book to my life came from a publisher. And the suggestion is irresistible even from a layman. Only think of it : your own, your very own life !

In a man of my years is it unseemly haste ? When Darwin postulated the survival of the fittest, he did not allow for street accidents. This taking of another man's longevity for granted I find insensitive. When I returned from India, spending a week in England before I again sailed for the United States, "Come," said a friend, "and lunch with me one day next week and tell me about India, or better still, lunch with me when you return from the United States, and you can tell me of your Indian and American experiences at once."

"Or if you would rather postpone the lunch," I said, "to include my experiences Beyond the Veil, you have but to wait till you read my obituary notice."

Nobody who appears here need resent it, since his appearance, I cannot make it too plain, is a guarantee of my approval, of my opinion that he or she must be preserved—rendered time-proof ; and so far from blaming me, they who walk these pages should rejoice at finding here an immortality not perhaps vouchsafed elsewhere.

Then there is yourself. You may speak of yourself without interruption—an indulgence which would be considered ill-bred anywhere else but in an autobiography. You have two things—yourself, on the one hand ; the universe, on the other. You have to ascertain, with scientific precision, what exactly the universe is to you ; and you have to suggest, with the retiring tact of an actor taking a curtain, or a menial dictating the extent of a gratuity with " I leave it to you, sir," what precisely you are to the universe.

The object of this autobiography, then (assuming the immortality of the subject), is to invite future biographers to take the author at his own valuation. In the matter of affairs of love and passion, affairs of the heart, it is intended to assist them by narrowing the margin of posthumous misinterpretation.

I will say at once that I am not a thwarted man of action turned man of letters. I have had no wish to free Italy or to liberate Greece. I have neglected to place myself at the head of the Soviet forces, and Fascist Italy, historians will note, has reached its present pass without my assistance. I have done nothing to unify the many godly but mutually suspicious branches of the Christian Church. Such pages as relate what I did in the Great War conclude my efforts in the realm of the deed.

PART I

MY VANISHED DAYS RETRIEVED

" Life as it flows is so much time wasted and nothing can ever be recovered
or truly possessed save under the form of eternity, which is also the form of art."

George Santayana.

CHAPTER ONE

THE BIRTH OF AN AUTHOR

I

HENRY

YESTERDAY, at dinner, it suddenly occurred to me what a fine fellow I was. How modest I have been! How good! How unduly unassuming! Arnold Bennett once confided to me that it didn't matter how you wrote: what mattered was whether you were a good fellow. How unerring that man's instinct!

In such reflections my thoughts turned to my ancestors who had a share in making me. I must here confess that I am a descendent of *the* Gerhardi—I mean of that remotely illustrious ancestor whom we all may reasonably assume to have been at one time or another a bright link in the infinite chain of the past and whose fame if it has not come down to us may be due less to his losing his way to posterity than to our historical rescue party neglecting to meet him half way. Or we may prefer to account for a fame which has not survived by postulating a deserved subsequent obscurity. The other day, however, I thought I had alighted on a clue when a casual acquaintance inquired with interest if I was a descendant of *the* Gerhardi, who, however, on further investigation, turned out, to my chagrin, to be myself. Unlike Napoleon, I don't prefer but resign myself to the necessity of being my own Rudolph.

Nevertheless, I have had ancestors. There was, for instance, my great-grandfather Henry Gerhardi, the first of us to come to England. He arrived by way of Belgium, about

1795. What prompted him to come I cannot tell. I visualize him buying a ticket at Ostend and after a rough crossing landing at Folkestone—perhaps at first not able to secure a room in a hotel, but staying on nevertheless eventually over four generations. This book, if so desired, may be regarded as a vindication of that perilous trip across the Channel.

There is always the temptation to make out that one's ancestors were grander, finer, richer, nobler than they were. But my fond aunts had no two opinions on the subject. So sure were they that the Gerhardis in Belgium and Germany and Italy had been aristocrats that it delighted me to question their assumptions by suggesting, on the contrary, that they may have been thieves, ponces, pimps, etc. My aunts contended that when an ancestor of ours left one country for another it was from heroic motives. Our family had left their native Italy waving the banners of the Reformation and preferring flight to submission, or death. I would suggest that they had left more probably to seek not glory but employment. Anyhow, the refugees seemed to have made themselves at home in Düsseldorf—or was it Hamburg ? —probably germanizing in part the Italian Gherardi by transferring the " h " to the middle of the name. Thereafter—or preferably before—according to my aunts, the Gerhardis were barons. But I regret that, after examining the evidence with benevolence, all I can trace in *Rietstrap Armorial Général* is the statement that they were " Chevaliers," followed by a detailed description of a coat-of-arms, the enumeration of whose composite parts would, I fear, be more satisfying to the author than the reader. This statement, though reassuring, perhaps errs a little on the side of modesty, and no doubt it will thrill my readers to learn that there was a Girardi who in 1633 became a Baron of the Holy Roman Empire. Another gentleman—perhaps two—of Verona, by the name of Gherardi, likewise answered to the name of Girardi, which suggests that the Baron might just as well have called himself Gherardi, and confirmed the theory that the name was susceptible to evolution, till it reached its dramatic climax in "Gerhardi." To recapitulate. If it was possible for Girardi to evolve into Gherardi, I hold that it is possible—on the ground that nothing is impossible—for Gherardi to evolve into Gerhardi. Once this is grasped everything becomes easy. Moreover, there was of recent years in Vienna a famous comic actor of the name Girardi, but, unless descended from the Baron, related to me, I suggest, only in a spirit of comedy. In Boswell's "Johnson" there is, under the year 1778, a mention of Marchese Gherardi of Lombardy attending a party at which Dr. Johnson was present. Stendhal, in his "De l'Amour," speaks of a beautiful woman called Madame de Girardi. These persons are related to me more by wish than by fact. But I discountenance any suggestion of kinship with Ambassador Gerard, and I am imperfectly connected with the Telephone Exchange of that name. These things, I hold, grew into being independently of me, and the philologist who devotes his days to the tracing of links will find his efforts defeated, but for one common discovery which he is bound to make in the course of his research—that "ger" in all versions signifies stone, and "hard" hard. In other words: "As hard as flint." Which, if qualified by "as soft as butter," is undoubtedly true of me. Thus far my ancestry is established. The only discord in the harmony is that when I requested my brother to supply me with a specimen of our arms it turned out to bear only a very faint resemblance to those of the gentlemen already referred to. A lady expert in heraldry, looking at our arms through a microscope, observed : " These things at the side *seem* to me to be supporters—though I wouldn't be quite sure."

" Indicating ? "

" Baronial rank."

" Thank you," I said. " That convinces me."

" My father was a moujik," says a merchant in " The Cherry Orchard," lamely, yet proudly, as if to account for the inherent simplicity of his nature.

" Your father was a moujik, mine an apothecary : and nothing whatsoever follows from it," answers the student.

If I have dwelt at some length upon my probable antecedents it is in order to suggest to what infinitely greater length one may go in these things with progressively smaller results. What I have stated is as nearly true as I myself know or can surmise : and nothing, or next to nothing, follows therefrom. " Experience "—which unimaginative people are wont to rate so highly—" Experience," says Goethe, " is always only one half of experience." And as with experience, so with knowledge, ancestral knowledge especially. The much you may know will just be enough to count for nothing. One Chink or Negro or even Jew ancestor a long way back will undo your Anglo-Saxon composition, of which you may claim an unbroken line of purely Essex stock, more thoroughly than if all your ancestors, from your parents back, had been Dutch, German, Swede, Dane, French, Russian, Portuguese, Italian, or any other easily assimilated Aryan race. And as heredity runs not, as one fondly imagines, on two parallel rails of daddy's and mummy's people, but diverges sidewards in algebraic progression to a bewildering number of contributing ancestors, so the probability of alighting on something unusual, enough to upset all your favourable preconceptions and disarrange your impeccable genealogical tree, is very considerable. Considerable enough to render the significance of the ancestors on the map, and their quota, surprisingly negligible. Were I then asked to contribute something really positive on the subject of my racial composition I would negative the proposition by remarking that no Chink, Negro, Jew, Kalmuck, Eskimo or other stubborn strain has, so far as records go, and if we may trust appearances, enriched the blood which circulates in me to-day.

The question so often posed by interviewers, whether heredity or environment is the stronger influence, seems to be one of those questions which demonstrate a truth rarely suspected by questioners on the look-out for wrong answers :

that questions, no less than answers, can be demonstrably wrong. For if environment may seem a stronger influence than heredity it merely seems so because, while knowing all there is to know regarding environment, we cannot know nearly enough regarding heredity. But because the influence of heredity cannot be accurately gauged, must it be less than that of environment merely because it is elusive and different in kind ? Elusive, moreover, because brothers and sisters of the same parents and environment are so often totally different. One brother has the instincts of a gentleman, the other of a cad. The manner, the style of the man, is plainly the influence of early environment. That I have spent my first eighteen years in St. Petersburg is something which five years in the British Army, three years at Oxford and the rest of my life in England can never undo. It is the direct contact of environment with the individual himself which determines his " style," so that the child born in the gutter and brought up in a palace will possess that " indefinable " feeling of ease and neatly disguised self-approbation which aristocratophiles are wont to associate with " blue-blood " brought about, as they claim, by generations of good living, plentiful food and spacious surroundings—that blue blood of a long line of men and women who have done themselves well, which often expresses itself in anæmia and nervous debility, a result hardly tallying with the other equally popular claim to good red peasant blood in one's veins, produced apparently by generations of want, under-nourishment and ill-ventilated homes : rival theories which seem to twit their protagonists by often producing a twelfth Earl of Somebody who looks unmistakably like a grocer, and an " aristocrat " with beautiful hands and features suggesting nobility and refinement in a son of the soil. But so adaptable are the heredity-mongers that when they find that a scion of an ancient house looks like the man in the street they assert that with an ancestry as distinguished as his he can well afford it and, in fact, see in him the perfect expression of the unobtrusive, unostentatious superiority by virtue of which a genuine aristocrat can afford to look like a genuine plebeian.

A perusal of Mr. Robert Graves' autobiography convinces me of the danger of dwelling unduly upon your antecedents. Mr. Graves harps on the fact, more interesting to himself than his readers, that he is of gentle stock, is at great pains to prove that on his mother's side he descends from a long line of German barons ; on his father's, from a high ecclesiastic dignitary. He tells us how inevitably he must strike everyone who comes in contact with him as a gentleman, and then fairly staggers you by a picture of himself, which might have been Carnera's, staring at you from the frontispiece with dumb, brutish wonder. But when, chastened by the image of Mr. Graves, I say that the " aristocrat " is a product of Nature aided by environment, and not of a family, hosts of people, I know, will raise their voices in protest. " Not at all," they will say. " Take our family. There is something we all have in common, though it may not be apparent to outsiders." There I have to agree. There is something common to all the members of my own family who bear the name of Gerhardi, some, shall I say, positive quality, so faint as to be " indefinable." But whether this heritage is something that others may see or which— as a vision of salvation to the true believer—reveals itself only to those who possess it, is a question on which it is in the circumstances idle to speculate.

Henry, then—for so this Columbus of ours was called— had ancestors who came from Germany, and they, in turn, had ancestors who fled from Italy. I stress the Italian or German origin of the name according to which country we are, at the time, in a state of war with. If, within the next decade, Mussolini renders Italy unpalatable to the rest of Europe, I will ignore the possible fact of my ancestors having been *nobil uomini* of Italy for the more topically agreeable news that they were *Ritter* of Germany. I neither claim nor deny a Flemish strain, for I have no means of ascertaining how long Henry remained on the Belgian coast before he purchased his ticket to Dover. Hence I am not sure whether I should cherish any special regard for that brave little people whom in 1914 England welcomed to its shores with a fervour of emotion only surpassed at seeing them go in 1918. It may be that Henry and his father and his father's father and mother had been citizens of Brussels or Liège or Dixmude ; but it is equally probable that he had arrived for the bathing season, found the plage dull, and crossed over to England. If these speculations may seem to the reader irrelevant to the undoubted fact of my present existence, I indulge in them to suggest with what whims, hazards, accidents and contingencies is fraught the eventual birth of an author. I would like anyone who may be inclined to treat this matter a little carelessly and light-heartedly to pause and reflect at how many points I might have miscarried even before I was conceived.

A benignant Providence, however, steered Henry safely into Folkestone harbour, and guided him to precisely the girl we needed, who, conceiving by him, delivered herself of my grandfather. He in his turn journeyed to Manchester for just the one woman capable of delivering herself, in due course, of my father. Providence then took my father by the hand and made him find my mother, and so, on the 21st November, 1895, I was delivered to a waiting world.

II

THE GOLD-STICK

My great-grandfather Henry cast anchor in the City and on August 31, 1818, married Caroline Genslin, daughter of a general of that name said to have held the office of Gold-Stick-in-Waiting to George III. Here a note of explanation may seem opportune.

Whenever the King himself appears in State—notably at the Trooping of the Colour—there rides immediately behind him a colonel of one of the Household Cavalry regiments, as his personal bodyguard. He carries a gold-crowned baton and from that derives his title of Gold-Stick-in-Waiting. Now there is nothing remarkable in itself in such an occupation, and I would deprecate its significance if another autobiographer laid stress on the fact that he was the great-great-grandson of a man thus equipped and thus occupied. But in a bleak ancestry like my own, with no other colour to troop, I feel it to be worthy of mention. The military element does not preponderate in our family. We can boast of but one gold-stick, not an unbroken chain of them, which would have suggested a rich variety of types : strong sticks and feeble ones, muscular and emaciated, a lion-hearted warrior, and a rat in uniform. As it is, that one, the only one, necessarily presents himself to my mind as a blameless knight, the inheritor of the gallant and martial virtues of the warrior caste, who has contributed his quota to what I myself am or am tending to be. So that when they said of me : " The lad is shaping," it may be that microbes of the gold-stick in me were closing ranks or forming two-deep as my jaw set itself in resolution, or advanced in extended order as my face relaxed into a smile. But do not let us be carried away by deductions more plausible than they are probable. It is as likely as not that this gold-stick, martially inconspicuous, gained his office for other reasons : because he was a sycophant, a sneak, or had been chosen as a make-shift, or because as a nonentity who aroused no opposition he was a natural compromise between two opposing candidates of military merit. But if so, must we again jump to conclusions and dismiss the good man as a dunce ? In his unobtrusive way—who knows ?—he may have had a quiet humour, a penetrating insight comparing well with the superficial daemonism of his more brilliant colleagues.

My readers may have grown impatient of all this speculative stuff. What is a gold-stick, to them, anyhow ? What is he to me ?

There they are wrong. Let me prove it. Supposing George III had been attacked during a state procession : the loyal gold-stick precipitates himself on the miscreant and decapitates him, while another assailant aims a stone at my potential ancestor. The gold-stick is flung from his saddle : they stoop, kneel over him—his heart has stopped beating. And the present book fails to make its appearance in this, or in any other spring list. Conversely, because the accident was averted I am here to say so, with joy, if not with accuracy, for I am a little doubtful about gold-stick. How the daughter of General Genslin came to marry Henry Gerhardi, a merchant of London and naturalized an Englishman, I cannot tell, nor can I presume to know how the gold-stick felt about it when he heard the news of the engagement.

At this point my mother, to whom I have read these paragraphs, looks a little sad. "I don't want," she says, "to spoil your book. But I am afraid your grandfather Gerhardi's mother was not the daughter but the grand-daughter of the gold-stick. And he was not a Genslin, but her mother's father—I forget the name." My mother had just been staying with my dead aunt's daughter in Paris, who is the source of all this gold-stick information, and this it seems is what my cousin said. "I shouldn't have told you," said my mother. "Does this put you back with your book ? I am so sorry, darling."

"Not a bit of it !" I cried. "We put back the gold-stick by one more remove, that is all. Which makes me the great-great-great-grandson of the gold-stick. What I lose in immediacy of kinship I gain in length of lineage."

And there, for a time, we must leave him.

III

WILLIAM ALEXANDER

Daughter or granddaughter of the gold-stick, Caroline gave Henry five children, my grandfather, William Alexander, among them, who was born in London in 1823, and to whom I owe my particular combination of names. It is not for me to question their beauty, but to state that few of my friends care to call me by either of them. Of that generation there survived, until a year or two ago, an old deaf lady called Auntie Carr. Of the following generation of Gerhardis there survives only my Uncle Willy, model of Uncle Lucy in "The Polyglots," though, unlike that gentleman, he did not hang himself in his sister's knickers but has emigrated to Canada where, at the age of seventy odd, he has started a farm.

William Alexander, my grandfather, is said to have run away from home—not, however, to sea but only to Manchester. In that city he met a supposedly accomplished, artistically cultivated girl, Belgian, it seems, also said to have run away from home and sustaining herself as a governess. He married her and set over half a dozen children on this earth, my father among them ; after which the whole family seems to have run away together to Russia. They travelled in sleighs ; there were no railways, and wolves pursued them. My grandfather eventually set up a small cotton spinning mill on the right bank of the Neva in St. Petersburg. He quickly prospered, even though he had little business acumen and no knowledge of Russian or cotton spinning to speak of. He had a Gladstone type of face, unless it was the whiskers which contributed to the resemblance, and there was a notion in our family that he wrote poetry, for he had placed two lines of verse on his wife's tombstone which, however, when I had sufficiently advanced in my reading of English poetry, I discovered to be borrowed. A true Gerhardi rolling stone, he had finally come to a halt on the banks of the Neva, and there gathering moss set his family on their feet. My father, who gathered more moss and enriched himself and his sisters tenfold, was yet sent rolling by the Revolution and died a poor man, paralysed, after nine years in a chair, in a cheap mountain *pension* in the Tyrol. And shortly before he died, when he was in great need of money, my poor father sent a story to the *Daily Mail* telling how his father on landing in Russia travelled with his family from Riga to Petersburg in sleighs and wolves pursued them. But the story was returned.

IV

WATERLOO

A contemporary of William Alexander, my paternal grand-father, was a Yorkshire man, John Wadsworth, who had come out to Russia in middle-age, and who was to become my maternal grandfather. My paternal and maternal grandfathers became close friends. Each possessed prestige in the other's eyes. Prestige is a big word. But it is no less great within each sphere of life because, outside that sphere, it may appear small. Prestige is essentially local : for if London prestige counts for more than Sydney prestige it is in London that it counts more, or with people in Sydney conversant with what counts in London : which means that it is local to London. If it were possible to live simultaneously on all the rungs of the worldly ladder one was someday destined to climb, one's capacity for correcting one's judgment regarding what may ·be deemed "smart" would be numbed and one's sense of elegance neutralized. An innocent's regard for the genteel table manners of a wealthy suburban family nibbling at their sumptuous meal would be upset by the spectacle of a millionaire only taking a little fish, and a duke eating like a ravenous peasant. But the rule of life is that different people, and the same individuals at different times, see the world with different eyes. And so there was a point in space and time when my mother's father enjoyed the prestige of being the manager of a very large mill, while my father's father enjoyed the dif-ferent prestige of being the owner of a very small mill, and when my father and mother, returning to Petersburg after their school days in England, met, fell in love and were engaged to be married, it was considered by their respective families that each could have done substantially better.

My maternal great-grandfather, William Wadsworth, fought at the battle of Waterloo, rising to the rank of corporal. He must have deemed this rank sufficiently responsible, for we have no record of his subsequent promotion. On the other hand, he was said to have earned the nickname of Billy Wits on account of his wit. I cannot pronounce on its quality; I accept it. His son, John Wadsworth, my grandfather, was never tired of relating stories of his father's long march in the rain, the long stand in the mud, and so on, producing medals out of a chest and locking them up again. And when, having joined up in the late war, I came to see him at Southport, expecting him to comment on my uniform, I was astonished by his indifference. He was now very old. My uniform and the war seemed unreal to him, but he talked, with faint glee, of his father at Waterloo, the long march in the rain, the stand in the mud, and so on. His one thought now was to get warm. " There is nothing like keeping warm," he would say to me again and again. " Ah, there is nothing like keeping warm," as he rolled the blankets around him. He saw me off at the station, but was preoccupied with his own thoughts, still of his father, and the war seemed to lack motive to him, as if it were a rag organized by a few rowdy young fellows. Though he shook his head sadly at one aspect of it : it would be the end, he opined, of old Francis Joseph, decoyed by foxy William of Prussia ; he would die, poor old man, of remorse. . . . " Ah . . ." he sighed, " ah . . ." Tears, either of pity or of cold and old age, stood in his eyes. The train pulled out. I never saw him again.

Like many men of indifferent achievement, my grandfather Wadsworth was generous with advice. But though incredibly cautious himself he had invariably contrived to be done. Before he migrated to Russia he had a wool mill in Yorkshire, which failed. Then he owned stores, a sort of potential Selfridge, which also failed. After this he grew more cautious than ever, advising us never to pour out our dirty water till we were sure we had obtained fresh. He once even advised me, when changing buses, not to part with the old ticket obtained on one bus till I had secured a new ticket on another. When I explained to him that the ticket obtained on one bus could be of no use on another, he said : " Even so, it gets you into good habits." Whenever he gave us money he said, " Now take care of it. Don't spend it foolishly." After Grandmother's death, Grandpapa Wadsworth came to live with us in Russia. Though old he was very helpful and a model of tact in domestic relations. He always said he would live till he was a hundred, but the death of a contemporary suddenly undermined his confidence and he sailed back to England so as to die and be buried in its soil.

Whenever, in Russia, he went to a shop and the price of an article for which he inquired appeared in excess of his anticipation he gravely shook his head and went out. When the shopkeeper, willing to come down, followed my grandfather into the street, my grandfather, still shaking his head, merely murmured in sorrow : " You have astonished me." The shopkeeper now offered him the article for one half the price. " You have astonished me," sadly murmured my grandfather, in soft, dulcet, pianissimo tones : " You have astonished me "—and passed on.

I often feel this economic Wadsworth strain in me rise to the surface to check the incurbing Gerhardi extravagance, and I believe that women dining out with me have very seldom witnessed a Wadsworth reverse.

V

INTRODUCTION TO PARENTS

My mother, who was born in Lancashire and came to Russia when she was three, first saw my father when he was eight. She sat on the steps and pretended to play the piano and sang at the top of her voice when he saw her. Her mother's name was Spencer, and I would tell this grandmother who later came to live with us that when I grew up I would build her a house of gold. My grandmother Spencer claimed to descend from an, evidently disinherited, branch of the

Earls Spencer. Lord Spencer, on the other hand, does not seem to claim a reciprocal relationship. My mother, who was irritated by her mother's claim and chaffed her for it, resented my own scepticism in this respect, for I was irritated by the claim, as, no doubt, my readers will be now that I, in turn, am serious in trying to put it over them.

When my father finished school in England he was placed in his uncle Gerhardi's office in the City. This uncle Charles— a son of the original Henry—was the managing director of the Direct Spanish Telegraph Company. He was somewhat of a Don Juan, and though married, kept a bachelor suite at the Hotel Cecil, and from time to time he would vanish for long periods from the office, leaving his address in a sealed envelope with his clerk and instructing him not to open it except in a case of special importance. On one occasion a telegram came from St. Petersburg to say that his brother William Alexander had died, and the clerk broke open the envelope and wired to acquaint my great-uncle of his brother's death, only to bring contumely on his head. " What the hell did you mean by spoiling my holiday ? Didn't I tell you to leave me in peace ? " The clerk replied that he understood his instructions were to wire my great-uncle if anything unusual occurred. " I didn't say unusual, I said *important !* " barked my great-uncle. My father modelled himself on his uncle. Alas ! For his uncle's sense of humour took a crude form of expression, as when he would call out for his clerk : " Preddle ! " and when Preddle, with inquiring tact, appeared in the doorway : " Yes, sir " : my great-uncle would reply : " You're a damn fool—that's all." My father imbibed some of his uncle's " style " as a youth. My brother and I, in turn, modelled ourselves on our father, whose style as " un gros industriel " seemed to us perfect. Years later, my ideal of the great business man was enlarged when I watched the smiling way in which Lord Beaverbrook controlled a vast net of business activities from an armchair in the drawing-room while entertaining his guests. Whereas my father, it seemed, could not run his cotton mill at a profit, without putting the fear of God into everyone a mile around him.

This imbibing of another's style in one's tender years which carries one along till one succumbs to a new influence, then a third, a fourth, until one's individual style is crystallized, is more important than one is likely to admit to the people whose personality one has used in turn and discarded. My father, even more spirited than his uncle, was in due course transferred to a branch office of the company at Brest, which proved a rich field for his gambling and amorous proclivities, till he was recalled to Petersburg by his father and put into the mill. My father, who was then barely twenty and had never been in a cotton mill, familiarized himself with the machinery as well as the commercial side in a week. If he put on a white coat to crawl under a machine he emerged spick and span. My brother, on the other hand, whom my father (as fathers do) put through the same experience, literally " through the mill," always looked incredibly dirty and oily at the end of the day. I, possessing no aptitude for or interest in machinery, was spared the ordeal, and I countered the humiliation of being considered a dunce by my family after the manner of President Wilson who in the early days of the war walked about with hands unstained by mud or blood because, as he gave out, he was too proud to fight. Taking advantage of a wave of industrial prosperity, my father in a few years increased the mill five times in size and twenty in wealth. My father's temper, the most awful in my experience, liberated him from his elder brother, my Uncle Willy (*alias* Uncle Lucy), who was glad to get out. This uncle of mine set up a bobbin mill of his own in Smolensk and found a ready market for his line of article in the cotton mill of my father, who preferred his bobbins to his presence, while my uncle favoured my father as a valuable customer and avoided him as a brother.

For some time my father and uncle vied with each other in prosperity, my father building himself a town house in the capital, while my uncle acquired land in the government of

Smolensk. One year it was my father who was ahead, next year it was my uncle ; and so for thirty odd years—till the Revolution got the better of both. Their meetings had been rare, and when they occurred were not a success : for my father could not bear to talk, and my uncle could not hear. My uncle would look over some tricky new stove my father had had installed in the house and murmur a few comments based on his own unassisted deductions, while my father, heedless of his brother and guest, lay on the sofa reading a newspaper. When, old and ruined, they met again in London in 1918, my father paralysed and confined to a chair, my uncle listening through an ear trumpet, their gravity and competitive spirit seemed to have left them. They talked excitedly and light-heartedly, like boys. My uncle, who had a large family, suggested that we should all, the entire clan of Gerhardis, start a poultry farm somewhere, and my father, though confined to a chair, was not averse to branching out into the broker business with his deaf brother on the few hundred pounds they had salvaged from the wreck of their fortunes in Russia. But their optimism was short lived. My father hung on for a few years more and died. My uncle and his family emigrated to Canada.

My father's four sisters, to show their faith in him, had retained their money in his mill and partook of his prosperity on a more generous scale than if they had been mere shareholders, their brother being eager to crown their belief in him with a bonus which he hoped might astonish them. But they accepted the windfall as placidly as he, to make it more striking, had offered it. And when, thirty years later, in the upheaval of war, their swollen capital degenerated to its original modest beginning, their brother acquainted them of the fact in a placidly worded document, winding up with the statement that he had had a brilliant career.

Perhaps success stands out in a more dazzling relief on the black background of failure. Ultimate failure which weighs decisively at the close of a career is, after death, balanced by early success : being dead and done for proves no serious handicap to perpetuating one's life in the memory of people, on the page of a book.   The end of a life does not neutralize the interest of its beginning ; and I can write with tender detachment of one who is dead, the other now old: my father and mother were married at the English Church in St. Petersburg in 1889 and, in the course of eight years, set six children on earth, I coming fifth.

CHAPTER TWO

CHILDHOOD

I

THE PETERSBURG HOUSE

RECENTLY my mother had occasion to visit Leningrad. One day she felt the wish to have a look at our old house. The surroundings had all changed. Many familiar buildings had been pulled down and the streets revealed vistas of space not unlike what the neighbourhood may have appeared in my grandfather's days. But our house was still there. My mother approached it. It had not, for many years, received its annual coat of paint which, in my childhood, had made it look so gay as we returned to it every autumn after summer at the seaside. Yet it looked fairly respectable. It had been turned into a museum and some public offices, and there was a brass plate on its walls. My mother hesitated. Then she caught sight of her curtains—the ballroom curtains. A heavy feeling overcame her, and she hurried away.

She would often say: "I imagine I ring the bell. Annushka opens the door and I go up the red carpeted steps of the vestibule, pass through the glass door. I am in the hall," thus, step by step, resurrecting the old life, lived heedlessly and not tasted in its full flavour till it had escaped her. In the same way my mother, on waking in the morning, would in imagination, review her six children, of whom the youngest is thirty, while the eldest boy, who died in childhood, remains a little boy of two. "I've come to you," he used to say to her. "Are you lonely?" My mother, addressing each photograph in turn, conducts each morning a private little conversation : " Now, Victor, what are you doing ? " And sometimes in imagination, together, we would conduct a tour of inspection of the rooms. Here on this landing I sat for hours on my tricycle which my brother had converted for me into a car, and waited for my elder sister to come back from school to convey her down the long corridor to her room. And so on, and so on. . . .

It was this house which, when I was about four years old, we used to watch from a neighbouring house we at that time occupied, as it rose and grew on steel rails—probably the first house in Petersburg to be so built. My father had intended to have a house reasonably large to accommodate himself, his wife, and his family of five children. Owing to some architectural miscalculation, however, the house came out on a loftier scale than was intended. It took several years to furnish the rooms, which were numerous and so high that several systems of heating were tried and discarded before the house became habitable. It was built as a permanent stronghold on a quay overlooking the Neva, a quay which, in Russian style, as in the early industrial period in England, accommodated several big " industrialists "—the Swede Nobel among them—each with his appropriate mansion next to his works. An unfortunate combination, since it suggested to the workers who worked in the mills that they were doing so to enable the owner to live in his mansion—an association of ideas which, during strikes and revolutions, prompted them to hurl stones through the windows of the mansion. We children would be drawn away from the windows, while a squadron of Cossacks, summoned by telephone, occupied the mill-yard, the officers quartering themselves on our willing hospitality. And so it came about that what was built as a stronghold to last for generations was taken away from us at the end of eighteen years. The mills and mansions are still there, but the kings and captains are gone—Nobel among them.

My father's natural irritation found a ready stimulant in

this huge house, which absorbed so much of his money and energy; and my mother, enjoying the services of many servants, a housekeeper, a competent German "Fräulein," and a French governess, felt exhausted, not so much in spite of as because of them, and sighed for a small house in England. The house, standing on the right bank of the Great Nevka, facing the Zoological Garden, was next door to the mill, which tended to spoil its ornamental appearance. The quay here was desolate and the river congested with barges of timber; and the baroque house, a replica of a wing of the Vienna Belvedere, looked completely out of place. Yet everyone envied us our house; and this is important to a child. In a city where large apartments were commonplace and everybody lived in flats, where only grand dukes owned palaces, such a house created in a schoolboy a sense of privileged well-being.

My father was a rich man. A rich man, judged by pre-war standards of wealth in Russia. Judged by the standards of John Rockefeller or Lord Rothermere, I gather my father could not be considered anything but poor. But all that matters here is that we thought, as children, that our father was tremendously rich because he travelled luxuriously, kept a racing stud, private horses, and lived in a house which, by a slight exaggeration, might be described as a palace. In so far as these things have affected my character the facts are important. The effect of early wealth cannot be taken away, as the Russian Revolution, which took it away, has shown. What you have had you retain, and what you have come down to you are inclined to regard as a period of transition. A cursory study of the cheerful (if sometimes foolish) hope-fulness of Russian refugees throughout the world amply bears this out. Though I have not as yet soared high enough above starvation level to take a bird's-eye view of it, the sight of wealth in others leaves me untroubled. A nos-talgia for a stately staircase alone remains with me. But that is all.

Socially we were not entangled—that is, we were looked

up to by people we knew, while knowing nothing of any people who might have cared to look down on us. For a sensitive writer this is half the battle. He matures quickly because his soul has not been distorted by envy and bitterness and suspicion, and he is born a free man with his nervous force unimpaired. In this he has the advantage over those who must exert all their strength in rebellion, with little humour or grace to dispose of in the service of art. The fighting and struggling, spiritually speaking, is of course always there. But fighting, like reading, must be economized. And I am better off as an artist living with detachment in the reign of George V than exhausting my strength in passionate, if poetic, obloquy on the regime of, let us say, Abdul Hamid. This much my father's money, my English birth, have done for me. After the Revolution my family landed in England with five hundred pounds. The rest of the fortune acquired by my father and grandfather in Russia reverted, by the decision of proletarian Russia, to the proletariat who had (indifferently) toiled for it.

I was born a little to one side, that is in a country of which I was not a citizen, on a bank of the Neva in a city of very broad thoroughfares, immense squares, wide bridges, lunatic dreams. Birth in Russia of foreign parentage does not carry with it the reward of Russian nationality, which, however, the English-born have no reason to regret. For in Russia (thanks to Peter the Great who, working at Amsterdam as a carpenter, had conceived a high idea of Dutchmen) a foreigner is at a premium—in fact as good as noble. I was born a British subject because my paternal grandfather was born in London, and British nationality thus acquired extends over three generations to accommodate the grandson—failing which arrangement I would have been lost for England. I was baptized in the local church of England by the Rev.— I think—Wilson, but neglected to be confirmed. I was born on a background entirely Russian ; and of the four languages taught me in childhood my knowledge of English was least and, until I was eighteen or so, quite abject. With our parents, as a matter of duty, we spoke English. But it was the language we children knew least—a language mostly confined to our parents in conversation with each other. Among ourselves we spoke Russian, and now that we have passed into the habit of speaking and corresponding in English, in a fit of sincerity we mechanically lapse into Russian. With our French governesses (of which there was a succession) we conversed, very unwillingly, in her tongue. With " Fräulein," who remained with the family seventeen years, we talked fluent German of the Reval variety. When in danger, as in a rocking boat or in an overturning vehicle, we, by association of ideas, exclaim in German. We expostulate, as indeed you must, in French. But English, peppered with Russian, is now our more or less natural mode of expression.

II

INFANT MEMORIES

I was born in such heat that the upper layer of my skin had peeled off, and revealed a thin, delicate, transparent new skin, so that my complexion thereafter was—though no longer is—the envy of girls. It is a favourite, if obscure, joke of mine—a " private " joke because not shared by other members of my family, who frankly do not see it—that my parents had tried four times unsuccessfully before they brought a masterpiece into the world, my young sister being an anticlimax.

My earliest memory goes back to a darkish dining-room in the old house (it was a few years before the new house was built). Lunch was over and I was sitting on the lap of my Russian nurse. My father's brother was on a visit from Smolensk, and my nurse exchanged impressions with the nurse of my Uncle Willy's children. I could not have been more than twelve months, yet I have a vivid impression of being interested, of being impressed by the weight of my nurse's general outlook as against that of the nurse of my cousins. What I understood, and followed with deep interest, was their attitude, the prestige, the position of one against the other on the background of a dark, wonderful, fearful feeling of the world which, to me, stretched from the distant and mysterious place from which my uncle had arrived to the darkish dining-room at the other end of the world where I sat, engrossed, on my nurse's lap, rapt and spellbound. But when, from the adjoining room, my mother came in, with that social laugh of amiability which emanates from her in the presence of strangers, and bent over to take me, like a parcel, and show me to my aunt, I, who had been comfortable on my nurse's lap, suddenly rebelled and slapped my mother's face. Then I became unpleasantly aware that I had spread horror—readily-advertised horror in the nursemaid; subdued, sad horror in my mother; and nicely-balanced horror in my aunt, as who might say : " He cannot be really bad being yours." For some time, the chorus of " Naughty ! Naughty ! " continued, with which idea I at bottom agreed, but, with the world against me, taciturn, abashed, helpless, I began to cry.

Then I remember my first attempts to walk within a wooden frame on wheels, interested spectators watching me and a shamefaced feeling in me at my half successful attempts. Later, a series of other attempts to adjust myself to my brother and sisters ; and very soon images identified with bliss, as a small ice cream cart on wheels with a real zinc tub filled with delicious ice cream was made for me by—I don't remember who. Never was there such ice cream as that sold by the Russian ice cream vendors who filled the tub. There was a particular flavour about it which no private chef could emulate—it may have been the dirt. This ice cream cart was my most treasured possession. It was identified with two desirable things : the scooping out of round balls of ice cream with a special long zinc spoon of my own, and the idea that all this was a contrivance which moved on wheels. Other possessions—a tricycle which my brother converted for me into a motor-car in imitation of my father's, and then my first pair of skis which, when the colour came off them, caused me to sob in the night and to feel, perhaps for the first time, that life was a mistake.

It is difficult to know where to stop when writing of the early impressions of childhood. The danger is that it might prove more fascinating to the writer than the reader. After all, if I digress on the pleasures of my first motor-car will it not irritate the reader who, quite properly, will feel that my emotion cannot compare with his own at the gift of his first locomotive? And where is one to stop? If one were sure that there was an invisible audience of readers around one who shed tender tears over my ice cream tub, choked with emotion and begged, " Oh, we want more of this, we can never have enough!" one might be induced to go on. As it is, I have to limit myself to such experiences as may be shown to have been productive of some value and significance in respect of my character, such as it is.

When I think of my childhood this is how it presents itself to me : " There was this, then there was that. Then there was my mother's '*jour*.' Then my father's first motor-car." Not that these things come to me in chronological order. They arise all round me like little jets of water which remind me that just here is an oasis. But what total worth can I extract from my childhood? That depends on the calm of my soul. When the weather is windy all that landscape seems blurred. But when the soul is clear there rise in me, as on a beautiful morning, picture-feelings more precious and crystalline than any I can beguile out of the later years.

There were five of us : a sister, a brother, a sister, myself, and another sister, all produced within the shortest intervals humanly possible. My eldest sister was dreamy and poetic and sensitive. My second sister, matter-of-fact and a good sort. My third sister passionately loyal to her friends, who, however, changed rapidly and the loyalty with them. We used to tease her by calling her, for some unspecified reason, " violoncello "—which, for an equally unknown reason, would send her into tears. My youngest sister and I used to play together, as did my second sister and brother, while my

eldest sister seemed always of an age to be preoccupied with
poetry and young men. I loved my youngest sister best.
We had a little garden we owned together, with a fence painted
green and paths cut through the lawn, and a small shed with
a bench in it and a tin plate on the fence bearing the inscription
" Villa W. & M. Gerhardi " ; and adjoining us was another
property belonging to my brother and the second sister with
a plate reading " Villa V. & D. Gerhardi." My father would
bring us tins of varnished paint for the fence, and we cultivated
all kinds of flowers, and when it rained sat under the shed,
which was the villa, eating strawberries and ice cream. The
smell of fresh paint always fills me with a sense of felicity
which for some time I was at a loss to account for till, pursuing
the special feeling that the smell of paint evoked in me, I
connected it with this love of our little garden. My second
sister Dora and I, when we were quite small, used to play at
barbers, in which game I was the client, till one day she cut
off my flaxen locks which were down to the shoulders, and
was suitably punished. My brother, older than myself by
three years, once told me mysteriously, as if imparting a
momentous piece of news : " And do you know, Willie,
that there's a big wolf under your bed ? Do you know ? A
big wolf." I listened with sustained attention till a mingled
sense of terror of the wolf and loathing of my brother caused
me to seize him by the shoulders and shake him. This unexpected reaction in me had the effect, more awful to me than
even the wolf, of filling my brother with such terror that we
stood there with our fingers embedded in each other's
shoulders, paralysed with fear and unable to relax our death-
like grip, shaking, shaking each other, till our elders arrived
and pulled us asunder.

The nearest regiment to us was the Moscow Guards, whose
commander became a close friend of the family and whose
children played with us. But they played at soldiers, while
we played at running a mill. We despised them for it. There
seemed nothing in soldiering. There still seems to me, after
five years of it in the British Army, to be nothing in soldiering.

Our games were far more intelligent and imaginative. In all such activities my brother was the inventive genius, and many were the things he constructed for us, though he quickly tired of the game itself. A string would be hung from one end of the room to the other, and suspended from it a wall made of newspapers pasted together. Doors and windows were cut out with scissors. Inside was the cotton mill "Gerhardi, Ltd." Bobbins and yarn procured from my father's mill were wound on and off, doubled and trebled. Wheels from a dismantled tricycle were set in motion by a miniature electric motor, the whole revolving by means of an impressive system of belts, and the finished article lowered in boxes from a crane and swung on to a lorry made out of a tricycle. I enjoyed the make-belief, the dream and atmosphere and imagination of being in turn the owner of this cotton mill, the proprietor of a theatre, the head of a school, the boss of a tailoring establishment, cutting immaculate tail-coats out of brown paper and selling stiff collars cut out of white cardboard. My brother did not care so much for the game itself, and his interest was exhausted with the invention.

When I was about six or seven we went on a visit to my mother's parents in England—my mother, "Fräulein," and five children. My father saw us off at the boat, which sailed from a quay in Petersburg. Some friends had come too. They were drinking champagne and shouting "Here goes!" The white boat at last left. She was very white, spick and span, and was called *Torneo* and was taking us to Hango. There we changed on to a larger boat. Brown she was and gold and proud and hooted ominously and was called *Arcturus*, and my little sister Marguerite, called Daisy, about three or four, said of her: "What a slippery house." And before she took off, as we stood at the rail and watched the narrow strip of water between her steep sides and the stone quay, there was the acrid smell of secreted fish. Cattle were being hauled on board who, as we later learnt, did not feel very well during the voyage. The boat called at

Copenhagen, where I remember sitting on a beautiful morning in the park, and there was a tram horse which could not move a tram that had come off the rails and was cruelly whipped for it by two men. When we disembarked at Hull it was raining, and we drove in a stuffy closed cab which smelt of stale leather. In Russia we used a closed carriage only when the weather was quite abnormally cold, and were usually sick at the end of the journey. Of the actual summer spent in England I remember but little. My grandparents had a little house somewhere near Selby in Yorkshire. There were some children who asked us to tea. Their father was a schoolmaster who, besides his own ten or eleven boys, had the charge of other men's sons, and his idea of educating them seemed mostly confined to using the cane. The boys were all cowed and a little daft from fright, and the tea party consisted largely of the schoolmaster, who entertained us while bellowing at the boys and flourishing the cane. My only other memories are of green country and buttercups and a merry-go-round, and the odd-looking half-crowns which, it was explained to me, were somewhat more than a rouble and bore the face of Edward VII instead of his nephew Nicholas II, and of a little girl next door who, when her mother went into the road to fetch her, cried, " Mammy, you go home, or else I'll kill you ! "

I have no recollection whatsoever of the journey back, except that on our arrival home we at once (as if we had skimmed the sea for that purpose) began to plant sunflower seed given us by our grandfather Wadsworth in England. We hoped to acclimatize sunflowers on the banks of the Neva, and discussed the probability that they would transfigure the riverside next year. As the years passed, whenever I caught some particular whiff in the air, were it only the smell of frying bacon, I experienced an extraordinary sense of felicity and found myself transported back to England. It is these things—the particular aspect of an autumn day in town as we arrived from the country, or the clearness in the air, the pink light over the Casino when in the spring we went to the seaside—which remain with me and vouch for an existence that otherwise

would seem never to have been, an existence which perhaps
but for these scents and lights, those tones and hues, has
little else to recommend it.

III

" LIEBE "

I remember an early feeling of responsibility, when I joined
a preparatory school and had text books and exercise books and
carried them in a satchel which had some nice fur on the flap.
The school belonged to an elderly spinster of Baltic extraction
called Fräulein Kaisar, and there was a limerick about her
which ran :

> *Gott sei Dank*
> *Fräulein Kaisar ist krank,*
> *Liegt im Bette*
> *Und frisst Kotlette.*

This Fräulein Kaisar who presided over luncheon was fond
of talking of a probably happy holiday she once spent in
Switzerland, and told us of the road signs common in that
country, which instead of giving the distances in kilometres
did so in minutes. A method in regard to which she invited
our criticism since, as she explained, what was the use of saying
that the distance between one village and another was twenty
minutes when there were men who might cover it in ten and
old ladies who might take half an hour. She explained that
the system could only work provided all men and women in
Switzerland were assumed to walk at the same rate of speed.
She explained again and again. But I could never see it.
My brother and I used to go to school together by horse tram,
the usual fare being six kopecks each way. One day my
brother evolved a brilliant scheme by which each of us could
make four kopecks a day. He explained that if we travelled
on top where the charge was only four kopecks we could
afford three rides for every two inside where the charge was
six ; and since three rides a day were one too many, by riding
on top we each made each day a clear four kopecks profit.

But I could not see it.   During the luncheon hour we were made to walk round and round in pairs, separating at one end of the room and meeting again at the other, to the sounds of the march of " The Double Eagle " played by a tall, dark-haired school teacher, Fräulein Eden, who had blue eyes and regular features and with whom I suppose I was in love, for the first time.

I was assisted with my homework by " Fräulein," whose intellectual expansion had been checked at an early age and whom the arithmetical tasks set me taxed heavily, and she looked red and worried and sad.   Our " Fräulein," who had come to us shortly before I was born and stayed with us seventeen years, was the most cherished soul in the household. We called her " Liebe " (which means Love) and there was no worse catastrophe than if she refused to kiss us good-night. The punishment was so barbarous, so unthinkably cruel, that we hated her and carried on like tortured maniacs, howling in sustained volume of protestation : " Liebe ! Liebe ! Kuss ! Kuss ! " (Kiss ! Kiss !), till she was forced to recant and give in.   The habit of being kissed good-night by her was so engrained in us that during her short absence my brother required a newly joined and very shy young housemaid to kiss him good-night, and when she assented at last, very blushingly, he told her that, on second thoughts, he perhaps didn't want it.   " Liebe," who did everything with the utmost thoroughness, had an extraordinarily vehement way of wash-ing our ears, and when the soap got into our eyes and she seized our recalcitrant necks between her broad knuckles and hissed at us : " Ach, du Viehstück ! " we spluttered back at her : " Alte Hexe ! Alte Hexe ! "   She used to take the five of us for walks and she dressed us so warmly, tying woollen hoods over our heads, that by the time the fifth was dressed and ready for an airing the first was nearly swooning, and either screamed hoarsely with resentment or choked in his padded coat and fur collar raised over the hood.   As a result of this we always caught chills.   She had two nursemaids under her orders but was so conscientious that she insisted on doing everything herself, and when she put away a thing she did it so thoroughly that no one else in the whole house could find it.   Occasionally my father would drink beer for dinner, and would treat " Liebe," who was fond of it, and her long nose turned red with delight, while we children watched, gloated, and teased her.   She came to us, many years ago, with a coffer in which she kept her few treasured possessions, and inside was a note to the men whom she expected in the course of a coming revolution to sack our house, informing them that this trunk belonged to a poor nursery governess and would they please not touch it.   She had never married because, when she was a young girl in Reval, she had been engaged to a young man whom she had the misfortune to pass one morning unexpectedly while she was going on an errand looking untidy and not at her best.   The young man was walking with some smart looking friends ; she did not want to shame him and pretended not to have seen him.   He thought she had " cut " him deliberately and never came her way again. After seventeen years she left us as the result of a silly quarrel foisted on my mother by Grandpa Wadsworth, something to do with the question of thrift.   She worked hard at anatomy, passed with great difficulty an examination and at last established herself as a maternity nurse in her home town, Reval. Recently my mother paid her a visit.   They were both old now, cried when they saw each other, tried to remember the past and parted probably feeling that what has passed can never again be recaptured entirely.

IV

SCHOOLDAYS

Other images come back.   There is a Christmas tree lighted electrically and making heavy demands on the dynamo in the adjoining mill.   We had returned from the English Church, festive on this occasion, with the Ambassador present, who is Harold Nicolson's father.   My father, in a morning-coat, walks about, irritable over the complete absence of letters and newspapers. The tree is lit, but nobody seems to enjoy himself save my mother, who enjoys "enjoying" us, and sings to her own accompaniment at the piano : " Glory, glory ! Hallelujah ! " hoping we may be induced to take hands and go round the tree. We refuse. No one joins in. My mother stops and begins distributing the presents. General resentment and disappointment. " What awful children ! " says my mother. " You should enjoy yourselves, you know." No one does, nevertheless.

Another scene. My father tries his first motor-car, procured at considerable expense from the United States. It has no steering-wheel, but a sort of handle and a bell instead of a horn. My father bids us sit at the back. We climb up, for the motor is about the height of a hansom cab, and we sit with our backs to him, doubled up, since the back of the seat in which he reclines is at a comfortable slope of some sixty degrees and ours accordingly at a reverse angle of thirty. My father, with great expenditure of nervous force, sets the motor puffing, and presently it sets off and runs along over the uneven frozen ground only to land into a bank of snow. We sit there perched behind him like frightened rabbits. My father wipes the snow off his pince-nez and, not knowing what to do with his irritation, applies it to the gears, with indifferent success. My father sends the car to us, at school, and we are terribly proud because it's the first motor to be seen in Petersburg. The motor shambles and bumps over the uneven cobblestones. My brother sits behind holding a bowl of gold-fish he had bought at a bazaar. The gold-fish get so shaken on their first and last motor ride that when we get home they are dead. My father for some time perseveres with the motor-car, but finds himself more and more stuck on the tram lines. The chauffeur in cleaning the engine chops off a finger. My father sells the motor-car and has to pension off the chauffeur for life.

At the age of eleven or twelve I passed from the preparatory school into a full-blown school—the Annenschule—one of four or five schools belonging to the Lutheran corporation in St. Petersburg, in which the teaching was done partly in Russian and partly in German. On the fateful day of the examinations, as I was coming down the stairs, my mother jumped out of bed and overtook me on the landing to bless me. I passed, as indeed I did all subsequent examinations, by the skin of my teeth. The new school, even more than the old, inspired me with a sense of awe. My brother had already preceded me by some three or four years and, no doubt to make his influence felt, walked with another big boy behind me and my pal, whom he kicked at intervals on the backside; but dispensed his own pal from kicking me. Thus we went round and round, my pal and I, followed by my brother and the other big boy kicking my pal, who found these periodic jerks interfered with the orderly flow of his conversation, and looked confused. My parents had decided in favour of the " Realschule " for both of us as against the " Gymnasium." This meant that classical languages were sacrificed in favour of mathematics and physical sciences, at which, moreover, I proved a complete dunce. I was always late for school and used to run at the last minute with my tongue hanging out, hoping to catch some specially swift tram, and the class master to whom I explained that we lived a long way off always said that this was no excuse since, on the contrary, it enabled us, if late, to make up on the length of the journey. I have not profited by his views, and to this day I regard punctuality—like chastity—as a beautiful ideal, something to aspire to, a dream realizable in a millennium, but not what we call practical politics, modern traffic and human nature being what they are.

English was at the bottom of the school curriculum and not begun till the fourth year. It was taught by an Englishman born and nurtured in Russia, who had difficulty in believing that my brother and I were English, but who, when he meant to say he would take down your name for some offence, said : " I shall inscribe you." I was very proud of the looks of my mother, whom, as a small boy, I used to

watch putting the last touches to her gown before driving
out to a ball or the theatre ; and I would say : " Oh, how
beautiful you are ! " which, since she was but a woman, had
a salutary effect.   She had very blue eyes, and generally conformed to my ideas of beauty.   I used particularly to like my
mother to call for me at school because I thought she must be
more beautiful than the other boys' mothers and because it
pleased me to show off that we had our own horses.   The
coachman used to drive up to the gate.   The gymnasium
instructor directs him to get out of the way of the boys playing
a ball game, but seeing my mother emerge from the building
with me, comes up and imparts to her with a cavalier bow :
" Dear lady, your carriage is round the corner."   This, in
the hearing of the other boys, is very satisfactory.

Sometimes my mother would call for me with a sister, and
then I thought : What a nice-looking sister and how envious
it must make the other boys to see what a sister I have !   But
this only happened now and again.   On most days of the
week I took the tram for the first half of the journey home,
and trudged the rest on foot with a satchel on my back and
dreaming of the future.   A vast grey granite building on
the Quay Peter the Great.   It is a bank.   Mine.   My brother
comes to raise credit with me.   I refuse.   That white house
by the side of the bank is my house.   Built by myself, for I
am an architect of genius.   Also a Cabinet Minister and, in
fact, the British Ambassador.   Also a conductor of orchestra.
I arrive on a diplomatic mission in court dress and a three-
corner hat.   Everybody admires me.   I conclude an advan-
tageous treaty with Russia, but am also asked to conduct.

I would, in these preoccupations with my future, neglect
my homework, and hope, the next morning, that Herr Tomson
will omit to test my geography.   But it looks perilously as if
he may, and so I request permission to leave the class-room on
the pretext of going to the lavatory.   It is a standing rule,
however, that you must be back at least a minute before the
bell goes and the class breaks up.   And so, as soon as I am
back, Herr Tomson, with his nose buried in the register as

if following down the list of names, calls out in a sly foxy voice : " Gerhardi ! " He has just time enough to ask me half a dozen places on the map, and I to prove my ignorance, after which he puts against my name a damning mark and the bell rings and the class disperses. Even now I often dream of this. I awake to find that my anxiety is unfounded, that I have indeed escaped him.

Perhaps one day, after they have left us in the grave, we shall awake to find that we have escaped it all.

V

THE BATTLE OF CYZICUS

In the year 410 B.C. was fought the battle of Cyzicus—a date unforgettable to all the boys of my school. Unforgettable, I say, since it was the crucial event of our school-days and one for which we waited three years before our ambition was realized in the Christmas Term of our fourth year at school. The event was historic in more ways than one. It was a small landmark in Ancient History, but a big landmark in the life of the school.

The Ancient History master had an impediment in his speech which prevented him from pronouncing the word "Cyzicus" without much stuttering and spluttering and nervous twitching of face.

" Herr Keisler, you've spat at me ! "

Whisking out his handkerchief : " I beg your pardon."

His nickname for thirty years had been " Cyzicus " or " 410." Once a year he had to come out with the word. Shortly before the break-up for Christmas, the boys in the fourth year, advancing chapter by chapter, reached that period of Ancient History when the mention on his part of the battle of 410 became imminent, and the word " Cyzicus " could no longer be withheld. The whole school knew of the event, and the lucky boys in the fourth year, who had prepared for it for weeks, arrived on the day armed with drums and wind instruments which they concealed in their desks. The master

knew he was in for it.   Nervous, twitching, he would proceed
with the task of narrating the chain of events leading to the
memorable battle, and, as the inevitable moment approached,
he would rise from his desk, stand in front of us armed with
the register bearing all our names, a pen already dipped in
ink, and warn us splutteringly that if anyone should dare make
a noise he would take his name down and have him expelled
on the spot.   The blackboards from an early hour had been
covered with the figures 410, which the schoolmaster would
cause to be effaced again and again.   As the moment approached there would rise from the back desks a low murmur :
" It comes, it comes, it comes . . ." interrupted by the
master's sharp : " Silence ! "   The murmur began again, rising
crescendo till again cut short by the incisive : " Silence ! "
Then a dead lull, the ominous stillness before a storm.   The
master was now at the point when it was no longer possible
to withold the news that we were now in the year 410 and that
a battle was preparing and that the name of the battle was . . .
He twitched all over, swallowed vehemently and blinking
nervously, spluttered as if to get rid of it : " In the year
410——"

" 410 ! 410 ! 410 ! " from the back benches.

The schoolmaster, savagely dipping his pen into ink, took
down names pell-mell.   But by now the whole class was a
raging orchestra of sound.   Better take the plunge.   " In
the year 410," he said quickly, with his head bent and blinking
desperately, " was the battle of C-c-c-c-cyzicus," spluttering
horribly over the word.

" Cyzicus ! Cyzicus ! Cyzicus ! " everyone stormed and
raged, and from the back desks came shrill whistles and the
sound of brass trumpets.   He was fiddling desperately with
the register, but nothing could stop the pandemonium the
word had let loose.   Boys from other forms stormed the
corridors and peeped through the glass doors.   Still the roar
of battle went on.   At length, the headmaster, the assistant
headmaster, and others rushed on the scene of disorder and
broke up the class.

Then, until the same time next year, the fatal name and date were not mentioned, and only a small boy, perhaps, sneaking behind a corner and spotting the Ancient History master walking down the corridor might shyly pipe after him: " Cyzicus! " But no more.

VI

MUSIC AND DRAMA

If my father did not bother unduly about us it was because he knew that our mother could be relied on to do so. She thought that music should not be omitted from our educational curriculum, and from an early age we were taught to play the piano. As there were five of us, each entitled to an hour's lesson with the governess and half an hour's solitary exercise, the pianos, of which there were two, were kept going pretty continually. My father, who could not play himself but was musical by inclination, was alternately irritated and enchanted by the sounds which graced his ears. When we were older our mother, who could sing a little and play a little, sent us to a music school which we attended regularly twice a week, believing as she did that music was a vital factor in the education of boys no less than of girls. No effort was spared to make us proficient musicians, and untold good has been done to our souls. Yet we grew up to be individuals who could play a little and hum and whistle a little, hardly more. My music teacher was a pupil of Rimsky-Korsakov, which makes me a grand-pupil of the famous composer; a fact, however, through which music has not gained. If this lady was cold and meticulous in her playing, like her master, her colleague, a Frenchwoman, was emotional and expansive. She was the author of a song to which she had written her own lines, both of which, at the time, impressed me as the highest expression of passion.

> *Ne me demand-e pas*
> *Comment je t'aim-e,*
> *Je ne saurais malgré mon desire mêm-e*
> *L'exprimer !*

Je ne sais qu'une chos-e
Infinement douc-e
Et que mon cœur os-e
C'est aimer !

Ne me demand-e pas,
Que puis-je dir-e,
Lorsque mon cœur fremit
Comme une lyr-e
De l'amour !
De l'amou-ou-ou-our !

This lady complained to my mother that I was much too inquisitive and had even crept under her bed—which to me, as I explained when censured, was quite a natural thing to do since I wanted to know what was there. At that period I suddenly developed a mania for objective observation, and could tell how many buttons there were on the tunic of this or that hall porter.

At the end of the musical year the two ladies who ran the school always gave a concert which they started by playing something of Mozart's together on separate pianos. The French lady, who was *not* a pupil of Rimsky-Korsakov, was subordinate to the Russian lady who was, both in teaching and in seconding the other in the Mozart piece. I forget what the piece was, but it was something very lovely. Following this was a recital by the pupils, and my brother and I appeared as soloists, for which performance my mother brought along my father, who, at the end of the concert, gave my brother and me each a rouble. I did not experience anything like it again till I had to lecture in America. I felt hot and limp in the concentrated gaze of some hundreds of individuals. I felt it was cruel that my fingers should be expected to move and my memory obey in such conditions. I somehow played, despite myself, to my own astonishment, in a cloud of forgetfulness ; my fingers seemed to say to my soul : " Buck up ! But we don't care if you don't."

My brother used to play the violin, too. The emotion

behind his performance, though felt, did not somehow get across, and the final effect was unrewarding. But he encouraged me to second him on the mandoline, while our sister Dora accompanied on the piano, and I must confess that even though the mandoline is a poor enough instrument at its best, I have heard it done better elsewhere. Yet I played with emotion—which must have been largely subjective.

If in the matter of machinery I showed no promise, the theatre and orchestra at once engaged my whole-hearted enthusiasm. My brother, in imitation of the symphonic orchestra we listened to every night at the seaside resort of Sestroretsk, cut 'cellos, violins, violas and contra-bassoons out of thin planks of wood. They were life-size but had no backs to them, and their tones were correspondingly meagre. The first time I listened to the Overture of Tannhäuser my mother at my side explained to me in a whisper that the string arpeggios connoted a storm. Not unnaturally, I thought, since I imagined Tannhäuser to be, literally, houses of pinewood exposed to the wind. When I learnt he was a man— a Mr. Woodhouse—I was disappointed. My mother still tells me things during performances and even explains to me what is happening on the stage, but with less success than when I was a child.

The conductor of the symphony orchestra—a Czech named Suck who hailed from the Moscow Opera House—was universally adored for the vehement way he conducted the loud finish of the Tannhäuser Overture. He shook his long grey locks and his clenched fists at the brass, exhorting them to burst themselves with sheer honest effort—an exhibition of musical temper which, at the end of the overture, brought forth handsome returns in the coin of applause. He knew that the fiercest possible gesticulation was expected from him and so dared not relax his efforts, though I daresay the orchestra did what it could and, however much he stormed and waved, could not do more than it did. But the conductor's frantic exhortations made it seem more, and there was no limit to the excited gratitude of the audience. At the season's

last concert the Overture to Tannhäuser was always the concluding piece on the programme. The audience stormed
and howled for the best part of half an hour, after which a
band of students and adult admirers advanced towards the
platform carrying an armchair shoulder high. The conductor was invited to transfer his person from the platform
into the chair and was carried all the way from the concert
hall to the station, where he entrained for Petersburg. I have
heard the Tannhäuser Overture hundreds of times since, and
the complacent wielding of the baton by all other conductors
as they bring the overture to its predestined finish must always
seem to me a tame anticlimax.

Suck—no doubt quite a plausible name in the original
Czech—sounds queer in English, and worse in Russian,
since, but for the omission of a final vowel, it means " bitch."
Nevertheless, what a musician! Not content with attending
all his concerts daily, I used to frequent his rehearsals, and my
acquaintance with orchestral music hence is not inconsiderable.
Those were heart-gladdening summers, with music in the
huge hall overlooking the sea, plenty of tennis and bathing,
and freedom from school. My interest in the orchestra was
furthered by my first visit to the Opera when, on the occasion
of my birthday, my father took a box. Labinsky, a then
famous tenor and a friend of my family, who on his visits to
us, I remember, would only drink milk, was singing. In
the scene in the first act, where old Faust turns into a young
man, Labinsky, his back to the audience while transforming
himself, whisked his mask off so clumsily that the white
beard remained, though Faust was now a youth. Vexed
with himself, Labinsky then pulled off the beard and threw
it on the floor.

A little later a very dear friend of the family died while my
parents were abroad, and my sister and I attended the funeral
as deputies. As the hearse entered the gates of the cemetery,
a distant chorus could be heard which grew louder as we
approached, and there over the open grave in the snow stood
four men, their faces red from the cold, singing something so

hauntingly beautiful that I often asked myself what it could be, till, not so long ago, I recognized the melody—it was the Venusberg Music—at a " Promenade " in the Queen's Hall.

After we had seen "Faust" my brother constructed for me a tiny Opera House. This miniature theatre made me conceive a new "Faust" which was to be superior to Gounod's ; but wasn't. On my twelfth or thirteenth birthday my mother took me to see a French play at the Théâtre Michel. An actress who had loved too much suddenly felt, after several harrowing scenes in which she entreated the young artist she loved to come back to her, that she could love no more, but must only be loved, and left the young man she adored for another man who adored her. She wept bitterly, and a woman weeping on the stage made me swallow—purged me with pity. I was impressed to the bottom of my soul and resolved to write drama.

My brother accordingly constructed for me a real theatre with real footlights, but instead of producing a work from my own pen we fell back on Gogol's "Inspector-General."

VII

THE DUNCE

Unwarned by the illustrious example of young Tolstoy, who was regarded as a dunce by his people, and of young Goethe who came home ignobly after failing at Strasbourg University, my family did not think much of me as a child. I was conscious of being looked upon by my brother, and to some extent by my father, as the fool of the family. At bottom this did not distress me because I knew it was not true. For I secretly despised their intelligence. Unfortunately, and naturally in the circumstances, parents do not inquire whether you are good at something they do not understand, but ask you how it is that you are no good at what they do understand. And it is our common frailty that we deem our particular understanding to exhaust all that there is to understand. And so they thought I was a bit of a dunce. But I wasn't. If I may be allowed to explain, if it be not presumptuous of me to speak of myself in the course of my own autobiography, let me say this. My family laid store by such things as being "sharp," "quick," noticing things on the spot and being able to find things when you were sent for them. Those of our family who were particularly good at these things in their childhood turned out, as adults, proficient at finding truths others had discarded, and at noticing what everybody else had noticed, and at saying things which had been said before. It is, of course, natural to suppose that observation, a keen eye for detail, a hunger for experience, are the natural equipment of a writer. Substitute "detective" for "writer," and these qualities apply. When I accompanied my mother, who was shopping in the Gostiny Dvor, I observed only two things: fatigue in my own limbs and tedium at what I saw around me. My thoughts, on these occasions, were preoccupied with other things and I could not have told my mother anything useful in regard to the price, size, number or extent of her purchases. In the same way I have never got any pleasure out of sightseeing. The born sightseer who neighs with joy as he beholds new places and retains all the information he can gather from the guides, always tended to intimidate me by his capacious intelligence, till I discovered that the flourishing sightseer was a barren artist. He noted and retained the surface aspect of phenomena, no more. As he would glance through a magazine of facile stories without bothering to read them, so the born writer looks at the outer world properly speaking without looking. He says to himself: "Nothing of this consciously observed and obvious to all phenomena is any good to me. I will absolve my mind from noting such trash." And the mind, thankful for such consideration, says: "Leave it to me"; and with its silent camera snaps an image in bloom, seemingly too trite to be worthy of serious notice, and stores the negative in oblivion, in that dark room at the back of our mind which preserves it from the light of day till we are ready to develop it. It may be some small trait—the way some shopwalker shrugged his shoulders, revealing a whole attitude to the world; or how a man hurriedly came down the steps with another, and observing a pretty girl at the telephone, said to her with a sort of beaming solicitude, which denoted his maximum anxiety to approach her in the minimum of time available, associate himself with her predicament, yet was sufficient to put her off by the apparent foolishness of the question: "So you can't get through, can you? Awful things, these telephones—(deliberately) aren't they?" These puerile nothings are in reality the most precious (because the most individual) receptacles of human truths. For it is the particular which reveals affectingly that which is general to all human kind and, in default of appearing to us through a particular lens, must remain what it otherwise is—a generalization. The woman we love, the precious exception conforming to the general laws of her species and sex, giving herself like another and bearing a child—her idiosyncrasies endear to us what is general in her and common to all. And it is her smallest traits, the twitch of her lashes, not her lengthy discourses on her mistakes and ideals, which, stored away in the dark room of memory, one day will bring her to life, her and a whole world of things, vouch, like a hall-mark, a kind of spiritual thumb-print, for her authenticity.

But these seeming trifles which I stored away, unsullied by conscious thought which might have vulgarized them into a kind of applied science, were so particular, so small, that I was unconscious of having acquired anything at all valuable, only something I could not communicate over the dinner table, and be told: "Yes, it's a good story." Still less would my listeners, expecting to hear from me an exact account of an event, have appreciated my reply that in fact I knew nothing, had seen nothing, absorbed as I had been by the one thought of economizing any mental exertion, being propelled into a state of coma by an instinctive solicitude not to tax my conscious mind, which was preoccupied in noticing things on its own. But it was what Goethe meant when he said that the whole of thinking was not a bit of good to thought.

Long before I knew I was to be a writer, I felt instinctively that what we human beings yearn for are the general things, and the particular things which contain them, and that particular things come to you *by the way*, when you are not looking. But my family did not know that this was the ideal state of mind for a writer, and moreover did not know that it was an ideal thing, for a boy so inclined, to make his way in the world as a writer. I was not " sharp "—so I was dull. My brother, who had his own room in the town house but shared a room with me in the country, would delight in telling me at night : " You know, I overheard Father and Mother saying that you were the fool of the family and that they didn't really know what they could turn you to as you seemed no good at anything." And when I stifled my sobs in my pillow my brother gloated, and when my sobs became loud enough to be inconvenient he would console me but only partly, just enough to reduce my humiliation to appropriate calm, not remove it entirely. If my brother and I, in subsequent years, cannot be said to have even bobbins to exchange between us, like my father and uncle, it is because the natural incompatibility of our natures is not softened by the recollections of childhood. To those of my readers who think I do not show enough forgive-and-forget, I would explain that this book is not a tribute paid to my family, much less a testimonial of character intended, if need be, to assist them in securing situations, but a record of pleasure and pain, joy and suffering as they impinged on the retina of a nervous system peculiarly my own. It is not therefore the Last Judgment. (And, for my own part, I should refuse to regard even *that* as the last ; so that if the Recording Angel reads out my sentence of eternal flames, he will have to record in the rubric against it that Mr. Gerhardi's solicitors have given notice of appeal.)

My childhood when I suffered from being thought a fool is far behind, and a reviewer in the *Spectator* writes that " Mr. Gerhardi is so clever that he threatens to become a bore." Yet even now if my best friend should chance to say to me, "You silly ass!" I wince and take at least ten minutes to recover. My father, who was a born financier and was attracted by banking, could not have wished, in default of cotton spinning, a more attractive career for me. When my brother continued to plague me about my future, the matter was brought before my father, who, very soothingly, said I would be a rich banker one day, and would refuse to grant my brother the necessary credits to enable him to carry on his mill.

VIII

FATHER

The nicest thing in my father was that he didn't bother about us. He was so busy, nerve-racked, unhappy by nature, that all he could do was to keep his own soul afloat. My mother would say: "Charles, *try* to control yourself! Other men have businesses and enjoy them." My father, evidently not finding that *trying* to do the contrary of what his exposed nerves required was soothing, winced and fretted more than before and, on occasion, even threw cutlery on the floor. He sometimes ignored a guest, and he insisted on always sitting on my mother's right hand and would not budge for anyone in the world. Usually he was silent at meals, eating his food with the air of a tortured man loathing and struggling with his executioners. Only very occasionally he would put a question to us, totally unintelligible, but which he would not repeat. A grand duke's son came to tea with us once, and my father, who had had business worries, never opened his mouth, except when the guest, in response to my mother's question whether he preferred his tea in a glass or a cup, declared in favour of a glass, when my father ridiculed our guest's fastidiousness.

Yet I still think that a father who doesn't bother about you while providing you with all the necessary cash is preferable to a father who tempers the cash with solicitude.

I have since had occasion to observe many types of fathers and, had it not been for the almost insane irritability of my own, I might have preferred him to the heavy educationist fiend, the duty-burdened father, the religious fanatic, and so on. Had it rested with my father, we might have never been sent to school at all. He didn't believe in schools—probably thought there was a snag in it. It is curious how fathers, who do not nag you with edifying precepts, inspire the most respect.

Yet I walked a little in fear of my father, who had the uncanny faculty of either talking in a whisper or bringing the roof down with a shout. Once when he was coming up the steps and saw me standing on the landing he whispered something, intimating apparently that I should switch on the light. I failed to catch his meaning. He shouted. I fled. This early fear of my father accounts I think for a certain nervousness of disposition in me, which, however, it has been proved unwise to take advantage of. My father was utterly incapable of repeating anything, and he explained badly. Half his sentences could never get across at all, but stuck in the roof of his mouth. But if you asked him to repeat his message he either shouted madly, or shook his head with an angry "Never mind!" Once my father, my brother and I were driving to the theatre, my mother and sisters in another carriage. It was New Year's Eve and this was a mournful attempt to celebrate it. And there was to be champagne afterwards. It was a moist evening foreshadowing an early spring. As we started my father muttered something we could not understand. When my brother said, "What did you say?" my father shook his head savagely and said, "Never mind!" My brother turned the matter over in his head and after we had crossed two bridges and were approaching the Opera House, a word or two in my father's inaudible sentence appeared to have given my brother a clue. "Did you mean the champagne?" asked my brother.

"Yes," said my father amiably.

His nervous irritation, moments of rage, and terrific energy were balanced by periods of perfect composure and relaxation —as if indeed nature were retrieving the forces she had thoughtlessly expended—when he lay on the sofa and smoked a cigarette in a long holder with the air of one whom nothing in the world could disturb. He was lean, tall, elegant and wore very thin-soled boots with elastic sides, and he had thick beautiful wavy hair and honest dog-like brown eyes. I remember him, as he lay on a sofa in his study, or in the glass veranda set aside for him as a resting place in the country, a strangely remote being, and how I watched his fine profile, as he lay there, reading—but only a newspaper. His gifts were financial, mathematical, technological. He could tell you in the twinkling of an eye how much 196 made if multiplied by 647, but he had no literary inclination whatever. He had little humour, and that little was not of the best quality. But my mother—perhaps thanks to " Billy Wits," her grandfather—enjoys a really first-rate comical insight into character. My father could settle a bill all in a moment, it would seem without effort. But I knew that was not so. The care he took to get the right change, to time departure and arrival, necessitated considerable nervous expenditure— which he took out of us. For our common enjoyment he would plan to arrange things to work out so smoothly that if the least thing went wrong we suffered from his rough temper. His plans were so detailed and intricate that, if one cog in the wheel got clogged, the whole mechanism was thrown out of gear—not unlike the German Army, which was said to be so meticulously organized that if one boot happened to misfit Private 666739502 of the 66th Regiment of the 55th Corps the whole German Army stopped functioning and had to retreat. My mother, on the other hand, grew more and more meticulous as the years passed, till all practical things connected with the expenditure of money developed into a sort of running sore of anxiety. Though I also wince at the contact of the outward world as expressed in waiters, porters, tips, and such-like worldly currency (the influence of Grandpa Wadsworth gaining in_me with the passage of years), my mother's chronic fussiness when I travel with her ridicules my own apprehension, identical with hers, and I exhort her to be calm. " That will be all right, depend on it," I say in response to her qualms, voiced aloud, that we should have seen whether they put our big luggage into the van at the junction where we changed trains. " We should have looked," my mother worries. " Please ! please ! " I say entreatingly, " Depend on it, the porter's seen to it, it is his job "—and our trunks fail to arrive at the terminus.

My father, so kind, so generous and well-meaning, had a knack of putting the wind up everyone unwittingly. An angry workwoman would barge into the office and shout at the cashier over a mistake in her wages. " S-sh ! " the cashier would hiss at her. " Karl Vasilievitch (Charles the son of William in the Russian idiom) is next door." She would grow pale, stammer, stagger, and vanish up her own sleeve. Yet all his workpeople liked him, for when he spoke to them at all it was in affectionate terms, in pleasing diminutives : " What is it, my dove ? " to a workman. A tender phraseology which, in Russia, contrasting with an equally usual violence of speech, goes straight to their hearts. An English manager in my father's works was shot through the eye by an embittered mechanic, and my father attributed this to the manager's thriftiness in the use of terms of endearment when addressing the people. My father himself was loved by his workpeople with a love that, however, fluctuated at times, for, in 1905 his men, who, he thought, regarded him as a father, tied him up in a coal sack and placing him in a barrel wheeled him along to tilt him into the Neva. They were, however, stopped on their way by an elderly workman who put them to shame by asking them what they meant by thus treating the English Socialist Keir Hardie. They then asked my father whether he was the English Socialist Keir Hardie, to which he replied that he certainly was. After which they released him with apologies.

Such presence of mind in my father won our whole-hearted admiration. But what finally established my respect for him is a story I heard much later from my mother. When, following on a love affair between my father and the wife of a Russian officer, the husband challenged him to a duel, my father wrote to him explaining that he was attached to life, attached to his own wife and children, and therefore felt that a man who could put forward a proposal having for its object the possible loss of my father's life was too despicable to fight with.

IX

DAISY

My most beautiful days at school were, then and now in retrospect, the days I stayed away from it. Sometimes I was ill ; more often shamming. " Liebe " used to call it " Schulfieber ohne Hitze " (Schoolfever without heat). My father, who did not believe in schools, also did not believe in staying away from them. But my mother was sympathetic about it. When my chill was definitely a thing of the past she would gently prompt me : " I suppose you will go back to school to-morrow ? " " I think the day after to-morrow—to make quite, quite sure." My father was seldom agreeable about it, though when one was genuinely ill he used to come up to our rooms and pay us a brief but not unsympathetic daily visit. My little sister Daisy was the one who managed him best. When she was very ill with inflammation of the lungs, he used to spend many hours of the night at her bedside and tell her of Nice, to which she was to travel on her recovery. He loved both Nice and Monte Carlo, as the paradise of gamblers, and used to go there each year, and sent us baskets of tangerines with the leaves on them. My father of all his children liked Daisy best. She was the only one of us who was not in the least afraid of him, and she used to sit on his knee and ruffle his hair. A daring deed in our eyes. But a crocodile suffers a little bird to sit on his snout—inspired by beatitude and a happy reflection on the essential goodness of crocodile nature. So tiny that droll little bird, and so daring !

In the same way we have no record of my father having devoured her.

I used to delight in buying my young sister little presents. Little pencils and rubbers and note-books and other such things, which she took but found rather useless. I was, however, very fond of her. On one occasion on our removal to the country for the summer I drove a horse van into the yard laden with luggage and my sister climbed up on top and sat at my side. Owing to my skill in driving the van turned over at the gate with my sister beneath it, who, according to all physical laws, should have been killed. But she was completely unhurt. I expected to hear about it from my father. He, however, said never a word ; we all dined at the seaside casino, and no reference was made to the incident.

Sometimes in the winter I would stay away from school on my own and spend the day driving a horse in the country. And coming back in the train I once followed a beautiful (or so it seemed to me) young woman all the way to her address in town without, however, taking any further steps to impinge myself on her consciousness. The seaside, especially in the winter, was happiness and freedom to me. When my small sister was a convalescent at a sanatorium in Finland I travelled there to stay with her ; the memory of it belongs to the same family of feelings. There is a quality about them identified with a smell of pines, and to this day I cannot hear a railway whistle without being filled with incredible well-being, a state of soul that does not seem to belong to the past or the present or mere memory, but which lifts one into a region immune from the fears and anxieties, the shackles and local irritations of Time.

Then my small sister, who suffered from weak lungs, was packed off to a school in Switzerland. It was a blow, something I dreaded to think of. We had been taught to play four hands by our French governess—the last of a succession, old, round and small and not unlike Queen Victoria in looks. The last day before my sister went, we played that dreadful Suppé thing together, she at the treble, I at the base, and the tears welled from our eyes. And in some way her going away for the first time marks the end of my childhood. Now that it is passed I never think of it. But recently in a hotel at Sousse while spending an April holiday in Tunisia I was suddenly plunged into a sea of pure and reasonless joy by the sound of a small dog yapping, and on analysing the source of this joy identified it with a long forgotten feeling of a summer's day in childhood by a deep black river, resurrected in me because connected by invisible links of time to the little dog we had that far back summer and whose yapping was in the same key as that which now came from next door. In the morning a disturbing-looking young woman stopped me in the corridor. " I hope my little dog has not troubled you by yapping in the night." " Oh, not at all, Madame," I said with passionate eagerness. " Vous êtes trop aimable ! " said she.

I look forward to the day when a small dog's yapping in a particular key in the treble will plunge me into a sea of reasonless felicity which, following the attempt to analyse the sensation evoked, will connect me with what occurred in Room 76.

And so these things are symbols of happiness, dreams grouped around persons and objects, perhaps essences of eternity. Dreams which flow on and, maybe, survive when the everchanging mechanism we imagined to have been ourselves has been replaced in all its parts too often and cannot again be overhauled. And what we had thought a dream is a reality, and the reality a dream.

CHAPTER THREE

ADOLESCENCE

I

DETESTED YEARS

MY eldest sister, who was fragile, rather lovely and a little hysterical, attracted a great number of men to our house. There were Infantry officers, Staff officers, Guards', Cavalry and Artillery officers, and youthful cadets and young men doing their compulsory military service as privates, all of whom we children graded alike. But certain guardsmen sniffed at the Infantry officers, an Artillery officer shrank in the presence of a smart cuirassier, and the young men who were merely privates stammered at the approach of a colonel. Two or three times each season my parents gave a ball, when the maître d'hôtel from my father's club, with a chef, cooks, bottle-washers, etc., would suddenly take charge of the house, banish our own servants from the kitchen and scullery, and begin to unpack many brass pots and pans as if disdaining the use of our own. My father, who favoured occasional gaiety, would come down the steps looking very smart and spruce in his tailcoat. The guests, for the most part, were a medley of uniforms—officers, students, etc., attracted by my sister. Also a few bankers and financiers with their wives, friends of my parents. We smaller children, while allowed to participate, felt a little self-conscious. You would stand there, at that wicked age of thirteen, in your sailor suit feeling utterly idiotic, and the guests as they passed you in the door said all and one, " Why don't you dance ? "

Who was there to dance with when you were thirteen and wearing a sailor suit with a ridiculous big bow and knicker-bockers showing off your thin legs—so thin indeed that when you went out, street urchins whistled and called after you : " Macaroni ! Macaroni ! " At supper when champagne (proverbially) flowed and speeches were made, a student in love with my sister, whose birthday it happened to be, compared her to a tender rose—a simile not unnatural since Rose was her name. This prompted another student, a tall, lean, cadaverous looking man of thirty who wore spectacles and an untidy mane of hair and was renowned for his wit, to rise and deride the sentimental flourishes of the young man who had anticipated him and to tell us that he, unlike the other, would confine himself to a few simple, unadorned words. Which he did and sat down. I was a little awed by this tall student, said to be a kind of Dr. Johnson, and I dreaded to speak to him lest he should find my intelligence very inadequate. But he came up to me in the doorway and said, " Why don't you dance ? " And I blushed and replied, for the twentieth time : " I don't like it." A man who attracted my little sister and me in particular was a tall, brilliant cuirassier colonel who arrived always a little late, wrapped in his sable cloak and wearing a magnificent silver helmet, which he would tell us negligently the Emperor's young heir had made sport of by flinging it down six flights of stairs. After supper the ball got into full swing. A real old-fashioned ball it was with the *grand rond* at the end, when cushions with buttonholes pinned on to them suddenly appeared from nowhere, and a tall shy young man from the Imperial Ballet, who acted as Master of Ceremonies, cried : " Avancez ! Reculez ! " and, I believe, was paid for his services, and a then famous pianist of light music, who had been chartered to do his best at the piano, now certainly did it. My father could not dance but delighted in playing cards, while my mother was one of these women one reads of occasionally in other people's memoirs described as a passionate waltzer. My mother at that time was very youthful looking and handsome, and I am not sure some of the men who came to the house were not attracted by her even more than my sister. As for my brother, my second sister, myself and my young sister, we were all of an age which does not profit by such a function. But by the time we were old enough to have enjoyed a ball they were, in our house at least, discontinued.

Meanwhile my eldest sister had grown romantic. One day when the windows were open letting in the noise of the street, which, in Russia where windows have double panes, is indicative of spring, I saw through the half open door my sister absorbed in intimate conversation with a young lieutenant. And I watched how this officer kissed my sister's hand and looked into her eyes with tender passion. But I didn't like his boots, and I thought that my sister's languid castdown glance was really a critical examination of his footwear and explained her hesitation to say Yes or No. And then there was another suitor, whom I also did not like, and my sister, who believed in candour, thought that he should know of it, and so this other suitor also came to me " to explain himself," as is the Russian phrase, with sincerity, which in the nature of the Russian soul is long-winded.

My three sisters are now what is called happily married. Viewing as I now do the matrimonial situation from another angle, my attitude to my brothers-in-law when I meet them is almost apologetic : as if I had palmed my sisters off on them, shifted a family burden on to their then unsuspecting, now creaking, shoulders.

II

FIRST LOVE

My very first love was at the age of eight for a little girl called Violet aged six. But the feeling was neither long nor strong nor yet profound and may best be described as negligible. I was conscious that she was an awful minx and that it gave me real pleasure to anticipate her wishes. When she was absent my thoughts of her were absent too.

Not so when, at the age of fifteen, I fell in love with a Jewish girl of sixteen, who intimidated me by being not only advanced in age but also at her school, and whose Jewish features appeared to me those of a Spanish noblewoman. This overwhelming experience happened to me one bright spring morning as we were playing tennis at a seaside club. It was enough for a certain stranger to enter with her governess and ask me how one joined the club to change my being. From that moment the sight of her released in me a felicity which did not seem new but as if my native sphere of being, the only real existence, but one clouded over all these years by another, a rift in which had always filled me with longing for now I knew what.

But she struck up a passionate friendship with an older boy of her own race aged seventeen, who had the same pale glazeless complexion, and it distressed me that I should have pink cheeks, which I imagined put me hors concours. I came across an advertisement in a newspaper of a " salon de beauté " extolling some new preparation guaranteed to give your skin a pale and shineless surface, and I betook myself there one afternoon, and a lady specialist applied the preparation to my face in front of a large mirror, while chuckles of suppressed giggling came from behind the curtain and I could see in the mirror female faces peeping at me through the chinks. The momentary effect was most pleasing, the pallor adding years and romance to my face, and I left the beauty parlour carrying a bottle of the lotion in my pocket. The cumulative effect of it, however, was less successful. Designed to cover the jaded skins of ageing women exposed to a strong artificial light, the lotion did not bear the scrutiny of daylight. Indeed, no sooner was it dry than it cracked under the stress of a smile and peeled off, so there was nothing for it but to scrub it all off.

My love had not been furthered by the application of the lotion, and the girl continued to treat me as a child. Everything she said to me—were it only " How is your sister ? "—seemed fraught with secret significance. She was a messenger of the mystery of life. Meeting her one winter day at the Yacht

Club in Petersburg, and mentioning, in timidity and for want of something better to say, a common acquaintance about whom I offered an opinion, she reinforced her own by adding : " I always go by first impressions." This stuck in my mind as an example of unparalleled profundity. Always I would carry away a new image of her which added a glow to the one I had before. My parents, for many years, had subscribed to two standing stalls at the Imperial Ballet, and as I grew up I tended to monopolize them, for I was nearly sure to meet her there.

I would sit there, hot and embarrassed, through ravishing music and dancing which was like a realization of what so far as she was concerned was less than a promise. She sat almost at the other end of the theatre. I could barely catch a glimpse of her. I waited for the interval, avoiding friends who might consume the precious minutes, and worked my way towards where she sat, when she would smile benignantly and say : " How is your sister ? " It is surprising how love can paralyse the will, how it can exaggerate in one's own infatuated eyes the intellectual fastidiousness of the being we love and who, we fear, may resent whatever we say or do. I had the rarest chance of seeing her, but every day of the week I would pace the street in which she lived for hours at a stretch, till I was exhausted and it was clear that I had either missed her or she was not coming straight home. Occasionally I would screw up courage to ring her up on the telephone, when she would inquire about my second sister (who was about her age but didn't like her), while to me even to ring her up seemed little less than an impertinence. On Sundays our parents sometimes allowed us to make use of the horses, and we would drive, if it was winter, up and down the Palace Quay, or in spring and early autumn to the Islands. Her parents were rising bankers and had just reached the stage of keeping private horses, and my Sunday drive was one long, strenuous sifting of carriages, a dream which degenerated into a sharp lookout. And so it came that the falling leaf of autumn, a quality in the cold Northern sky, is to me identified with that ravishing, consuming, and largely painful feeling of first love. And likewise the aspect of elegant St. Petersburg, the driving to and fro along the red granite Palace Quay, the broad iron bridges sprung across the quiet, beautiful, intimidating stream—these things, inseparable from Pushkin who had sung them are, to me, also tinged by my first love.

There followed another summer, when we all went tennis mad and spent all our days at the tennis club. The then Austrian Ambassador, Count Berchtold—who, with others, shares the distinction of having caused the War—and his son, a tall, lanky young boy of about my own age, often played against me and my sister, who, when she was losing was wont to justify herself by saying, " I am not trying." At a Junior Men's Doubles match I won the championship, which was a dressing-case presented by the said Count Berchtold and which, unlike the Count, survived the War.

III

ANCESTORS OF THE SPIRIT

My love, thrown back on itself, sought an outlet in poetry. It was more love than poetry. When the love ceased the poetry ceased with it. Yet it was musical and elegiac, with notes in it reminiscent of Pushkin, Lermontov and Apukhtin. Ah! Russian poetry! Russian poetry! Other poetry, French, and German, and English seem, to me at least, as if you strained to read it under a magnifying glass. Russian poetry flows of itself like the natural spoken language of poets.

I fell under the spell of Turgenev, for no one else can give that feeling of being in love so well as Turgenev, unless perhaps Apukhtin in his charming, one and only story, " The Diary of Pavlik Dolski." Tolstoy fired me with a desire to write novels. When I read " Anna Karenina " and " War and Peace," the simplicity of it addressed itself to me : How true to life. How faithful in detail. That's exactly how life presents itself to me. I must write. I must communicate my feeling of things to others. Gogol had been an early and lasting favourite. But Goethe, with his "Werther's Leiden," so like my own, brought me down, as later I was brought down by "Tristan and Isolde." Goethe, who was the pet of all our German masters, was always a hero to me. Tchehov and Proust came much later.

The English of me and my sisters was so embryonic that, at the English Sunday school which we frequented, the teacher had to explain to the other English children, sons and daughters of foremen in local cotton mills who hailed, at a recent date, from Lancashire and whose knowledge of languages was confined to that of their county, that if we seemed to cut a poor figure at the Sunday school it should be remembered we were at home in three other languages. For my part I could not keep up with the class, and while they were learning Collects by heart I was invited to learn a simple psalm—"Now the day is over . . ." The first English book I was given to read was "John Halifax, Gentleman," and it was either a prize or a Christmas gift at the Sunday school, I don't remember which. I must have been ten or more. I read it with great difficulty. I thought John Halifax a great bore. In late adolescence, through sheer intellectual starvation, I took to Wilde and Bernard Shaw. Oscar Wilde inculcated in me the feeling that "the artist is the creator of beautiful things," and Shaw completed my detachment. I had always been interested in the theory of things. But now, under the spell of Shaw, having driven my young sister to fury by taking sides against a professional musician in whom she was then especially interested, I was preoccupied, as I stood beside her on a railway platform, with the question whether, if in her present state of agitation she threw herself under the wheels of the approaching train, I would not be inclined to exaggerate my blame : which I decided would be slight or non-existent, since I was genuinely opposed to the musician's views, and her wrath and excitement and love, if she must have them, were surely her own affair.

By now my poetic elder sister was married, and my brother and other sisters, thrown on their own resources, cultivated friends in the British Colony who assembled twice weekly at our house, forming a ballalaika orchestra, whose taste in music, and interests in life, I found uncongenial. In their arguments they used expressions of emphasis like " You can't deny it," " There is no denying the fact," thereby proving, not, as they thought, the indisputability of their proposition, but merely their unfamiliarity with a civilized form of discussion.

I was by now engaged in secret literary activity, writing a book, chiefly in Russian, comprehensively entitled " Joys and Sorrows." I would cover it up hastily if anyone came into my room, and this secretive conduct led my mother to believe that I was engaged in some subversive revolutionary or atheist or worse activity ; so one day she found her way to my locked archives and examined my manuscripts. Betrayed, however, by my young sister, my poor mother was placed in the position of either owning up to her " Okhrana " methods or blankly denying them in the face of my little sister, who yapped protestingly at her, like a small fox-terrier : " I did ! I saw you ! I did ! I did ! " Which was she to do ? My mother, I believe, did first the one, then the other, then both, and when unable to reconcile the logic of her statements, did the only logical thing left— got angry with my sister. My resentment against the inconsistency of parents, sharpened by a perusal of George Bernard Shaw, became vocal, and my implicit independence of parental moral judgments was thus achieved and completed.

My mother, if not exactly inspired by my manuscript, was reassured by what she read. As a matter of fact, I had been writing my autobiography. In her opinion I moaned and sighed too much in my records, as though I were really unhappy. Which, if true, was news to her.

Since I have become a professional writer, my mother's attitude has undergone a complete metamorphosis and she approves of my books to the extent of being angered even by

a " but " in an otherwise favourable review ; and is disposed
to suspect critics indifferent to my merits of being animated
by professional jealousy. " Victor," she writes, " has brought
Rosie ' Jazz and Jasper ' and ' Pretty Creatures ' to read.
We are reading the first together and getting many a laugh
out of it ; then we come to some beautiful part full of deep
and beautiful meaning and we stop to wonder and ponder
over it."

My father when " Futility " appeared and the collected
batch of some hundred press-cuttings made him think the
world had suspended all other news to write of me, was
indeed impressed, and said, erroneously, that while it had
taken Dickens forty years to establish himself I had done so
in one. He enjoyed " Futility " and such passages from
" The Polyglots " as my mother read aloud to him from the
manuscript (for he died before the book was out), but I don't
think he enjoyed my critical study of Tchehov, poring over
it rather angrily, munching with his mouth, for want of
anything better to do.

The attitude of my family varies on the subject of my works.
An illiterate connection, who had " Futility " read to her by
her husband, asked him to write : " We consider Willy's
book very fair." My housekeeper came to me one morning,
beaming. " Oh," she cried, " I asked my hubby (a policeman)
' Oh,' I asked, ' What do you think of Mr. Gerhardi's novels ? '
' Rotten,' he said. ' Oh, they are rotten ! ' " All this with
a smile of enthusiasm.

But recognition, in whatever form, was not yet at hand.
Whatever the view held of a printed book, there is no opinion
of an unpublished manuscript.

IV

EVADING THE UNCONGENIAL

My first love was presently supplemented by a schoolgirl
named Alice, half English, half German, whom I used to see
in the tram on her way back from school yet never spoke to,

but loved from afar. She heard through her mother, by way of my mother, that I was in love with her, and her adorable face blushed when she saw me. Alice did not displace my love for the Jewish girl, but was like a bourdon melody—what a viola is to a violin. My heart usurped my attention, and I got stuck at school. Whereupon my mother went to see the headmaster of another, if anything better, school, the Reformierte Schule, and employing her utmost talents of persuasion got him to transfer me to his school without my losing an extra year. At this school I brought my studies to a successful, if far from brilliant, consummation.

Having done but poorly at school I had no convincing argument for passing on to the University. My parents had long since settled that as my brother and I were apparently to inherit my father's business, and my brother was clever at machinery, I had better be trained to take over the commercial side. I rarely cared to fight an issue, unless thoroughly roused, but preferred to evade and circumvent it, and so in the end nearly always got what I wanted. My naïve, touch-me-not air was, though few people knew it, but the other end, the disguise, of considerable cunning. I had expressed the wish to go to England and had advanced a plausible excuse—training in *soi-disant* financial and commercial sciences which would fit me for the *soi-disant* commercial side of my father's cotton-spinning business. My father, off-handedly, wrote to Mr. Preddle in London—the young clerk whom his uncle used to call in to tell him he was a damn fool—now a man in the seventies and the secretary of the firm. And Mr. Preddle caused inquiries to be made, and great batches of prospectuses began to pour in on us with every post, ranging from laconic handwritten letters from a schoolmaster who said : " I shall be glad to have your boy at £150 a year," to a " secretarial college " which boasted that it stood in its own grounds. My father could not be bothered with this mass of prospectuses and turned them over to me to decide for myself which school, if any, I wanted to go to. I turned down resolutely the schoolmaster who would have me for a hundred and fifty pounds a year. I would not have him as a gift. Comparing one building with another I finally decided in favour of the one which stood in its own grounds.

The humiliation of being relegated to commerce, as the duller son is consigned to the Church, made me detest the whole idea. I wanted literature, not commerce, and if my relatives had not the perspicacity to detect my predilections and set them in train I was, I judged, entitled to go to England and escape from the uncongenial life at home, even if my father had to pay for a commercial training I was not going to absorb.

Before I left for London, grandfather Wadsworth volunteered to start me on my commercial career, although his only qualification for doing so was that a nephew of his was a bank manager. He read out excerpts from a manual of Pitman's commercial correspondence with great relish and gusto, a deep unctuous pleasure in his voice, and smacking his lips :

" Messieurs F. T. Smollett & Co.
" 17, Leadenhall Street,
" London, E.C.

" Gentlemen,—I have the honour to inform you that I have just established myself in this town as a Commission Merchant for Japanese goods. I was for many years with Messieurs Brown, Potter & Co. of this city, and had control of their export department. My connections with the manufactures of all varieties of Japanese goods are both numerous and extensive, and you can be sure that any order you may send me will be executed at the most favourable market prices, and in the best class of goods obtainable.

" I hope to receive your inquiries when in the market,

" And remain, Gentlemen,
" Your obedient servant,
" James Scott."

My grandfather delivered these lines as if they were a model of oratory, or a human document of poignant integrity. He thought I ought to be a banker or, in default, marry a rich woman.

My father ordered me a number of expensive clothes and linen as well as a " globe-trotter " trunk, which has since accompanied me twice round the world.

These were my last days. That autumn I strolled about with a camera I had been given for Easter and snapped pictures of Petersburg, suddenly become dear to me, the river, a corner of the Winter Palace, the little house which Peter had built with his own hands. I visited museums and picture galleries I had omitted to see, as if I would never again have the opportunity. And once I saw the Emperor of Russia in a small but elegant brougham driven swiftly across the dusky snow-covered streets. His face looked kind, his eyes had a soft, intimidated look, contrasting with the heedless speed of the horses and the stern look of the coachman and footman, as if driving something precious that they were afraid to spill.

Then came the day of departure. You were driven to the station. You said good-bye to the coachman, to the horses. I was travelling with my mother and young sister, who was being taken back to her school at Territet. The mahogany coupé is hot and stuffy, but luxurious looking. My father stands at the window with that infinitely human look which music and emotion lights in his eyes. My parents urge each other to " take care of yourself." There is the first whistle, followed by the second and, dramatically, the third. The train, according to this warning (in that country habitually disbelieved), yet pulls out, runs past factories, and fields, and more factories, and more fields. A cemetery flashes by, and the factory chimneys of the darkling capital are left behind.

Good-bye childhood, good-bye Russia, constraint and innocence and youthful dreams, and all and all . . .

PART II

HEROES NOT MINE

" A society of convinced disciples of Christ is needed to support each other in resisting that confederacy of co-operative guilt with limited liability which the New Testament calls the world."

Dean Inge.

CHAPTER FOUR

THE LONDON ALIBI

I

WESTWARD

THE train went faster, darkness set in. We were now grazing the dominions of the Tsar of Poland. And now the dominions of the Emperor of Russia lay behind us, and the dominions of the Tsar of Poland (the same person) lay in front. Then, at the frontier of Verzhbolovo, we crossed an abject little stream on one side of which stood a docile looking Russian infantryman facing a smarter if equally docile German " Pickelhaube "—tragic representatives of tuppenny-ha'penny nationalities which, nine months later, were to set the world aflame.

Eydtkuhnen, the German side of the frontier, was as spotlessly clean as the Russian station was bespat and belittered. We sped through Königsberg, home of Kant, and, as dusk fell, rolled on to Berlin. This, my first visit to Germany, threw Russia retrospectively into relief. I had always been conscious of the beauty, the widespread majesty of the town of my birth, childhood and adolescence, St. Petersburg, and was therefore exceedingly curious to see what other towns were like. I had, at the age of seven, on my first visit to England, seen Helsingfors, Copenhagen and Hull. But it was great capitals which attracted me. And now, on my journey to England, I was to see them in this order : Berlin, Paris, London. Berlin struck me as satisfactory in a " towny " sense. But the streets were too clean—almost as if they were

67

floors constructed for the purpose of roller-skating. And I could not quite get the hang of Berlin; the river was too insignificant to make the plan of the town intelligibly attractive. There were too many streets like the Friedrichstrasse running into each other (whose shops, it was said, catered not for local inhabitants but for Russians at exclusive prices called "Russen oder Narrenpreise") unlike St. Petersburg where there was but one Morskaia, and therefore more noted and cherished. But the Unter den Linden impressed me.

From Berlin we went south to Montreux. And, waking in the morning, suddenly I saw the mountains, for the first time in my life. Depositing my young sister at her school in Territet, we stayed on at the hotel about a week. Everything about me absorbed me. I would talk about it to my mother at meals, who begged me not to speak so loud—everybody, she remarked, could hear me. Even now when my mother and I give expression to our contending views in quite the same volume of voice, suddenly, as she feels she is losing ground, she will say, "Please don't talk so loud. You don't want the whole house to hear you."

Next came Paris, the very thought of which excited me. I watched its approaches from the train as I had always watched the approaches of Petersburg, a few distant-lying factories, fields, gleaming domes and spires, a brief glimpse of the capital's outlines. Then steaming up, with much delay and perplexity, under the frozen snow-bespangled station roof—Petersburg! The approach to Paris, as indeed to London, was less rewarding. An accumulation of incredibly mean, dingy houses with washing hanging out of the windows, a forest of them—then a network of railway lines diverging, flinging themselves out right and left, and running into the Gare de Lyons, almost before you were ready for it; and a vain, fruitless hunt for porters who were apparently few and strolled with their hands in their pockets as if disdaining their job. "This is scandalous," said an American lady. "No porters!" "Hein?" inquired a stray individual —maybe a porter, maybe one willing to try his hand at the job.

The romance, the splendour and shabbiness of Paris engulfed me as we came out into the streets. The Paris of Zola, of Maupassant—it went to my head. And when, in the evening, I managed to get away from my mother, I let a prostitute stop me and conversed with her, half fearful of her power, thrilled, but resisting her invitation : " Viens avec moi, mon petit chou," but continuing to converse with her, which I deemed was good for my French. Then my mother and I were hurrying to the Gare du Nord in a ram-shackle taxi. I had to hold the door to prevent it from banging about. The taxi-driver dashed across at hair-raising angles, cutting corners and pulling up within an inch of another taxi dashing out at us from another direction, and pulling up simultaneously, after which both drivers indulged in an excited colloquy : " Toi ! Quoi ! Toi ! Quoi ! " and, like a splash : " Merde ! "

The crossing over to England, where I had not been but for a brief summer at the age of seven, excited me. The smooth train journey across parcelled green fields, past tiny brick houses, neat and toy-like—all rather like a Saturday afternoon of cricket. But whereas the propinquity of Paris was sordid, the approach to London, with its rows of thin, soot-covered, dingy, incredibly ignoble houses turning their pipes and backyards on you as you whirled into the greatest of metropolises, amazed me, astonished my soul. I remember, as our cab-horse slithered out of Charing Cross Station into the Strand, my first impression of the heaviness of London— so heavy that the streets, it seemed, crumpled under its weight into little hills and valleys. The narrowness of the chief streets, the uncertain line of Oxford Street, the utter planless-ness, the higgledy-piggledy of it all distressed me, especially Bayswater, where I was destined to live.

But already on my first vacation home I thought with tenderness of that clumsy, sprawling, lovable old thing, that absurd big fellow, London, who tries to look like a townee but remains the burly village lad who can't adapt himself to city uses. Petersburg was wide, cold, sprung, elegantly poised. London was neither poised nor sprung but heavy, narrow and growling. But it was endless, oscillating with life, teeming with faces; and so much more friendly than his cold sister of the Neva. And the trees! These green open breathing spaces whither you fled from the heat and burden of the day! I discoursed before my Russian brother-in-law, weary and travel-eager, on the easy customs of the city, the tolerable climate—no Russian winter! the charm of the girls who, if they gave you the " glad-eye " in the street, you joined forthwith as a long-lost brother. Girls who, though they were not prepared to travel the whole length in love, did not disdain the joy of going as far as they decently could without inviting disaster; unlike their sisters of the Continent with whom it was either the kiss complete or no kiss at all. Yes, I admired the national spirit of compromise. I praised the debates at street corners, the liberty of speech in the parks, the intellectual curiosity of open-air audiences, the complete political detachment of citizens, so that, according to the military captain at whose house I was a boarder, you could go up to any soldier on guard outside Buckingham Palace and say to him what you liked about the King, and his smile would imply that it was a matter of opinion.

My mother and I, walking up Porchester Terrace in search of the secretarial college, examined the houses with interest, thinking we were looking at Park Lane. The head of the college, on receiving us the first time, impressed us adversely by an immediate request, conveyed with a smile as affectionate as it was unconvincing, for our photographs. We were asked to tea. There was a long table surrounded by girl students, and my mother records that she had never before seen me more perfectly at my ease. I was to lodge with an old retired army captain who kept up an air of gentility, dressed regularly for dinner and liked to sit long over his coffee talking of better days, while his wife, emaciated and hardened by life, slapped him in the face with his own napkin and bade him rise and be gone into the smoking-room as she wanted the table cleared. Meekly resentful, he did as he was told. She had been his father's housekeeper, it was said, and he had married her, forty years ago, against his parents' wishes, who resented her rise and his fall; and she had ended where she had begun, as her husband's housekeeper. Busy and acrid, she relaxed into a state of humanity after meals, when she would inquire from me whenever I passed her: "And what do you think of my pussy-cat?" Her husband had a sepulchral, scarcely audible, voice, and the first day we dined there he talked at length of Händel, Mendelssohn, of sonatas, cantatas and oratorios, while my mother exchanged occasional glances with me which denoted that the soup was abject and the fish worse. My relations with the retired captain were entirely amiable. They never touched any subject less gross than Mendelssohn's "Elijah" or Händel's "Messiah," but for one lapse, when the veteran soldier, having run across me on my way to the pictures with a shopgirl from Arthur's Stores, conceived it his duty to report the matter to the head of the college, to whom he said with a stiff, blank, hitherto unknown to me, expression on his face and avoiding my glance: "I saw him in the street the other night with a low woman." The head of the college, who had a naturally sly face, looked very, if unconvincingly, grave and said: "I shall have to write to your father." At which I burst into tears.

When, ten years later, I suddenly chanced to run into the old captain in the Queen's Road, he appeared in no wise surprised. His blunt nose seemed to have got blunter, his voice more inaudible, more sepulchral. He did not greet me, made no reference to the war, the Russian Revolution, the armistice, but shuffled up to me, stopped, looked up with mild glassy eyes and murmured: "Ugh—ugh—they are giving Mendelssohn's "Elijah" in St. Giles Church at three o'clock to-day. Would you—ugh—care to come?"

I thanked him. And we parted for ever.

For the rest, I confined myself to long solitary strolls across the length and breadth of the magnificent London parks. I must confess that if at first I cherished ideas of taking the City by storm, by virtue of my secretarial training, such dreams, together with my interest in secretarial training, were soon set aside. The old captain had made it clear to me that with the money spent on me my father could have sent me to Oxford, but the explanations involved by such a change of plan were too arduous. If I wasted my father's money, at least I was in England, about, as I imagined, to impinge myself on the artistic consciousness of London. I strolled and strolled athwart the parks and dreamed with the empty vanity of youth. Here, the sight of a piquant-looking girl inflamed my senses and I would set off in hot pursuit of her. There, a military band deepened the lonely sense of paradise deferred. The conductor, a major, sword and red sash round his waist, tries to sway and bend like an artist, but remembering he is a soldier, restrains himself. The truth is that he is neither one nor the other.

I had such a poor acquaintance with written English that at first I wrote my letters home in Russian. When after the first term I returned to Petersburg for my vacation my parents were a little surprised to find no perceptible improvement in my command of their native tongue, and I explained that if I had not improved my English I had become strangely fluent in French, since the only other " foreigner " in the college was a Parisian sent by his father to England to acquaint himself with the language of the country, and with whom I pitted myself against the intrusion of the Anglo-Saxon world. During my second term I began to prick up my literary ears and read the whole of " The Picture of Dorian Gray "—never having, since my distasteful dip into " John Halifax, Gentleman," essayed an English book in the original. The pronounced and distinctive cadences of Oscar Wilde sunk into me ; from whom (as seems inevitable for Continentals) I passed to Bernard Shaw, whose incisive, deliberate sentences also commended themselves to my groping literary sense. Thereafter I began to employ the English medium in correspondence with my parents. When I could bring out a " nevertheless " or a " notwithstanding " I felt instinctively that my command of their language was now such as to allow me to use it like a master. I decided I would write books simultaneously in Russian and English. I measured my knowledge of written English (which my friend Hugh Kingsmill describes as " brilliant but uncertain ") by the increasing certainty with which I fingered the opaqueness of the, to me, more remote and ambitious words. If a sentence balanced nicely and came down with the awaited emphasis on the last word I deemed it in itself a reason for inclusion. I caressed words like a sculptor, remembered them, used them for their own sake, transposed them indefinitely. I ceased to attach undue importance to difficult words since I noticed that they were the everyday coin to others. My use of them was now lighter, but still tangible and caressing. And when I read to-day that I write " carelessly " I begin to wonder how it is that " carelessness " is not a synonym for " taking pains."

My homecoming at Christmas was marred by my losing, before I reached Dover, my London-Petersburg return ticket. I had to borrow money from an acquaintance in the train and I felt very miserable ; strains of Tchaikovsky's Sixth (Pathetic) Symphony dogged me all the way as an echo of the tragedy of human fate on earth, that bitter night especially as I paced the streets of haughty freezing Berlin. When I reached home, I wondered how I should break the news. When I came to acquaint my father of it, he was stretched on the sofa, smoking with the air of a man whom nothing could disturb. He inhaled, puffed out the smoke, said gently : " It's experience." And that was all he said.

During the Christmas vacation my father did have one go at making me his secretary. He gave me a letter to type on a typewriter which looked and worked like a watch. My long pauses disappointed him, and his impatience handicapped my efforts.

After the Christmas holidays I travelled back to England. Bishop Bury, the official shepherd of the Anglican flock dispersed through Central Europe, was in the train with me, and, as if holding out a cake or sweetmeat to me, said : " Come to my class in South Kensington. I will confirm you." On the same journey I also met a family called Tolstoy—unrelated to the novelist.

II

THE EXCUSE

At the end of the summer term, July 1914, I again travelled home for the long vacation by way of Berlin. I had not acquitted myself with any too blatant distinction. When the report came in it proved disappointing. My father was a little astonished, but said nothing. He had recently broken his ankle, was laid up in town, conducting his business by telephone—an instrument which tended to arouse his anger ; in which circumstances no good report could have appeared to him appreciably better than a bad one.

It was a sultry summer, and most of us were in the country, at a seaside place near Petersburg. Thunder in the air. Reports that Sazonov had been seen taking his luncheon at the Restaurant Content, looking worried. Count Pourtales doubtful. M. Paléologue listless . . . And then, almost at once, came the war. As if at a signal, all the local worthies became patriotic, and marched in processions, united by a feeling that all the shortcomings inherent in the scheme of things, which had hitherto prevented them from being happy, were due to a malignant cancer, now to be eradicated, a cancer which—the newspapers left no room for doubt—was the Empire of Germany. Patriotic wrath was unanimous. A small gentleman, who had behaved with marked restraint for nearly a lifetime, beholding his *vis-à-vis* in the train reading the *Petersburger Zeitung*, a paper catering for the Tsar's German-speaking subjects (but read also by many an orthodox Russian for the superiority of its financial page), now snatched the offending rag from the stranger's hands and flung it on the floor. The Germans, it was already being rumoured, diverted themselves by throwing returning Russian baby passengers out of express trains. Who but a moral outcast would in the circumstances read the *Petersburger Zeitung*?

An aspect of the war, not usually commented upon by historians, was that I could not go back to my secretarial studies, the direct route through Germany being blocked. My father accordingly put me into his head office, where I was given a ledger. He had recently merged his business with two others into a combine which, with the backing of two banks, was to be the largest textile company in Petersburg. As one of three active directors of the new company, he displayed a beau geste in fixing a nominal salary for me at less than the minimum rate, and though the other directors politely suggested an increase my father magnanimously waived aside the suggestion. As the son of the guiding force of the concern, I was treated with indulgence by the other employees, and nobody minded my coming late to the office. I put up an unconvincing show with the ledger, at the same time scribbling surreptitiously beneath a blotting pad a play in three acts entitled "The Haunting Roubles." The theme was a condemnation of money. A young Russian prince compelled by his rapacious relatives to marry the daughter of a wealthy merchant, curses his fate and his wife, who he believes has only married him for his title. The idea haunts him and prevents him from confessing his love for her, till, in the last act, she confesses to him that she had been kept back from avowing her love for him by the haunting thought that he had only married her for her money. Hence the appropriate title—"The Haunting Roubles." When their mutual error is discovered there is no further bar or limit to their love and happiness and, as I hoped, the ecstatic tears of the audience.

When, three or four months later, "The Haunting Roubles" was completed I was anxious to travel to London to give Sir George Alexander the opportunity of producing it, but as I could not urge this as a plausible reason for returning to England, since literature carried no weight with my people, I pretended I was anxious to resume my secretarial studies, at which, as a matter of fact, I had made a poor show. My father proved unenthusiastic. On the other hand, my activities at his office inspired him even less ; and he agreed to let me go. I won over my mother with even less difficulty, for she and I were generally on the best of terms. We had the same comical appreciation of human character. She used to read aloud to me now " Tartarin de Tarascon," now Gogol, or Tchehov or Dickens. I would amuse her by recounting in the evening the characteristic traits of the people in my father's office observed by me during the day. My father, tired, would come up into her bedroom while we sat on her bed, laughing a good deal. My father rarely laughed except when relating some old anecdote of his own, when the laughter would precede the story and drown it. So that though we had heard the same anecdote many times before the story remained tantalizingly unknown to us. He would rarely smile, but just come in for a few minutes and retire early to his room. And we all had a feeling of compassion for that tired giant whose shoulders supported us and to whom we owed all the amenities of life. To this day it is a mystery to me why my father should have, once again, and in the midst of war, financed my unconvincing zeal for secretarial knowledge. But the war had paralysed one's will. The central heating in the house was not working adequately. My father's resistance to life must have been low. There is no other explanation.

He did once feebly suggest that I should rather join the Anglo-Russian bank with which he was connected. " They know," he said, " you come from a respectable family and in a few years' time you might become a director." I, with the completed manuscript of " The Haunting Roubles " in a drawer of my writing-table and with my mental eye on its forthcoming production by Sir George Alexander, was determined to have a pretext for returning to London. Nothing would have induced me to disclose the real reason, since that might have led to a domestic scrutiny of my play.

The complicated journey through Sweden and Norway, and the sending of school fees, necessitated some preliminary calculation, to which my father devoted an hour after dinner, and wherein I was not at my best. Previously, when he had intended to employ me as his secretary, I had not acquitted myself with any credit at the new watch-like baby typewriter, the ingenuity of which hampered rather than helped me to show off my skill, never great, at an ordinary typewriter. Now, it seemed, I could not as much as calculate what my fees for next term, living expenses, and the travelling money I needed amounted to. A poor mathematical gift is not assisted by a distracted father deploring aloud that you cannot do simple sums in your head. And when your father's distraction turns to despair and he splits the problem for you : " Now, come here : how much is twenty-seven times seventy-three ? " the whole of the problem is not clarified but further confused by your excited inability to solve a part of it. " Now come," cried my father excitedly, " calm yourself. To-day is the 8th of January. How many days till the 9th April ? " My request for a calendar angered my parent who thought I ought to be able to divine the answer without artificial aid. " But let me look at the calèndar," I implored. Now the innocence of this request was made sinister by my mispronunciation of the word, which revealed to my father that despite my twelve months in England at a secretarial college intended to prepare me for a commercial career I was unable to type on his typewriter, calculate my own expenses without resorting to a calendar, and unable to pronounce correctly in English the very article to which I aspired. And, in addition to all these things, declining to remain at his head office, negativing his proposal to join the staff at a bank which conducted a part of his business, and proposing to travel by a costly circuitous route to a country absorbed in waging war, with a view to continuing, at some considerable expense to himself and at a time when his business was suffering heavy losses, my *soi-disant* secretarial studies at which I had clearly proved myself useless. Now it is not impossible for an incurious youth to spend twelve months in England without ever hearing the word " calendar " ; the more so as, having spent most of my days with a Parisian youth, the language I had polished up was not English but French. My father might have appreciated that a young polyglot like myself, having to choose between the Russian pronunciation of " calendar " where the accent is on the last syllable and the German which is on the second, and not yet aware of an English version, with the accent apparently on the first, a polyglot youth, I say, might show a philological sense in grouping together two Saxon languages. But my father, irritated by the muffled mutterings of a baffled son, showed no such appreciation—instead a wincing irritability at my repeated mention of the word " calèndar." With inherent generosity, he, for some-time, ignored the word, which seemed to grate on him painfully. But at last his endurance was overcome. " Calèndar ! Calèndar ! " my father shrieked savagely and seizing his head in his two hands howled aloud : " Oh my God ! What have I done to have begotten such a fool of a son ! "

I rushed out of his room and up into my own and turned the key in the door. My father's words had taken the stuffing out of my soul. And by the law of spiritual com-pensation I constructed a future in which I would be some-thing when my father was nothing. Who was he ? What did he know of Nietzsche, of Schopenhauer ? Had he written poems ? Books ? Had he conceived " The Haunting Roubles ? " That fragment of a novel he once began as a young man of which my mother had told me and where he lorded it with superlative qualities, calling himself " our hero." Laughable !

My reflections were cut short by a knock at the door. I turned the key. It was my father. " You shouldn't mind what I say. I am an irritable fellow," he said, " and I have little patience. But you should try to keep a cool head and then everything will be easy." As my father's previous words had taken the stuffing out of my soul, his present ones took the stuffing out of my avenging thoughts. I felt a little cheated, yet appeased.

III

SIR GEORGE ALEXANDER DECLINES

At the Finland Station, where he saw me off rather dubiously, my father said, probably thinking of the railway tickets I had lost on a previous occasion and the cheque on another: "Keep a cool head." My mother was also there, and my brother, and all looked dubious as if they were at a loss to account for my journey to England and, as I thought, for my existence in the world. It was the last time I was to see my father on his feet. When, two years later, I saw him again he sat paralysed and helpless in a railway carriage and, perhaps remembering what a different man he had been when I last parted from him only two years before, he cried.

I travelled by way of Helsingfors and Stockholm, completing one part of the journey on sleighs. Rolling on through the snow-covered hills of Norway, I read Ibsen. On the night journey between Christiania and Bergen I had just opened at that passage where Professor Ruebeck in "When We Dead Awaken" speaks of being able to "hear" the silence, in those wistful moments when a train stops at a wayside station in the dead of the Norwegian night: when suddenly the train did stop and I too fancied I could "hear" the silence.

The day before I sailed from Bergen a rather beautiful Norwegian girl I used to know in London recalled herself to my memory by the fact that she lived in Bergen; and I was consumed with the desire to see her again. Her name was Miss Jansen, and my endeavour to elucidate her address from the Town Clerk caused a score of women, all answering to the name of Jansen, to call at my hotel; when I realized that Jansen was the Norwegian for Johnson and scarcely less popular. It was only a few minutes before I sailed that a young man came on board and introducing himself to me as the brother of the authentic Miss Jansen, informed me that his sister was in hospital with appendicitis.

When I arrived in London, "The Haunting Roubles" manuscript in my trunk, it was evening. War-time London looked dark, anxious, and unfriendly. I repaired to a Bayswater boarding house which styled itself a " residential hotel." I hated the idea of returning to the secretarial college, and as I was certain they had received no intimation from my father as to my return, I stayed away a fortnight to put the finishing touches to my play. The " residential hotel " was, on the whole, rather comfortable and it contained an assorted and not uncongenial set of people. There was a charming American woman with whom I was a little in love. She had a big bully of a husband who did not share her taste for literature but played billiards, and punctually at eleven retrieved her from our musical and literary company. He barely opened the door and bawled : " Kate ! Bed ! " He called me, with much secret relish, Sòzonoff. The humour of it appeared as ebullient to him, ignorant of Russian, as it was obscure to me, who saw no point in the repetition of a name foreign only to him who was himself a foreigner in respect of a language unknown to him. Nor did I see any fun in his unconscious mispronunciation of the name. But had I acquainted him of the correct rendering : " Sazònov " he would have been disappointed to the extent of finding that the Russian language was " not a sport." His wife was terrified of him, and though she seemed to like my company she did not yield to my advances beyond consenting to travel alone with me on the top of a bus, which she thought very daring.

The " residential hotel " excelled in tall men, and one morning we were incensed to find that the shaving mirror in the bathroom had been lowered from its accustomed position by a foot, apparently by a newcomer of short stature. This was before Strube's Little Man had endeared himself to the British Public, and the tall men's blood was roused. Why should the Little Man have it all his own way when all the other men were tall ? Time after time we unscrewed the mirror and screwed it in again at its former height ; and time after time the Little Man unscrewed our work and screwed in the mirror at a height to suit his own stature. One day we found a message which the Little Man had scribbled on the wall. It read : "Do be reasonable." But no one had ever set eyes on him. He rose early and returned late. Then, one morning, we lay in wait for the Little Man. We heard sounds ; we burst into the bathroom after him. The Little Man turned out to be an exceptionally tall man who shaved sitting in front of the mirror.

There was an over-ripe grey-haired woman of forty who made shy advances towards me and even knocked at my bedroom door. She, however, inspired purity in me, as the young woman who would not yield inspired desire. I maintained the best traditions of decency and would not open the door. Her son was an officer in the regular army, and she resented the detachment and sanity of an elderly naturalized Austro-Hungarian whose wife and family had been English, but whose own position as the war progressed became increasingly unenviable.

When, at last, I put in an appearance at the secretarial college I found the place almost exclusively populated by girls. My interest in secretarial knowledge having dropped to zero point, one day, with portentous solemnity, I handed my English teacher " The Haunting Roubles," inviting him to correct it. He brought the manuscript back two days later, looking a little confused, as if not quite knowing what to say about it, but intimating that at all events it was good exercise in English syntax. I asked him if he had corrected it, but he hinted that correcting it was apparently more than the manuscript was worth and gave it back to me with a kindly smile.

Still I was hopeful. One of the old ladies in the house who watched me copying out " The Haunting Roubles " in black and red ink seemed also hopeful. Everybody, she said, wanted a good play. I had paid six pounds to have it typed, for it was a long play. Enclosed in an extravagant cover it looked more hopeful than before. My first impulse was to protect it from the possibility of being stolen. When I sent it out to managers I was afraid they might crib my plot. A touring actor in the residential hotel warned me of this. When my play had been returned to me a dozen times or so I became less nervous ; and when it came back for the fifteenth time I lost all sense of fear and became quite reckless in the way I handled it. My first step had been to write to Sir George Alexander at the St. James's Theatre to ask him if I might send him the play ; and Mr. Adrian Vivian (or some such fastidious name), the stage-manager, replied that he was desired to say by Sir George Alexander that he would be delighted to consider my play if I kindly sent it to him at the St. James's Theatre.

The word " delighted " encouraged me unspeakably. The clerk at the post office accepted the package addressed to the illustrious actor-manager with a look full of meaning ; and I felt that there had now been established certain relations between myself and Sir George Alexander. Mr. Adrian Vivian promptly replied on a printed form that Sir George desired him to acknowledge the receipt of the play (which I thought a good sign), and the printed form also stated that Sir George could under no circumstances whatever hold himself responsible for accidental loss or damage to it. This, I thought, was quite reasonable on the part of Sir George Alexander. I also thought that I rather liked Mr. Adrian Vivian. They were fateful days. Once I could not contain myself. I strolled down to the St. James's Theatre and stood beneath the lighted windows, gazing upward ; and I thought that Sir George Alexander must be reading my play now . . .

But in the morning I perceived a large square envelope on my breakfast table ; and Mr. Adrian Vivian informed me that he had been desired to say by Sir George Alexander— etc., etc.—and (already on his own initiative) requested that my safe receipt of the manuscript might be acknowledged on the card enclosed for the purpose. And that morning I went for a very long walk.

Henry B. Irving was hardly more encouraging. He wrote : " If you will send the play with an envelope for its return, I shall be pleased to read it."   In a later letter he said : " I will read your play this week-end without fail and return to you," on second thoughts striking out " return " and substituting " report " in ink.   Marie Lloyd, who had tarried six months and then lost the manuscript wrote, after I had already joined the Army : " I am happy to say I have found it this morning in a disused cupboard and have devoted the afternoon to reading it, so that I might return it to you at once, having kept it so long."

The residential hotel, as time went on, became increasingly patriotic. The tall men began to join up. The extremely tall man, I later learnt, changing from a sitting to a standing position, exposed himself above the parapet and was finished ; and his desire to sit in front of the shaving-glass assumed, in retrospect, a tragic significance. There were two very tall, very British spinsters called the Misses Colonel, with a hook-nosed old father and a delicate, bird-like mother. And one day a tall young lieutenant in kilts came home on leave and called on them and took the girls to a dance ; and thereafter the elder girl was renewed ; the old maid's cloud that hung over her had dispersed, her prestige had gone up and her contempt for civilians became marked. More families appeared on the scene with more second-lieutenants about to go out to France. There was a canary-haired widow who all day long knitted khaki-coloured things for her son. And presently she began to expect him to come home on a four days' leave and made detailed plans for him, only leaving him free the last day in case he wished to spend it surreptitiously with some woman unknown to her. Her boy arrived. A nice, dutiful son of a second-lieutenant, he spent his leave as planned by his mother. But the last day he spent alone and in mufti. And next morning he went back to the war and was killed. The canary-haired widow that day, and thereafter, did not come down to her meals but had them sent up to her.

IV

THE NO-EXCUSE

The drums became more active, the call to manhood more urgent, the secretarial college more dreary as the days went by. There were posters stretched across the street with: " Who dies if England live ? " The sentiment evoked was one of noble self-sacrifice. Yet it did not occur to us when reading this appeal flung at us in the form of a question, the rhetorical nature of which was liable to escape attention in the whirlwind of patriotic excitation, that there was no question of England's survival, since her national spirit would, if anything, become more pronounced in the event of defeat, while there was also no doubt about the extinction of those individual Englishmen who fell in a quarrel as dignified and impartial as the squabble of street urchins : " He kicked me." " No, s'e kicked me first."

The theatre apparently not being ready to receive my plays, with nothing in front of me and everyone absorbed idiotically in the war, I suppose my judgment was momentarily warped. I too had a patriotic heart-beat and decided to join up. I wrote to my parents to acquaint them with the momentous step I was contemplating, curbing my patriotic excitement and sense of personal heroism. I said I would join the Navy were it not that the sea made me sick. I acquainted them with the fact, not previously disclosed, that I had, with the backing of the old Army captain with whom I had lodged (now suddenly become influential) dispatched an application to the War Office offering my services as interpreter, and courteously acknowledged by the Secretary at the command of the Army Council, which letter ranked in my mind as a document of State. But this, I argued, valiant as it may seem, was not enough. Join I must, and forthwith.

I half expected my parents, while admiring my bravery, to hold me back from the madness of it. Instead, and some-what to my chagrin, they readily agreed, adding the usual cliché about king and country, and apparently regarding my idea of going to the war as a solution of the financial problem, recently become acute, of supplying me with funds. This much I read between the words of the telegram I received in response to my letter : " Proud join up King and country," the wording of which disgusted me. But youthfully anxious to live up to it, remembering that my paternal great-great-great-grandfather was George the Third's gold-stick and my maternal great-grandfather William Wadsworth a corporal at Waterloo, I inquired, irritably, as to the whereabouts of the Inns of Court O.T.C. and was directed to the recruiting office at Lincoln's Inn. I passed expeditiously through several hands of junior officers till I came to the colonel, who was struck by my name, which ominously recalled another—to wit, von Bernhardi, just then considered the arch-author of the war ; as well as by my curious, more Petrograd than London, intonation. Given these two factors he advised me in the kindliest terms, while understanding my natural wish to do my duty, etc., against joining up, at least as an officer, for fear that my men might in their ignorance identify me with the enemy. My patriotic impulse having thus received a cold douche, despite the warm, almost fatherly tones in which the colonel discussed with me the inadvisability of my sacrifice, I returned, I remember, on the top of a bus to the residential hotel, telling myself that no man in the circumstances could do more.

In the hall a letter from my father awaited me in the rack. He somewhat recanted his hasty telegram and tried to modify the grievous mischief it might cause his son. "I advise you," he now wrote, "to go to the War Office and see Lord Kitchener personally and tell him you are not suitable for roughing it in the trenches, but are good at foreign languages and could be best employed in a sedentary capacity at the War Office, to the benefit of all concerned."

For a time, at any rate, I thought little more could be expected of me. I strolled about with a pleasing sense of having nobly volunteered my life for my country, a feeling difficult, however, to convey in view of my country's strange refusal to accept my sacrifice. Each time I called in at a sweetshop in the Queen's Road the man behind the counter as he wound the paper bag containing my little purchase of liqueur chocolates, said : "We're closing in from the West, the Grand Duke Nicholas' steam roller comes crashing down from the East, and the war will be over next month—I thank you, sir," dexterously twisting round the paper bag.

One day I saw a pretty girl on the balcony of another Bayswater house, found it to be a boarding house and removed there forthwith, only to find later that the pretty girl who was the cause of my removal did not hold my interest for the whole time I was to spend there. The house was owned by the girl's sister, a rather beautiful young woman, secretly subsidized by a florid looking young Jew connected with the film industry. But no one was aware of their relations till one night a Zeppelin dropped bombs close by and the young woman fainted in her lover's arms, after which several of the older ladies left the house out of protest. There was a rather lovely American woman, a zealous follower of Bernard Shaw and delighted when, in the lecture hall, he inadvertently stepped on her toe and apologized to her. She helped me with my writing, and one night during an air raid sought protection in my arms ; which moment I judged psychologically right to kiss her. She had, I can still feel them, rather dry lips. The young Jew and I shared a table in the dining-room and he suggested that I might try my hand at writing scenarios for the films ; though not for his own firm. Whereupon I wrote to my father that I intended to discontinue my secretarial studies altogether, and devote myself to the writing of film stories. My father, whose own business at that time was undergoing a financial crisis, heartily approved of my decision, implying that the film industry held a future while his own appeared to be on the decline. His allowances to me ceased, I think, from that date. I wrote a dozen scenarios, all of which were rejected.

The film magnate in the boarding house told me to be of good cheer, but offered no practical help. My Aunt Mary (Aunt Teresa in "The Polyglots") had taken refuge on these shores from the Germans who had invaded Brussels, and my father, ever a devoted brother, was sending her fat cheques through my own banking account, which, except for these large sums that passed through it, was conspicuously bare. On one occasion when I was very hard up I retained ten shillings out of the £100 which I was taking to my aunt in notes. This caused my aunt to express some concern, till, having sold my Russian astrakhan coat for thirty-five shillings, I was able to return her the ten.

The Austro-Hungarian had followed me to the new boarding house. He had lived thirty years in London and built up a business in the City. But now his English wife was dead, his home dispersed, his business confiscated, and he obliged to report twice weekly to the police. One evening at the cinema, to which we had gone together, we saw a drama depicting a once successful man grown old and deserted in adversity; and my Austro-Hungarian companion by my side began to cry.

It was therefore not as extraordinary as it may now seem that about November, 1915 (on a third wave of patriotic exaltation), I again offered my services to my king and country. My people at Petrograd, probably imagining by now that Lord Kitchener had taken me under his wing and provided me with emoluments even more covetable than those obtained in the film industry, had altogether ceased to support me. This time I enlisted under the Derby Scheme and walked about the streets of London wearing a khaki armlet, and wondering incidentally why the girl I had taken to the pictures did not look at me with the eyes of one beholding a hero. For a month or so I walked about with the khaki armlet, and I really felt that my Belgian relations should be very proud of me and give me the place of honour at their table. But these relations had sons and nephews in the war, some already grazed by bullets, and accordingly they were wont to take my khaki armlet for granted, which irritated me, and I argued with them in favour of the Germans.

Then came the fateful day when I received an official notification that I was to proceed to York and report at the Cavalry Barracks there. The only one to see me off was the old Austro-Hungarian. He came to the station, and I can still see him, a small, squat figure with eyebrows and gold-rimmed spectacles like Rudyard Kipling's, waving a patriotic good-bye to me as the "Flying Scotsman" pulled out of King's Cross.

CHAPTER FIVE

FOR KING AND COUNTRY

I

CAVALRY BARRACKS, YORK

I WAS met at the barrack office by a smart corporal with a gleaming silver eagle in his hat, who, learning from me that I hailed from the banks of the Neva, said I absolutely must join the Scots Greys because the Tsar of Russia was their Colonel-in-Chief. When I told him that my maternal great-grandfather was at the battle of Waterloo, the corporal stressed this as an additional reason for my joining the Scots Greys, as opposed to the 1st Royal Dragoons, because the Scots Greys' badge was Napoleon's eagle. Attached to the 5th Reserve Cavalry, composed of 1st Royal and 2nd Dragoons (Royal Scots Greys), were Yeomanry units of Yorkshire Hussars and West Riding, recruited from a more gentlemanly section of British manhood. Unhappily, however, I yielded to the Scots Greys corporal's wishes and donned his badge. At that period I had succumbed to the elegant pose of Dorian Gray, and I wore a languid, blasé, æsthetic look, an Oscar Wildish collar, a cane, and longish hair under a bowler hat —an appearance which was not enhanced by the khaki armlet. Together with me arrived a freckled East London dairy boy in cap and muffler ; and throughout our barrack life together I remained an object which excited spontaneous mirth in him. This took the form of chucking cakes of mud at me in the dark when we slept in a tent ; however, in no spirit of malice but through sheer ebullience of humour. I was

supplied with what the corporal described as a palliasse, which
I learnt was a mattress, though at first the word inspired in me
pleasing associations with " Pelléas and Mélisande." I was
given three boards and two trestles and two blankets, which
I rigged up in one of the barrack rooms over the roof of
the stables. And then for some hours sat on these bare
boards waiting for developments. There was an astonish-
ingly fat man, an old soldier in charge of the barrack room,
whom I asked where the dining-room was. This question
provoked general mirth. From the barrack square came
barking shouts of command and the sound of soldiers at
drill ; and presently a number of men marched into the
barrack room, divested themselves of their accoutrements,
and occupied the thirty or forty bed boards. The fat orderly
dragged in a huge pail of ready-made tea and milk, loaves of
bread, and margarine, and the men scrambled around him,
dipping their mugs, and sometimes hands as well, into the
pail.

I waited two days before I was taken to the stores and
supplied with the complete uniform, which was designed
at first to fit one approximately. Afterwards the regimental
tailor, for a fee, harmonized the uniform with the lines of
one's body. He immediately took an interest in me. I
found him reading Chesterton's " The Man who was Thurs-
day," and learning French by a self-taught method. A
tailor, even a regimental one, may relax with impunity.
And here in the Cavalry Barracks at York was a regular
British soldier who was a real Dostoevskian character, a tragic
type—an intellectually inclined youth run away, long ago,
from home through unhappiness, and become in middle-age
the regimental tailor, brooding, as he stitched a button on a
tunic, over Pascal's " Pensées." But at night he smartened
himself up like another and left barracks for a drink in town.

My immediate bed neighbours were a young regular
soldier and a police constable called up from the reserve.
Both seemed impressed by my knowledge of four languages.
The police constable's patronage—he was the senior corporal

in the room—stood me in good stead. The 5th Reserve Cavalry, it appeared, was almost exclusively a regular force, and such men as had joined for the war were, like the old soldiers, of the lower, and sometimes by the look of them, criminal, classes. There were two exceptions in the whole regiment—a Canadian college boy, a disappointed idealist, and a young clerk from Pinker's Literary Agency, who told me stories of Arnold Bennett and Joseph Conrad and other literary news, congenial to the author of " The Haunting Roubles." On hearing that a literary agent had agreed to " handle " " The Haunting Roubles," which, she wrote, " had atmosphere," I immediately had myself photographed for the newspapers astride a horse, only to find when I called on the lady in London that she was taking a keener interest in me as a soldier than a playwright.

To most of my companions I was a source of curiosity and, as they had an idea that my people in Russia were inordinately rich, of possible profit. They never ceased asking me to " lend them a tanner." The great hunger provoked by exertions in the open air made the nauseous food, of which, moreover, we didn't get nearly enough, almost palatable. The last meal, however, was tea, and it was as early as five o'clock. For the rest, we men were supposed to feed ourselves at our own expense at the canteen, or go hungry. Considered to be very wealthy by my companions, yet with nothing but my trooper's pay to support this reputation, I avoided the canteen, in which demands on my hospitality were frequent and heavy, and often went hungry. There was a tall, " well-spoken " sergeant, a Dubliner, who discussed literature with me in the washhouse, confiding to me at the end of our conversation, which I divined had been introductory merely, that he had just lost two pounds playing cards in the Sergeants' Mess, and would I square it for him ? When I revealed I had not the money his tone of deference changed and he ceased to exercise any favouritism on my account. Another corporal, a Welshman, hinted to me that my soldier's pay was a superfluous bagatelle to me and offered to become its recipient. When I negatived his proposal he began to pick me out for every toilsome fatigue. Whenever he saw me coming back from drill he pointed his finger at me and said: "Fatigue!" I did all fatigues but one—washing latrines—for which I always found a deputy, at a fee. For an hour I had to turn the handle of a machine which cut straw into chaff, or burnish rusty door knobs, clean windows, the corporal exhorting me not to spare " elbow grease," or work in the sick-lines. To-day I read of the hardships endured in the Foreign Legion, of conditions on " Devil's Island." For me, after my experience of British cavalry, they hold no terrors !

There was a nice young corporal called Willie Taylor, son of a Scottish farmer, who used to take me of an evening to a friend of his whose name was also Willie Taylor and whose profession was that of a tailor ; and I, too, was a Willie. The tailor was a socialist, very intelligent and well-read, and he viewed the whole war with a scepticism which in my dislike of barrack life appealed to me. His wife used to regale us with hot chocolate and home-made pastry, while I played the piano and the Scottish corporal sang " Asleep in the Deep!" He had a fine, resonant voice and got excited at the loud passages, exhorting me to emphasis : " Willie, play like hell! " As the war progressed our host became increasingly susceptible to Zeppelin raids and, I was told, concealed himself with his entire clan under the table in the cellar.

I liked the solitary nights when I was " on guard," a lonely sentinel left at last with my own thoughts, pacing up and down the long rows of stables, rats scuttling past, a cat sleeping peacefully on the warmly gleaming back of a horse. Pacing up and down, rifle on shoulder, with a pleasant sense of gravity, " guarding " something. What ? From whom ?

Once some obscure soldierman dressed himself up as a brigadier, blew in suddenly at midnight, turned the guard out, told off the Adjutant, sent for the Colonel, and generally raised a hell of a dust, and got away with it, too.

But how I loathed " Stables "—the tenderness of the
N.C.O.'s for the horses, and the spiteful brutality to the men.
The greedy, ill-mannered horses who stamped for their
food, and when you gave it to them first tried to devour the
food of their neighbour, to eat their own at leisure thereafter.
These kicking and biting brutes had to be brushed by you
till their coats shone, while at least three N.C.O.'s stood
by and idly looked on ; and when, after an hour of it, the
horse was led out into the sunlight to be watered, a young
lieutenant in shining riding boots (" put on " with the elbow
grease of his soldier-servant), came up and passed a gloved
hand across the monster's back : and if there was a speck of
dust on it you paid for your efforts with six days' C.B.

Sometimes I would be detailed with other men to fetch
remounts from the station, and would be leading them in
the early hours through deserted streets, past windows with
drawn blinds and the occupants—how I could imagine it !
—sweetly asleep on soft pillows, between white sheets.
Presently they would wake and demand their delicate break-
fasts.   O God ! O God !

II

IN DEFENCE OF PEACE

By the end of the second week I already felt that we were
paying too dearly for the war. What indeed had induced
me to join the cavalry, where I had to look after a horse, when
I could not even decently look after myself ! After the
second or third day, when my initial curiosity had been
exhausted, I began to feel as if all this had happened a long
time ago : that I was Joseph, sold by his brethren into slavery.
I was detailed by the corporal who did not get my pay to
carry sacks of oats across the barrack square which were too
heavy for my back, and when I fell I almost felt that the
drama of Golgotha was repeated. Why was I here ? And
the reply came in the ditty the Tommies sang while they

burnished their spurs or polished their buttons : "We're here because we're here : because we're here : because we're here," the words appropriately embracing the whole tragic helplessness of the conflict. We were indeed here because somebody in the Balkans had put a penny in the slot which started the music, and there was no one to stop it, for no one would own to having called the tune.

In " Journey's End " there is a moving scene when a great big sergeant-major drags a screaming German prisoner, captured at the cost of seven British lives, into the dug-out, but consoles him affectionately : " That's all right, sonny. You'll be all right, my son," and so on. In this line lies all the tragic impotence of humanity unwittingly plunged into war. For compared with the fierceness of the punishment borne and inflicted, there was surprisingly little resentment against the enemy, who, one realized, was in the same predicament. It were better for the race of men if they resented more bitterly injuries less fierce. But there is no bitterness, only complete charity of understanding. Total strangers blown into smithereens with not the slightest ill-feeling—bombs dropped on towns from a high sense of duty—a bayonet plunged into another's vitals from sheer love of one's country and without bearing him a grudge. No ill-feeling against battalion orders which tell you to advance, for it is realized that the battalion has no choice but to submit to orders from brigade headquarters, the obedient slave of the division, the latter at the mercy of the army corps, which carries out the will of G.H.Q. And so further back till, one supposed, the real decision rested in the hands of Mr. Lloyd George, who had taken over the war as a running concern, rather like a man who has a baby thrust into his arms in a public thoroughfare and does not know what to do with it beyond continuing to hold it. And we were here . . . because we were here.

The discomfort of sleeping in your underclothes, the hard boards, the mattress called " biscuits," the absence of sheets, no pillow, only very occasional baths, a room full of unwashed humanity, the unbelievable stink of perspiring feet and the urinals placed in the corridor outside each barrack room, some dream of a remote and happy time, and then the réveillé, hasty dressing in the dark. Shouts of " Show a leg ! " and the cry " Stables ! " Hasty saddling of kicking horses in pitch darkness, and riding school in the open.

From rough work my hands had got sore and full of blisters, and for a week I was excused duty. When I returned my riding school class had already advanced to riding on mere blankets, and I was expected to hold on as well as I could. I remember these cold early mornings on the snow-covered marshes of Yorkshire. At six it was so dark you could hardly distinguish one troop from another. My horse and I were not on the best of terms. I would lose sight of my troop and be carried along at a gallop, unable to control my mount, for I was not at home on the blanket. My horse, perceiving a troop at a distance and, in his inferior judgment, considering one troop as good as another, would barge into the middle of the closed ranks and set the whole troop agog. The sergeant-instructor would ride up with extended whip and yell ferociously, " Get out ! " whereupon my horse, resenting the whip, flung off, I clinging to it as to a schooner tossed about in a storm. Then into another troop, and so on till at last we barged into our own. The sergeant-instructor, ignoring my week's absence, made me ride with the rest, and every time I came near him lashed my horse with a voluptuously sardonic cry, borrowed from, I believe, the title of a contemporary revue : " Baby Mine ! "

" There's a war on ! " they reminded me. By God, I was aware of it !

After another fortnight of it I felt that the war had been declared (as it had been in truth) on an impulse and ought to be stopped forthwith. But Mr. Asquith, the Kaiser and M. Clemenceau thought it ought to go on. After a little while I reported sick (and, mark you, I was no less than disgusted with it all), and the medical officer, barely looking down my throat, sent me to the hospital across the road.

This military hospital happened to be full up, and without further investigation I was put along with a few others into an ambulance and conveyed to a beautifully equipped extensive hospital overlooking Rowntree's chocolate factory. On the way thither the ambulance collided with an apple cart and several old women surrounded us, gave us apples and expressed the view that it was beautiful to see a man die for his country. At the hospital I suddenly developed flu. Tender nurses attended me, ladies of York brought me flowers. They asked me where I had been wounded. That they might not be disappointed I kept silent or, if pressed, invented plausible names on the spur of the moment. "Antibes," I said once. As soon as I was allowed to take afternoon strolls, I quickly struck up passionate friendships with several Rowntree girls. I really had the time of my life. The two weeks I spent in hospital, first as an "invalid," then as a "convalescent," may be reckoned as among my happiest days of the war.

In the same ward with me was a grocer boy hailing from a village near Selby in Yorkshire, who told me he knew my Grandfather Wadsworth—knew him unmistakably—who didn't? "Why," he made his point clear, "he was the greatest miser alive!" When I came out of hospital I at once applied for sick leave, which was, to my surprise, granted, if a little grudgingly. I spent a week with my aunt and Grandfather Wadsworth in Southport, who talked at great length about his father at Waterloo and scarcely realized that a contemporary war impairing the comfort of his own grandson was in progress.

How I hated the return from leave! I daresay some of my readers would prefer to see me expose myself without delay to shrapnel fire and high explosives, whatever my own view of a foolish world. I, however, felt about the war then much as most people think of it now. What were the old ladies who felt so keenly on the question of " duty " actually demanding of one? This—the surrender of one's private universe to a formal, nominal quarrel pluming itself

with patriotic feathers, only to become, when the real life
has been offered up to it, a tarred and feathered object for
laughter and contempt. The Canadian idealist was likewise
disappointed. The thieving—"pinching," they called it—
that went on in the barrack room appeared to him inconsistent with regimental solidarity, or what is called "esprit de
corps," and seemed indeed to expose the whole idea of a united
front to mockery. To me, on the other hand, it seemed
more natural, more consistent, that men who presently were
to stick bayonet-blades into human beings with whom they
were not even on terms of nodding acquaintance, should
not be ideal but, if capable of murder, also capable of minor
theft. I had no illusion about the essential ignominy of
the war in which everyone seemed to do admittedly unneces-
sary acts of beastliness in the name of some assumed necessity.
Not all the human touches of the war could, I knew, redeem
its inhumanity. Though I wore uniform I felt, from start
to finish, that there was neither rhyme nor reason in it all,
and those who talked earnestly of national honour, which
required a continuance of contemptible acts to prevent their
repetition in the future, were precisely those who seemed
to me like grinning idiots in an asylum. But the other day
while dining with a friend at the Cavalry Club, a grey-haired
colonel in the Lancers came up to us, and my friend, to
emphasize my congeniality, said : "You know, he joined
the Scots Greys in the war—as a trooper," which brought
forth the white-moustached colonel's hearty bark : "Dam'
fine show!"

But I can only say that I acquired such distaste for my
immediate companions, especially my Squadron Sergeant-
Major, that the distant Germans seemed to me inoffensive
almost to the point of friendliness. True, if a sudden force
of Germans had poured into the barrack square, I would,
in the ensuing panic, have automatically fallen into line with
the odious sergeant-major and corporals, ranging myself with
them against the Germans, of whom I knew nothing except
that they were apparently trying to kill me. But that wars

do not last for ever (or not, at any rate, without a change in the distribution of belligerents), proves in itself that the panic, having dissipated itself, our loves and hates are redistributed according to personal and known criteria. Were there anything really consistently serious about racial hatred (and it is hardly reasonable to ask us to lay down our lives for less), man to-day would continue to carry out the idea of primitive man, his lineal forebear. Because the mammoth had chased primitive man, we to-day, out of loyalty to our race, would wreak vengeance on our prehistoric enemy, the elephant—and perhaps the horse. Then each of us could at least have the moral satisfaction of pounding himself on the chest and saying : " I have not swerved." But since we do swerve, since history is nothing but a record of changing loyalties, then, each time we unsheathe the sword in the name of undying hatred, we are the dupes of our own fervour.

Thus ran my thoughts, as I carried out bodily the cavalry axiom that " rear rank follows his front rank wherever he goes." *Wherever !* How uncritical ! It occurred to me that if consistency in the matter of national loyalty were of such stuff, consistency of vision in the realm of international economics, in pursuance of which some men claimed to have entered the war with their eyes open, was if anything a thing more hazy and incalculable. A far-sighted statesman might consider war with another state an economic necessity, to stay the commercial rivalry between them, only to find that, for a multitude of reasons which no mortal eye could foresee, the vanquished state, owing to a general depreciation in wages and standard of living, is capturing all the export trade of the world. I found my general scepticism confirmed by the events which followed the armistice. The war began as a concerted action of democracy to crush autocracy, only to end in Bolshevism on the one hand and Fascism on the other. Morally the war proved even more comically unrewarding. The splendid response of our women folk in staunchly shouldering the work of the men away at the front had a sequel in their no less staunch refusal to vacate their posts when the men came back. A vast roll of dead would, one had feared, arrest the wheels of industry in this island : actually it seems to have thrown two million men out of work. Must I therefore be blamed if my interest in the war, as an intellectual, spiritual, and economic adventure, was exhausted as early as August, 1914 ? Instead, what gained in force, with the passage of days, was the sickly nausea I felt for the Squadron Sergeant-Major.

He would say : "Who told you to think ? You're in the Army now. You haven't got to think but do what you're told." But if your implicit carrying-out of his orders did not, in the ensuing result, please him, he would turn on you : " Can't you *think* ? Can't you use your discretion ? "

The sergeant-major reciprocated the feeling I had for him. At first his dislike of me was mingled with curiosity. " Jeerady," he would say to me, " pull yourself together, so that when you go back to your Czar he will look you over and say : ' Jeerady, you've become a smart man.' " In sloping arms I was, however, always a little behind. In common with Chopin, I could never keep time. About Chopin's *rubato* playing, Berlioz says in his autobiography : " Chopin could never bear the restraint of time, and, I think, carried his *rubato* too far ; he simply *could not* play in time." In the same way the drill sergeant also thought I carried my *rubato* in sloping arms too far. When the command " Slope arms ! " was rapped out there would come the unanimous sound of the squad's concerted movement, followed two seconds later by the individual sound of my own. In the Army, however, individuality is not encouraged. " Jeerady," the drill sergeant would shout, " you innerve me." Or, with reference to my equivocal movements, the hesitant figure I cut on the parade ground, he called me " that Chinese puzzle." My inefficiency was not cunningly planned, but was pure lack of interest in my surroundings. As in childhood I was unable to devote attention to that which others considered important, but unconsciously stored away trifles which illustrated particular aspects of the general, so here also I would note individual aspects which illustrated the tragic comedy of mankind at war. So interested was I in the expression on the drill sergeant's face that he said : " I've got a picture of meself in me pocket. I'll show it to ye afterwards." In a thundering voice : " And *now* will you look to yer front ! "

I was put back and back, so that an officer, reviewing the ranks many months later, was surprised to find how long I had been trained and to what little effect. Why did I linger ? Why did I not hurry up to relieve my hard pressed countrymen in the trenches ? some kindhearted ladies will ask. Well, I will confess that after a five days leave spent in London, so awful was to me the idea of returning to York that the day before the expiry of my leave, I quailed in disgust. I then did a hasty thing. I actually wrote to a person at the War Office and asked him to use his influence to get me transferred at once from the Cavalry barracks at York to any unit in the front trenches in France. When I arrived in York it was four o'clock in the morning. It had stopped raining but was cold and damp as I trudged to the barracks. I was told to sit in the barrack room till réveillé, which I did like a man waiting to be shot at dawn. The men in the guard room were new and unknown to me. Presently, when réveillé had sounded, I trudged back to the barrack room to resume the soul-killing round of military routine.

Having established my inefficiency as a private, I applied for a commission. My Squadron Major, who on a previous occasion, when sentencing me to six days' C.B. for a dirty rifle, had said that " coming from a lucrative family," I should have been an example to the other men, now readily agreed to recommend me. In writing out the application I mentioned the fact that previous applications had already been filed at the Intelligence Department of the War Office. Through writing the application I was a little late in saddling my horse, and as the sergeant-major came along to inspect his squadron he stood a long time looking at me and my horse, at the twisted reins and the crooked blanket and the incorrect way I had buckled the girth. His look from a profound meditativeness changed to a sarcastic smile round the edges of his huge, waxed moustaches ; his pale eyes became cold and inhuman. " ' *Intelligence !* ' " he said with a sardonic nod, and swung on, his cane under his arm.

There was only one other man in the regiment who applied for a commission and, when asked whether he had private means essential to an officer, replied : " Money is no object." Two months or more elapsed before I was transferred to an Officers' Cadet School. When, after having distributed my private's kit among my comrades, I proceeded, in answer to an urgent summons, to the War Office, no one there knew who had sent for me. Somebody in the War Office thought it must be Major-General Cowans and I was instructed to wait for him outside his room. After waiting four or five hours, I was told that General Cowans did not wish to see me, and I was sent back to York. A little later, while I was on parade, a telegram arrived from Headquarters, directing me to proceed forthwith to London and report to a certain Colonel Leslie who, at the suggestion of General Poretchkin, a Russian friend of our family and now acting as some sort of liaison officer with the Admiralty, had applied for my services. When I reported to Colonel Leslie, he murmured : " Yes, yes. . . . Yes, yes . . . " and suggested that the next time I happened to be in London, I might give him a call. Again I returned ignominiously to York, where I had to buy back from my comrades the kit I had given them on going to London to take a commission. A few weeks afterwards I was again sent for by the War Office and instructed to report to the Russian General Poretchkin. He was vague about it all, but over lunch remembered that he had in actual fact mentioned my name to someone at the War Office as a likely man to sail with Kitchener to Russia as an interpreter, but that as they were in a hurry they secured another young man, a second-lieutenant called Bobby MacPherson, who had been at school with me in Petrograd and whose father was also a friend of the Russian

General. And it so happened that MacPherson's father,
who was a stockbroker, went to see my father in Petrograd,
and in the course of business imparted, not without pride,
that his son was coming out on Kitchener's staff.   On leaving
my father's office, he bought a newspaper and learnt that the
Hampshire with Lord Kitchener and his whole staff had
been sunk off the coast of Scotland.   He staggered back
into my father's office who, if he had envied him a moment
earlier, now helped to bring him round with brandy.   And
there is this anomaly for which Fate must account as it can :
there is he who is dead and better off but yet unable to enjoy
the sense of his advantage ; and here am I abandoned to a
fretful and foredoomed existence which I would not willingly
forego.

III

CADET SCHOOL IN IRELAND

In due course papers arrived which I was to fill in and
forward for signature to some headmaster who could vouch
for my character. I wrote to the head of the secretarial
college who, remembering an article of mine in the college
magazine in which I defended in certain circumstances the
telling of a lie, as well as questioned whether the secretarial
college did indeed " stand in its own grounds," asked me if
I still clung to that " philosophy," in which event I was
putting him to a struggle with his conscience in requiring him
to place his signature to an affirmation that my character was
one compatible with that of an " Officer and a Gentleman."
I wrote back, very uncomfortably on my knees in the tent,
while wishing Mr. A. to hell, that the sort of lies I felt
morally justifiable were of the kind you told, through your
maid, to a bore who called on you that you were not at home,
while really meaning you were not at home *to him*.

Mr. A. found my reply compatible with that of an " Officer
and a Gentleman " about to fight in the cause of Empire.
Mr. A. tended to drop the article and spoke of " Empire "

instead of "the Empire." He telegraphed on the occasion of a dinner messages of loyalty to the King-Emperor and then reprinted the acknowledgment from Lord Stamfordham, "I am desired to say by His Majesty." Altogether he was great on loyalty—loyalty to the college especially, which he interpreted as eagerness on the part of his students in getting fresh pupils for him.

He hoped I would always prove worthy of the confidence he reposed in me. Two members of the college had already laid down their lives in the cause of Empire, but my philosophic mind, he was sure, would realize what a small fraction Time formed of Eternity ; he was looking forward to that muster in the Great Beyond (reminiscent of the "musters" at the secretarial college which I instinctively avoided) when we would all meet again under the auspices of the Holy Father and he was ever, would I please believe him, my sincerely.

After the forms had been duly dispatched there was again a good deal of waiting. In the meantime I had been moved with others to a camp some thirty miles from York for a course in musketry training, during which it was explained to me that I was to try to hit the bull's eye on the rifle range. I don't think I ever got anywhere near it, but I may be wrong. It was spring now and all around was soft, beautiful green country. From physical exercise and an open outdoor life I had become very strong, wiry, strapping. This was possible, it seemed, on the abject food we consumed. I had even grown to a full six foot and had completely shed my æsthetic look. On one of my strolls round the camp I came across a Belgian young woman who, separated as she was from her husband, I thought would be glad of me. But, as we strolled alone in the wood, she said you couldn't have love like that : you had to pay money for these things. Then I chanced to alight on a little cottage inhabited by a very old couple and a pretty young girl to whom they could not make themselves understood and who did not understand them. She was a little Belgian girl their soldier son had married, and brought home when last over on his leave, and who already had a baby by him ; and they were glad of my services as interpreter.

During my stay at the camp I was taught " jedging " distances—a science which, as the sergeant-instructor explained, consisted of appreciating the illusion that, " when things are further off they seems nearer to yer : I mean ter say, when things is nearer they seems further off, ye know what I mean." A willing lecturer, he also explained the meaning of patriotism to a squad lined up before him : which was to lay down your life for your country. " You can't do more than that," he said lamely. I agreed that it was difficult. What was the object of bayonet drill ? he also asked us, a nonplussed audience, who suddenly felt we didn't quite know. " To kill," he said definitely. It was the same sergeant who made his drift clear to a headstrong recruit unable to catch the meaning of the command, " As you were." " When I says as you were," the sergeant explained, " I means as ye was, understand ? "

The day did come when the order for me to proceed to No. 2 Cavalry Cadet Squadron at Kildare, Ireland, was telephoned through from the barracks at York, and, it being Sunday, I trudged the thirty miles on foot through beautiful sunny glades, regaling myself at wayside taverns, on my way to York, where I entrained for Manchester, Liverpool and Holyhead. Before I left the camp my friends said to me : " Willie, when you're a —— —— officer, don't you —— —— forget the —— —— 'ardships of a —— —— trooper's —— life ! "

I hope I have discharged my trust. If I have not hitherto made my meaning plain, I do so now, viz., that a trooper's life is —— —— awful.

What a release ! In the train between Liverpool and Holyhead (the latter place was later to become a symbol of happiness, for it was there I spent the " honeymoon " night with the girl described as Sylvia in " The Polyglots ") I found myself sitting by the side of a very pretty young Scottish girl, bound, like myself, for Dublin ; and on the boat she lay in my arms, thus identifying in me a feeling of passion with a sense of release. When we came off the boat at Dublin some elderly woman belonging to a mission for the protection of girls from male strangers approached the girl, and benefited her with advice. This recalls to me another woman who distributed pamphlets to Tommies home on leave, in which they were urged not only to abstain from sexual intimacy with women, but even to ban any such thoughts from their minds, since, the pamphlet urged, thoughts like these deflected the blood from the brain and made them less efficient soldiers in the cause of their country. The pamphet urged that they wanted their soldiers, if they were to win the war, to remain clean in limb, which was perhaps a little exigent in view of the foul task they had imposed on them. Soldiers, apparently, made restless in the trenches by the absence of women, aching in limb and mind for the proximity of womanhood, were to banish the pleasure that they most needed and thirsted for, and were to return after a bleak leave to be cheerfully, " cleanly " killed. It will be remembered that General Smith-Dorrien on his recall from France devoted his energies to raising the morality of the entertainment dished out to soldiers home on leave. My own view is that it would have been more charitable if the women who urged the men to lay down their lives for their common country, in return laid down their virtue at the heroes' feet.

I loved Ireland. There was something about Dublin which reminded me of Petrograd. The maidens exuded a charming speech. The slowness and inefficiency of the Irish trains were also Russian. The Cavalry Cadet Squadron was in every respect more congenial than the cavalry barracks at York. We were quartered in pleasant army huts. My companions were mostly educated youths and men, a large proportion coming from the public schools. The food, again, was quite civilized. There was porridge in the morning, real milk and butter, eatable bacon and eggs. Everything was more pleasant. We wore white bands on our hats, and our uniforms were those of officers. Every afternoon we rode in the country. I remember the fragrant fields, scouting, manœuvres in extended order, all of which was more like a picnic; pleasant, congenial companions, interesting conversations. And once, in the field, I saw a beautiful young Irish wench, the daughter of a Curragh trainer, the beauty of the village. I spoke to her. She ran. I overtook her. Oh, she was nice to touch! This was about Easter, 1916, soon after the Irish Rebellion, and one afternoon as we rode through the village an old Irish woman called after us: " The English swine ! " To a polyglot like myself of vaguely defined nationality such precision was pleasing.

No. 2 Cavalry Cadet Squadron was commanded by a major who combined gentleness with rather a drawling, affected voice. He gave lectures on various aspects of military life—topography, scouting, care of horses, saddlery —always beginning with the words : " Gentlemen cadets." On one occasion, discussing the merits of military equipment he took off an ankle boot of his own which was passed round the class. A wit turned on the tap and filled it with water. When the major got back his boot thus filled, his voice became peevish. " Gentlemen cadets," he drawled, " I thought you were gentlemen, but now I realize you're merely cadets."

Once, a sort of manœuvre took place. In turn we had to place ourselves at the head of the squadron. I remember galloping and shouting orders with much gesticulation and expenditure of voice, according to what I believed to be the best cavalry style, only to learn at the end of it all that my squadron, by all the rules of the military game, had been annihilated by the " enemy."

IV

COMMISSIONED

My time at the Cavalry Cadet School was not allowed to run its full course. The application for an interpretership I had lodged with the War Office in 1915 was brought to light at the end of 1916, when the dearth of Bulgarian-speaking officers caused the War Office to lay its hand on everyone knowing Russian. I was directed to proceed to London, and report at the barracks of the Royal Horse Artillery, to which a handful of us, mostly English boys I had known in Russia, were now attached. But we were quartered, very delightfully, in the Masonic Hall adjoining a public-house off the Finchley Road. A diffident Bulgarian prisoner-of-war, looking not unlike, and having the peculiar courtesy of, M. Maurois, had been instructed to acquaint us, in as short a period as possible, with the rudiments of his language, for which purpose we assembled every morning for an hour in a lecture room at King's College, Strand. Bulgarian struck me as a sort of degraded, contorted form of Russian with a few Turkish words thrown in for ornament. It differed from Russian as Scotch from good English. As my knowledge of Russian was probably better than that of any other member of the class, I confined myself to distorting it at will, which seemed to meet the case, and spent the remainder of my time at my aunt's, where, I remember, we gave, together with the other Belgian family who shared the house with her, a French performance of " The Importance of Being Earnest," in our own version, I taking the part of Dr. Chasuble. It was not since my early return to London that I enjoyed such freedom coupled with entire financial ease. For we were well provided for at the public-house, at the expense of the War Office. Apart from the Bulgarian hour in the morning, and occasional rides in the Park under the supervision of a R.H.A. sergeant, which for all that we enjoyed, I had all the day to myself, as well as the night, for no record was kept of our comings and goings. The other cadets were all pleasant youths acquainted with Russia, and there was a brilliant Etonian boy who subscribed to homosexual views and, when I explained I was going out with a girl, wrinkled a fastidious nose and said : " How disgusting." In addition I had, to assist me in intimidating the young womanhood of London, such dubious advantage as my cadet's uniform could procure. I was happy. But just as rich men tend to become richer, happiness, once it has favoured you, delights in astonishing you more and more. My commission having now come through, I strode about with one star on my shoulder straps, and in some West-end shop I was startled by the smart and rattling salute of an elderly grey-haired soldier. He turned out to be a brother of the canary-haired woman in the residential hotel, whom I had known at the time when my first attempt to join an O.T.C. had been cold-shouldered by the tender-hearted colonel. On the eve of my proceeding as a second-lieutenant to Salonica, I was again instructed to report at the War Office and told to proceed at once to Petrograd at the British Embassy, who had apparently applied for my services.

My military career was on the up-grade. I was provided with the necessary funds and equipment, and proceeded in charge of a Foreign Office bag to Newcastle and across to Bergen, and by way of Christiania, Stockholm and Helsingfors to Petrograd.

CHAPTER SIX

WITH THE DIPLOMATISTS

I

WAR DE LUXE

TRAVELLING with me was an elderly Englishman returning to China, a pampered, painted and scented Rumanian lieutenant proceeding to Bucharest, and in the train from Helsingfors to Petrograd an elderly Russian second-lieutenant who turned out to be the father of an old school friend of mine. His weary pessimism about the war, which on arrival in Petrograd I found to be typical, astonished one like myself just emerged from among a bull-dog race which had set its teeth into Germany and was worrying her. My friend's grey-haired parent, a subaltern like myself, seemed to think the war was a mistake and would lead to nothing.

I was met at the station by my brother, who seemed impressed by my uniform. I wore all the equipment I could reasonably put on, including a cavalry sword of unusual proportions which I had bought second-hand in a Charing Cross Road shop; and my cap had a peak not unlike those worn by Roman warriors. My turnout rather erred, I confess, on the side of the martial and bellicose. I may say that the Military Attaché, rightly knowing that the Russian military tradition could not imagine an officer without a sword, had instructed the War Office in London to impress the fact on all officers sent out to Russia. But the size of my sword, its enormous length, its bulging guard seem to

me now, in sober retrospect, to have been more ludicrous
than impressive. British cavalry swords require for their
background a saddle and a horse ; they do not look at their
best when buckled to a raincoat. How ridiculous we can
be in our youth !

Our coachman was outside, and we drove quickly across
the glittering snow, down the wide thoroughfares, up the
quay to the old white house. My parents were away in
the Caucasus. My brother, who had recently got married,
beholding me in my martial splendour, turned to his wife
and said : " I still don't regret," implying, apparently, that
he still preferred a wife to a sword.

This respect from my brother, who had held a poor opinion
of me as a boy, did not displease me. I was back in the
town of my birth, having what is vulgarly known as "made
good," though God knows I was the greatest fake of a soldier
alive. In matters of love, he felt, referring to the Jewish
girl whom I had loved, I would now carry everything before
me. She was, I learned, married to a young barrister of
pure Russian stock. I rang her up on the telephone and she
asked me to dinner. This must have been two or three
months after my arrival in Petrograd, following on the
outbreak of the Revolution, because I remember I argued
heatedly with her husband who was in favour of letting in
the Germans to restore order. This seemed to me shock-
ingly unpatriotic. Later, at the time of Allied intervention
in Russia, the war having terminated, the British War Office
played with the idea of inviting the Germans to assist them
against the Bolsheviks. When it is remembered that the
idea of Allied intervention in Russia was to restore the front
against Germany, and the idea behind the war was the stamping
out of imperialism, it was a little disconcerting to hear the
war lords in all countries, of late mutually engaged in vomiting
abuse and high explosives, now calling across to each other
like brothers for help against their own people. But such
comedy I could not as yet anticipate, and the idea of my
love's young husband, of so purely Russian stock, preferring

German militarists establishing order in Petrograd to the disorder of native communists did not greatly appeal to me. All my long-suppressed passion for his wife, my long-suffering timidity of youth (for she was a little older than myself and when I loved her, seemed so much wiser), now came to the surface, so that I spoke with fire and ire and recrimination, resenting the complacency of him who was her husband. And she seemed impressed. When I turned to go, she, curious about my unfamiliar uniform, put on my British-warm and looked at herself in the glass as if conscious of the pleasure she must be conferring by this act on the man who adored her. But she looked hateful in it. Her nose was too much like a rudder. I had seen too many young Jewesses as good and better in the Tottenham Court Road to mistake her for a Spanish noblewoman. Love, I realized, was subjective and therefore transferable. The recognition that our love does not belong to the being who inspired it is painful but salutary. Why? "Because," says Proust, "our love is not only that of a Gilberte, nor yet because it is also the love of an Albertine, but because it is a part of our soul more durable than the divers selves which die successively in us but would selfishly retain it—a part of our soul which owes this love, the comprehension of love, to all the world, the universal spirit, and not to this woman, then to that in whom this, then that, which we had been successively, would like to merge itself." The self in me which had loved her was but a tenant who had vacated my house, and the new self made no call on her. No obligations, moreover, had been incurred by the old tenant on behalf of the new tenant ; and the new tenant took his leave and his hat and wound his way downstairs to the front door.

I did not go back to the room of my childhood, but was installed in my father's bedroom, which was L shaped and looked out upon the Neva. My brother had half the upper floor partitioned off for himself as a flat. My parents were expected back from the Caucasus, where my father had been taken for convalescence after his stroke. Six months earlier, while I was still at York, my father had had a sudden attack of paralysis. He had been worrying a great deal over the new company he had floated, whose shares were steadily declining. Two of the directors proved fraudulent, and my father suddenly found himself saddled with problems which weighed on him heavily. The day he had the stroke he ate his lunch silently as usual and, if anything, displayed more composure than customary. Lunch over, he rose heavily, carrying his cup of coffee, which it was his custom to finish in his study. And suddenly he fell on the floor, his limbs and features grotesquely contorted, lying there among the spilt coffee and splinters of china. Weeks passed, and he recovered his memory and his face assumed its normal expression ; but his right hand and leg remained paralysed and he could never walk again.

A few days later my parents returned from Kislovodsk, and my brother and I went to the station to meet them. As the train drew in I saw my mother's face at the window. Then she led me into the coupé. " Well, well," she said, " there he is." And my father cried. Already in his over-coat, all buttoned up as if in readiness for removal, his hat at an unfamiliar angle which denoted that it was not put on by himself, sat a patient shrivelled up figure, contrasting so painfully with the man I had known, eager and nervous with initiative. And just because we had never been really intimate, I now felt so sorry for him. When we were back in the house, the change in my father struck me even more forcibly. The living rooms on the ground floor, except the ballroom, had been turned into bedrooms for him and my mother, to avoid climbing upstairs. He sat, a little depre-cating, in the ballroom and listened to the gramophone, and to every casual conversation, with a naïve, new-born air of one who no longer had responsibilities. Our " Liebe " had come on a visit, and for a moment the family atmosphere seemed recreated, never again to be repeated.

II

IN THE LAST DAYS OF TSARDOM

It was January, 1917, just after the Rasputin scandal had blown over, an incident unimportant in itself but which has received more than its due share of melodramatic publicity. Rasputin was no more a villain than Prince Yusupov a hero. He was not so much—who is ?—a saint as a man of splendid virility, and if he exercised a magnetic fascination over certain women attracted by such qualities, we must assume that they were recompensed by what they found in him. If others, notably men, found in him something else, it does not follow that he must be at once in the pay of the devil and of the Kaiser.   But jumping to conclusions is the alacrity of a weak mind.   And it is characteristic of human courage that, when the world has been safely won over to the view that the cold-blooded murder of a befuddled monk is the act of a Siegfried slaying the dragon, the author of it at last comes forward to make his public bow : " How I Killed Rasputin."

Russia was by this time spending the last of her wrath, energy, and resources in that fight of Democracy against Autocracy in which, though flagrantly the latter, she was trying to convince herself that she was fighting for the former. It had been the practice of every English ambassador, as soon as he arrived in St. Petersburg, of every statesman, monarch, soldier and sailor, however reactionary, every crusty portwine Tory, to urge the Emperor to grant his people a measure of self-government through the Duma ; and it had been the habit of the Emperor of Russia to wish them, with kindly dignity, to mind their own business.   If the Tsar had enjoyed a keener sense of humour he might have neutralized the British Ambassador's well-meant, if unpalatable, representations by expressing, as a friend and well-wisher of England, and a cousin of King George, his concern for the King-Emperor's Indian subjects, and uttered kind, grave words of warning as to the unwisdom of withholding self-government from Ireland, and all the while ignoring the more blatant case of Poland. That the Emperor was by no means without a sense of humour is proved by his reading aloud, with obvious relish, Gogol and Tchehov to his family. It is quite probable that uninvited advice from abroad merely irritated him and confirmed him in his own opinions. If left alone he might have begun to develop liberal views, which, however—as in the case of Asquith, who shot the Irish rebels of Easter, 1916—are not inconsistent with what is called " a strong hand."

As the Russian national effort slackened, the British military machine put on steam. After Lord Kitchener's ill-fated journey, Lord Milner and Sir Henry Wilson arrived at Petrograd ; and the Russian Generals agreed that, yes, they could do with more munitions from England, and came forth with stupendous plans. There is nothing petty about the Russian mind. If it errs at all, it is on the side of the grandiose. The disproportion between the scale of conception and the amount of achievement is apt to be considerable. The would-be dictator would have a hard time of it in Russia. Conceiving, for example, the idea of electrifying all the industries of Russia, his procedure would be to jot down on the margin of the ministerial report : " Electrify Russia forthwith." And the contractors would proceed at once to bribe the authorities, supply rotten material, grow rich ; and the scheme would be crippled at birth. In this lies the humour and genius of the race.

I remember Sir Henry Wilson with his ugly face, but lovely peace-time sword, worn in deference to Russian military opinion, and a huge cigar sticking out of his mouth, stamping his feet in the Military Attaché's office at the Embassy, and cursing a Russian Grand Duke who had failed to turn up to dinner : " That swine Boris ! " And then I remember the Grand Duke's elegant aide-de-camp sitting down in our office and taking down figures fastidiously and as if born for better things.

With a practical efficiency as excellent as the theoretical basis of the war was weak, British supplies began to arrive very regularly at Russian ports. The Russians, however, war weary yet all the while clamouring for more, did nothing to remove them, but left them where they were dumped, to rust and rot in the snow. In one instance a Russian General, jealous of the successes of his rival, deliberately misdirected the supplies so as to check his rival's victories.

I enjoyed my work for General Sir Alfred Knox, the Military Attaché, for, though I worked hard, he worked harder still. He had great personality, a fine presence, spoke Russian fluently and, after seven years at the Embassy, still retained a freshness of mind, an eagerness to get in touch with every phase of Russian life, so that he was the real link with the country, the most authentic channel of information for the Ambassador. Though by tradition a Tory, he said *vous* to his Russian batman, not *tu*, like the Russian officers (to give the French equivalent). If a Russian soldier stood to the salute before him, as prescribed, General Knox invariably lowered the man's arm. All of which argued a fine sense of human dignity. He was full of fun, too, and when I showed him a paragraph in the *Daily Sketch*, describing secretaries of embassies as glorified clerks, General Knox wrote in the margin : " How true ! " and sent it up to the Chancery. The diplomatists, from Sir George Buchanan downwards, were charming, cultured people and on the best of terms with us. But the Ambassador knew not a word of Russian. The secretaries were so shy about displaying their knowledge that for a long time I was under the impression that none of them knew any Russian, till, long afterwards, I was surprised to find how much they did know.

Bitter criticism has been levelled against the British Embassy in Russia ; some critics accusing it of bringing on the Revolution, others of obstructing it. To my mind the British Embassy at Petrograd is a perfect illustration of what can, should, shouldn't and cannot be done by an Embassy. I know the hollowness of corporate emotion which vents itself in some such terms as : " A more splendid set of fellows I never knew." But at the Embassy in Russia you had the pleasing spectacle of loyal teamwork under a sensible, intelligent chief. When the Revolution had run on for a little while, the British Government, imagining Sir George Buchanan to be tinged by old régime prejudices, thought that Mr. Henderson might be a better man for the post. Curiously, however—and I have an idea that this holds good of not only the British Diplomatic Service but the entire Civil Service and is an argument in favour of bureaucracy and even Socialism—Sir George Buchanan, whatever his politics at home, displayed a completely open and flexible mind in regard to Russian politics. Like a spiritualist medium, the Ambassador had cleared his mind of all personal baggage and merely gave voice to the opinion of Downing Street. Simultaneously, like a telephone service equipped with two lines, he transmitted to London the persistent asseverations of Kerensky, Miliukov, Tereschenko, even Trotsky, that the one thing which could possibly save Russia from a separate peace with Germany was for all the Allies and enemy countries to stop fighting and be friends again like good children. " Liebe Kinder zankt euch nicht, lieber spuckt euch ins Gesicht." But having had it drummed into him by the Home Government that nothing, Russia's ruin included, mattered so much as winning the war, he used all the arguments he could muster to induce the statesmen of Russia to flog the weary Russian Colossus into putting up a last stand against Germany. For a time they did so, till each Prime Minister in turn found he was flogging a dead horse. When arguments arise as to whether Sir George Buchanan was right in advising the Russians to continue the war, his judgment in doing so must be set off against his advising our own Foreign Office first to make peace all round, and their urging him, in diplomatic language, not to be a fool but tell the Russians to get on with the war. It is often in circumstances like these that the man on the spot, told by authority not to make a fool of himself, then acquires the reputation of having done so.

III

INNOCENCE—DECLINE AND FALL

Returned to Petrograd, it was natural for a healthy young man to take steps to stabilize his condition.

I do not consider that any subject is unfit for print. But I think that there is a fit and unfit manner of presenting it. The matter is simple. Sex is as legitimate a subject for literature as any other subject. But literature is concerned with the component emotions which precede, surround and follow the purely physical sensation (whether of sex or, for that matter, of drink or of gluttony). Pornography (unadvertised by censorship) is apt to make dull reading because its object—the excitation of the senses—is necessarily very limited. There is no more scope for reproducing it in literature than for reproducing the actual sensation of eating a meal. The meal may be a banquet. Even so, the writer can say no more than that the caviare was delicious, the champagne delicious, the meringue glacé even more delicious. "We believe you," we say as we read. "But nothing short of eating and drinking ourselves will make us appreciate the delight implicit in the word." That is why most pornographic novels (whose spiritual home is in France) are peppered with meaningless words like *délices*, *volupté*, and so on. The only healthy thing to do with lust (since as often as not repression is the father of it), is to give it expression in its own medium. A sensible artist avoids pornography in his books as he avoids melodic reproduction of music, or the colorific quality of painting, leaving these to the arts to which they properly belong. Now the moment a writer depicts a component emotion arising from sexual union (be it tragic, comic or otherwise illuminating or beautiful), his work ceases to be pornographic and becomes literature.

It is in this spirit that I wish to write of a young man's innocence—its decline and fall. Whatever my wishes, I doubt whether you can read my books in any other spirit : whether the most inflammable soul can get erotic excitation from my writing. The reason is artistic, not moral, even though it may seem that in this respect art and prudery are allies. Morally, everything is better for being ventilated, especially sex, which thrives on suppression.

I am not of those, then, who consider sex a blight, a shame, and a weakness. In this doomed world impelled by the force of gravity of bodies, in the name of what god should we resist the impulsion ? But I differ from those high-minded disciples who, like Miss Ethel Mannin, for example, consider " Lady Chatterley's Lover " the most beautiful book of our generation, and look forward to the time when men and women will give themselves " cleanly and proudly," without equivocation in full daylight, conscious of the sublimity of human passion—and rubbish of that kind. The sexual passages of "Lady Chatterley" are as high-minded as you may aspire to below the hips. All this sublimity about sex seems to me about as appropriate as a novel of crime in which detectives and criminals, horrified by the murky duplicity of the past, henceforward resolved to confide in each other and to commit and detect crime side by side as befitted an enlightened and courageous generation. So much for the advocacy of " clean " sex which, like crime, appeals to the lower rather than the higher instincts and, to produce a deeply satisfying flavour, must be nurtured in the dark recesses of our natures. It is through the keeping apart of the sexes that this desire brews and passes through all the different stages till, like old wine, it is there to be enjoyed.

Not the least of the salutary consequences of affording your sexual instincts a reasonable outlet is that it ensures a periodically clean mind. My parents, perhaps not un-naturally in those days when Freud had not yet shed light on the causes of many human ills, had done nothing to canalize my early passions. Our governesses were elderly, few of our maids were handsome. Though doubtless my father's mills swarmed with pretty girls who would have been glad to ensure, at a fee, the sexual poise of the son of the owner, any such *rapprochement* would have been considered in advance of current traditions. Like the town-councillors in Bernard Shaw who, roused to action by rampant intemperance in the district, broke up the meeting, feeling that drunkenness was not a fit subject for gentlemen to discuss, my parents felt that incontinence was something to pursue more properly outside the home. There had been isolated incidents of realization : a girl in the woods suddenly conceiving that she was a wood nymph and enjoining me to impersonate a hoofed and hoary-haired satyr ; another on the river who gave herself while singing to her own accompaniment on a guitar. But an episode here and there, which sustains our memories, is not enough to sustain us in the present. The greatest excesses are—or aren't ?—committed in wedlock ; and what is a bachelor's occasional night out compared to the married man's three hundred and sixty nights a year spent in sin ?

In short, returned to Petrograd, I inquired from a very worldly and elegant friend of mine, an official at the Ministry of the Court and a bachelor, to what impeccable arrangements he owed his poise. He took out a gold-edged note-book and gold pencil and jotted down the name and address of a "maison de rendezvous," where next day I sat facing a really hideous-looking old woman, with her skin hanging loose from the chin, like a pelican's, to whom I explained rather bashfully that what I wished was to get married—though not quite, not really (this with a foolish smile), not actually, did she understand ? She understood. She would—and did—bring me into contact with a very fair lady who, she felt sure, was everything I could desire—maddeningly passionate and, for what she was, inexpensive. I remember my first adventure with this very ripe lady, curls bleached with peroxide of hydrogen. She looked at her watch. She was in a hurry. We set out in a cab to her flat. I felt full of misgiving. Arrived, she repeatedly exhorted me to be careful, and the preponderating impression I had of it all was that of precaution. Then, suddenly, she said she must hurry : she was due at a ball, her lover was waiting for her ; and she whisked the notes off the table negligently, like a doctor. My only pleasant memory is how I stepped out on to her balcony, and it was a beautiful sunny day, snow melting on the curb.

I dispensed with her favours, and a young girl from the provinces was brought to my notice who, because she had a penchant for the schoolmaster at home, turned out the light and said, " Don't talk, if you don't mind. Let me think you're the schoolmaster." I thought her request reasonable and complied—the mute executive of another's will ! But whenever she happened by mistake to touch my chin she withdrew her hand in a kind of horror. From her gesture, I, though no Sherlock Holmes, concluded the schoolmaster wore a beard. It was not given to me, however, to discover its colour. Beardless, I yet continued to impersonate him ; and when the light went on and our eyes met again we smiled as two human beings who had done each other a good turn.

There was a youth of about my own age who had been doing his military service in the Moscow Guards, a unit commanded by his father. I managed to second him from his unit to the Military Attaché's staff so as to spare him reprisals at the hands of the men of his father's regiment, after the father had been relieved of his command by a revolutionary tribunal. My friend described the position he held at the Embassy as that of " Envoy," since I employed him by sending him on errands—notably to the " patronne " in order to fix up appointments for the evening. My friend, though reduced to an errand boy, accomplished his errands in his private carriage in the best of style. All day I would work very hard at the Embassy, deciphering the Military Attaché's telegrams, receiving visitors, writing letters, and so forth. But two or three nights a week I would repair to the " maison de rendezvous " to keep the appointments my friend had made for me. The provincial girl having gone back to the provinces, two others were brought to my notice : a pretty girl who desired to supplement the wages she earned in a grocer's shop, and a colonel's wife who desired to supplement the pin-money she received from her husband. And I was struck by the respect shown by the " patronne " for the colonel's wife, and her curt manner with the girl from the grocer's shop, so much prettier than the other.

I remember these satisfying hours, so agreeable, so good for the nerves ; and then, warmly wrapped in my furs, the journey home, the sleighs gliding swiftly across the frozen river ; then a bath and to bed ; with clean thoughts between clean sheets. Blessed are they who, by purging the body of sin, achieve a clean mind !

One evening, chancing to arrive without an appointment, I was informed by the " patronne," with a look of solemn benignity, that business was suspended for that night : a wedding was on, her daughter had been married to a civil engineer and the flat arranged to receive the guests. To this ceremony I too was invited, in a private capacity. When, some time afterwards, I paid her another call I found that, though there was business as usual, the " patronne " shook her head at the Revolution, which was steadily " deepening," as was the phrase. She expressed a doubt whether, in the general loosening of morals, her own trade could hope to hold its own much longer.

One summer evening, walking along the beach at a seaside resort near Petrograd with a monocle in my eye, in imitation of Edward Cunard, Third Secretary, who I considered had " style," I beheld a number of naked bathers, several of them women, and a bearded chap, evidently a man. The idea of young naked womanhood in the sea, the thought of their life, unknown, mysterious, but revealed to me in its purest intimacy should I wait for them to come ashore, stirred images in my mind which were not displeasing. But the bearded man in the water divined my intention, and began to relieve himself of long strings of words which, taken singly, or in their context, could not be interpreted as other than abusive. "And wearing a monocle, too!" he sneered. Realizing this was a situation which could not be improved by repartee bandied back and forth between the one on the beach and the many in the water, or indeed by mute exposure to further contumely, slowly, sadly I turned and went away. It seemed to me irrational that I, unlike himself, should be deprived of the nude girls' so congenial company merely because we had not been previously introduced. And turning over in my mind the insults which had been cast at me, wondering what to do with them, I decided to disperse them in mystical speculation. Lord (then Mr. Bertrand) Russell, whom I once asked if he ever resorted to mysticism, said: "Yes, when I am humiliated." I had been humiliated. And so I reflected that I was not and he was not: that both of us were in perpetual becoming: a bundle of fleeting qualities and faults passing each other like clouds. And what was it to me, or God, if a bearded figure in the water, a form distending itself in the twilight, had popped, as it were, its head through the window of a vehicle to shout a word of insult at another passing shadow in that constant traffic in the dusk which is the flux of life, the Eternal Relative?

IV

THE REVOLUTION COMES

When it came I was not really interested in the Revolution, but was writing a war comedy entitled "The Khaki Armlet; or Why Clarence Left Home." I have given my impressions of the First and Second Revolutions in Petrograd, as well as the Allied Intervention in Siberia, in my novels "Futility" and "The Polyglots." I therefore must refrain from covering old ground.

A week before the Revolution I had been dining in the company of Colonel C. B. Thompson (later Lord Thompson, Air Minister), then Military Attaché at Bucharest, with the

Moscow Guards, whose barracks were quite close to our house. The Commander was a friend of my parents, and his children our playmates in childhood, and two weeks later I was to rescue his son from the vengeance of the revolted regiment by employing him at the Embassy as "Envoy." Colonel Thompson, who was the guest of honour, discovered that as he knew no Russian and the Russian Commander no French, they must converse in the language of the common enemy, to whose speedy destruction they raised their glasses. A Russian captain, who had lost a leg in the war, conceived a passionate wish to seal undying comradeship with Colonel Thompson's assistant, an equal in rank, and in a sacred moment of trust he begged his comrade-in-arms to accept his regimental badge, his most treasured belonging, he vowed, as a token of friendship. But the English officer, engaged in conversation with another, did not understand the Russian and requested him not to interrupt. When he did at last take the badge, the Russian captain expressed glum doubts to me whether the other would value it. The episode in "The Polyglots" is derived from this source. While we ate and drank—and our hosts insisted on our doing much of each—there were soldier songsmen who had been woken up at midnight and ordered to sing in the Officers' Mess. The whole party had started casually by Colonel Thompson wandering into the wrong box at the Ballet, and a Moscow Guards officer, a friend of mine, asking me to insist on his joining them for supper. The songsmen looked sleepy and glum as they sang and there was a light in the eye of one of them, eloquent with revolt. You could have seen the Revolution coming. (A week later, at the first signal, they went over as one man.) As we were leaving I dropped a handkerchief. A soldier picked it up.

"Thank you."

A terrible volley of sound was fired off at me. It was the soldier rattling off the regular formula: "Glad to endeavour, your highwellborn—*Rad staratsa vashe visokoblagorodie!*"

The relation of officer to man is everywhere more satisfying to the officer; but far more so in Russia. A condition which lasted until the Revolution; after which it became more satisfying to the man. It was not unusual to see a Russian officer, having ordered a delinquent soldier servant to stand to attention before him for an hour, himself recline on his bed and gently stroke his guitar while singing, a beatific expression on his face, some greatly emotional song. An officer in the Moscow Guards conceived, as a punishment, placing a hot boiled egg in the palm of a soldier and ordering the man to crush it. When the Revolution turned the men into masters, they did not lag behind their late officers in inventiveness.

Within a week from the midnight party at the Moscow Guards, our host was ringing our front door bell late at night for shelter. When a maid opened the door, she saw him running away. He afterwards said he felt he could not expose our house to attack from his troops by taking shelter there. Nor did he know that a scullery-maid of ours had a soldier lover in the regiment who would have been sure to give him away.

I suppose what connotes a revolution is shots; they have a way of giving a sense of importance. Another thing is enthusiasm. In the first days there was not one Englishman in the Embassy building who was not enthusiastic. It is exhilarating to see something cumbersome at last overthrown, and the long suffering underdog yelping with delight. It was a change; and most changes are deemed for the better. The Tsar fell like Humpty Dumpty—so quickly and painlessly that his best friends could not suppress a smile. The first day the police force resisted with strength; then, as all force, crumpled in impotence at the first blow aimed at its self-confidence. Policemen were said to shoot at the crowds from the house roofs. It is more probable that they had fled there for refuge. To attract attention to themselves by such tactlessness was the last thing they could wish. Such as were found were brought down and lined up in queues; a hole was hacked in the ice on the river, and they were pushed under the ice one by one with barge poles.   No blood was spilled.   And the First Revolution was accordingly called " The Bloodless Revolution. "

Sir George Buchanan was quick to associate Britain with Russian Democracy now that it had won its spurs ; and from the balcony of the Embassy he delivered, through the mouthpiece of Professor Sir Bernard Pares, a speech the sense of which was that Russia now need have no scruples in fighting side by side with the Western Democracies against German Autocracy.   I was just leaving the building on my way to lunch, and lingered a little in the crowd to see how they took it.   And this was the opinion of a portly shopkeeper as he beheld the slender aristocratic features of the British Ambassador on the balcony :   " A talented individual," he said.   " Seen him before.   Never drives, you know ;   always walks on his flat feet.   A distinctly talented personality ! " One night, during the first unsuccessful attempt of the Bolsheviks to crush Kerenski, there was a rumour that firing would take place from the Peter and Paul fortress with the Field of Mars, behind the Embassy, as objective, and a secretary woke up the Ambassador to advise him to vacate his bedroom for a safer room at the back of the house.   " I wish," the " Old Man " sighed wearily, " these people would put it off till a little latah ! "   He turned on to his other side and relapsed into sleep.

It is an essentially English trait to refuse to be perturbed in one's habits even by a revolution.   General Potapov, the first to command the Petrograd garrison which had gone over to the Revolution, later confessed to me he had ruined his digestion because, when in charge of the Revolution, every time he ran to the lavatory he was stopped and called back on some matter brooking no delay.   A British organizer, on the other hand, would begin a revolution by introducing a first-class chef on to the premises and generally installing himself for a long stay.

As things got worse the Embassy applied to Kerenski for a guard, and a detachment of cadets from the brilliant

Corps de Pages, youths training for crack regiments, were detailed for duty inside the building; and they were the kind of patriotic youth later to be singled out for ill-treatment at the hands of the mob. As everybody knows by now, the King had offered the Emperor and his family refuge in England. The latter, however, took some time to make up their minds, and by the time they decided in favour of Denmark, the authority of the Provisional Government had already been severely undermined by the Workers and Soldiers Soviets. The Russian Provisional Government was, moreover, a little afraid lest the emigration of the Empress, German by birth and no doubt disgusted with Russia, to a neutral country might lead to leakage of military information; and by the time the Emperor had made up his mind to leave the country the Government would not, or probably could not, let him go. It was because Petrograd was becoming rampantly revolutionary that good-hearted Kerenski decided for their safety to dispatch the Imperial family into the quiet depths of Siberia, where he presumed they might be forgotten. And it was when the Bolsheviks, having thrown over Kerenski, were losing ground against the Czechs in Siberia, that they executed the Emperor and his family, lest the Czechs should deliver them to the White Army and the Romanov dynasty receive a new lease of life. And so another page of brutality has been added to the history of man's struggle for freedom, already rich in blood. A hundred years before, Goethe remarked that, since liberty, when crowned with authority, invariably turned into an oligarchy, one would think it not beyond the wit of man to devise a system whereby the balance between freedom and coercion could be adjusted automatically, and the violent swinging of the pendulum of politics perpetually neutralized. But apparently it was not given to man to achieve it, and God did not seem to want it.

V

MR. ARTHUR HENDERSON ARRIVES—IN A BOX WITH KERENSKI —THE WOMAN'S BATTALION

I remember that when Mr. Henderson arrived in Petrograd, and departed without achieving anything more noteworthy than to have his clothes stolen in his room at the " Hôtel d'Europe," I sat on a table in the Chancery swinging my legs ; and Sir George Buchanan who came in with Mr. Henderson gave me a somewhat baleful look. I suppose I should have stretched myself to some form of attention at the passage of a Cabinet Minister. I am now so firmly convinced that the poet takes a natural precedence over the statesman, their stations in life being, respectively, those of the wit and the half wit (the latter seeking to complete himself in action), that I make a point of not removing my head-gear except to kings, ladies and viceroys. Any display of respect to a man of action, who represents but himself, has, even as a youth, been irksome to me. On the other hand, I would willingly raise my hat even to " Beachcomber," who daily represents in the *Express* the comparative triumph of spirit over matter.

Kerenski, contrary to the opinion of Lenin, who called him " the boy braggart," was a first-rate Prime Minister for the initial period when the Revolution could still be maintained on a certain *niveau* of idealism. When it drifted into a more realistic setting, Lenin was the man for it. My acquaintance with Kerenski began and ended when, to my great pride, I was sent by the Ambassador to represent him at a meeting of all the contending political delegates at the Alexandrinski Theatre ; where I sat with other Allied representatives in the Imperial box just behind Kerenski's chair. Kerenski took no notice of me, as if preoccupied with things of greater moment. The delegates delivered their speeches from the stage, and presently Kerenski himself appeared in that theatrical setting which spurred him on in his acting, a rôle that was natural to him.   There he was strutting about in his riding breeches, calling upon the delegates to prove themselves worthy of their newly acquired freedom, not to be revolted slaves besmirching it.   An impassioned speech which appealed to the romantically minded, but was interrupted by jeers from the wing of the theatre occupied by the Bolsheviks, who were intermittently shouting abuse at the opposite wing occupied by the Mensheviks and Social Revolutionaries.   Tsereteli, Tchkeidze, Skobelev, Tchernov, Gotz, Kamenev, Trotsky and others followed.   Their delivery was not as romantic and impassioned as Kerenski's, but was mealy-mouthed, and about as graceful as the run of Hyde Park speakers.   Next morning I handed the Ambassador a statement I had prepared of the proceedings.   He thanked me, but after perusing it, said that the morning papers, he had been told, differed materially from my statement, indeed to the extent of asserting the exact opposite.   Who was correct : I or the newspapers ?   The golden mean, I suggested, was probably nearest the truth.

On another occasion I attended a concert of Wagner when, during the interval, a fierce-looking little officer came on to the platform and began to denounce the treason of playing German music, while his comrades at the front were shedding blood for Russia.   His words brought Miliukov, then Minister for Foreign Affairs, to his feet.   The Minister delivered a graceful speech defending German music as exhibiting a side of the Germans which, far from quarrelling with, they all admired intensely.   Miliukov was a professor of history, an enlightened man, a fine orator, and the first Liberal to occupy the post.

The Provisional government—the First Liberal Government in Russia—struggled on through spring and summer into the autumn, trying to persuade the people who had won the Revolution that they must win a war on top of it.   It was the easiest of tasks for Lenin to crush Kerenski by representing to the people, whose heart was not in the war, that if they wished to cease fighting the way to go about it was to fight Kerenski instead. Kerenski, however, still clung tight to the rapidly spinning wheel of the Revolution, till he was displaced from the dead point of it by Lenin. Half an inch sufficed: off he came and landed with a bump far away somewhere—either in London or Paris. . . .

It was significant that the Woman's Battalion should be the last unit to defend a romantic Prime Minister; and a blameless knight like General Knox, the first to demand the women's release from the men who captured them. General Knox confessed afterwards that he had no arguments at hand with which to persuade the commander of the Soviet troops to release the women prisoners and came out with the first thing that happened to enter his head: "If you don't let these women go at once, I will set the opinion of the whole civilized world against you." The vague threat proved devastating enough for the Bolshevik commander to release the women prisoners. Yet, quite unconsciously, General Knox was right. For had the women been kept captive in a camp, converted, let us say, into a sort of recreation and refreshment ground for the soldiery, it would have proved a more popular topic than even Rasputin. Yet if it comes to the point, I don't see why the impinging of lust on them should be any worse than plunging cold steel into them. The first holds out a possibility, however faint, of enjoyment; the second none. Such a war between men and women would have introduced a new sound into modern warfare—that of a sigh, a groan of love. And there would have been a more lively response for volunteers, in the male camp at any rate, when a raiding party was required to bring back a prisoner. Such a state of affairs might popularize war, and really hold out those " glittering prizes for men of stout hearts and sharp swords," in that famous phrase of Lord Birkenhead which was accorded so chill a reception. They were a queer sight, that Woman's Battalion, marching along with quivering calves, raising jeers from the sloppy soldiery who lounged in the streets with their hands in their pockets, spitting out sunflower-seed shell. The soldiers had won the Revolution; the women, by their example, wanted to shame them into carrying on the war. The soldiers who had done one thing well declined to do both.

VI

NIGHTLY CONTEMPLATIONS OF LENIN

Every evening on my way home I passed Kshesinskaya's house where the bearded prophet Lenin, among others, could be heard speaking from the garden wall. I would linger a while, but not for long, for there was nothing in the man's speech or looks to give an inkling of his future career, and I was more concerned with thinking out the plot of my comedy, " The Khaki Armlet; or Why Clarence Left Home."

A friend of mine, a young officer of the British Military " Control," whom we affectionately called " The Spy " (a designation which he resented on grounds of secrecy with a scared " Sh ! "), and whose work consisted chiefly in passing little notes to other noodles of his calling all over the world to warn them of this or that innocent and bar their exit from or entry to all and sundry countries, had actually let Lenin through into Russia. True, he acted on instructions from the liberal-minded Kerenski, who a few months later was fleeing from Lenin in disguise. The same young officer served with me later, on the British Military Mission in Siberia, and we, the intelligentsia of the mission, twitted him for ever after : " You're a bright lad, locking the stable door when the horse was out, or, rather, in." He felt the responsibility of having caused the Soviet revolution acutely. Were he a Japanese he would have committed hari-kari.

My father, invalided out of his directorship in the new company, was requested by his old colleagues to vacate the house which he had built for himself and his family eighteen years previously, but had rashly thrown in to the new combine, with the mill, in exchange for shares. To break the fall we first moved to the country and, on returning to town in the autumn, went straight to the new flat, avoiding the old house and gratuitous heart-breaks.

After the Bolshevik Revolution in November, 1917, things began to look so sinister that I advised my people to pack up and go to England. On the morning of my family's departure, fighting had broken out again in some of the streets. No cabs could be got. It was drizzling with snow and still dark when they set off at last in a broken-down taxi driven by a man who looked like a thief in the night as he sped them through the dark wintry dawn of Petrograd. The capital looked ominously deserted. Our family doctor, an old friend, came to see them off, holding up my father on one side, which enabled him to hobble a certain distance, and expressed sorrow at their departure. But my father, in no mood for emotion, only said irritably that they were in a hurry and afraid to miss the train. I went back to the Embassy, where we carried on for another four months, till no further purpose was served in remaining. Germany was advancing swiftly into the Baltic Provinces, and the Allied military authorities were concerned lest military stores should fall into German hands and later be used against us on the Western front. Krilenko, then Soviet Commissary for War, expressed his willingness to blow up the ammunition, and when advised by Colonel Thornhill, our acting Military Attaché, to be sure previously to clear the town of the inhabitants, assured him that he need have no qualms, since the majority of Reval's population was bourgeois anyhow, and so no doubt counter-revolutionary.

General Knox, deeming that he would be of more use growing potatoes in Ireland than remaining in a rapidly dilapidating State, left for England. I was to stay on with the acting Military Attaché who took his place. In parting, General Knox thanked me for my work for him and supposed that when he saw me again I'd be a general. He gave me a mock punch in the ribs and said that if I did not come to see him in England he would kill me. I was so attached, so devoted, to the man that when I was alone in the street

I hurried against the biting blizzard, which blinded me as I tore on, and sobbed. And if you think it " unmanly " of me, let me tell you that the " *larme facile* " is again in the fashion. All true humorists, moreover—Dickens, Gogol, Tchehov, Mark Twain, Proust, Averchenko, to name only a few at random—are lachrymose by the natural balance of things.

VII

THE MILKMAID

In March, 1918, the remainder of the Embassy, with F. O. Lindley, the Chargé d'Affaires, set out on our journey back to England. Lunacharsky, then acting Foreign Commissary, travelled in a railway engine to the Finnish frontier to ensure us a free passage. I remember Karsavina, looking very beautiful as she stood there on the platform seeing off her future husband, Henry Bruce, the handsomest man at the Embassy and the ornament of ballet goers. At Tammerfors, after several days in the train, we made a dash for the public baths. I fancied the novelty of being washed by young female attendants, the young womanhood of Finland, as I understood to be the custom of the country. I accordingly got into a bath. The door opened and an old, old hag, thin as a skeleton, came in and, averting her face, scrubbed me with her bony fingers. For several days more we lived in our train, which stood on a siding. Intermittent firing went on in the town. One afternoon I saw a pretty milkmaid and, by signs and mimicry, for I am ignorant of Finnish, arranged to meet her at dusk on the top of a snow-covered hill. I feared she would not turn up, but she did, and began at once to cajole me to part with my wrist-watch, and then wrestled for it. She proved so powerful that, by shoving her knee into my chest and nearly stoving in my ribs, she all but got away with it. Below, in the town, denoted by a few lights, fighting was going on between the Finnish Whites and Reds, while dusk fell and the hill sank into darkness.

Next day, two of us rode ahead, waving a Union Jack and a White flag. Our party on sleighs was allowed to cross the firing line unmolested, and a few hours later we crossed the Swedish frontier. As there seemed difficulty in securing accommodation for us on the boat, for a week or so we lived in various towns in Norway, and I devoted the time to writing my war comedy, " The Khaki Armlet; or Why Clarence Left Home."

CHAPTER SEVEN

ROUND THE WORLD ON A MISSION

I

WELLINGTON BARRACKS

WE reported at the War Office to the D.M.I., General McDonagh. He treated us as men who had gone through a great deal and deserved a good rest. There was some possibility of our being sent, at an early date, on another mission to Russia, and he desired to keep those of us who, like myself, knew Russian perfectly, close at hand. I was accordingly attached to the 3rd Battalion Scots Guards, stationed at Wellington Barracks; another young officer called Steveni, to the Grenadiers. Hitherto I had been coached in cavalry drill. I had, for instance, grasped the notion, uncritical though it seemed to me, that " rear rank follows his front rank *wherever he goes.*" Suppose, I thought, he goes where he shouldn't—wildly, irresponsibly astray? Oh, the hazards of military life! Now it seemed that what I had learnt I had to unlearn in favour of a drill designed for pedestrians who formed fours and two-deep. My people had on the few hundred pounds they managed to smuggle out of Russia rented a house in Notting Hill Gate. The morning and afternoon I spent at Wellington Barracks, first training with, then training, a squad of recruits, shouting at them at the top of my voice: " F-h-h-om fho-h-s ! " or " Slope hipe ! " while friends of mine collected behind the railing and watched me with impish curiosity. The evenings I mostly spent at home, concluding my war comedy, " The Khaki Armlet; or Why Clarence Left Home."

When it was completed, I wrote to Miss Horniman at the Repertory Theatre in Manchester, asking her with the greatest possible diffidence (for I was unknown to her) whether I could persuade her to read my new play. To my astonishment, she answered by telegram : " Please send your play at once. Will let you know immediately whether I can produce it successfully at the Repertory Theatre." I lost no time in sending her the manuscript, and she lost no time in returning it. An unflattering letter accompanied the rejected script. " I have read your play," she wrote, "and must tell you at once that it is *entirely* unsuitable for my theatre ! You do not seem to have grasped the rudiments of dramatic probability. If the Army be anything like what you describe, all the more honour to the Navy and the Air Force for keeping the enemy out. But I know," she concluded, " that farce writers find it difficult to realize that exaggeration does not always take the place of wit." In a postscript she added : " Read William Archer on play construction."

I pictured her from her letter as a dried-up old spinster seriously affected by war hysteria, and I courted the idea whether I might not indulge in the fun, perhaps the greatest in the world, of behaving like an arrant fool with pretentious persons whom you exasperate with your assumed foolishness, while secretly deriving enjoyment from theirs. In this instance, you thank Miss Horniman for her advice about reading William Archer. After a week you write suggesting that William Archer, whose book you have read on her advice, is a fool. She writes back to say that you are one yourself. You write back that you don't think so. And so on, and so forth.

While attached to the Scots Guards I had an unexpectedly good time. Though wearing my own General Service uniform and therefore looking on the parade ground like a duck among fowls, everyone treated me delightfully. Just as the diplomats at the Petrograd Embassy deferred to me because they thought I must have had an adventurous time as a soldier, the guardsmen were charming to me, perhaps because they thought I had gone through hair-raising adventures while with the diplomats. Of this I was glad. For I would sooner be undeservedly than deservedly rewarded, preferring a gift to mere payment. There was a married captain with an amputated arm who lunched me at the Ritz with his wife and spoke of Continental royalty as though referring to common friends—an assumption I neither confirmed nor disputed. Once or twice I was told off by the Adjutant for being late in the morning. He thought there was no excuse for it, and I found it difficult to make him understand that it was something not deliberately willed by me but inherent in my nature. But even he was interested in what had happened in Russia; and he would say, with that obscure private humour derived from ignorance peculiar to the humorist and not apparent to the informed outsider: "I suppose anybody who is anybody in Russia is a Bolshevik!" And he would laugh, choke, from a too-abounding sense of humour. In my Russian school, when after inviting me to come out with a few words in English, boys would remark that it sounded to them as though I had hot potatoes in my mouth, I was not amused, nor did I share the fun of the Scots Guards Adjutant when, after listening to my quotation from a Pushkin lyric, he expressed the view that Russian was a rum sort of tongue full of itches and bitches, pop-offs and ditches. I understood that the humour of an ignoramus may indeed be exclusive.

II

ANTICIPATING DEAN INGE

Recently I read an article by Dean Inge who expressed himself doubtful as to the future of Russian communism and predicted that in Russia, as in France, communism would be succeeded by a military dictatorship after the Napoleonic pattern. The Dean has evidently overlooked the unsuccessful attempts of Kornilov, Kolchak, Denikin, Yudenitch, Wrangel, and others. In the exercise of prophecy one is inclined to expect history to describe the same pattern as before, forgetting that if the initial curves are sometimes the same, those which follow often diverge, forming the initial curves of a new pattern. In short, " Napoleonic " dictatorship in Russia, as in France, followed on the Social Revolution ; however, to be speedily overthrown.

In June, 1918, my connection with Wellington Barracks was severed. With a handful of other officers I was ordered to proceed to the outer fringe of Siberia. We formed the nucleus of the British Military Mission sent out at the inspiration of the War Office, whose ideas as to the historical propriety of a " Napoleonic " dictatorship for Russia were the same as the Dean's.

We started off from Euston, quite a small band, our original mission to Siberia consisting of half a dozen officers, headed by General Knox, under whom I had already served when he was Military Attaché at Petrograd. We sailed in the *Aquitania* to New York, where our uniforms caused unknown women affected with war hysteria to stop us in the streets and take us for joy rides in their cars. Bell-boys in the Hotel Vanderbilt, where we put up, asked us if they might shake a hero by the hand—a request I invariably accorded. We crossed the Rockies on our way to Vancouver ; and at Victoria, B.C., we boarded a Japanese boat, the *Kashima Maru*, to cross the Pacific to Yokohama.

Among the officers composing the original military mission there was a journalist called Francis McCullagh who, beneath his dry and shrivelled-up exterior, concealed a good deal of subtle humour which sustained one during the journey. His was one of the three friendships I formed during the two years we stayed in Siberia, and he was one of the first to encourage me—though quite unnecessarily—to write. I had with me a copy of " The Khaki Armlet ; or Why Clarence Left Home," which had been rejected by the majority of West-end theatre managers. McCullagh, while declining to read it himself, advised me to send it to his friend Maurice Baring, then a major in the Flying Corps. I don't know why he advised me to send it to Maurice Baring, since the latter does not produce plays. He might just as well have advised me to send it to the Aga Khan or Mr. Reginald McKenna. Major Baring returned the play with the easy courtesy of a being whose energies had not been expended in reading it.

After a pleasant fortnight in Japan as guests of the British Embassy, we sailed from Tsuruga to Vladivostok by s.s. *Penza* of the Russian Volunteer Fleet. There is something perennially ironic about these distant voyages and the great expectations of change they arouse in us. To cross the sea from anywhere to anywhere else is to stand at a piece of rail looking ahead at where damp cloud, with mortal unmeaningness, touches damper water ; to hear the piston thud of the engines ; to note the seaman look of a ship's officer ; and the same, always the same sea, whether the strip of water you cross lies between Tsuruga and Vladivostok or Folkestone and Boulogne.

When I look back on the two years I spent on the staff of the Military Mission in Siberia, what fills me with wonder is not what was done—some people were killed and maimed, a few towns changed hands—but the dead matter of history. I feel already that the future is looking back with historical wonder on this little phase, when, owing to arguments no doubt very plausible at the time, a number of very variegatedly foreign troops massed themselves in a small sea-port on the Far Eastern fringe of Siberia ; and while they were sending on stores and discussing what they ought or ought not to do, individual lives were gradually shaping themselves. Officers observed a certain orderly routine of living, thinking, eating and drinking, falling in love, getting married occasionally. This sort of thing must often have occurred in the past—at Tilsit while the armies were waiting, and elsewhere. Yet to-day when we read the life of, let us say, Goethe, it seems difficult to realize that months and months of the poet's life were spent at a camp while a certain campaign, between perhaps the Prussians and Saxons or Austrians, was in progress : and that the campaign seemed then so imperative as to compel thousands of men to leave their homes and risk their existence, but now, in retrospect, strikes us principally as a waste of Goethe's time. Or—another analogy—what lends the life of the sixteenth-century pirates off the Algerian coast its chief, perhaps sole, interest to me is the thought that Cervantes was inadvertently captured and held as a slave for several years in Algiers.

III

I AND GENERALS

We remained in Siberia exactly two years. My inmost beliefs not being bound up with the re-establishing of an obsolete régime in Russia, my efforts were chiefly directed to resisting the perfidious attempts of senior newcomers from England to oust me from my influential post as the officer in charge of the " General Staff Office," an appointment largely of my own invention. My career as a private soldier was retrogressive, my rise on the staff meteoric. Before we left Liverpool I had become a full-blown lieutenant, and on arriving in Tokio I was a captain and drawing pay at the rate of a G.S.O.3. I displayed some little gift for organization, but I suppose I would come under the category of young officers described by somebody in a book of Hugh Kingsmill's as " generals' pets, bleating nuisances." Colonels and generals were far more in my line than sergeant-majors. A general is a man of action already sufficiently elevated above the deed to desire to crown his achievement with some apothegm. (Napoleon : " From the sublime to the ridiculous is but one step.") This desire of the man of action to complete himself in thought is responsible for the steady output of generals' memoirs. There are three natural steps in man's development. The brute aspires to become conqueror ; the conqueror aspires to become administrator ; the administrator, reviewing himself, mankind, and God, pronounces himself a philosopher.

Yes, I was at home with generals, bearing myself towards them as a disciple seeking a revelation. I would ask questions

more abstract than " What is the object of bayonet fighting ? "
which might have brought an echo of the sergeant's axiom :
" To kill." I would inquire discreetly whether my chief's
work was not comparable in its complexity to that of Cromer's
in Egypt. At Petrograd, where more than one British
general passed through our office on the way to G.H.Q., a
dear old man asked me what honour I thought the New
Year's List had in store for him—a K.C.B. or promotion to
brevet rank.

" Which would you rather have, sir ? " I asked, as if ready
to accord him his own choice.

" Well," he said, " I am already Sir Eric. I can't be Sir
Sir Eric, can I ? On the other hand, brevet rank . . . though
I don't know. A K.C.B. is not to be despised. Which
do you think they'll give me, what ? "

I thought hard. " I think *both*."

" Oh, no, no, no, not both," he said, shaking his head
disapprovingly. " Not both."

I have dealt in " Futility," and again in " The Polyglots,"
with the business of interfering, on an international scale,
in other people's affairs, the sample I dealt with being known
to history as the Allied Intervention in Russia of 1918-1920.
When, having depicted the scene in " Futility," I was re-
proached for pouring more water into the same teapot for
" The Polyglots," I might have replied that no extra water
was needed, since it was a large teapot and " Futility " was
only one cup. I used the background of this theatre of war
to throw into relief the theme of my novel, " Futility." I
was chiefly concerned to achieve a cumulation of certain
artistic effects, and the characters of my novel were composite
creatures, for the most part combinations of several real
people I had known, not necessarily in the surroundings in
which they appeared in my books. The genuine writer
avoids psychological invention like poison. Nor is he concerned with living characters as such. They impinge on
his consciousness, and become the nucleus of new beings,
who soon develop out of all recognition. Real people

recognize one or two traits of themselves, and the rest which is taken from others they regard as a calumny. I have lost not a few friends through " putting them," as the phrase goes, " into books." They cannot understand that they have merely served as nucleuses, that a week after I have begun work on a book I cease to think of them as they are. How tired we authors are of being accused of malice. Proust says : " The very stupid manifest by their gestures, speech, and sentiments involuntarily expressed, laws they do not perceive but which the artist surprises in them. Owing to the nature of this observation, the vulgarian considers a writer malicious : but erroneously, since the artist sees a beautiful generality in the ridiculous ; he imputes no more discredit to the person thus observed than a surgeon would misesteem a patient for being afflicted with a fairly frequent trouble of the circulation ; also he is the last man to mock anyone."

Of the prominent officers on the Mission, two have since committed suicide, and another is dead. There was a charmingly courteous colonel, Sir Edward Grogan, who, for a time, was my chief. He was meticulous to absurdity, but kind, and very nervous—and now no more. He had red palms, like a monkey, and if anybody looked at them, blushed and turned his hands down. He was a great enigma. Then there was General Blair who died in Serbia. I worked with General Blair when he was Assistant Military Attaché at Petrograd. He was overwhelmed with duties, but always nice, considerate, helping me to decipher badly mutilated telegrams, always ready to do a good turn. He had his wife and young boy in Petrograd with him, and used to carry her things, her overcoat and umbrella, holding her up with the same arm, because on the other he carried the boy, who gripped a cage with a canary in one hand and a vessel with goldfish in another. General Blair possessed perhaps the noblest nature of any man I have known, not excepting my father, whose inherent nobility of soul was neutralized by an insane irritability. A Czech officer once said he had often heard of the traditional English gentleman but had always believed the idea to be a myth, till he met General Blair. Light came to him then, suddenly, as it had come to Saint Paul on his way to Damascus, and now he knew what an English gentleman really was.

At the Mission's headquarters I held an appointment similar to that of the Permanent Under-Secretary of State in relation to the Cabinet Minister. I saw four chiefs succeed each other, while I initiated each in turn into the mysteries of local politics, only to bid good-bye to him at the wharf or the station. I was twenty-one, and I must say I enjoyed the whole foolish business; and the combined efforts of several officers to dislodge me from my powerful position proved to the last unavailing.

IV

LOVE AND REVOLT

Because I begrudged the expenditure of efficiency on a meaningless cause, I always saw to it that the seriousness of my own practical effort was not above the level of the seriousness of the idea behind it. As I read the political situation, I was convinced that my own work left nothing to be desired. "*A partir du 8 du mois courant,*" the Japanese *communiqué* announced, "*il y eut ça et là des petits engagements contre les bolshéviks dans les régions amourienne et maritime, mais sans apporter de grands changements aux situations antérieures.*" And an entry in my diary reads: "Played tennis this afternoon, love, then a bath, and afterwards witnessed a revolution."

First about love. She was the willing wife of some Russian officer unknown to me, and she would await me in my room at the officers' quarters. We were quartered in a low one-storey building, formerly used as a house of ill-fame, with one long corridor, on each side of which were cubicles. The building, for all its abject appearance, bore the name Hotel Bristol; and when the wife of an officer stationed there wrote to him from England: "I am always thinking of you, dear, sitting in the lounge of your hotel, listening to the band," his reading of the letter provoked bitter mirth in us. The heating of the building having broken down, we were provided by the Army Ordnance with little kerosene stoves which smoked wickedly. One night, coming back to my room, I found the Russian lady asleep in my bed but so covered with soot that at first I mistook her for a coloured woman. When I woke her she was so angry and begrimed that our love-making was discontinued forthwith, never again to be resumed.

The revolution, a coup d'état of General Gaida's followers, ended in a battle royal, having Vladivostok, and particularly our Mission headquarters, for battle ground. The shots breaking the tense atmosphere which had lasted several days filled one with a mixture of exhilaration and gravity, and one exchanged gay looks with others, as if to say: "There! Didn't expect that, did you?"

The grey air of a slightly dull winter afternoon. As I watched a fearless recruit in full view on the railway bridge rattling off his machine-gun, I thought that the truly awful thing was that the man who now exposed himself so recklessly might be grinding a barrel organ after all the pain of losing an eye or a limb. And I remembered that some people still talked of warfare—of the dropping of bombs on capital cities—as " human nature," a sort of Müller physical exercise to keep manhood in condition.

When the fighting became fairly general, the Allied Missions convened a conference, to which meeting I accompanied my chief, Colonel (now Sir Charles) Wickham. Our car awaited us round the corner, and to reach it we had to cross a good part of the square which was being pelted with the rat-a-tat-tat of machine-gun fire. Colonel Wickham did not increase his leisurely pace, and I conformed my step and composure to his. But when we drove off in the car, he remarked to me, with a smile, " My nerves are not what they used to be." He did not inquire about mine.

While we were in conference, a report was handed to the

president, General Nagasaki, the Japanese Chief of Staff, that fighting had ceased; and it was resolved that this being so, the question was now one for the diplomatic representatives to determine. The diplomats, who sat in conference above us, after an hour's fruitless deliberation, sent down word to us, that fighting, having just resumed, the question was again one for the Allied military and naval authorities to settle between them.

V

THE SITUATION

When a set of people in Russia, who believed in the War only as a prelude to the Revolution, concluded a separate peace with Germany, they behaved very creditably from their own point of view, but inexcusably in the opinion of Imperial Russia's Allies, who felt they had been let down at a critical moment in a war launched jointly. Clearly the Soviet Government put themselves in the wrong in our eyes by not resisting the Germans in their attemps to re-equip themselves with Russian resources and British supplies, to be used against us. But no less clearly the Soviet Government put themselves in the wrong in German eyes in failing to resist effectively the passage of Czech prisoners of war, whose avowed purpose was to fight against Germany on the Western front. It was natural that the Soviet Government should fail to please either ourselves or the Germans, for they were helpless. It was natural that the Czechs, most of whom had deserted from the Austrian Army to their brother Slavs, should now wish to leave Russia, which looked as if it might soon be dominated by Germany, who might conceivably hand them back to their hated masters. It was natural again for the Russian Whites to imagine that the object of the Allies was to overthrow the Soviet Government; and it was natural for certain Allied officers in sympathy with them to wish to do so. And it was equally natural for a democratically-minded autocrat like Mr. Lloyd George, who controlled the situation, to resist such unwarranted folly, and

for a man of Mr. Churchill's somewhat irresponsible tempera-
ment to condone it. It was only common humanity on the
part of the Allies to protect the White crusaders, who had
helped us to resist German recuperation while the War
lasted, from Bolshevist revenge after the War. But it was
swelled-headed stupidity on the part of the Whites to refuse
to meet the Reds at a peace conference on Prinkipo Island,
when everyone else was agreeable. And it was our own fault
if we put ourselves in the wrong by not dropping our White
Russian friends like hot bricks when they refused our invitation to Prinkipo, but by continuing to help them half-heartedly
in the name of a *soi-disant* national Russia when all the moral
strength was on the other side.

History persistently evades any assignation to individuals
of responsibility for events. Let us assume the impossible.
Let us assume that the Russian White armies had, thanks to
the Allied intervention, effected a swift and crushing defeat of
Bolshevism and re-established a strong nationalist government. The career of Bolshevism would then have seemed but
an abortive and ominous adventure, which had met with a
swift and well-deserved retribution at the hands of the orthodox forces which stood for God, country, and home. As it
is, the protracted struggle made all the Russian national cause
seem a band of disgruntled adventurers, struggling, mainly
against one another, on the coasts and outskirts of Russia and
mocking by their medley of nationalities the ideal of a national
Russia, for which they had set out to fight. The international
Bolshevists, on the other hand, defending the citadels of their
own country against a host of foreign invaders, gradually
assumed the aspect of national heroes guarding their land
against miscreants who were ready to barter it to foreign foes.
The dream of the Cromers of the world was not to be. True,
Mr. Winston Churchill was indefatigable in appreciating the
menace of communism. To me, however, a Churchill mind
was in itself a calamity so formidable that the idea of its being
preoccupied with " menaces " and " dangers to civilization "
seemed as grotesque as the anxiety, let us say, of a cancer for

the welfare of the human body, and the more so because Mr. Churchill was not an ironist enjoying the paradox of an incomparable situation, but was sincere about his value in the scheme of things. The danger of a mind like Mr. Churchill's is that it is no more "malignant" than cancer is malignant, but like cancer eats itself unconsciously into the body politic. It is not the brutality, but the chivalry of these gallant knights of the sword which ensures the continuity of slaughter. I mean this sort of thing. Men in a Zeppelin are dropping bombs over some vulnerable spot in London. Children are maimed. Then the Zeppelin is brought down. The German crew is surrounded by a crowd thirsting to tear them limb from limb. But the gallant airmen are saved by their own type of men in the British camp, who understand instinctively that these are heroes ready to risk their lives for an ideal identical with their own ; and the men who agreed to kill children are safely interned, on their leisure evenings show themselves lovers of Shakespeare, shed a sigh for Chopin.

There are those who applaud intermittent violence followed by fraternization ; and there are others who regard it from first to last as criminal lunacy. The first say that war having broken out, defence of your own country becomes inevitable ; and that there is a time for war and later a time for peace, and that both testify to the glory, the heroism, endurance, and finally, the wisdom of man. The second say that if this beastliness and waste and folly be glory, then what is shame ? The first retort that, anyhow, a war will probably again become inevitable—and not so bad, for a change. The second reply : It need not and would not be, but for the attitude of the first, who should be locked up for breach of the peace or for " causing a disturbance." And so on.

No, I do not think the world has ever seriously suffered from the dearth of patriots. And the Russian White Guard nationalists, as was shown by subsequent events, deteriorated into disgruntled sentimentalists invoking every country but their own to assist them, while the Bolshevists, who would not allow the word " Russia " to slip into their reports, turned out to be the real patriots who stood against the world for Russian integrity. In the end it is not patriotism but the upper hand in experimental economics which is at stake ; the eventual advantage of Socialism or the immediate benefit of Capitalism (which as we know also has its depressions). And there is room for both, or a new combination of principles, cloaked by sentimentally obsolete terms. For my own part, if it were not for some of my friends who are neither allowed to accept relief from the outside nor to leave a country in the throes of an experiment in which they do not believe, I would favour not a five but a ten-year plan. I have but a mild interest in that glorified form of housekeeping, that squabble below stairs, called politics. I prefer not to live in a socialist state undergoing alterations and repairs. On the other hand, a few more bank crashes might cause similar uncertainty and discomfort throughout capitalist countries, and who can say whether at the termination of the five-year plan, Russia may or may not be a more ordered community than our own ? But if so, they who live and suffer privation to-day will pass into the unknown martyr's grave, to be forgotten, not mourned. They are the generation living on its memories and soon to die. The Russian humorist Averchenko, who died a refugee abroad, writes with a heavy heart of two old men, an ex-senator and a former manager of a foundry, now employed in unloading and sorting cartridges in an artillery depot in Sevastopol, who meet at sunset on the seaside promenade and recall their beloved St. Petersburg.

" And do you remember our Petersburg sunsets ? "

" Don't I ! "

" The sky ashen and pink ; the water a rosy mirror ; the trees silhouettes as if each cut out separately. The dark etching of the Kazan Cathedral against a pearly background . . ."

" Oh, don't speak of it ! Don't. But when they light the lamps on the Troitski Bridge, what . . . ? "

" And that bit of canal there by the Spasskaya . . ."

" And the heavy arch with the clock at the end of the Morskaya . . ."

" Don't ! "

" Then will you tell me, please: what have we done to
them ?   Whom did we hinder ? "

" Don't ! "

Averchenko's book was published abroad, but Lenin
recognized its merit. " A great part of the book," he wrote,
" is devoted to themes which Averchenko knows exceedingly
well, having lived, thought and felt them. And with extraordinary talent he depicts the impressions and moods of
a representative of the rich, gluttonous, landed proprietors
and industrialists of old Russia. So indeed the Revolution
must have appeared to the representatives of the ruling classes.
A fiery hatred makes Averchenko's stories sometimes—
indeed, for the most part—quite extraordinarily vivid. Some
of the stories, in my opinion, deserve to be reprinted. Talent
should be encouraged."

The book was printed by the Soviet Press, in spite of its
mordant criticism of the Revolution. In one sketch Averchenko likens the Russian Revolution to a place of amusement
in Petrograd called Luna Park, containing scenic railways and
other rib-breaking devices, a place, he declares, where only
the congenital Russian fool really enjoys himself. So the early
ministers of the Provisional Government, Lvov, Miliukov,
Gutchkov, Tsereteli, Kerenski, and later Trotsky too, are
seen scrambling for a secure position on the " devil's wheel,"
and gradually, as the wheel sets in motion, coming off with
a bump. Kerenski, pushed an inch from the centre, is thrown
off far beyond the barriers of Luna Park and crashes somewhere with a thud . . . " either in London or Paris."

But it is a sketch called " The Great Movie Stunt" which
is the most poignant. " Let us rest from life. Let us dream,
shall we ? " The old exiles sink into deep easy chairs, throw
more coal on the fire, and fill their glasses. One of them tells
of a film he once saw, depicting the ordinary actions of a
human being backwards. A man has finished his lunch and
strolls to the sea shore to dive from a rock. By reversing
the handle, a man is shown jumping out of the sea on to the

rock, backing home to his dining-room, spewing on to his plate bits of food which grow into a chicken. The chicken is carried back to the kitchen, where it rapidly grows plumage. The cook touches its throat with a knife, and the chicken comes to life and runs gaily down the backyard.

" If only our life also were like an obedient film and could be reversed and flow back ! " sighs the narrator. Both men are lost in images. The reel unwinds backwards. The writer's nib moves backwards, erasing his writing. He takes his hat and stick and backs to the door, into the street. It is September of the year before last. He gets into a train which rolls backwards to Petersburg. In Petersburg wonders are happening. Bolshevist posters peel themselves off the walls, leaving the houses clean and smart. Behold, full speed back, there dashes up in a motor-car Alexander Feodorovitch Kerenski and enters backwards into the Winter Palace. Lenin and Trotsky have backed out of Kshesinskya's mansion and drive backwards to the station, board an unsealed coach, which is sealed forthwith, and roll away backwards into Germany. Quickly the February Revolution passes before our eyes, and the machine-gun cartridges fly out of dead bodies back into their barrels, and the dead jump up and run back, waving their arms. Out flies Rasputin from the Tsar's Palace, and rolls back to his native town. Commodities get cheaper and cheaper. Quickly the Fourth, Third, Second, First Duma succeed one another, and strangers are seen kissing one another in the streets. They are overjoyed about the Constitution granted by Nicholas on the 17th October, the happiest day in the lives of Russians. . . .

And here one of the exiles begs the other to stop turning the handle. "Don't, for God's sake," he pleads, "turn any more." And the Soviet preface writer, officially bidden to prepare the stories for Communist consumption, at this point ironically asks : " What, to be sure, does the White writer deem a suitable event for history to linger over ? " and he quotes the irresponsibly happy passage depicting the exiles hailing a cab at pre-War tariff and repairing to a restaurant to celebrate with champagne the Emperor's grant (subsequently withdrawn) of the Constitution. Is it on things like these, he asks, that the author wishes the history of man to rest indefinitely? The desire for change and progress makes light of the poetry of other people's memories. But the preface writer omits, perhaps intentionally, the lines which follow and, for all we know, explain the real reason which moved Lenin to say, in the teeth of high politics, "one should encourage talent."

"Don't turn any more!" the exile cries. "Enough. Please stop here, if only because we're fifteen years younger, youths almost. Ah, our hopes! and how we loved, and were loved, too. . . ."

.   .   .   .

"Why don't you drink your brandy? The fire's gone out, and I can't see in the grey dusk . . . why is it your shoulders are shaking so queerly: are you laughing or crying?"

VI

EXODUS

My memories of Siberia, put to rest by "Futility" and "The Polyglots," are now pale ghosts; and if survival is indeed bound up with personal memories my two years in Siberia can do little to sustain me in the other world. A few images remain. I remember how Admiral Kolchak, passing through Vladivostok, entered my room with General Knox, and as there were no chairs sat on my bed. I surveyed him with interest as a potential Napoleon, little knowing that his career would be cut short by execution, some eighteen months later. But when I heard Lenin bombarding the capital with what seemed to me idle words I had no prevision that in some two years from then the capital was to change its name from Peter's to his.

For the rest, our existence was diverted by dances on British and American battleships, and at the various Allied

Missions in turn. There was an engineer-commander on one of the British ships who never went ashore. Why should he? he asked. He had his wife's photograph in his cabin. What did he want ashore? At one of these dances I met a Russian girl, with whom I fell painfully in love, and remained so three years till I dissipated my love for her in writing "Futility." "Nina" of "Futility" first taught me to dance jazz. The plaintive music, so inviting, so expressive of what you felt towards the lovely, lithe creature with the sidelong look—but words failed one and one asked oneself how it was that she did not respond to what one, through the music, was saying to her.

In the Mess I was but moderately popular. And once I saw the gleam of the collective spirit in their eyes, when a group of my brother officers, outraged by my frequent absences from the Mess, and general intellectual assertiveness, burst into my room and carried me in my bed out on to the roof of the house. I pretended to be enjoying it more than they, and so I was not exposed too long to the rigours of the Siberian winter night, but was duly carried back, still comfortably tucked away under my blankets. There was a Hussar major who disapproved of me and suggested that a " dose " of riding-school would do me good. When I told him I had been through riding school as a trooper, he did not believe me. To make him a little more flexible, I reminded him of a concert at the British Embassy in Petrograd, where two hearty Naval officers who sat behind him indulged their sense of fun by kicking his seat incessantly, while he, in the unhearty accents of a hysterical young girl, begged them to stop their foolery.

There was a very brilliant young officer on the Mission, whose friendship I cherish to this day. His name, Zilliacus, was of Greek origin. But he was born in Japan of a Finnish father and an American mother, was educated in England and America, and married a Polish lady in Manchuria, and their children were born in Switzerland. Another friend of mine was Captain Sandelson, the financial adviser of the

Mission, who, in addressing letters to his wife at home, gave such prominence to the sender's rank, name and address, that his letters came back, the post office concluding that they were addressed to him.

Once, a year after the armistice, entering our waiting-room, I saw a Russian peasant woman sobbing loudly, and two Russian interpreters looking on and grinning foolishly. I inquired what was the matter, and was told she had come to have a letter translated, believed by her to contain news of her son in Canada, of whom she had not heard for years. The letter, it seemed, had arrived that morning, and it bore an English stamp. She had come tearing up to the British Mission, and the Russian interpreters had bluntly translated the letter, which turned out to be a much travelled communication from the Army Council, dated more than a year back, and informing her that her son had been killed in action and the Army Council sympathized with her in her loss.

I have a recurring dream. The war, though most people have forgotten about it, is still on. Everyone has agreed it should stop, since neither the Germans nor ourselves take any further interest in it. But the Government has other, more topical questions on the schedule list—Unemployment, Trades Disputes Act—and the war must wait its turn. So drafts are still being sent out from Victoria Station to the trenches in France, but nobody comes to see one off. The war, it is now agreed by all, is a bore; and so the casualties are no longer reported. On one such draft I am going out, much against my will, fully equipped, with gas mask and hand grenades. . . .

Though the war was over in November, 1918, we stayed on in Siberia and did not return to England till August, 1920. After a time the whole thing bored me. I applied to go home, but was told my services were indispensable. I then began to write a novel. It developed into " Futility." For my services I was awarded the O.B.E.; the Czecho-Slovak Croix de Guerre; and earlier the Stanislav order of Russia; mentioned in dispatches; and recommended for a G.S.O.3.

General Knox, after realizing that the bottom had been knocked out of the Intervention, telegraphed to London : " General Knox presumes that his further stay here can serve no useful purpose and recommends recall to England."

The reply read :

" General Knox's presumption is correct."

Another time, when General Knox had been for several days impatiently awaiting a reply to an important telegram, I handed him a wire, which read : " A certain Captain Knox suspected of German and Bolshevist sympathies claims to be a relation of General Knox. Please confirm. He has protruding chin and sandy moustache."

General Knox took a pen and wrote : " I recommend that the man with the chin be first arrested and then shot."

In May, 1920, we began our journey back to England. It took us through Manchuria and China, and lasted three months. We lingered in Mukden, Tientsin, Peking, Shanghai, Hongkong and Canton, sailing home by way of Singapore, Colombo, Aden, and Port Said, this journey later forming the closing chapters of my " Polyglots."

PART III

LIFE: A VOCATION

" And I understood that the materials of my literary work were my pas
life ; I understood that they had come to me in frivolous pleasures, in laziness,
in moments of tenderness, and in suffering ; they were being stored for me
while I could no more guess their destination or even survival than the grain
which stores all the aliments that will later feed the plant. Like the grain,
I could die when the plant had developed, and I would find myself having lived
for it without knowing it, without my life ever seeming to me to come into
contact with the books I wished to write and for which, when formerly I sat
down to work, I could not find a subject. Thus my whole life to this day
could, and could not, be summed up under the heading : A Vocation."

—Proust.

CHAPTER EIGHT

OXFORD

I

CULTURE AND INERTIA

A GRATEFUL country, in the form of accrued Siberian allowances, a bonus, and a gratuity on demobilization, crowned my career with the sword with a credit balance of £1,000, upon which money I proceeded to educate myself at Oxford, which I had always felt to be my spiritual home.

My wish to take degrees in Arts and Letters was dictated by a sense of propriety, since it struck me as incongruous that I who was to express myself in Arts and Letters should not, like the scholar, who, carrion-like, feasts on the dead flesh of my kind, be a Master of one and at least a Bachelor of the other. Going to Oxford was merely for me a sort of inoculation against future academic snobbery. Degrees were valid only in so far as they would be missed if they were denied oneself. I felt that if I had once been to Oxford, I could afford henceforth to dismiss it from my mind ; as indeed I did : that if I obtained a M.A. and a B.Litt., I would no longer attach the slightest importance to them ; as I don't.

I went to Worcester. I had never before seen Oxford, and my first impression, arriving as I did at the end of the Long Vacation to be interviewed by the Provost of Worcester College, was one of extraordinary peace, gentleness, melancholy brooding ; a seat of learning without parallel, an ideal place for meditation.

When I passed through the porter's lodge into a delicious quad and rang the bell at the Provost's lodging, I was in another world.   I found myself in a quiet study overlooking the garden.   The chestnut tree was like a gigantic burning bush : but the flowers looked sad after the night's frost ; and the swans were a little bedraggled.   The Provost, Mr. J. F. Lys, came in quietly, and questioned me gently.   He asked me what I intended to do when I went down.   When I said, bashfully, I wanted to write, he said nothing, concealing a look of scepticism.   He very kindly inquired if, in view of my military service, I did not require any State aid, just then forthcoming for demobilized officers.   I had a feeling that I should have been sent to Oxford earlier by my father and I (foolishly as it now seems to me) relied entirely on my thousand pounds and disdained any aid from the State which would, I then felt, make my presence in Oxford merely an accident of the war ; as in any case it was.   When a little later I discovered that quite a number of undergraduates were in receipt of allowances from the State, my squeamishness on that point vanished, but I was too shy to go back to the Provost and claim the money.   I venture to hope this is a point which Income Tax collectors will learn to appreciate more and more with the years.

I left Mr. Lys and his quiet study.   I strolled through the streets and looked at the beautiful colleges and felt so proud to be, at last, a member of the great ancient University.

The essence of education is the acquirement of a capacity for the transvaluation of values ; and in this respect I was assisted by Oxford.   My career there may best be characterized as " quiet," or what in social phraseology denotes merit —" unobtrusive."   I took my degrees of B.A. and B.Litt. and M.A. quietly, without exciting the University.   I neglected to win prizes.   What I was really doing while there—my chief work in the English school as Mr. Nichol Smith pointed out to me in a generous letter—was to write my " Futility."   I was fortunate in having Mr. Nichol Smith as my tutor.   He said that my accent was not un-English, but my intonation was, largely owing to the speed with which I spoke, and he advised me to talk more slowly.   I

rejoined that if I talked quickly it was because I did not wish
to take up too much of the time 'of so eminent a scholar.   He
replied that by talking too rapidly I often failed to convey my
meaning clearly, and, in the repetition which ensued, wasted
more of his time than if I had spoken slowly.   There was
an undergraduate who appeared to lay down the law every
time he opened his mouth, putting undue emphasis on every
word in his speech, shoving it down our throats—till we, his
table companions, protested.   Then suddenly going red and
stuttering hopelessly, he explained that this was the advice
given him by a throat specialist—to stress every word when
he talked as an antidote to stuttering.   " I-I-I-I am so sssss-
sorry," he said, blushing crimson.

I attended regularly, and with pleasure, the lectures of
Sir Walter Raleigh, Doctor Carlyle, and Mr. Nichol Smith.
I remember Sir Walter Raleigh saying, with that ready smile
of his which disclosed that he was coming out with something he knew himself to be good :   " Milton compares
unseen things with other unseen things."   Tremendous lofti-
ness !   Another time, with the same smile, he said, in a
lecture on Swift :   " I suppose that anyone among you who
has not read ' Gulliver's Travels ' may pride himself on his
originality."   Of Bernard Shaw, Sir Walter Raleigh said that,
unlike Dryden, Shaw tried to get his laugh in first.   And
Raleigh's lecture on Farringdon lingers in my memory because
of Farringdon's mania, who thought his perspiration turned
to flies and bees.   If a fly crept out, he said :   " There ! "

The English School, had it not been for philology which
overburdened it, was peculiarly congenial to me.   It allowed
one to indulge one's natural taste for literary criticism on a
long range of English writers, in whose life and works one's
interest was continually stimulated by discussion and a secret
comparison with one's own problematic fate as a writer.
Most of my contemporaries in the English school were not
themselves writers.   When Mr. Nichol Smith, a teacher of
literature, asked his pupils what they intended to do when
they went down from Oxford, and was told that, like

himself, they intended to teach other men literature, he looked really shocked, as if he thought they were not making proper use of his instruction.

I loved the freedom of Oxford, the unassuming attitude of the dons. Once, I remember, I barged in upon Sir Hugh Allen, at Paddington, in the train for Oxford, and discussed with him, though I had never met him before, the merits of Wagner and Tchaikovsky; and Sir Hugh, with that perfect pose of the Oxford don who treats an undergraduate as an equal, listened seriously to my opinions and told me where and why he differed from me. Another time I went the round of the Oxford Colleges with Sir Hugh Allen and Sibelius, the latter in a fur overcoat, and Sir Hugh with that habitual angry look of his which seems to say " Bah ! "

You wander down Holywell, and you see two youths arm in arm, discussing Schumann, and you think that perhaps this great matter-of-fact nation of shopkeepers and mechanics is, where the cream of it is assembled, really interested in unapplied science and the theory of art. Adorable Oxford ! Proud, humble seat of learning where you sit on the steps of the altar of culture and hear as much as, and no more than, you are inclined.

II

MONASTIC DAYS

Your life at Oxford, as everybody knows, is not confined to your college, but extends over all the other colleges. To me who found loyalty, except to myself, to those I love, to mankind at large, and to God, repugnant, this was a welcome arrangement. My experiences in the Mess had taught me how to avoid the wrath of the collective spirit. That, I learnt, was achieved by neither too intimate an acquaintance with the hearty men of the college who, on finding that you were constitutionally not hearty, would soon learn to dislike you ; nor by ignoring them, which would speedily make you seem singular and a fit prey for their wrath when in the collective spirit mood. To ensure inconspicuousness, the best course was to adopt a cheery " Hello-feeling-fit-eh ? " attitude. That esprit de corps, which consists in extending inhospitality to newcomers, did not assert itself to any extent at the University. But a certain young Etonian named Reade, who subscribed to Bolshevist politics and flaunted a red tie, invited wrath from a small but strong-limbed group of athletes ; and one day when he came back to his rooms they were all waiting for him with a gleam of the collective spirit in their eyes. Reade offered the raiders beer, but the leader of the raiding party observed : " There is not enough to go round." " Then," said Reade, " I suggest that those who dislike me most should drink the beer." The leader reiterated : " There is not enough to go round." And later again, during a bonfire celebration on the occasion of the College victory on the river, he was " de-bagged " outside the College (that is to say, had his lower garments removed), which was intended to confer ignominy on him instead of, as one would suppose, on his captors. This University disapproval which finds itself expressed in removing the lower garments of an individual and letting him run home along the streets exposed to public ignominy, is not confined to the immediate members of the University. Krassin, then Soviet representative in Great Britain, on a visit to Oxford, escaped this fate only owing to a stalwart bodyguard, drawn from Liberal and Socialist opinion in the University. Even Asquith, it was suggested, when the ex-Premier visited his old University, should be de-bagged.

Krassin, by the way, on his Oxford visit, which was on behalf of the Famine Relief Fund, was tackled after the meeting by an English millionaire, who had lost his property in Russia, and now exhorted Krassin to see the error of his ways. While Krassin was struggling with his chaotic English, the rich man fired out in quick succession a string of words : " Death, ruin, desolation, famine, vice, corruption, shame, lies, filth," etc. Finally, defeated by Krassin's ignorance, which he had first tried to take advantage of, the rich man tackled Krassin in faultless French, and then they really came to grips. Next morning a " blue " in some reactionary den delivered himself of these words regarding the incident : " I hear," he said, " that Krassin spoke very broken English until he demanded money for the maintenance of the Red Army, when he suddenly dropped his crippled sentences and showed remarkable fluency. These Bolsheviks are up to all sorts of tricks. You can't be too careful with them."

While avoiding the more uncongenial sports, I habitually played tennis, to me the most attractive of games. A French-Canadian, who partnered me, after beating his English fellow-undergraduates in a match, addressed them as follows : " I congratulate you on the staunch resistance you have put up and the gentlemanly way you have behaved throughout."

The Americans, Canadians, South Africans and Australians at Oxford generally went about together, and were a little put out by the English undergraduates who showed no interest in them, or, at most, an uninformed curiosity, expressed in a casual question, like " Are there any railways in Canada ? "

During Torpids or Eights' Week I would indulge in a modicum of college patriotism. Arriving at the riverside just in time for the finish, I would dash in front of the other men of my college, exhausted by their long run, and cheer voluptuously : " Worcester ! Worcester ! " What attracted me so about Oxford was its vague and loose organization. University discipline was not hard to bear, except that access to women was not encouraged. Most of the women undergraduates were so plain, so chastening to the senses in their black cotton stockings, that the deprivation could be borne without strain. Dances at the Masonic Hall with town girls, who, on the contrary, tended to be pretty, were forbidden. On one occasion a friend of mine and I were pursued by a Proctor. I escaped, but he got " progged." Next morning he was fined £2 for going to the Masonic and five shillings for climbing a lamp-post.

I have memories of a midsummer Sunday. A Salvation

Army band makes you feel you are suffocating. Your libido fixations are, to borrow the language of Sigismund Freud, circumvented and forced into the conscious. From the chapel come dissonant voices of choir boys, and of the choir-master cursing them in the name of the Lord.

Sex, unless you respect it, seizes you by the throat. Oxford offered little assuagement in this respect. But I remember a lovely blonde " undergraduette " in my punt, brimming with desire, which, the presence of her chaperon notwith-standing, found some partial expression.

One afternoon, at the cinema, I found myself by the side of a pretty girl; and gently, insinuatingly, I pressed my calf against hers, harder and harder, emboldened by her seeming response. After an hour of it, she rose, and I found I had been pressing the velvet side of the chair.

Another day, spreading myself in my seat with no thought of women, I was shocked when my neighbour, a plain female, rising to go, said as she squeezed herself past me : " I won't thank you for pressing your leg against mine."

What attracted me in my own College was the beautiful garden and the cottages on one side of the quad. Among the men of my College I had two or three friends ; and when some little time ago I came across a young tutor who re-marked heartily that we were both Worcester men I could not think what to say except that the men there, in my time at least, were rather dull on the whole : which brought forth from him : " I like dull men."

Lord Lovelace and De Quincey, however, had both been Worcester College men. There was a College dramatic society which on a midsummer night gave a performance of Bernard Shaw's " The Devil's Disciple " in the garden, and I heard an old lady in the audience remark : " One gets so tired of these American authors ! "

My contemporaries at Oxford, who have since achieved a degree of distinction, were Richard Hughes, Beverley Nichols, Edward Sackville-West, John Strachey, Victor Cazalet, L. P. Hartley, Bob Boothby, Edward Marjoribanks,

Basil Murray, Louis Golding, Alan Porter, Edmund Blunden, Joe Brewer, Malcolm MacDonald, John Rothenstein, Athol Hay, and, inevitably, others, if more meritorious at any rate less striking. Some of them I did not meet when we were at Oxford, and others I have not met at all. I associated myself with a certain literary movement, supported by John Strachey, who published a magazine called *The Oxford Fortnightly Review*, for which I wrote several short stories, the first I ever published, and the worst. L. P. Hartley, who edited the *Oxford Outlook*, also published a short story of mine. I wrote most of "Futility" at Oxford, and an exhaustive essay on Tchehov, which I later included in my book on that author. My retired life gave me a certain literary reputation, and friends of mine would bring their friends to my rooms, intrigued by the rumour that I subscribed to some utterly new view of life and literature. And once while I sat and wrote, a fellow undergraduate burst into my rooms. Was it true—he understood as much, but wanted first-hand information—that Tchehov was . . . *passé?* I assured him that the rumour was unfounded. " I will be able to uphold him, in the face of adverse criticism, without appearing out of date? "

" Absolutely ! "

" And without making a fool of myself ? "

I could give him, in the latter case, no such assurance.

Edward Sackville-West was the first to tell me of Proust. Apparently, so I gathered, Proust was a man who had never written a line till he was forty, had gorged himself with reminiscences till he had reached bursting point, and now had opened the safety valve, and all this pent-up stuff was gushing out in long sentences without stops.

" Without stops ? " I asked.

" Without stops," he replied.

Just as every political party considers itself a " centre-party " threatened by revolutionaries on the left and reactionaries on the right, so every young writer tends to think his talent is compounded from the choicest ingredients. One hopes— and on what little ground !—that one incorporates the lucid sanity of a Bertrand Russell, without any of his liberal smugness ; the bitter incisiveness of Bernard Shaw, without his sterility ; the rich humanity of H. G. Wells, without his splashing-over ; the analytical profundity of Proust, without his mawkish snobbism ; the elemental sweep of D. H. Lawrence, without his gawky bitterness ; the miraculous naturalness of Tchehov, without that sorry echo of the consumptive's cough ; the supreme poetic moments of Goethe unimbedded in the suet-pudding of his common day ; the intimations without the imbecility of William Wordsworth ; the lyrical imagery of Shakespeare, without his rhetoric ; the pathological insight of Dostoevski, without his extravagant suspiciousness ; the life-imparting breath of Tolstoy, without his foolishness ; Turgenev's purity in reproducing nature, without his sentimentalism ; the lyrical power of Pushkin, without his paganism ; the elegiac quality of Lermontov without his " Byronism " ; the humour and epic language of Gogol without his provincialism ; the spirit of Voltaire, without his tinniness ; the human understanding of Dr. Johnson, without his overbearingness ; the dash of Byron without his vanity ; the faithful portraiture of Flaubert, without his tortuous fastidiousness. The list could be prolonged.

When you went to tea in the rooms of some rich and fashionable young man at the House and his friends, of a similar type, came in every few minutes, you had a sensation as if you were watching a stage play, so exactly like actors in a society play did they look and talk. The sustained insincerity of the whole thing seemed somehow incredible. Astonishing fluency was the chief characteristic of this type : a brain unable to cope with its output and speed. I was struck by the feebleness and timidity of the undergraduate mind, so easily intimidated by bad argument. It was so interesting that after going to tea one was tempted to write to one's host : " Thank you so much for giving me an insight into your mind."

It cannot be said that you have reached a stage of maturity until you have ceased to regard yourself as a personality. At Petrograd I still imagined I cut a certain figure. I was impressed by such things as the Ambassador, who tendered his card on which was engraved : " L'Ambassadeur d'Angleterre," secretaries, attachés, the Minister of Foreign Affairs, etc.   But by the end of Intervention I lost all interest in myself as a personality ; and by the time I went to Oxford I turned the corner.   It was for that reason that the little airs and graces, the little conceits of the undergraduates irritated me then, whilst I might have been impressed by them before, and condoned them afterwards.

The borrowing habits of Oxford scouts, usually destructive to wine and cigarettes, in my case, as I neither smoked nor drank, were diverted to marmalade.   I was inspired to the following poem, my only expression in rhyme and metre.   " Whether I eat the marmalade or not, it sinks daily in the pot."   Nor did the scout do much work.   Of a morning he would flap my three chairs, each once, and the mantleshelf, with a duster, and retire, slamming the door.   Each little act and conversation he would punctuate with " Thank you, sir," so that when he emerged with a dish we invariably thanked each other for some time, and he would then retire, thanking.   At the end of term he would murmur " Thank you, sir.   If you want to give me some money, sir, you can do it through the Bursar, sir, thank you, sir.   You don't mind me saying so, sir ? thank you, sir."   And he would flap a chair with a duster and retire, slamming the door.   My rooms in College were not comfortable.   If I sat by the fire I was in a draught ; and if I moved out of the draught I was a long way off the fire.   The situation, no matter how much mental application lent to it, could not be bettered.

III

NINA AND SYLVIA

One night in June, 1918, before I sailed for Siberia, while I strolled down Westbourne Grove I saw a girl with amber locks.   " Hello," I said.   " Hello," she replied.   And this was my meeting with " Sylvia " of " The Polyglots."

We resumed our friendship in 1920 on my return from Vladivostok, and it continued while I was at Oxford. " Sylvia " was not, as in " The Polyglots," my cousin. Nor had she ever been to the Far East. She was a beautiful Irish girl who lived with her sister in London. My monastic days at Oxford were relieved by an occasional run to London, Colchester and Holyhead, for a brief honeymoon. I remember dashing with her in a taxi to catch the 10.30 from Paddington to Oxford : brief oblivion cut short by the sudden opening from without of the door of the taxi : " Porter ? "

" Oh, go away ! Don't want you ! The impudence of these fellows ! In Paris you can shout yourself hoarse, only to see porters strolling past you with their hands in their pockets."

" Good-bye, darling."

" Good-bye, darling."

And I would get one of those marvellous letters from her saying that a girl friend of hers had just come back from Oxford where " flowers, etc., are in full bloom."

I wrote of " Nina " in " Futility," while consorting with " Sylvia " of " The Polyglots. " I wrote love letters to Nina, vowing not to forget her for ten years, and to-day, a month before the expiry of time, I received a letter from her, now a married woman, and just arrived in Paris after ten years in China—and perhaps we shall meet.

When I was writing " Futility " about Nina, and spent my leisure moments with Sylvia, it always struck me, each night we parted, how impossible it would be to write a book about Sylvia. What *was* there to say—since she had absolutely nothing to say ? And it did not occur to me that neither had Nina. That neither has any woman ; and least of all when she thinks that she has.

I won Nina by telling the story of the man who cut off his nose while shaving, dropped the razor and cut off his big toe, and in the confusion which overtook him clapped his nose on the stump of his toe, and his toe on his face, so that whenever thereafter he happened to blow his nose, his boot came off. She laughed freely, and felt herself drawn to me. But beyond that story there had never been any real contact between us. When I asked her why she did not write to me, she replied she didn't know how.

When I have complained to women of the sort of stupidity which seems typical of their sex, they invariably exclaim : " Ah, but you have but yourself to blame. Look at the women you consort with. Why don't you choose for companions intelligent women," presumably such as themselves ; and I invariably found that the stupidity of the women I had complained of, and which had shocked my listeners more than myself, was precisely of a kind indistinguishable from their own. The poet, the man of intellect, detests the sophisticated woman, but loves physical beauty, fragrant simplicity, the naïve and natural, behind which the wonder of life seems concealed, and which lures him. Owing to her comparatively recent emancipation, or her instinctive subjection to the higher intellectual integrity of man, even the cleverest woman reveals herself as a parvenu in the sphere of the intellect. The first-rate mind of a woman must, to the first-rate man, always smack of the second-rate. If he wishes pure, unadulterated philosophy he will be drawn away to discuss it with a man. The artist approaches women (whatever he may pretend to them) as he approaches his art, the profundity of which is not inherent in the subject, as it may seem to some young critic, unseasoned in understanding, who might consider Sinclair Lewis's attempt to explore the mind of a scientist in " Martin Armstrong " a more difficult and worthy feat than his revealing the souls of the people on Main Street, erroneously deeming that a higher mentality in the hero must correspondingly lift Mr. Lewis's novel into a higher realm of art than were possible if the author were conducting his literary investigation again on the *niveau* of a Babbit ; or that literature in the hands of Michael Arlen, who writes of Mayfair, must be a more decorous affair than in those of Gorki depicting the dregs of humanity. On the contrary, a woman does not fully exercise our spirit unless she be attractive enough for us to desire her and so stupid that her ways must seem to us inscrutable. Intelligent women only attract men more stupid than themselves. A stupid woman is always a wonder. An intelligent woman reasons like ourselves and, by sharing our beliefs, merely confirms our own doubts. We read of such legends as the spiritual influence exercised on a Goethe by a Frau von Stein, and so on and so forth. And then we read that the same illustrious Goethe, " for fifty years the undisputed sovereign of European literature," as Byron put it in a letter to him, tires of the " spiritual influence " of the said Frau von Stein and transfers his affection to a pretty factory hand, with more inward profit than before. As Proust says, " A woman we desire, by causing us to suffer, draws out of us a series of feelings differently profound, differently vital from those inspired in us by a man of superior intelligence who interests us." And a woman we do not desire, however intelligent, is to us like a man of middling intelligence who does not interest us. And it is those barren mouthpieces, touching no chord in us, who are loudest at dismissing our precious fleeting moments, which fertilize us a whole lifetime, as " just one of those silly little affairs with some young girl of no intelligence."

When an object, like Sylvia, who has no visible subject, appeals beyond all analysis, we may assume that the divine spirit itself has found in her a happy home.

Little did I guess that so far from finding it impossible to write a book about Sylvia, I not only made her the heroine of " The Polyglots," but, her charm still haunting me, gave her a second run in " Jazz and Jasper " as Eva.

When I sent Sylvia a copy of " Futility," she asked me, with the air of one expected to be a little jealous : " And who is Nina ? "

When I discovered Sylvia was neither more nor less articulate than any other woman, I understood that, if only I knew how to listen, I could write indeed a very charming book about Sylvia. I understood that there was not a being alive

or dead who did not reveal beauty if we only saw deeply
enough.   But when I told Sylvia, just as we came out from
a movie play, that I was writing a book about her, she only
said : " Darling, I'm not interested. I'm not interested,
darling."   When " The Polyglots " was completed, and I sent
it her to Australia, no reply came.   I learnt later from her sister
that Sylvia since leaving England had never written home to
Ireland, till her parents, communicating in their anxiety with
the police, heard from her on a postcard that she was happily
married in Melbourne and had a little boy, eighteen months
old, of whom she promised to send them a picture.   But
she never did.

The last letter to reach me was from the Canary Islands on
her way to Australia.   She had met some man who knew
me at Oxford and "'Oh,' I said to him, 'did you know Mr.
Gerhardi,' and ' Oh,' he said to me . . .   I won't tell you
what he said—but just you wait."   I have waited in vain.
But I have no regrets.   She still lives in me.   " What a
dreadful person I am ! "   I hear her say this again and again.
It brings her to life.   She is, in this way, and this way alone,
an acquisition for ever.

IV

" FUTILITY "

When " Futility " was finished my agents, Curtis Brown,
hawked it round a dozen of the leading publishers, all of
whom rejected it without comment.   I began to think that a
passionate recommendation from an established novelist might
not be amiss ; it would at any rate draw from one of the next
dozen publishers some comment.   Hugh Walpole was in
Russia at the time of the Revolution in charge of an Anglo-
Russian propaganda bureau and, as such, in frequent touch
with the Embassy.   I, however, had never actually spoken
to him till the day before he left Russia, when I was present
while a loud, blatant British subject implored Hugh Walpole
to look after his wife on her homeward journey to England,

and Hugh Walpole promised, with correctness and an unconvincing simulation of enthusiasm. I hoped he would
remember me, and wrote him a letter, with flattering, if
insincere, references to his two Russian books, and asked him
whether he would kindly read my own, likewise on a Russian
theme. He replied, gravely misspelling my name, with no
reference to our meeting on the Embassy steps, and lamented
that he was up to the eyes, what with novels and what with
lectures, and would six months hence do, and would I write
to him again ? I did not see Hugh Walpole till eight years
later, at a party of Arnold Bennett's.

Aloud I said : "Is that Hugh Walpole ? "

"I know who you are (stretching a manly hand out to me,
as if to save me out of water) : How do you do ? "

Then blushing, to H. G. Wells : "Is that how to say it ? "

H. G. (inattentively, thinking of other things, but smiling
vaguely) : "Yes."

Disgusted, I wrote to another novelist—this time to one
Arnold Bennett. His secretary replied that Mr. Arnold
Bennett was cruising in the Mediterranean and would have
my letter laid before him on his return. And, as good as
her word, eventually came Mr. Bennett's reply that he would
have liked to read my novel but could not do so. He had
every year over five hundred manuscripts sent to him by
people chiefly unknown to him. He congratulated me, in
the absence of other data, on my prescience in first writing to
him before sending the manuscript. Arnold Bennett's reply
touched me. The established author was anxious lest he
should miss a genuine disciple of his art. But he was only
human after all and could not shoulder single-handed the
burden of existence : talent had to take its chance. It was
Arnold Bennett who had spoken of the agonies of finishing
a novel. He knew, yet he could not help. "I would have
liked to read your novel." It really seemed to me that he
would have liked to, but was prevented by some iron implac-
able fate. Since I flowered into print Arnold Bennett has
not ceased to encourage me by reviewing every one of my

books, in a bright, cheery manner which was among my greatest delights. When " Jazz and Jasper " appeared, Arnold Bennett said the appearance of a novel from my pen was as interesting . . . as the accouchement of a political duchess. In it I amiably caricatured him as a novelist by the name of Vernon Sprott, who is the foreman of British fiction. Arnold Bennett, in acknowledging the copy I sent him, signed himself " Ever yours, Sprott."

One day Professor Walter Raleigh, who himself boasted of coming from the " Eastern University," announced that Oxford always believed in inviting lecturers from outside, and the editor of the *Athenæum* would this term deliver a series of lectures on " Style." I don't know why he should have referred to the lecturer, who was himself a graduate of Oxford, as coming from " outside." Mr. Middleton Murry, however, lectured without a gown—but superbly and engrossingly, and not a word of his fell on stony soil. At a literary club he also spoke on Tchehov. He spoke very quietly, seated in a low armchair stroking the carpet pensively while he searched for some phrase which, when found, really expressed the secret of Tchehov's enchantment. He also made some shy allusion to the work of his wife, Katherine Mansfield ; and when I read a story of hers I was so pleased with it that I wrote her a letter. The kaleidoscopic exuberance of her " Je Ne Parle Pas Français " increased my admiration. What dash ! How supple—acrobatic. Many months later, ignored by Walpole and Bennett, it occurred to me that Katherine Mansfield might like my " Futility," and if so, find it a publisher. She was in the mountains of Switzerland, dying of consumption. I was unknown to her. But she replied by return, read my book within a week, and found it a publisher by the end of a fortnight. My mother began to like Katherine Mansfield's stories.

Mr Richard Cobden-Sanderson, who published it, came to Oxford to see me and we sat too near each other on the small sofa and felt a little constrained.

I was very pleased with our conversation, and when my

mother came up to Oxford to see me, I told her what a fine man my publisher was. "He is so tactful. I mentioned that I was writing a new book and he never said a word. You see, I explained, "it is the practice with grabbing unscrupulous publishers to commit you to giving them your next. But that man hid his emotion behind a mask of indifference." My mother looked dubious. However, "Futility" was published.

Some little time after "Futility" appeared Katherine Mansfield came for a brief stay to London. I was at the time laid up in Bolton, and by the time I was able to go down to London she had already gone to Paris and died at Fontainebleau, eight years before Mr. Spahlinger discovered his cure for tuberculosis.

V

"DISTINGUISHED VISITORS"

An immediate neighbour of mine was John Rothenstein, son of Professor Sir William Rothenstein, the artist; which caused me to inscribe in a book I gave him:

> "*From the son of a merchant*
> *With the soul of an artist*
> *To the son of an artist*
> *With the soul of a merchant.*"

An inscription which, to this day, he repudiates. It was he who was responsible for my nickname "Baron" at Oxford, based on my imperfectly established descent from Baron Girardi auf Castell zu Weyerburg und Limpurg, of the Holy Roman Empire.

In political discussions I would tend to take the liberal view. "The Feudal system was good while it lasted," said an opponent. And I would contend: "In other words, it was not good enough to last." I conceded that the reactionary impulse was to delay a reform, while the radical attitude was to anticipate it. There would be no need for either were it not for the other.

Of the public men who came to speak at the Union while I was at Oxford, I heard Mr. Asquith, Lord Birkenhead, Mr. Horatio Bottomley, Mr. Ramsay MacDonald, and Mr. Winston Churchill.

Mr. Asquith was very red, very old, and when I saw him trying to run up the stairs like a young man I understood how old he was. When the President of the Union rose and called on the distinguished visitor : " The Right Honourable H. H. Asquith, member from Balliol," he articulated the H's, as if drawing flame out of them. The only similar effect I noticed was when, years later, Lord Beaverbrook's butler articulated with the same emphatic pauses, as if counselling you not to make any mistake about it : " Mr. H.—G.—Wells." Mr. Asquith finished his speech in the Asquithian tradition. " Will you," he asked, and the question had poignancy, for a bust of his own son, a former President of the Union who had fallen in the War, had just been unveiled in the building, " Will you be content with cenotaphs and memorials, or will you live and let live ? " And he brought down his fist on the *soi-disant* treasury box.

Lord Birkenhead I heard twice. He had a beautiful voice, oddly enough, for a man devoid of any sense of music. He struck me at once as a bully of genius. When an undergraduate interrupted him with : " Question," Lord Birkenhead turned on him sharply. " There is no question," he said. " I know, and you don't know. I am a Cabinet Minister, and you are an undergraduate." He offered to instruct " one of his secretaries " to show the honourable member the figures in question, though he doubted whether the honourable member's conduct deserved such courtesy on his part. Or words to that effect. He described the Sinn Feiners as a gang of murderers, and when someone protested that a party like Sinn Fein which represented the best part of Ireland could not be called a gang of murderers, Lord Birkenhead promptly cried : " I don't care ! In that case they're a *large* gang of murderers ! "

Mr. Horatio Bottomley charmed the Union with his

candour. We had expected him to ape great learning. He did nothing of the kind. " I have been educated," he said, " at the University of . . . Life." He opened his speech by referring to the end of term notices issued by the librarian, requesting honourable members to return the books borrowed from the library. He supposed that the honourable members had received private notices, in view of his coming, to leave their watches at home. This remark at once put the captious audience in his favour, and his speech was a rousing success. When Mr. Bottomley, on his return, addressed himself to the task of arousing public opinion against prison life, I, who had just brought out a book called " Pretty Creatures," which contained a story " A Bad End," dealing with hanging, sent Mr. Bottomley a copy, with a complimentary letter, desiring (a) to identify myself with his humanitarian movement ; (b) to invite his commentary on my book in the Press, which would give it publicity. Mr. Bottomley did not have leisure to acknowledge my letter and book. Some months later, however, I received a circular letter from him, inviting me, in view of my being one of the many people who had shown kindness in writing to him on his return to public life, to profit by the opportunity he was now offering of taking up shares in his new paper, *John Blunt*.

Mr. Churchill, who, like Mr. Asquith, wore a black waist-coat with his tails, was very bellicose, if occasionally stammering, about the ignominy of any surrender to Ireland. " What ! we (apparently excluding the Irish who fought for the Empire), after having won the greatest war ever known, allow the Irish to dictate to us ? " Or words to that effect. It seemed to me poor stuff from a grown-up man.

Mr. Ramsay MacDonald, whose son Malcolm, of Queen's College, was anxiously watching him, made the initial unforgivable slip of addressing the audience as : " Ladies and Gentlemen," instead of the traditional " Sir " to the President, a " sir " which, according to local tradition, must be included in the first sentence. Mr. MacDonald's speech was forceful but not graceful. His opponent, an undergraduate from

Balliol, had made some remarks which, in Mr. MacDonald's opinion, proved his gross ignorance ; and Mr. MacDonald kept on heavily and very Scotch : " A Balliol maan ought to know," very angry, apparently, at what a Balliol maan did not know.

Another speaker I heard was Stephen Leacock, who started off humorously, kept up a continual run of fireworks, then suddenly lapsed into a serious tone and administered an earnest moral lesson in those unconvincing tones of Canadian oratory the gravity of which makes an Oxford audience always feel uncomfortable. This difference of tone between the moral earnestness of speakers on the other side of the Atlantic and the flippancy of Oxford was very marked when the members of Yale University Debating Society came over for a debate. They seemed almost hurt by the levity with which their points were turned against them. When an American speaker pleaded for a recognition of the fact that the two countries had a common language he was interrupted with shouts of " Question ! "

The difference of speech was again exemplified a few days later when two American undergraduates went to the Clarendon Hotel to ask if they could have a " bàeth," and were brought, after a few minutes of waiting, two bottles of Bass.

The incident seemed to lend a degree of reality to the fine shades of philology to which Professor Wild was treating us. " The overwhelming majority of the world to-day," he said, " is of opinion that ā was pronounced ăe in the sixteenth century." I tried to picture the world divided on that issue ; and it occurred to me that it had been divided by lesser things.

Research in Old English is not dissimilar, in method and general interest, to Sherlock Holmes' efforts in the detection of crime. The philologist clutches at a vaguely familiar vowel which has hidden itself in an unfamiliar place. " Got you there, my boy ! " he cries. I believe philology could be put successfully on the screen. " Detectives of Syllables " should be the title of the film. Captions : " On the Heels of a Syllable." "Tracking a Vowel across Five Centuries and Three Continents."

There were other speakers I heard at Oxford. Mr. Bertrand Russell on China; Lord Buckmaster on Divorce. Once I attended an address by Dr. Nansen. A bluejacket was among the audience. He had come in because it cost nothing; but went away after a time, bored.

I had a passion for philosophic speculation; for reconciling inconsistencies between one philosophy and another, for doing away with the difficulties of the Trinity or the Immaculate Conception and fitting them, as a plumber fits a pipe, to Kant, to Einstein, to Schopenhauer. We talked a good deal in my rooms and listened with that coy *good* look we have when we expel all thoughts of self and revere pure theory. But there was an American whose literary criticism would take the form : "*I* say 'Madame Bovary' is the biggest novel of the bunch, and I don't care what any of you sons of bitches has to say to the contrary—not *that* !"

But for the most part, I was as lonely at Oxford as elsewhere. I sat in my lighted College rooms and watched the pinnacles, the spires and towers gradually dissolve in the gathering gloom. And sometimes—often—it rained.

Oxford curbs enthusiasm. Of course, one reads a great deal there, but one can read as much anywhere else, with the same amount of leisure. There is this to be said for reading at Oxford, however, that when you go down you find that your reading of books has received recognition, been certified for others, if not for yourself, by the University degree. But I distrust them—definitions and abstractions, reputations resting on past laurels, titles and degrees. I am afraid of forms, of "courses," institutions, universities, academies, which, like clowns in circuses, sham great activity when the object of their chase has already turned the corner.

The value of Oxford is in the emotional retrospect. You like to think of it, as the time recedes, of the brilliant undergraduate days you believe you have, but have not, spent there. And you like to think how, when you are an old man, perhaps

a well-known writer, you will go up and see your son at
Oxford, how you will walk about the old familiar grounds,
under the old pillars, and perhaps point with your stick to
this or that sight, and say, " In my time ——" And you will
stand on his hearthrug, your hands clasped behind you,
warming them at the fire, your grey distinguished head thrown
back, and talking simply to the youth of 1960. Oh, let us
get old ! quickly get old !

I visited Oxford again a year or two after I had gone down.
My mood was that of " the hero returns." Now, I felt, they
will all come out to meet me. . . . *Pas un chien !* Not a soul
about I knew, except a scout or two and a few estranged dons.
After a midnight stroll in the rain, I found I was locked out
at my hotel. " Ring at the back," says a street drunkard.
" Will they open ? " " Don't know ; ring at the back."
Rain.

CHAPTER NINE

THE CAREER OF LITERATURE

I

VACATIONS IN BOLTON

MY father, though he had no more money, continued from habit to support his sisters abroad, who noted in their letters to him that he was paralysed, but were happy he was not, like themselves with their neuralgia, in any physical pain. My parents' Petrograd funds having evaporated, they came to Bolton, where there were some remnants of Grandfather Wadsworth's friends, and my mother started a shop of "Parisian" hats and gowns which my young sister, who lived in Paris, sent to her from time to time. My mother ran this shop single-handed, as well as looking after my father, who was entirely dependent on her as he could not move from his chair. There he sat day after day. Formerly he had only read newspapers. Now he began to read books, too. When tired of reading he would begin to brood on the past; and when tired of thinking he read again. He sat there, pulling out his watch at intervals, waiting for the evening paper, restless, anxious to get time on, to "kill time."

He had extravagant hopes of making money by sending every pound or ten shilling note he could lay his hands on to dubious brokers in London, who advertised for likely victims. His old financial perspicacity seemed to have left him and he was invariably cheated by those sharks of the mart. He said he had to make a thousand pounds, to enable him to go off by himself, to London and Paris and Vienna, with a manservant. His right hand was twisted and paralysed, but with his left he managed to type letters to these sharks with one finger on a rusty old typewriter of a primitive model; and sometimes the keys would jam, when my father would angrily tear out the sheet and, his left hand propping his chin, sit sulkily by the fire.

When my mother refused to give him any more money for his speculations, he would keep up a sustained scream at regular intervals to force her hand, or compromise her with the neighbours. Nothing, however, would damp his hopes, which we recognized was a good thing for him as it kept up his spirits. But as every little bit of money we gave him was immediately lost in these financial transactions, one often wished that his spirit might be kept up in some other way.

I would spend my vacations with my parents, revising or, otherwise, waiting for news of " Futility," which, as we all hoped, might, when published, prove so successful as to lift us out of the fogs of Bolton altogether. The publishers, however, continued to return it as if it were a kind of tennis ball sent over to them for that purpose. This was long before Katherine Mansfield had found a publisher. It seemed interminable, that time at Bolton when " Futility " was being rejected by one publisher after another. My mother would bring the ominous envelope to me with a look of the utmost commiseration, which provoked in me the utmost irritation. For it is a fact—and the more unaccountable because I am so easily upset by the slightest reverses in love, in travel, in financial dealings, by a scratch on the wall, which fill me with soul-consuming anxiety—that the rejection of my work or the failure of a book has never caused the slightest depression in me, but, on the contrary, has filled me with a strange, sinister exhilaration. Any commiseration with me, so desired when I suffered from unrequited love, which my mother would smile away, was, whenever the packet containing " Futility " came back to us, most bitterly resented as an insidious attack on my literary morale. Much as I abhor the waste of money,

I have, I notice, never begrudged any child of my pen its failure in earning its parent a satisfactory livelihood. On the contrary, when this or that story came back empty-handed, I merely spent less on myself. I did not eat less, but more cheaply. It is surprising how adequately one can eat at, for example, an Express Dairy or a Lyons' shop. I have, in regard to the art I practise, the same natural ascetic attitude as a born priest to religion or the athletic man to sport. I, who have given you the sad record of my soldiering, my dislike of school, my bleak childhood, take almost the same delight in risking failure in literature, as other men take in risking their necks in dirt-track racing. I may honestly say that nothing has tended to irritate me more in the past than any interest from the public in what I am going to write next, since I have always felt that only through temporary failure, which induces your readers to mind their own business, are you sufficiently thrown back on yourself, in your renewed obscurity, to come out with something compellingly good.

At times it seemed to me that the easiest way to get my book published would be to besiege the city of London and then force the publishers to accept it. After "Futility," and under the influence of Tchehov, I wrote about a dozen short stories, all of which were, and now I know, deservedly, rejected. The great point in favour of a novel after all was that it was not returned so rapidly as a short story. I then sounded a publisher, who advertised for new authors, to whom I sent a few of my stories. I had a letter from him by return of post. "These," he wrote, "are capital. Fresh, original, capital." And he asked me to put down the sum of £95 "towards the cost of production." The publisher's offer amounted to this. You were to write the stories, then hand them to the publisher, and pay him £95, and afterwards buy them from him at 9d. a copy. I wrote for his booklet called "Tips to Authors," which told you that your first task was to procure paper to write on, unless you preferred a copy book, and that you could write either in ink or use a pencil. Stories, the booklet further informed you, could be either short, or else they could be long. Then there arose the question of employing an agent or doing without him. Well, this was a matter where it was difficult to advise. There were authors who preferred to employ an agent; there were other authors who preferred not to. In conclusion, the author of the booklet asked permission to be allowed to wish you the best of luck. I read this booklet, but declined the £95, whereupon he instantly lost interest in the freshness and originality of my stories.

Then an idea occurred to me : if publishers wanted thrillers I would write them a thriller indeed. In two months I completed the book, a composition full of purple patches, entitled : " The Amazing Honeymoon," and, to disguise my responsibility for such a production, I took the pseudo-name Basil M. D'Azyll. The story pivoted on the plot of a man whose memory, owing to an operation to his brain, moved forward rather than backward, so that he " remembered " his own future and accordingly tried hard, but unsuccessfully, to avoid certain events and disasters. The book, when submitted, was rejected whole-heartedly by six publishers, one of whom, however, offered me tuition in novel-writing from his reader, at a fee of five guineas. " I know the book is rubbish," I wrote in reply, " for if it wasn't rubbish you may be sure I wouldn't have offered it to a firm of your reputation. It may be of interest to you to know that when I had completed the work I submitted to you I wrote to a friend of mine, a man thoroughly at home in the world of publishers : ' I have a sixth-class novel. Could you suggest a likely publisher ?' He wrote back: 'All publishers publish rubbishy novels, but Messrs. X.Y.Z., Ltd. do more in that line of drivel than anyone else in the world.' " To another publisher who abused the book, I replied as follows : " I know something of the puerility of it : I wrote it for men of your calibre. I like that affectation of yours that it's not good enough for you. Why, it's miles above what is presumably your head ! " Another publisher's reader suggested in his report that I, the author, was no doubt a very young man but extremely clever. I wrote back that I was an old man and a damned fool. After this my literary agent advised me to discontinue " Basiling," as he called it, and to devote myself once more to serious literature ; and I allayed his anxiety by telegraphing to him : " Basil dead."

After that there was nothing for it but to give the " system " a trial.

II

TRYING OUT THE " SYSTEM " AT MONTE CARLO

My father, conceiving the idea that, in proportion to the collapse of his body, his mind had developed to the highest degree of mental acuteness, declared one day that he had solved the riddle of how to make a fortune at roulette. He grew more and more insistent till I, knowing nothing of gambling, wrote to Gamage's for a roulette, after which my father and I spent many weeks in testing his system. The initial results were favourable. My father immediately began to make extravagant plans as to our future. We would proceed to Monte Carlo ; he, I, my mother, my sister and husband would all assemble daily at the Casino in the gaming rooms and, putting his theory into practice, grow rich, happy, independent. My mother, always sceptical, at first ignored the whole business. Though very plucky in adversity and wary in prosperity, she was easily discouraged and easily consoled. After a time the novelty of her Parisian hats palled on her Bolton clientele, who began to boast of buying their hats in London and Paris. Her shop after the first twelve months became more and more a place of meditation and repose, rarely disturbed by the ring of a client ; and as my father reported the unbroken record of winnings on the roulette my mother, as she sighed for the purchasers who would not come, began to look round at us, envying him the vast, if nominal, sums he was raking in. My father, as his hopes of a successful " system " increased, tended to get out

of hand, regained some of his old temper.   My mother began
to think that a reasonable and sustained income, if played
for with system and caution and loyal perseverance by half
a dozen members of the family, including my aged and
infirm aunt, was perhaps within the scope of happiness
humanly realizable.   If an adequate sum should be made,
she insisted that it must be put aside, and the hazardous game
discontinued.   But my father flew into a rage and said, since
his system had proved infallible, money was no longer any
object, it was there simply to provide pleasures and luxuries
on an increasing scale.   He deprecated my mother's spirit
of defeatism, so liable to damp energy and enthusiasm at
the outset, and advocated spending what money we had
forthwith.   After an unbroken run of luck, my father's and
my luck turned, and the system proved capable of occasional
losses, nevertheless balanced by gains.   My father deprecated
the losses, ascribing them to our unfair and excessive demands
on the roulette.   We had tested the game for a fortnight, he
said, and it had proved capable of providing us with a fortune.
Why go on tempting Providence ?   Why not be modest and
reasonable and proceed forthwith to Monte Carlo to put
theory into practice, dreams into reality, numbers into money ?
My father and I were accustomed to treat each other like
gentlemen, and out of pity for him I also professed to deprecate
the recent losses in our tests.   He was so eager I should go,
so anxious I should not drop the scheme, since there was no
one else to try it out, that I had not the heart to disappoint
him.   My father slyly over-emphasized the sportingness of
gambling.   And when he wanted some money to put on
a horse he told me that he was prompted by the love
of sport, and that sport was the backbone of the country.
The obvious pleasure which he felt in thinking that he had
found a way to get round me prevented me from questioning
either that gambling was sport, or sport the backbone of
England.   I gathered such resources as I could lay hands
on and proceeded to Monte Carlo.   My father, who was
impatient and eager of results, advised my flying there since

expense was no object.   In the old prosperous days he used
to go to Monte Carlo for relaxation, a relaxation full of
irritation and nervous storms, punctuated during the brief
moments of rest by telegrams from Petersburg which appeared
under the bedroom door at night.   But the place for him was a
private paradise, and it gave him obvious pleasure to instruct
me, who had not been there before, how and where I was to
get out and by which platform I was to cross to another.   I
did not travel by air.   I took the train at Victoria and committed the error of getting into the first of the three trains,
due to leave in rotation, thinking it to be the third; and then,
having had my luggage, coat, hat and stick placed on the rack,
going out to buy something or other.   When I returned the
train was not there.   I remonstrated with the guard, but to
no avail.   The train would not come back.   On arrival at
Dover I had some difficulty in collecting my belongings,
for the three gentlemen who had travelled with my luggage
had all taken a kindly, if individual, interest in my misfortune,
and my things accordingly had been deposited in three
different parts of Dover Station.

When, rushing and roaring through Northern wet and
bleakness, I turned at daybreak the windy corner at Marseilles and the train raced gaily along the sunny Côte-d'Azur,
past the sort of villas our " system " would procure us, I
felt the moment approaching.   The scene was just a little
unreal, a little deceiving.   The benignant luxury of the
approach.   Can it be real ?   Can it be true that this little
pantomime place will solve all our monetary troubles ?

A French gentleman was holding forth to me on the evils
of gambling at Monte Carlo.   When the train stopped at
Nice he waited for me to get out.   " This is Nice," he said.
" I know," I answered, " I am going on . . . to Monte
Carlo."

He was dumbfounded.   He couldn't speak.   " Ah," he
said and shook his head gravely, and then added, " Mais il
ne faut pas jouer.   Il ne faut pas jouer."

He went and then came back again just before the train

started, and standing at the window said, " Non, il ne faut pas. Il ne faut pas jouer. Il ne faut pas."

Then he went.

As is usual on such occasions, I found that my conception of the place was totally at variance with what it was really like. What I had imagined to the right was to the left, what down up. And the atmosphere, too, was utterly different. Indecent luxury. The luxury of a lavatory de luxe. There was no poverty to counterbalance this opulent magnificence, no visible reason for its existence ; it was unnatural, as the vice it throve upon. Even Blackpool, even Bolton, even Edgware Road, yielded to it in sheer vulgarity. For vulgarity is something that *need not* be. What is characteristic is no longer vulgar. But there was no character in this crowded opulence among the rocks.

In the hotel lounge an infernal old man with an infernal foreign accent kept on telling everyone that he was an Englishman. It was mid-August, and the room at night was full of mosquitoes who fed on me, so that I almost felt ashamed to kill them, for they were after all my own blood. The proprietor of the hotel had a curious custom, which he thought remunerative, of coming up to everybody in turn as they sat at dinner, and bowing ceremoniously and saying a few kind things about the weather. He came up to me and smiling said something nice about my appétit, to which I retorted that my appétit came " en mangeant," and his eyes lit up, as though he were struck by the fine originality of my thought. I then said something about the weather, but my sentence hung in mid-air : the proprietor had already departed to another table.

The hotel looked out upon the sea all right ; but the view was rather obstructed by a railway bridge. To see the blue Mediterranean, one would either have to live on the roof, or peep at it under the bridge.

The gambling saloons at Monte Carlo are a replica of human life, a microcosm of the fortuitous outward circumstances and limited human possibilities latent in the individual who confronts them. It is a little world within a bigger world, but more meticulous, more accurate, even less incalculable. At least, the outer circumstances, which in life are represented by such unforeseen events as a fire or a war, a millionaire acquaintance, an uncle falling off a roof and leaving you a fortune or a mortgage, are here carefully graduated in more or less successive and symmetrical runs of red and black, of odd and even numbers ; so that instead of having dangers and opportunities hurled at you indiscriminately, as in the world without, you are here allowed to choose the kind of chances you prefer to grapple with. The seas of life are mountainous, and at any time you may go down through no fault of your own. But here is a sober sea of graduated waves, and whether you plunge into the depths or paddle on the surface is left to your choice, your capacity, and your judgment. That is the difference. And indeed the croupier at the green table looks like a sort of cox sitting at the helm of a boat loaded with human fate. This world within a world is in the image of the old, and its laws are as stringent. They may be only coins and plaques that are raked in, distributed and exchanged : but they are symbols of happiness. The human soul stands on tiptoe, awaiting fulfilment, realization. For in our world of appearances one symbol is as good as another. These men and women, perfumed, overdressed, young innocents or hardened cocottes, are all human beings, and it is the hope of fulfilment, a need to appease their souls, which has brought them here, far more than the greed of gold.

As I took my seat to try out my father's " system," which, on the whole, had shown such promise in Bolton, I was put out by a florid, excited individual who stood beside me and shouted to the croupier, " Allez ! Allez ! Allez plus vite ! Allez toujours ! " The rate at which he was shorn of his wealth did not seem to him fast enough. A young woman put a hundred francs on red. Black came up, and she began to cry softly. The Bolton " system " was interrupted by various outward events, such as a sudden confusion, the

failure to reach over in time. At the end of three hours'
effort I found myself the winner of five francs. On a bench
in the garden a harassed-looking old gentleman was explaining
excitedly to another that all the mischief had come about
because the expected " 13 " failed to come up when expected.
" Et pourtant," he said, as if in justification, " il y avaient
beaucoup de treizes ! "

On another bench several little French children were
comparing their mummies.

" Votre maman vous donne le goûter ? "

" Mais oui, il faut pourtant que j'aille le chercher."

When in the afternoon I resumed the " system," I was
let down at the start. Our " system " did not provide for
losing at the start, and I could not retrieve my losses ; could
not either that afternoon or on the following morning when,
unfairly as I felt, further losses were added to those of the
day before. The gentleman at the door of the gambling
saloon asked, with inquiring charm, as I came in again in
the afternoon, how I was doing ; and when I said I was
losing, " Alors," he said, " il faut jouer." Advice which
struck me as uncritical. It became quite clear to me that
our " system," which had not been proof against ultimate
defeat during our trials in Bolton, now also provided for
losing at the start. I sat down in the Casino writing-room
and wrote a long pathetic letter home, explaining that it was
no good, that I had decided to waive my last year at Oxford.
After all, I said, what good were degrees in my case ? I
would use the balance of my money to enable us all to live
cheaply abroad, etc., etc.

So I cut my losses and left Monte Carlo, that city of shim-
mering black and gold, that very night for London.

In the train, nearing London, an infallible method was
suddenly revealed to me, based not on mathematics, but
on mysticism. I saw gambling as a spiritual exercise with
mundane rewards ; the successful gambler as a being temporarily in a state of grace. My method was simple. I
would watch a successful gambler who did not follow any

system but who seemed to be inspired by sheer good luck. Success gives him confidence, confidence style. He feels in contact, in harmony with fortune. He is in grace. I sit and watch and do nothing. Sooner or later his luck turns: he is beginning to lose. At once he is put out, tries to retrieve his losses, grows nervous and now consciously attempts to follow some system of his own. No good; he is out of touch with luck: he loses all the time. Now's my chance. I play against him. I back the opposite colour, numbers, etc. He loses. I win. He is ruined, I walk out a millionaire.

The porters cried " Victoria ! "

When I arrived in London there was a letter for me from my mother saying that there was no need for my sacrifice, that I must finish my course at Oxford and get my degrees which meant so much to me, and that I should come home and we would all have a good time.

When I arrived there was a general mood of generosity in all members of the family. Each offered to do his best, each held out his savings ready to throw them into the common pool. My father, who had twenty pounds' worth of shares in some Paris concern, could be dissuaded only with difficulty from selling them to make up part of my losses. " It was all my fault," he said. " I thought I'd discovered a system, but it's this damned roulette "; and suddenly he cried. In spite of what I'd lost, I had just enough to carry on for another year, and I returned to Oxford, and took my B.A. and B.Litt. a year later. As soon as " Futility " was published, my brother and I arranged that my mother should give up her shop, and we went to live in the Austrian Tyrol, where, owing to the collapse of the currency, we were able to live at a pleasant *pension*, overlooking gorgeous scenery, at something like two shillings and sixpence a day a head.

Recently when I left Antibes, there were two English ladies in the train who said you could make a steady income at the wheel provided you were steady, knew when to stop, etc., etc.

" Yes," I said gloomily. " Ye-e-e-s. . . ."

III

THE LITERARY DEBUT

When your novel is in typescript you feel like telling your friends how you have, after much misgiving, deleted a comma and made one sentence out of two by joining them with a semicolon. In vain you hope to find any response. But long after you have ceased to take an interest in a book, a casual observer will point out some little detail to you. In vain! You no longer care.

I think the greatest moment in a writer's life is when, having packed his finished novel into a parcel, he deposits it behind the counter of the post office and obtains a receipt for it. I am not one who is given to jubilees and birthday celebrations, centenaries, or festivities of any kind. But on such a day I shave more scrupulously, I dress with care, and put on a white tie. The registration receipt in my pocket, I go home, prancing. Then I feel like calling on some quite unknown person and saying to him, smilingly : " Well, how *are* you ? "

When the publication of my first book, " Futility," was announced I felt as if the revolution of the globe would be arrested, that planets would hang still in space, the normal activities of man subside : that there would be a lull : all the traffic would stop on the streets, trams and omnibuses would cease to run ; more than that, that they would never run again, or at least they would not run in the same way. " We did not know," was to be their attitude. " How could we know? But now we know." Absurd? So it is! But something like this is experienced, inarticulately, by the virgin writer.

What happens *after* publication is far less exciting, and grows progressively so with hope and royalties deferred. The calm which follows on the storm of a novelist's expectation begins on publication day. You go out and you find that everything is quiet in the city. You expect to see more policemen on point duty ; you don't. Fail to see your book in the bookshop. Nay, fail to see any damned bookshops ! Nobody apparently interested in your novel. You brood, and at last hit on the idea of placing your novel on the roof of a house. A crowd collects. Finally mounted police have to be called to disperse the mob. At the close of day the Superintendent of Police sits down to write his daily report to his superior : " Thanks to Providence," he concludes, " I have been able to avert bloodshed. The city is again quiet."

CHAPTER TEN

FATHER'S DEATH

I

IN THE AUSTRIAN ALPS

AFTER " Futility " had appeared, though it was selling what the publisher called " steadily," which meant about a couple of copies every couple of days, I suggested to my mother that she should shut up shop for good ; and, armed with confidence based on future books rather than a meagre bank balance, I worked out a scheme by which, if we took ourselves off to some country whose money had reached unprecedented depths of depreciation, my parents might exist in tolerable comfort on what my brother and I were to contribute jointly. I went off on a reconnoitring journey to Austria, for economy's sake spending only one day and night in London, my first visit there since "·Futility," and accordingly my first taste of lionization. From Innsbruck I reported that I found that town suitable for our abode, tending to exaggerate the amenities of the *pension*.

" The *pension* comprises two houses," I wrote to my parents, " an old one, like a Russian *datcha* inside, and a new stone villa, with two rows of balconies practically surrounding the house. You and I will live in the latter, but if you wish we can live in the old one ; but we shall scarcely want to ! There are very few people in either of the houses, but the stone house is ideal. There are three storeys : i.e. the ground floor and two others. We can have the whole front row of the middle storey if we take three rooms, which are all in a row with communicating doors, and each with a door into the corridor, and each room likewise having a double door on to the balcony. Bathroom on the ground floor. We would have the whole of the middle (i.e. lower) balcony to ourselves, and both the balcony and our windows face South. We are moderately high up, and are screened from the wind by enormously high mountains, North, East, and West, while towards the South the mountains are somewhat lower and occasionally a breeze comes up a wide valley from Italy, wo die Zitronen blühen . . .

"I sit here on the open balcony outside my room, and the view from here is magnificent. You can see the river, the beautiful turbulent Inn, and the bridges, you see also the funicular going up the mountain slope, and all around are pine-trees, birches, roses, beautiful villas in lanes lined with foliage; and at night when you walk by the river, where lanterns shine between secretive trees, you feel as though you were somewhere in China, in Peking. It is quiet; you hear only church bells and the silvery sounds of cow bells. There are no motors, only horse carriages, and you can cross the street almost with your eyes shut: it is so quiet and slow, so neat and respectable; an ideal place for wheeling Papa round. Yet it is not a bit dull. There are theatres, cinemas, museums, the old Imperial Palace which can be inspected, and which I have seen. At the theatre they are giving Goethe's 'Faust.' The old villa here has a garden. And in the winter, if you like, dinner can be served for us in a drawing-room (with a piano) which we can have to ourselves, without any extra charge, or brought up to our rooms. I have a dinner-table in mine covered by a white tablecloth slightly mended in places. The maid is a very nice girl, but not pretty. Everybody is so polite, it is all 'Bitte schön,' 'Danke schön.' There is only one other visitor in the *pension*, a thin, intense Englishwoman. She is violently pro-Bolshevik, anti-British, and a little unbalanced. However, she will be good company. I only met her yesterday at lunch, and she at once asked my advice as to how she could recover a trunk she had lent to some skunk of an English major who had since returned to England and was ignoring her letters. I said, 'Write to Scotland Yard.' She thanked me profusely. 'Thank you, it is *so* kind of you. I'm very grateful *indeed*. I shall do so at once.'

" The *pension* is on the edge of a little village called Mühlau. If you go down by a rather steep lane, in a few minutes you find yourself in Innsbruck, on a beautiful suspended bridge, where, if you wish, you can take the tram to almost any direction; or the funicular. If you don't care for a steep lane, you go down by a slightly longer but imperceptibly ascending road, by which the carriages come up, and in ten minutes you find yourself in town. If you go by another lane, you have an Austrian reproduction of Bubwith—pigs, roses, cottages, little children playing in the street, a hen crossing the road . . .

" While I write, a very angry old woman rushes out after a child calling it ' du Scheussal '; the child is very frightened, and runs into the little chapel, which is opposite our balcony almost. But the angry old woman runs into the chapel and fetches the child from there and carries it home, cursing all the way : ' du Scheussal du ! ach du Scheussal !'

" I am afraid I can't write any more : I am jaded ; and so I am going out to post this letter. I am sure that when you come here you will find that for the first time in your lives you will really begin to enjoy yourselves. Monte Carlo and these other fashionable artificial places are simply ridiculous compared with this lovely place."

Three weeks later I went down to the station to meet the long, much-travelled, exhausted, dusty train from Paris which contained my father, my mother, and a maiden aunt, a daughter of Grandpa Wadsworth. We drove in an open cab, at first through the old mellow town with its cloistered streets, domes, turrets, and pinnacles ; then by the side of the river, angry and turbulent. A faint hazy summer afternoon was drawing to its close, and as, at sundown, we came to the hanging bridge between rocks and the foaming green river rushing angrily under the horse's hoofs, my father, though not a lover of nature, looked at it all with new awakened wonder, as if a little dazed with rapture.

There were inns in the hills, and my father liked to be wheeled to them in his chair to drink beer or coffee. "It's my turn to-day," he would say, when the bill was brought. We would wind our way up the Schillerweg and sit down in a beer garden, amidst the beer and wine-drinking peasants, with chamois beards like shaving brushes stuck in their coloured hats, and the women in Tyrolese peasant dress, taken in tightly at the waist and showing off their figures to advantage, and sit still and look down into the green folds of the valley and up at the jagged summits of naked rock. Fowls, chickens, strutted all over the place, jumped on the chairs. The little serving maid, bare-legged, would call them : " *Zip-zip-zip !* " The sun, as if making a last effort, shone with a tragic brightness ; then, unable to sustain the effort, diminished its light. The bare-legged maid went in. When she came out she wore a pair of brown stockings. The sun set behind the hill and left the valley cold and unfriendly ; only the tips of rocks still gleamed in the sun. Far away, a train whistled, and then coiled below, like a serpent, on its long journey to Vienna. All the peasants, save for one old man, had already vanished down the hill. He drank his big mug to the bottom, smacking his lips. Having paid for the beer and lighted his pipe, he rose, and at once there came sounds of his jolly accordion, as, with twinkling eye, he strode to his own happy tune out of the courtyard. Fresh and alert, he went down the road making his own music, till his long curved pipe, and his knapsack, and the plume in his hat, ducked by the hill, and only the jolly tune spoke of his fresh onward strides.

The sun had long set behind the hills. It was very still. My father coughed and expressed a desire to be wheeled home.

He also loved to be wheeled down to town, to be assisted into a café called " München," order a glass of beer and listen to the music. But having drunk his beer, he at once wished to be off again. To wheel him up the hill was an arduous task, a truly uphill business. We ordered him an elaborate mechanical support for his paralysed leg which we hoped would enable him to walk eventually; and he told us of a dream in which he had walked on it by himself to the Casino at Igls, to give our " system " another try. But when at last the expensive new " leg " was ready for use, my father would not give it a fair trial, and when I asked what I was to do with it, said: " Throw it out of the window."

In Innsbruck I found local society comically punctilious about calls. When I went to tea with a family of young girls and grown-up boys, the call was returned the next day by the head of the family, aged seventy. We lived at the top of a very high hill, and as I sat at my table by the window and wrote " The Polyglots " I saw an old man with silver locks, in goloshes and astrakhan coat, puffing up the steep incline. Another day I was invited by a woman to tea, and next morning while I sat in my portable bath the lady's husband was already knocking at my bedroom door. I explained I was in my bath. The baron stressed the fact that he was returning my call. A desultory conversation took place through the keyhole, I explaining I could not that moment admit him; he evidently offended. Within half an hour of being dressed I dashed to the baron's house to return his call, but found he was out. Late that night he came tearing up the hill, to return my call, only having seen my card, he explained, ten minutes before, on his return from an excursion in the hills, and dog tired.

When I was struggling with " The Polyglots," full of literary compunction because I could not tear myself from the life around me, it did not occur to me that in my truant hours I was absorbing impressions for my future books, " Donna Quixote," " Pretty Creatures " and " Jazz and Jasper." Years later, a young woman journalist in Montreal spoke to me enthusiastically of the nature scenes in " Jazz and Jasper," and recalled the passages I most treasured, but which no one had noticed.

II

MOUNTAIN SPRING

Innsbruck was a retreat of impoverished Austrian nobility, a wistful valley whose hills looked longingly across to the dissevered South Tyrol. " You couldn't be seen in the street with an Italian," they told you. Nevertheless, they cultivated the society of the Consul-General for Italy, Count Pravana. He had an American wife with a lovely niece staying with them, with whom I was more than a little in love. And at everything I said she gave a delighted expression, as if I had tickled her, and said, " Oh, Willy ! " The first time I came to see them I surprised her drying her hands in the process of manicuring them ; they were still pink from the water, long, tapering, girlish, lovely. The scene cannot be obliterated from my memory. Were I to drown and my whole life to pass before my mind's eye (as it is said to) that scene would start up before me.

The walks, the dances, the excursions into the hills, are bound up with my memory of that girl. The Inn valley stretches deep beneath us. More mountains, like ghost ships on an uncharted sea, loom into sight as we climb the spiral grass-edged path, meeting more flowers on our way : snowdrops, buttercups, daisies, bluebells, primulas, violets, while little brooks skurry down head-over-heels to announce that Spring is already come. An hour's distance from our goal we spread out our mantles on the green slope of a sheltered warm valley, where daffodils grow in profusion by the side of a brook, and stretch our limbs and doze rapturously in the sun. Rising, we set out on the last but one stage in our journey, climbing hills without paths, cutting across pastures where frisky young cows, turned irresponsible on these heights, jump over the moon ; now clearing gurgling brooks which still run hurry-skurry down to the valleys to tell the glad tidings ; now stopping to drink the cool water. By two we reach the top of the shaggy mountain slope : above looms the gleaming naked dead rock of the summit. A separate journey, after an hour's repose.

We lie on the edge of a plateau projecting perilously over the void and look down at Innsbruck, miniature as on a map, the river Inn bedded in the soft, green folds of the valley, the parcelled fields, the dotted villages, the spired churches, all lucent and serene in the spring sun. We climb the steep rocky way to the peak, clinging to loose stones and sending them rolling a mile or two till they rebound with a heavy earthen thud in the abyss. No more shrubs or alpine roses ; nor a human habitation anywhere. The last was the Gasthaus, which is now lost to sight. On we climb till, in the first dusk, we reach the flat rocky mountain top : there is nowhere higher to go. The air is amazingly light. I sit on a rock, struck speechless by the mighty spectacle ; the neighbouring mountain-peaks, all level now and grandly equal, look into the gathering dusk, heavy with unspoken utterance, listening, straining over, pricking their ears. On these heights they commune. Hush ! Can you hear ? " We shan't say anything . . . shan't say anything. . . ."

She stayed in Innsbruck one brief spring and summer. But her correspondence was long and pregnant with memories. " Do you remember so-and-so and so-and-so and so-and-so ? " she wrote. " And how the storm came on, and how you helped me up, and how it rained and we ran together to hide in the cave ? "

I remember everything ; and in these memories of the fleeting moment seems to lie the permanent, the unforgettable, the sustaining, for ever, for ever !

" I like being married," she writes. " I wish I could show you my little son. James (my husband) is the image of you. It is such a striking resemblance that I feel sure I must have told you of it. What a funny meeting we had in Toulon—just a glimpse of you—tea in the *pâtisserie*—do you remember ? "

On my way back from India I came across an American couple mother and daughter, of Philadelphia, who knew

Phyllis, had recently seen her in China. "And what is her husband like?" I asked eagerly.

"A very nice man," they both said, "absolutely charming, and *so* devoted to her!"

"But to look at?" I asked.

"Oh, very plain."

III

EDITH WHARTON'S VANISHING TRICK

My acquaintance with Mrs. Wharton began with the receipt of a letter from her, shortly after the publication in England of "Futility." She had paid her annual visit to England, and at the station a Cambridge don gave her my book, which she began very unwillingly in the train from Victoria, only to finish it with the utmost enthusiasm on nearing Paris. Her letter to me was worded with the unstinted praise of a generous soul. I am ashamed to say that I had, at that time, not heard of Mrs. Wharton! I hoped she might be a lovely flapper polishing off her French at a Paris finishing school. I was about to reply to her in a manner acceptable to a flapper, but that day I happened to stroll into the Bolton public library, and the name of Edith Wharton suddenly touched some obscure literary association. Hadn't I seen it somewhere—in the columns of a literary review? I inquired from the lady behind the desk, with the diffidence of one who is inquiring concerning the improbable, if she had ever heard of a writer called Edith Wharton. In reply, she directed me to two shelves and a half, in a corner marked "Fiction," devoted to the works of that author. I took out two of them, and was thus able to reply to Mrs. Wharton in the tone of a young pupil and aspirant, who had kept his passionate admiration of her works too long to himself, and was overjoyed to be at last able to give expression to an en-thusiasm which he insists she must now at last share with him.

Our friendship for some time took the form of corre-spondence. But when I had transferred my residence from

Bolton to Innsbruck, Mrs. Wharton, rightly observing that the rolling surges no longer divided us, invited me to come and stay with her at her château at Hyères. I had every reason to be grateful to Mrs. Wharton. She not only allowed my American publisher to make use of her enthusiastic letter, but actually wrote a preface for the American edition of "Futility," which attracted considerable notice and gave the book a propitious send-off. "Futility" leaving me with more praise than money, I could not afford the restaurant car and so set out for Hyères laden with sandwiches. Sandwiches prepared by the Tyrolese *pension* contain more bread than meat. Finding it impractical to throw the bread out of the window, for the train was already running into Toulon, I put the bread in my bag. Mrs. Wharton's car conveyed me from Toulon station to Hyères. When I drove up to the house, Mrs. Wharton was already in bed and welcomed me from her window. I could not see her face in the dark. Reflecting that my bag contained large chunks of bread and butter, and that an immaculate butler would be sure to survey them with critical thoughtfulness, I threw them where they belonged and pulled the plug. Early next morning there were noises, anxious faces, and on inquiry I was told that plumbers were at work, some unknown person, the butler said, having thrown bread down the lavatory which had swelled and blocked the pipe. When a few hours later I advanced to meet Mrs. Wharton in the garden we both smiled unconvincingly. If the truth must be told each thought, as we shook hands, of the bread in the lavatory. Edith Wharton, I heard afterwards, told people that I, coming from Siberia, had brought bread with me thinking there might be a shortage of food in her house.

After lunch I spent the whole day with her in the open air, during which time she, of course, wore a hat. When I came down in the evening there was a woman in the drawing-room with yellowish hair whom I thought I had not seen before.

We sat there waiting, as I thought, for our hostess.

Presently we went in to dinner and I found myself sitting by the side of the woman to whom I had not been introduced, because of the absence of our hostess, I supposed. It seemed odd to me we should not have waited for our hostess, and after the soup I said to the woman at my side : " But where is Mrs. Wharton ? "

She looked at me with sad, inquiring thoughtfulness and said—very pertinently, as it seems to me now : " I am Mrs. Wharton."

" Oh," I said, " are you Mrs. Wharton ? "

She looked at me as if she thought I couldn't be all there. " Of course I am," she said. " Oh . . . good evening," I said.

Mrs. Wharton writes in bed, having contracted the habit as a young woman when she was ill. " Of course, the great advantage you enjoy over me," I said, while Mrs. Wharton looked suspiciously at me, " is that you needn't shave in the morning."

She thought this a trivial point. But it gives women novelists a good start on us men. When I told her what a heart-bleeding business it was writing a novel, " And let me tell you at once," she said eagerly, " that it doesn't get any easier as time goes on."

Mrs. Wharton asked if I pronounced my name with a soft or a hard " g." I said it was soft, after which she instantly dropped the " h " in the middle, calling me " Mr. Gerard-y." When I protested, she said I couldn't possibly have it both ways : it was either " Gherhardi," or " Gerard-y." The soft " g " with the " h " in the middle, as I had always heard our name pronounced by the people who bore it, she dismissed as impossible philology ; as Mr. Nichol Smith, of Oxford, had done before. My name offers no difficulties to the French or the Germans, the Italians or the Russians, the Spanish or Portuguese, who pronounce it as to the manner born. As I am the last person to wish to deprive a name, susceptible of several pronunciations, of its genial complacency, I have decreed that, to satisfy divergent opinions, the correct way of pronouncing my name is : " Jerhardy " on Mondays, Wednesdays and Fridays ; " Gherhardy " on Tuesdays, Thursdays and Saturdays ; but on Sunday, which is the day of rest, let it be " Jeerady."

IV

THE FAREWELL

By the following spring we moved from the *pension* at Mühlau to the other side of the valley. We took the little mountain railway to Igls ; and my parents entrenched themselves in a *pension* at Andras, and I at Ambras, a station lower down the hill, half an hour's walk from Andras, far enough away to enable me to concentrate on " The Polyglots," which I was just then bringing to a conclusion. Another novelist, Archibald Marshall, was groaning in another room, bringing forth a child of his brain in pain and labour. My father, in his *pension* higher up the hill, for the most part sat out on the balcony in the sun, till it declined towards evening, when suddenly the landscape shone forth with a crystalline clearness, as though you had adjusted your binoculars to the required focus. Nature here was, if anything, even more rapturous than on the other hill. Tired of writing, I would stroll for hours through the pine-wood. Suddenly the sun came out again and shone through the trees with a dazzling whiteness such as only acetylene lamps can produce. On the edge of the wood I stood still ; below was a lake surrounded by firs : a little lake, like a plum dipped in water. Sky, firs, hills, water, all was blue, each just a shade darker ; all blue and motionless, as if waiting for something. I stood still, my heart beating, till the sun sank, and the first silver stars twinkled feebly in the sky. One night I walked on and on till the sky grew threadbare, the moon paled, and a small peevish sun looked out, sleepy, red-eyed. Then a shaft of light licked a fugitive cloud. A cock cleared his throat in the yard below. The rich odour of mown grass and the rays on the ricks of straw bade one live. I blessed my fate, which did not require that I was to be hanged at dawn, that I had sufficient to eat, and could go home and sleep in clean sheets on a feather bed.

When the summer was over, and the sun failed to appear, my father sat angrily in his room by the stove and tried to kill time with a book. He had from of old a habit of punctuality, and now that he had nothing to do he still pulled out his watch at frequent intervals to see if it was time to hope for the arrival of the post, which might bring—he had ceased to expect letters—at least a newspaper. He was now impatient to " get time on." I remember seeing him there reading my Tchehov book to himself angrily, munching and swallowing as he always did through restlessness, which since he had to sit in a chair had no other outlet.

But lo! a shaft of sunlight. The wet valley glittered with gaiety ; it spread to the hills, then the whole vault of heaven burst into sunlight. My father's spirits rose. He would cheer up at the prospect of being " taken out," which for him now was just sitting on the balcony in the sun.

A week before I left for Vienna, where I intended to spend the winter, my mother read aloud passages from " The Polyglots " in manuscript. When she came to the description of Natasha's death she began to cry and my father kept saying : " But this is only a book. Don't cry. It's not real. It's only a book. Willy has invented it." My father remarked several times that the concluding chapters about the voyage home were " instructive." Through sheer boredom, he looked forward to my mother's readings. But one is shy of one's work in manuscript form ; when a book is in print it seems to assume a concreteness, a responsibility of its own. I discouraged these readings. The book would be out in less than three months, I argued. And how was I to know that my father was not to survive that time ?

He was now very fond of sugar, which everyone kept telling him was bad for him. He would ask me to buy him a pound at a time, which he kept surreptitiously in his drawer. He used to put nine or ten lumps into a cup, as if to sweeten his declining days. By that time everything he liked was deemed to be bad for him. When I came in to say good-bye, before I left for Vienna, it was an early afternoon. The winter sun looked in and suddenly lit the room, dwelt on the brown wrinkles of his face as he sat there, composed, resigned to his uncharitable fate. How he would have loved, himself, to have gone to Vienna !

We sat still, as one does before parting. My mother remarked that my little hand-bag, which was Count Berchtold's tennis prize, won thirteen years ago, was too dilapidated to be of any further use and, with that wifely habit of sharing her husband's property, said : " Papa will give you his." My father's bag had accompanied him on all his journeys, and he seemed to attach a sentimental value to it. He said : " Of course." But I could see he was not willing to part with his bag. He would have been quite ready to sell it to me, perhaps. For he was still keen on gambling whenever he could, and he was now dependent on any little money one gave him from time to time. I could not afford to buy the bag, even if I had wanted it. My book on Tchehov, a year's work, had brought in £12 10s. in royalties. I had already, before leaving, given my father some little pocket money to last awhile. I had barely enough to take me to Vienna and keep me there for a month. " No, no," I said. " Papa doesn't want to part with his bag. I'll borrow it. May I borrow it ? I'll bring it back next time."

" Of course," he said.

My father sat there in front of me, transparent, unearthly in the sun, so tranquil and beautiful. I rose to go. " Well, good-bye." " Bon voyage," he said. This was the last thing he said to me. When I saw him again, he was dead. I had not seen his eyes for a long time. Now, in the burst of sunlight, I saw them again. Tranquillity filled them.

I trudged down the hill. At the end of the path we stopped. Here my mother and I kissed. " You never know nowadays," she said, " that your parting with him may not be the last."

V

VIENNA

In Vienna I put up at a *pension* near the Votivkirche, which stretched its two towers heavenward and at night seemed as if made of lace. The Opera, the intellectual curiosity and the architectural gesture of Vienna, charmed me, though the Viennese were a little absurd in their self-love and self-praise of the Wienerküche, which, good as it was, was not as good as all that. Still, they kept up a certain style ; and the arts were held in esteem by them. And one afternoon, passing along the Kärnthner Ring in Vienna I saw a massive statue of a tall, big, strikingly good-looking man seated in a ponderous armchair, his arms resting on the sides and his hands hanging down perfunctorily. A clean-cut profile and wonderful large eyes. I guessed him from afar. As I came up I read : Goethe. I stood and wondered.

Unlike in Innsbruck, where I had been absorbed by the somewhat prim but art-loving remnants of the local nobility, in Vienna I landed right into the middle of Bohemia, nearly all Jews, and at that mostly Czech, Serb, Pole, and Hungarian. The names were all like Vinzens, Hneika, Nachòd, Ida Sika, Herr Smolka, or Fräulein Trŝzka. There was a poet who read his own verses at the meetings of those many little clubs which have no premises of their own but assemble regularly twice a week at one of the innumerable cafés. At some unearthly hour, as we returned in a taxi, packed like sardines, he would be declaiming at the top of his voice :

> " *Es ist der Wind ! der Wind ! der Wind !*
> *Der ka-a-alte November Wind !* "

And the November wind was, in truth, uncommonly sharp, unwarrantably bitter.

The informality of the Viennese is famous. The first day I did not know anyone. On the second, on the platform of a tram, I stepped inadvertently on a lady's foot, and as the lady was beautiful excused myself profusely, again and again, touched her ankle to ascertain that the pain had gone and asked leave to call on her to-morrow to apologize again. She invited me to a Kegel-Klub. From that evening I seemed to know everybody. I commented on the amiability of Viennese, and they laughed and said it was a point of honour with any real Wienerin to extend hospitality to a foreigner if she as much as spotted one in the street. Emboldened by this statement, next morning I followed a rather lovely lady down the Ring and, catching up with her, asked her to direct me to the Kolowratring. " Ask a police-man," she said irritably. I myself, however, never failed to impart information. And once an Englishman who was groping his way towards the Rathhaus, stopped me and said : " Pardon me, which is the way to the rat house ? "

Girls did not lack, either. When in Innsbruck I asked what the much-praised Viennese woman was like, I was given conflicting ideas. " Gross und schlank," said some. " Rund und mollig," said others. They were just like daughters of man and woman elsewhere. There was one Jewish beauty, who caused me great exultation and great tribulation as well. She was the daughter of a jeweller who, however, had not much jewellery in his shop window. He was really a watchmaker ; and once, when I turned back the hands of my watch, she was alarmed. She told me that " Never ! Never ! Never ! " should I do that : always turn forward till the requisite adjustment was completed. A family of ten (eight of whom were boys), they were of modest means and small position, but for a distant uncle on their mother's side, a retired general whose visit was deemed a rare honour. The two girls thought they had to do as the boys, and stood up clicking their heels and bowing stiffly like their brothers.

At first I did not know how to get on with Trudl ; then I discovered. One day I had watched Hans, Trudl's original lover, and saw that Hans was silent with her. I adopted Hans's attitude, with a measure of success. But Hans had the misfortune to die. And I had to suffer for it. At night, in my arms, she would entreat me not to speak (so as not to break the illusion of my being Hans), only to awaken and cry when she realized that I was William.

" My darling, my love," I would try to console her.

" Don't speak." More tears.

" I am tired of pretending to be a dead man."

"I will never find another like Hans. I will live on my memories."

I did not mind silence, especially her own. Physical passion can do more for the renewal of a man's spirit than all the ethical discourses of a clever mistress. The compulsory posing as a dead man was less pleasing. But I was the dead man to her then and did not become alive till, a year hence, my own passion for her was dead.

She looked not unlike a youthful edition of Pola Negri, and did not see why she should not repeat her prototype's success. I wrote accordingly to the florid young Jew I had known in the Bayswater boarding house, who had encouraged me to write scenarios for film companies other than his own. "I am anxious," I wrote, " to secure her for England and thus forestall an American offer." He, however, did not in his reply share my anxiety. A year later I told Rex Ingram I would do my best to secure her for the film he was making. He begged me not to put myself out on his account, but have a drink with him instead.

And there was the young wife of an amiable Viennese, who appeared inordinately flattered by my infatuation for his wife. It seemed I could do no wrong in the eyes of that young husband. He had a touching way of delighting in every commonplace observation I might make, such as " Spring is a beautiful season," or "I hate rain, don't you?" as though they were oracles of wisdom. "You have an extraordinary understanding (Verständnis) of these things," he would say, or "You've hit the nail on the head there," and tap my shoulder quietly, elastically, with two of his long, tapering fingers. And even when discovering his wife with me in a situation that admitted of no doubt, the amiable Viennese seemed not at all displeased. " I've noticed it ! " he said to me afterwards, beaming at me through his spectacles. " Ha, ha ! You must approve of my wife ! " He touched his hat politely. " My high consideration ! (Meine Hochachtung !) " When later I intimated to the husband that I was about to take his wife on a long spin in the hills and that we would not be back till next morning, the latter only said : " Yes, yes. You are quite right. You have an extraordinary understanding of these things. My high consideration ! "

And there was a girl with thinnish legs, a product of war food—or the lack of it—called Gretl, who looked at herself in my glass and when I said, " You're so pretty," replied, " Denkst du ? " She had Gypsy blood in her veins and sang an interminable song : " Er war ein alter Zigeuner, lebte nur für Musik," the burden of which was that the music-loving old Gypsy died, was buried and mourned as " ein alter Zigeuner " who " lebte nur für Musik," died and was mourned in those slow, deliberate tones which assured us again and again that he was " ein alter Zigeuner, lebte nur für Musik."

And there was a polyglot porter who said : " Das, ladies und gentlemen, ist nicht le business ! " And when at night you returned with a girl, he took his gate money and wished you " Angenehme Ruhe."

VI

THE BLACK SUIT

I remember that day I was to go to a party to meet again a rather beautiful young woman. She had been married a few years, had found the experiment unsatisfying romantically, and was ready for an adventure with a poet. I should explain that writers, novelists, in the German language, are, if presumed creative, designated Dichter—that is to say, poets. I was her poet, writing in a language she could not read and so the more incalculable in appeal. And that night, following on two or three other preliminary, preluding nights, was to be decisive. I should add that a dinner-jacket in Bohemian Vienna is often deemed excessive ; a morning coat is more usual or, if the occasion is quite informal, the dress urged upon you is " ein schwarzer Anzug "—a black suit. I had accordingly, a week previously, ordered such a black suit and that day—it was a Wednesday—had called on my tailor for a final try-on. Though—or because—the tailor from the outset disparaged the English tailors and said that there was nothing to beat a Vienna tailor like himself, and, moreover, disdained trying-on, claiming that he could cut a suit after one glance at a client, the " black suit " turned out to be the worst it has ever been my misfortune to wear. Nevertheless, the " black suit " was required for this especial night and, distrustful of promises, I brought it back myself. When I returned to the *pension*, there was a letter from my mother which informed me that my father had not been very well over Christmas but had since recovered somewhat. There was also a letter from a friend who required a small loan of money ; and, following my disbursement on the " black suit," this request made me feel how little my friends appreciated my poverty and how much better off than I actually was they thought me. I put on my " black suit," and the fact that it was too tight under the arms, too short in the sleeves, too loose round the ankles, confirmed my impression that tailors also were only out for what they could get out of you.

Just then I was called to the telephone. It was, I was told, a long distance call from Innsbruck, and there was my mother, by the sound of her in great distress, informing me that my father was very ill indeed. My impulse was to console her. However ill, I suggested that he would recover. But no, she implied, he was unconscious, had been so for several hours ; the doctor had been and gone, having apparently given up all hope. Why had the doctor gone ? It seemed incredible to me that the doctor should have gone away so

complacently. The doctor, my mother informed me, lived
a long way off. There was nothing he could do, he said,
and his staying would not help matters. I said I'd jump
into the next train and come. My mother said, " Do."

In old novels grief is treated as a one-melody emotion.
In real life this is not so. And anything which is simulated,
which is false, becomes a cliché, a piece of self-deception,
which can no longer deceive others and which literary
criticism rightly labels " sentimentality." When an experience
is given to us at second or third hand we invariably react to it
in a simple, single manner. " Grief, intolerable grief " is
the emotion expected of us in such a moment. In reality,
grief comes much later. I remember that as I faced the
husband of the *pension* proprietress, I was filled with a sense
of the gravity of my position, not so much racked by my
own feelings as expecting him to be overwhelmed with sorrow
at my words : " I've got to leave at once for Innsbruck. I've
had a message from my mother. My father is dying. Could
you please look up the next train for me ? "

To my surprise, the old man did not comment on the
tragedy of my position but merely began to look up the
trains. Two things emerged. First, that he was not conversant with the technique of looking up trains ; second,
that he tried to conceal his ineptitude. It emerged from his
prolonged turning up of time-tables that there was no
train for another hour and a half ; and it is a twelve hours'
journey from Vienna to Innsbruck. I threw a few things
into my bags, including the little bag which was my father's.
Then, with time to spare, I rang up the lady whom I was
going to meet, and told her. She took in the news and
expressed herself appropriately, hoping for a meeting later
in the season. Probably feeling that such a meeting, coming
after the loss of my father, might seem to me trivial, she
expressed the hope that my father would recover. There
were several people in the *pension* who had heard the news
of my precipitate departure, and they all expressed, as if
unwilling to pamper my feeling of tragic gloom, the view

that my father would have recovered his consciousness by the time I got to Innsbruck.

When I arrived at the station I found that, the *pension* proprietor's time-table being out of date, a train had just departed for Innsbruck and that the next was not due for another two hours.

I remember pacing up and down the platform, filled with a sense of tragic importance, looking at all the people hurrying past me, unconscious what I, unlike them, was going through. At last the train left. As I sat there in an empty coupé, the assurance came to me that my father would pull through, as he had once before pulled through. But when, at midnight, I flung myself on the couch and lay awake in the dark and empty compartment, I felt certain that he had died, that it was over, and I cried without restraint.

I saw him again as he had been in my childhood, in his full power and success, how well he had borne himself, how vigorous he had been ; then his decline, and now the end.

As dawn lifted the night and the sun smiled on the Tyrol snows, I ceased to think. I resolved I would not speculate any longer, but leave the decision to Providence.

Towards mid-day the train arrived at Innsbruck station. The whole country was deep in snow and the sun shone over dell and hill benignantly. As there was no conveyance, I took the tram to the foot of the hill, and then set out quickly, girdling my way past Ambras to Andras. As I climbed up the hill, the snow-clad pines looked expectant and everything waited and watched. In the winter silence of frozen brooks, suddenly, as I listened, it seemed to me I had come near, quite near, the initial mystery of existence : that if somehow I could hold on for one more minute I should be touching the fringe of eternal being.

I was carrying my father's little bag which I had borrowed unwillingly. "I've brought you back your bag." He won't say anything, but he will be pleased. I was now more or less sure that on reaching the top of the hill I would find my father sitting in a chair and smiling at the danger through which he had passed successfully. Lear's words, " O, I have ta'en too little care of this . . ." occurred to me. I wondered indeed how it was that we had done so little for him, why I had not taken him to town more often. In future it would be a pleasure to drag him up the hill, whatever the effort. He must know that and give us another chance. All the daily fatigues, personal handicaps, when all that an individual can reasonably do is to combat his own gloom, rekindle that battery of life which daily runs down and has to be recharged with your own hopes and dreams—all this vanished. It would be quite easy now, I thought, to devote all one's life to one's father, since he could not—how could this have escaped us ?—have very much more to live, to relieve the tedium of his days. Another ten minutes ; and how glad would be our reunion ; and what a lesson !

A car came tearing down the hill, raising much snow in the doing. I stepped aside to let it pass, but it halted quite near me. Inside was my mother, draped heavily in black crêpe. I approached. My mother explained that the chauffeur—to whom she made an effort to introduce me— had very kindly volunteered to take her to town as there was so much that had to be done, the people at the *pension* naturally feeling——

But what of father ? My mother told me the news, some-how confining the interest of it to the time—he died about one in the morning. Would I step into the car with her ? The people at the *pension* were so frightened to have a dead man in the house. They wanted him removed as quickly as possible. I got into the car beside my mother. The snow flew into my face as the chauffeur put on speed, and the tears streamed from my eyes, all the way, in one mad rush down the winding mountain road. Why rushing ? What was the hurry now ? My mother, who had gone through it all and whose tears had run dry hours ago, seemed quiet and sensible as she recounted to me the details of his death : how she kept vigil over him during the long hours of the night, gave him the drops prescribed by the doctor who

had refused to wait, how she had stroked his head and, as he
ceased to answer, called him by a pet name not used since
they were newly married—" Carlusha ! " she called to him,
but he was impervious ; how she said to him again and
again : " Willy is coming, Willy is coming ! " news which
had apparently not seemed to him worth the pain of recrossing
the boundary of unconsciousness : that antithesis of consciousness which refuses any longer to have to treat with
our world. I listened and cried. I could not stop my tears
even when we called on a Lutheran pastor, who did not
despise my weakness but affected to regard it as natural and
of a passing nature. It seemed that if we, as Anglicans,
insisted on a Church of England burial, there was, hidden
somewhere amid the hills, a veteran Englishman remotely
connected with the cloth, who might be willing to conduct
a service for us. But his health was frail, the winter rigorous,
he had recently damaged his foot and—the Lutheran pastor
asked us as reasonable beings : Was it worth while ? To
me, now that my father was dead, no activity, which apparently
could not revive him, seemed very worth while. The pastor
was no worse than another—we'd have him. He seemed
pleased with our decision and when we, shyly, asked him
for terms, qualifying our clumsiness by our total inexperience
in such matters—no one in our family had died before—the
clergyman, already a gentleman, pulled himself up into a
christian. There would be nothing to pay, he implied. Of
course if, as foreigners, we desired to contribute anything
towards the poor of the town of Innsbruck we could do so—
that was all. He would regard it as a privilege to conduct
the burial service over the departed man, whom he regretted
not to have known when he was alive. Moreover, he would
give orders that during the service all the churches of his
denomination should toll the bell. I could not help, even
before my tears were dry, visualizing my father, who abhorred
any kind of officiousness, shrugging his shoulders and wishing
the clergyman, his parish, his poor, and his bells to hell.

My mother and I, who really were inconceivably poor at

that time, were agreeably surprised at the news that the burial of my father was not going to cost us anything beyond a voluntary contribution to the poor.   But we were mistaken. The clergyman's altruism did not, as we later discovered, include the actual burying of the dead—" Oh, no," he smiled blandly and, sitting down to his desk, produced a blank sheet of paper and wrote us the address of an undertaker which he handed us with the air of a dandy who recommends you to his tailor, deeming you a person worthy of first-class clothes—" You will find him entirely satisfactory."   We thanked him, and stepping into the car of the chauffeur who had volunteered to take my mother about her funeral business, drove in search of the undertaker.   The undertaker, a nice, sensitive but ill-shaven individual, at once assumed that we desired to invest all our liquid wealth in a really gorgeous sarcophagus.   He also unfolded a map of the available cemetery ground at Innsbruck, and suggested our purchasing a sufficiently large plot of land which might later absorb my mother as well as myself.   As he calculated the plot necessary for three individuals, he involuntarily cast a glance at us as if determining our meterage.   My mother and I were very averse to burying father in a land which we would not care to visit again, and I was revolving in my mind whether there might not be some sort of travelling cemetery which would follow us wherever we went, when the undertaker, divining our difficulties, suggested that in the circumstances we might like our relation cremated.   We jumped at the idea, and the undertaker at once selected a special zinc coffin and arranged to send his men for the body, get in touch with the parson, etc., etc.   This reference to " the body—*Die Leiche*— " at first shocked me a little.   It—the body who overnight was he—my father.   From the undertaker's we proceeded to the florist's, took a meal in town and, at dusk, our volunteer-chauffeur called for us as arranged and drove us back to Andras.   It was dark when we reached the *pension* up in the hills.   We walked up to the room.   My mother, as if to prepare me, said : " Now don't be shocked."   I went quickly to the bed on which lay my father, his head thrown back on a pillow; a napkin covered his face, and that suggested two thoughts in succession: that he could not breathe with the napkin over his face, and that he no longer needed to. My mother gently lifted the napkin and said: "You see, he looks quite nice." My father's brow looked austere and composed; his eyes were closed, the mouth slightly open: but not a breath came, and the stillness seemed uncanny. The dead are said to look as if they were asleep. But he looked more than asleep. His brow seemed to have contracted in a last concentration; yet it looked as if the thought behind it, the thought that had been him, had flown away, only leaving the carcass in which he no longer retained a proprietary interest, but had left behind for others to dispose of, almost like a lodger who had cleared out of a room he had long occupied and not bothered to take with him some superfluous, if characteristic, garment. We do not recall the spirit of a man by thinking of his spirit; no strenuous recollection will resurrect the nature of the dead. But we come across a suit, a tie that he has worn, and our heart melts into tears. And, as I stood there and looked at the fine outlines of that brow and nose, the thick wavy hair, it reminded me of the man who had once owned all this and who would never speak again. I suddenly understood that there had never been a shadow of meanness about him, no desire to hurt or even score in an argument; that none of us in this respect could quite come up to him, and that if in a crisis I myself sometimes was prompted to a generous decision it was his nature that was speaking through me. There had been, especially since his stroke, something child-like about him, confiding, perennially hopeful. And how well he had taken his defeat! He died before we could really help him, before the appearance of "The Polyglots," before I was at all on my feet. He just sat there, uncomplaining, day in, day out, in a chair. His one desire of late seemed to have been to "kill time": and there, at last, he had killed the enemy.

Towards nightfall two ruffians arrived with a coffin and proceeded to tear off my father's clothes rather roughly, as if angered by his stiff recalcitrant arms. A dead body was nothing new to them, and they looked like body-snatchers. They had lost their way in the mountains and were in a hurry to get back. But we did not care about that, nor did we see any sense in undressing the dead, and we told them to leave the coffin behind and be gone.

It was a sleepless night for the *pension* proprietors who, frightened of a dead man in the house, huddled the whole lot of them in one room till daylight. By the morning my father looked utterly disinterested in life. At noon a motor hearse wound its way up the mountain. The men came noisily up the plain wooden steps, hauled down the coffin, placed it on the hearse, and quickly drove off down the hill into town. I thought that my father would have approved of this quick business-like arrangement, characteristic of his own procedure. My mother, who, for the last nine years, had had him on her hands, and until this moment had been preoccupied with his removal, now, having followed the men with the coffin downstairs, did not seem to realize, as they drove away so quickly, that he was already off her hands, there, speeding away as he had always wished in life, by himself! Now as she saw him vanish quickly downhill in charge of strange men, for the first time it came to her, the loneliness of her position. Left standing there, wan and hatless, under the freezing porch, she began to sob.

But we consoled ourselves that we should see him once more. After lunch my mother and I went down to Innsbruck to the cemetery mortuary, where my father lay in the open coffin. But when, at dusk, we left him, the thought that he was to spend the dark winter night alone at the mortuary, seemed strange and inhuman, though natural and conventional. Next day a service was held in the mortuary, attended by a few of our friends, and by the elder boy of the *pension* proprietors, who was going to be a priest, and, as his mother said, was " interested " in funerals (even though scared to death of the dead). The Lutheran pastor, with a strange, almost malignantly ironic look at me when he said : " Dust to dust, ashes to ashes," read the funeral service in sonorous German. I stood beside my mother in the " black suit " which had been completed for me in Vienna on the day of my father's death. The eyes of the congregation were fixed on us. But I had by now spent a good deal of tears and emotion, and had little feeling in me at the time other than being sensible that I was, with my mother, occupying the centre of the stage ; the malignant look in the pastor amazed me, the solemn sonorous German (a language my father despised) was beautiful ; my thoughts strayed. What was I thinking about ? All kinds of things. I even gave a thought to my mistress in Vienna.

Some little time after the condoling visitors had dispersed, the doctor arrived to pierce my father's heart. A year or so before, in discussing the awful danger of being buried alive, a few of us, in the presence of my father, had agreed that this precaution should be taken for all of us. He was at that time already on the downhill of life, anxious to secure such little enjoyment as he could in being wheeled down to town, ordering a glass of beer, or backing a winner, and did not particularly appreciate the consideration to be shown to his corpse. But I was very insistent that the undertaking should be rigorously carried out, and I hope my relatives will do as much for me. The doctor, not looking to right or left, stretched on a pair of red rubber gloves, uncovered my father's chest and, unsheathing a stiletto, pierced my father's heart, who, was it yesterday, had sat on the balcony in the sun. And when the narrow blade went in, there was a dry, rustling sound as if my father's body was a trunk of frozen meat. And not a drop of blood came. I was not horrified ; I only felt this was strange, unimportant : that the importance, the reality of things, therefore, was not here but elsewhere. The doctor took off his red rubber gloves, replaced his stiletto in the case, and was gone as stealthily as he had arrived.

Outside stood the hearse. The sympathetic undertaker busied himself, in a friendly, leisurely way. He looked considerate and rather well disposed and cheerful with his " Now it's all over " look, as if pleased with my father for having behaved well in trying circumstances. Dusk had fallen. The snow was yellow from the lamp of the mortuary. Coffins with bodies reposing in them would remain here through the black winter night, while the motor hearse with my father would set out on the solitary long road to Munich.

My mother and I, arm in arm, trudged back through the snow to the station. Suddenly we felt relieved.

We took the little mountain railway back to Andras. It wound and wound, girdling the snow-covered hills in a spiral. It was now quite dark. We got out at the little station, and shuffled through the dark forest on our way back to the *pension*. The pines laden with snow and swaying in the wind seemed to be telling each other something. For a moment we looked at them and wondered.

VII

THE URN

Next day, because we are really so fond of each other as to express a constant and irritating solicitude as to the other's welfare, my mother and I were already quarrelling and throwing father at each other's heads. " Fancy," she said with scorn in her blue eyes, " in this very room where, not three days ago your poor father . . ." " Fancy, in this very room where, not three days ago your poor husband . . ." My mother opined that my father would have hated to hear me speak thus, and I agreed that he was fortunate and, if conscious, glad to be out of it. Our common interest in him reunited us. " God grant him rest," said my mother, and sighed. " Rest ! " she repeated doubtfully. " Does he want it ? Why, he was restless from so much rest. The poor fellow wanted a little excitement." I said that I felt sure, however, that he did not require excitement of the kind

provided by our quarrel. "No," she laughed, "but oh——"
She sighed, in pity for him.

After three days, we went down to town to fetch the urn,
and surprised the pastor exacting his pound of flesh in the
guise of church charities from the undertaker, who was
preparing a long bill. Between them they set aside a sum
for charities which caused both my mother and me, incredibly
poor as we were at that time, to raise our brows. At dusk
the mountain train took us back to Andras. There was a
full moon as we crossed the forest. The trees laden with
snow leered evilly, conspiring. I carried the urn, not three
pounds in weight, along the path up which only eight months
before I wheeled my father to the *pension* which was to prove
his last abode.

My mother decided, as soon as my father's urn returned
from Munich, to leave Innsbruck with it for the South of
France, while I was to return to Vienna to finish reading
proofs of "The Polyglots." Meanwhile I refreshed myself
by squeezing the pretty maid in the *pension* in which I
succeeded by trading on her sympathy for me. At night
I thought of the Hungarian mistress I was going to meet
again in Vienna, and how I wished it was all over.

Count Pravana, the Consul-General for Italy, advised us
that travelling through Italy with the urn, as my mother
intended to do, was an ambitious project; and after some
inquiries I was put in touch with a transport agent who
offered to assist us. This man, an Italian, explained to me
in fluent German, shouting at the top of his voice (though
I showed no indication of being deaf to his words), the
well-nigh insurmountable difficulty of conveying the urn
in a legal way into and across Italian territory. The only
practical thing, he said, and in the end the least expensive,
was to smuggle it through some person he was willing to
find for me, at a fee. Hardly the thing, I thought to myself,
for a descendant of a *nobil uomo* of Italy to have his ashes
smuggled into the country of his distant origin by a member
of the underworld who deals in dope. Hardly compatible.

But the agent again began to shout very loudly, intimating that there would be no trouble at all : the urn would be collected by an unseen individual and delivered as mysteriously at the other end. I need entertain not the slightest anxiety. There would be nothing for me to worry about—only, I gathered, a small fortune to pay and the urn handed to me in return all ready for burial.

Good. But how, assuming that I was willing to have the urn smuggled across Italy into France, was I to account for its arrival in that country when the formalities of burial would have to be complied with ?

That was, he said, with much expenditure of gesture, another side of the problem, to be attacked in its own good time. No good meeting trouble half way. If, on the other hand, I resolved to do it all legally, there were a number of formalities I must comply with. The agent again began to shout very explicitly what I must do before my mother could embark on so hazardous an undertaking as to travel across Italy with the ashes of her husband. A declaration must be obtained from the Italian Ministry of Finance that they had satisfied themselves by cutting open the urn that it contained no gold, platinum or jewellery. Next I required a permit from the Prefecture of Police, whom I must satisfy that the urn contained no revolutionary literature ; a visâ from the Ministry of Foreign Affairs applied for respectively through the British Embassies in Vienna and Rome ; a certificate from the local Medical Association, the Chief of the Italian Railways, the station master of Bolzano, the Ministry of the Interior at Rome, and the sanitary inspector at Ventimiglia.

I began to laugh violently. I could not stop laughing. I must have laughed very infectiously, for the transport agent, who at first could not think what was the matter with me, at last caught my laughter and also began to laugh loudly and violently as if his sides were splitting. When he finished, still hiccoughing, he said, after drinking some water, looking again serious : " Yes, this is what you've got to do."

I went back to my mother, who is a reasonable woman, and told her everything; and we decided in the circumstances that I should take my father's ashes to Vienna, whither I was returning for a few months, and later bring them to Paris, thus avoiding Italy altogether, a country apparently not propitious for the transit of mortal remains. My mother was to travel through Italy to the South of France alone, where, if I made any money with " The Polyglots," we might build a house and have my father's ashes buried on our own plot of land. The idea appealed to my mother, and as she parted temporarily with the urn she was consoled by the thought that we were not parting from him but that he was still with us, travelling, as he had always wished, first to Vienna with me, then to Paris and the South of France. Before we left we thanked the people who had been kind to us; and we gave the chauffeur who had taken us about for nothing in his employer's car my father's dried-up cigarettes as well as my father's artificial leg to pass on to any German war invalid he could find, always provided the leg could be made to fit him.

As I stood on the station platform at Innsbruck, with my father's urn in my haversack across the shoulder, an acquaintance of mine called Miss Hobhouse came up to me and inquired what I had in my haversack. I told her. Suddenly she began to laugh. I inquired, painfully, what was amusing her, and she told me an aunt of hers had been cremated and her ashes, in compliance with her will, were strewn over the garden lawn. Her hip bones, however, had remained proof against the fire of the crematorium and found themselves flung on to the lawn, where a dog came and ate them.

I thanked her for her appropriate wit and boarded the train for Vienna.

From now on my father, reduced to a few ashes in a zinc receptacle, began to travel furiously all over Europe. He had, poor man, wished to do so when still alive and confined to his chair. Now he covered mile after mile with a vengeance.

When I returned to the *pension*, each guest shook me

solemnly by the hand and said the one word : " Beileid "
(sympathy).   Once, in a tram, a young student with relations
in Innsbruck, sitting beside me and talking quietly of the
charm of the Austrian Alps, heard from me that I had just
lost my father.   Without further warning, he sprang to his
feet, clicked his heels and, like a pistol fired into my ear,
came the word : " Beileid ! "   Then he sat down again
quietly by my side.

The door porter's wife in Vienna was shocked at the
idea of cremation.   At the last trump, the cremated dead
would be hard put to it, she implied, to collect and assemble
their parts and answer the call of their judge.   I pictured
the trump, followed by hasty putting together of disintegrated
parts.   A man who had lain long in his coffin, with the
flustered air of someone dressing for dinner, whom the
gong reminds he is late and who is unable to find his black
tie : " Where's that left hip of mine !   Oh, God, the worms,
the worms ! "

When I came back to Vienna, my Hungarian mistress made
an appointment, but we missed each other.   " I waited for
you, I distinctly said——"   We did not meet again.

I placed the urn on the top shelf of my bedroom cupboard,
and resumed my normal life.   My mother and brother,
however, mistakenly concluding that I could not part from
the urn, hugged it day and night, and led a life of morbid
grief, wrote advising me to take it to the local crematorium
till I left Vienna.   What was the good, they wrote, killing
yourself like that ?   I felt that the urn was as good in one
cupboard as another, nevertheless complied with their wishes.
One bleak winter afternoon I wrapped up the urn in brown
paper, tied it with a string, and carried it to a tram, which
conveyed me to the crematorium at the Zentralfriedhof.
When I carried it, I could hear the waistcoat buckle rattle
in the urn.

I could never understand why a humorous aspect of a
thing should be deemed to diminish its tragedy, just as I felt
no reality whatever, for example, in the jovial recommendation

to put all your troubles in your old kit-bag—and smile, smile, smile. A forced smile, I felt, would only add weight to the kit-bag. The humour of a situation did not to me alleviate one whit of its pain, for a sigh came after it. A glimpse of humour, indeed, was like inhaling oxygen only to have to release it in a sigh of carbon hydrogen. My growing grief at the loss of my father, so strong that it seemed to me natural that it should have dislocated my work, and that I should wince at the scant sympathy I got from correspondents, bored by my mention of it, was something unrelated to the disposal of his ashes, before which the superstition of a savage would, on the contrary, have prostrated itself in solemn and complicated funeral rites. A photograph, though imperfect, for it interfered with my mind's various memories of him, was so much nearer. If I had asked my father what I was to do with the urn, he would have said, " Throw it away."

The crematorium of Vienna lies in a distant suburb ; the tram which conveyed me thither rattled on for the best part of an hour. It moved along a street as straight as an arrow, and as my journey progressed the shops on either side were more and more undertakers, stonemasons who exhibited marble crosses and angels of peace, and florists exhibiting wreaths. And more and more this long street which led to the cemetery received funeral processions ; they converged from various side streets and by-ways, only in the end to travel down the same sordid straight road. At the crematorium I watched a burial service. Not a word was uttered, no priest was present ; only the organ pealed out its sorrow. A few relatives occupied the front rows of seats in the amphitheatre, and in front of them on a platform was a coffin. The music had sent me into a trance, and my eyes wandered away from the coffin ; and it was the sudden crescendo of sobbing which brought my look back to the coffin steadily sinking on the platform ; and when it came up again, closing the cavity, with an air of finality, it was empty. The music grew fainter, the people moved out.

I rented a niche for my father's urn, which I would visit from time to time to renew the flowers; and each time the attendant took out the urn from the niche and patted it with a bland smile in his eyes, in which I could read solicitude for a tip.

But only later, perhaps three months after he had been burnt to ashes, one bleak Sunday when I was alone in the Vienna *pension*, did the full force of our loss strike me. He had been so quiet, passive. Yesterday he was there, now he was not.

VIII

PYSTIAN

I was convinced that I would be subject, at some future date, to rheumatism. But the doctor, who said there was nothing the matter with me, nevertheless, to satisfy my own wishes, prescribed me a lengthy cure. Every morning I was packed from my toes to my ears in hot mud, and later I splashed about in an enormous sulphurous bath. One of the bathers was a tall bearded Hungarian who, discovering I was a writer, began to cultivate my acquaintance. He sought my company more and more, and one day he organized an elaborate picnic to the top of a hill, providing horses, Hungarian dishes, wine. At dusk, as we sat on the hill, strains of music, growing louder, attracted our attention; and we saw a gipsy band, hired by the Hungarian patriot, marching up to provide us with music. National toasts were drunk freely, and there was much said about the Hungarian cause. I was invited next day by my host to throw myself with zest into the cause of Hungary, and write articles in its support in the British press. I explained to him that I was a novelist, not a journalist; that nationalities, as such, stirred in me distaste rather than inspiration. A few days later I learnt that the Hungarian patriot was grievously disappointed in me, and had said that he would never have invited me had he known I did not write for the newspapers.

His lavish picnic (a contribution to which at the time from myself and the other male guests he rejected with scorn) had exhausted his resources, and he could not continue his cure at the baths.

Pystian, Pystiani, Pistchani, or Pestigen (to give the same place its various names) is a remote village in Czechoslovakia with a couple of grand hotels, and the sulphurous baths to attract visitors. There is a broad swift river along which you wander dreamily into the wilds as far as you care to go. And when you wandered far out the river divided itself, the country lay flat, and there came upon you hundreds of geese. And one day as I went out to meet the geese there was a lovely young girl who came out after them, and I discovered that she lived in a white cottage tucked away beyond the river. I came again and again, and every time I saw the geese advancing like a white blanket waving on the horizon I hoped that the girl was there too. And one day I helped her with some obstreperous geese, and we became friends. She was a Hungarian girl who understood German, and from the films she had seen at the village cinema she had built up a romantic picture of the outer world. She longed to see Vienna, and thought it would be wonderful to run away from home and the geese and travel with me to Vienna and Budapest and live the kind of life people led on the pictures. But I, when I was in Vienna and London, often thought of that lovely girl with bare feet and her loose hair in the wind, coming out for the geese and living in that white cottage where the river branches out widely; and it was she and her life which seemed to me romantic.

And there was a young woman, a strange blonde who walked with a borzoi on a leash, with whom, when we spoke, it seemed we could not converse in any mutually known language. Her own was Czech; and after a time I found that by mutilating my Russian, and she her Czech, words formed, the sense of which was that she was the wife of the reception clerk at my hotel and not averse to a love affair with a man other than her husband so long as her husband

and the hotel management were not permitted to share her secret.

And there was a most attractive young German woman whose German officer husband had such a high regard for the English and his own country that he thought in future all wars should be confined to England and Germany, who knew how to fight each other like gentlemen, and that the French should be kept utterly out of it. His wife had such a high regard for writers, whom she considered the salt of the earth, that she told me there was nothing I could do wrong, since however boorishly I chose to behave to any German woman, whatever I did would be interpreted in terms of originality.

In the same luxurious hotel, where on the walls of the ballroom hung notices " Guests are respectfully requested not to spit on the floor," I met a crippled old woman who informed me, with a strange, astonished expression, as if herself unable to account for the fact, that she was simply swimming in money, having once written a novel entitled " The Diary of a Lost Soul "—that is to say, of a prostitute—followed by several other books, entitled the " journal," the " life," the " drama," the " love," etc., always of the same " lost soul," which had run into countless editions on the Continent, but, characteristically, had not taken on in England. There was an old German General, too. He was just like an English General except that he clicked his heels. If there is an English General who clicks his heels, I would like to meet him.

IX

THE URN AGAIN

A month or so after the publication of " The Polyglots," I received a letter reading : " Dear Sir,—If it would be convenient for you to call on me here I should like to see you." The signature, when I deciphered it, read : " Beaverbrook." In my reply, in which I said I would be returning to London in October, I endeavoured to combine pleasure at hearing from a man whom, having never met, I regarded less as a personality than a power, with legitimate curiosity as to the object of the invitation. Returned to Vienna, I prepared to vacate Austria, where, but for Lord Beaverbrook's letter, I might have remained several more years. The British Consul, an old acquaintance named Wilton, supplied me with a certificate for my father's urn. With this document I repaired to the French Legation, which, uncertain about regulations relating to urns in France, would not commit itself to more than stamping "*vu*" across the document. I also obtained permits from the Vienna police and the Swiss Consulate, and started off on my journey to Paris, where I hoped to hand over the urn to my French brother-in-law who, when he returned to the South of France, would convey the urn to my mother. I had the urn in my haversack, which I placed on the rack. The Austrian frontier officials failed to make an appearance at all. The Swiss, it being night, looked in and went out. When we reached the French frontier, a very officious functionary, accompanied by a gendarme with a sword, strutted into the compartment and asked me if I had anything to declare. Nothing, I assured him, nothing at all. "*Bon.*" He looked round. "And what's that thing on the rack, if you please?"

"Une urne," I said.

"*Quoi?*"

"Une urne," I repeated, and hastened to produce my passport and all the documents I possessed relating to the urn and how and why I came to be in possession of it.

The man handled the urn, which looked like an anarchist's bomb, suspiciously, but presently thanked me, assuring me that everything was in order. In a minute the gendarme returned; requested to have another look at the urn; satisfied himself that it was *plombée*. "*Parfaitement, monsieur*," he said, highly satisfied with me, and retired.

I was profoundly relieved. When in the evening we were approaching Paris I began to wonder what I was to do with the urn if I failed to find my brother-in-law, since, having an appointment with Lord Beaverbrook for the following day, I could not stay on in Paris. After a few unsuccessful attempts to get through to my brother-in-law's hotel I discovered that he had not yet arrived. Unwilling to take the risk of handing my haversack with the urn to a hotel porter, who might forget to deliver it, or even refuse to accept it when told of its contents, I judged it the safest and simplest course to leave it in the station cloakroom and send on the receipt to my mother for delivery to my brother-in-law who, on his arrival in Paris, could call for the urn. This I did, and hurried to the Gare du Nord to catch the boat train to Calais.

I was having a wonderful time with Lord Beaverbrook in London. Since I published " Futility," " Anton Tchehov," and " The Polyglots," I had not spent a single day in London except on my way to the Tyrol, and now I was having my full share of hospitality from editors, publishers, and hostesses. It was in the midst of all this excitement that my mother's letter arrived, expressing horror at my having left the urn at the cloakroom in Paris. My brother-in-law, to whom she had sent the cloakroom ticket, resolutely refused, she wrote, to handle the urn, and she begged me to return to Paris at once and take the urn out of the cloakroom. My sister Daisy was incensed at my putting her husband to a task so distasteful to him as a Roman Catholic. And I was urged by all my relations to go back to Paris at once. But I was at that time suffering from a cold in a tooth. I had important appointments fixed ahead with American editors. Lord Beaverbrook was entertaining me and introducing me to the great and the beautiful. I knew that if I had asked my father what I should do with his urn he would have told me to chuck it away, and I sent back a telegram to say I was ill, I was dying, I could not return to Paris, and would they please force my brother-in-law to be a man and go to the Gare de l'Est and claim the urn with the cloakroom ticket. My sister's attitude to her husband who, she deemed, should in no circumstances be exposed to a slight inconvenience if any blood relation of hers could be exposed to a great one, determined my refusal to return to Paris, which I had just left for London. Few things irritate one more than the spectacle of a devoted wife, when one happens not to be the husband. My sister, when you don't agree with her husband's views, does not understand that you disagree with him, but merely puts it down to your intellectual incapacity to comprehend him, and explains to you in quiet, patient tones what you have heard already, and with which you don't agree. My brother-in-law and my sister lead a life of exquisite harmony. He, like a perfect human being who is above all else interested in the things of the mind, drifts about all day and expatiates on tendencies in philosophy, sociology, politics and life. Till my sister one day says : " Jean ! We have no more money ! " " Ah ! " he exclaims, and puts on his best suit, while my sister hurriedly wraps up a Buddha (which god he imports in stone from Siam) and takes it to Paris by the next train, and returns in a few days with money to carry on with for a bit. During this short absence they write endearing letters to each other every day, about the child, and telephone and telegraph. Then he returns and they live in pecuniary ease for a while.

My mother had written to me that my father's death had affected my brother-in-law very painfully. He came to meet her at the station wearing black clothes, black gloves, and, for want of black boots, a pair of brown shoes dyed that colour. A sensibility, she urged, which contrasted favourably with my own. My letter enclosing the cloakroom ticket had upset them. They had all spent a perfect Sunday together, the first peaceful day for a long time. The weather was beautiful, the baby unusually well-behaved. All was perfect. After this long, sunny day of perfect harmony by the hearth, my brother-in-law, very happy and wearing his new light-coloured spring suit, had dutifully accompanied my mother to the terminus, where she was to take the tram back to her hotel, when suddenly a big dog rushed out at him through a

garden fence, tore his suit, and bit him in the calf, so that he
had to go to hospital twice a day for a month to be examined
for hydrophobia. This marked the end of a perfect day.
My letter next morning with the cloakroom ticket seemed
to them the last straw in a life dogged by ill-fate.

While I tarried in London, letters began to reach me
from my brother-in-law in Paris, sounding an increasingly
earnest note. He assured me that the matter was of the
utmost gravity, that no urn could legally have reached Paris
without being conveyed all the way from the frontier in a
full-sized coffin. " I don't know what will become of
your affair," he concluded ominously. And again : " The
longer you tarry the more sinister the outlook." He
solicited immediate replies. And every time he omitted to
give his address, which might have enabled me to reply
to him.

I was meeting and communing with Wells, Shaw, Bertrand
Russell, Bennett, D. H. Lawrence, Middleton Murry—all the
men who have kept the spirit alive, had been handed and were
handing on the torch. Was there any sense in busying myself
about an urn containing ashes ? " Let the dead bury the
dead," I repeated to myself, " but you, go and proclaim the
kingdom of heaven ! "

" Your opinion," I wrote to them, " differs from my
opinion." But there came an ultimatum from Marseilles :
If I refused to go, then my mother would have to, and at
once, as the matter had now reached a crisis. I replied
that if anyone chose to interpret the situation as critical, he
was the right person to deal with it. My sister, perturbed
at the idea of putting her husband to any trouble at all, and
incensed against me, but unwilling to proceed herself,
persuaded my mother to carry out her threat ; and my mother
got into the train at Marseilles and arrived next morning in
Paris. She was met by my brother-in-law, still wearing his
black gloves and black boots, who impressed on her the
seriousness of the predicament in which I had involved them.
My mother, fully expecting to be arrested, repaired to the

station and handed in the fateful receipt; whereupon the haversack with the urn was forthwith handed out to her.

My mother then turned to my brother-in-law and said, wistfully: "Well, Jean, couldn't you really have done this yourself?" After which a long *passade* took place between the French Jean and his English mother-in-law, the burden of which was that Jean begged his mother-in-law to realize that the laws of France were not the same as those of England, whereas my mother tried to make him see that in the matter of claiming a piece of baggage deposited in a cloakroom against a receipt obtained therefor they were identical. And I was re-established in my mother's esteem.

My mother proceeded with the urn to the British Embassy Church, where the chaplain very kindly agreed to place it in the mortuary. As "The Polyglots," contrary to expectation, did not sell any too well, and the house and land in the South of France did not materialize, and we continued to be homeless for several years, the chaplain of the Embassy Church, after a number of years, perhaps feeling that we were presuming unduly on his good nature, began to hint that he was not averse to having the ashes removed at some future time convenient to ourselves. And on one of her journeys from Paris to England my mother brought the urn with her; and it was at last buried alongside of Grandfather Wadsworth and Grandmother Sarah at the cemetery of Bacup, near Bolton, in the county of Lancashire.

X

DEATH AND TRANSFIGURATION

"He was dead. But for ever? Who can say? It is certain that neither spiritualist experiments, nor religious dogmas, bring us proof of the survival of the soul. What one can say is that everything happens in our life as though we had entered upon it with a burden of obligations contracted in an anterior existence; there is nothing in the conditions of life on this earth to make us think ourselves obliged to be good, to be sensitive, even polite ; nor for the artist to feel himself compelled to begin a passage twenty times over again when the praise it evokes will matter little to the body devoured by worms. . . . All these obligations, which have no sanction in our present life, seem to belong to a different world, a world founded on goodness, on scruple, on sacrifice, a world entirely different from ours, and whence we come to be born on this earth, perhaps to return there and live under the rule of the unknown laws which we have obeyed here because we carried their principles within ourselves, without knowing who decreed that they should be ; those laws to which every deep intellectual labour draws us nearer, and which are invisible only—and not even !— to fools.

"So that (Proust continues) the idea that Bergotte was not for ever dead was not without verisimilitude."

The beautiful passage I have translated seems to me as far as it is safe to go. It is at least as far as I am myself inclined to take belief on faith. If I were asked what confidence I have in my survival, I would reply that I was fully confident. "Fully confident," that is, as a father would say to his son concerning whom he entertains doubts, but wants to put on his mettle : " I firmly believe that you will acquit yourself with honour and fulfil in a high degree the lofty aspirations your old father cherishes on your account." My confidence in immortality is of about that fullness ; my belief in it of about that firmness. I would not care to stake £5 on it, if it came to the point.

When a man gives up his abode at No. 10, Downing Street, we assume that he has ceased to be Prime Minister, though he may still be Mr. Stanley Baldwin. But when his residence is permanently transferred beneath ground, we assume that he has ceased to be Mr. Baldwin, or Mr. Jones, who was Mr. Jones by virtue of his constant anxiety to be helpful to the said Mr. Jones, to go out of his way to serve Mr. Jones, and of whom all that is left is a soul-liberating feeling which cares not two hoots for the late Mr. Jones. You may argue that this same impersonal feeling has always been the integral, immortal, *real* Mr. Jones, who, having shed his bodily shackles, is at last able to be his unrestricted self, Mr. Jones *in excelsis*. You may say this, or you may say the reverse : that the immortal spirit which breathed life into his corrupted loins has now lost the little contact it ever had with Mr. Jones, has shed his soul and memories like dirty linen and will not hear of being reminded of its former associations. Or, again, you may say that it is Mr. Jones's soul which was and still is the real Mr. Jones, suffused with memories mellowed at this distance of time into poetry, rightly defined as " emotion remembered in tranquillity "—be the memory of a basement flat in Edgware Road and the emotion an irritable colloquy with his landlady. Even if Mr. Jones's longing for a cloud, a tree, is so completely fulfilled that he is merged with the object he longs for so as to be himself a tree, a cloud, never-theless, to realize the happiness of fulfilment, he must be able to see, all while merging with it, the outlines of the object he longs to lose himself in, and thus remain eternally the unique Mr. Jones. You may say all these things and they are all, perhaps simultaneously, true and not in the least contradictory or mutually exclusive ; there is no need for you to stand in the doorway of expression and chuck out a seemingly discordant thought because you have just let in its cousin. A stupid conversationalist would proceed to argue your head off by endeavouring to prove, as in this argument, that *either* personality survives *or* it does not survive ; whereas the real decision, as any seasoned conversationalist will see, depends upon how far up or down the scale that lies between the personal and impersonal you choose to shift the definition of " personal " immortality.

The immortality I desire I cannot imagine ; for the immortality I can imagine I am wise enough not to desire. My hope is that, if there cannot, must not, be a heaven according to my present liking, there will be one according to a view of things to which I shall be won over. A way of looking at things so different from mine that it may well be defined as God's.   And to be able to agree with God is, in effect, to have become God, to have entered on the unimaginable day.   Such immortality (which is all but synonymous with extinction) I hold is not without probability. For I cannot say that I share that feeling, so often claimed by people, of being taken care of by some ineffable Being : I have rather the feeling that He is taking care of Himself. But—this I will concede—His taking care of Himself is identified with that other dormant but larger being in me who does not care what becomes of me.

> " *In the world ye shall have tribulation :*
> *but be of good cheer :*
> *I have overcome the world.*"

In the concluding paragraph of " Pending Heaven " I attempt to express symbolically the paradox of transfiguration :

" He felt he was out, out of the narrow house, and could go where he liked, be what he liked.   A blue, sunny sky stretched above him, trees fluttered in the breeze, and he went, stick in hand, over dell and hill without looking back. And the farther he went the more clearly he understood that all these things—himself—were but symbols and metaphors of a miracle by whose dim candle he had read in the book of life a sorry page, confused and deceptive : and a nameless usher had closed the book and carried it away.   ' Yes,' he thought, ' I don't want it.   I don't want anything.' "

> " *Now I am no more in the world,*
> *but these are in the world,*
> *and I come to Thee.*"

The reality of things is not contained but reflected in a being.   If so, are " we " the perishable mirror, or the reflection of an imperishable light ?   I think that if we are intent on the idea of survival we had far better identify ourselves with the least personal interpretation of immortality.   For the odds are against the survival of anything in us, individual, peculiar, what kindly critics are apt to call the " inimitable " in us. Our " personality," moreover, was even in life only properly discernible by others.   The owner was only conscious of a certain always changing combination of feelings as registered by his senses, themselves in process of change.   For we are not, have never been, " individuals."   Rather we are little limited companies, each of the many shareholders who has invested in us all the while stealthily replacing his shares, slinking away to do things on his own.   What is death ? A liquidation of a limited company kept together for a time by the limited liability of its members, ostensibly on behalf of one another, actually for the sake of amenities in their nature essentially separate and not interchangeable. When the directors and shareholders have dispersed, what of the company ?

It is not our habits, noticeable chiefly to others, but some undifferentiated spark of life in us which we ourselves are most conscious of.   And it seems that it is just this un-differentiated something which survives, because, like a ray of the sun, it does not depend on the mirror, which merely reflects or reflected it, but on itself alone.   It is that impersonal, universal light we reflect which, in life, makes us understand one another, suspect that we are essentially one and the same.   This consciousness of the one in the many is the mysterious spring, the most profound and moving element in literature and in art.   It is for this reason that mysticism in art is best suggested by the uncommented presentation of the realistic—that is, the strange.   I described how when the doctor, putting on red rubber gloves, pierced my father's heart, who yesterday had sat on the balcony in the sun, I was not horrified, but only felt that this was strange, unimportant : that the importance, the reality of things, evidently, was not here but elsewhere.   " What shall I do with the body of this death ? "   Death had a body ; bodies were pledged to it. But if somehow we refused to take in the grievous com-pleteness of death's victory, it was because we felt that the victory was only apparent, that it was not the full story. For it is strange that we, who attach such importance to our temporary welfare, haggle over leases, worry over old-age pensions, should care so little about our fate, removed only by some ten, twenty, thirty years. Our resignation is strange. What really inclines us towards a belief in after-life is that the manner of our end, the whole fortuitous character of our destinies here, does not seem serious enough. "Voyons, messieurs, soyons sérieux!" is how we feel when the doctors intimate to us that our haphazard life has come to a medically logical conclusion. It is now for God to deny the aspersion cast on Him that in humbugging us He is Himself hardly more than a humbug. If all the world be unreal, by what high standard of reality is it so? If we are to be dead for all time, by what living truth is it to be?

Tchehov has a story in which he describes, with many humorous details, how a consignment of oxen are entrained by a cattle-dealer for a distant town, how the tired oxen walk dreamily in the twilight from the railway station to the market and slaughter-house, along streets they had never previously seen, and will never see again. It seems strange, unwarranted. And this uncommented presentation of what is strange, unwarranted, by itself inconclusive, is cavernous with promises belonging to a different world from this, where we are held to ransom, a world which has the power somehow to equate the balance, for if there exists a half world there must also exist a world which is whole.

·PART IV

THE VISIBLE WORLD EXISTS?

"I have always been one for whom the visible world exists."

—Gautier.

". . . worldly pleasures which cause the kind of ailment provoked by the ingestion of abject nourishment ; or friendship, which is a simulation, because for whatever moral reason he may do it, the artist who gives up an hour of work for an hour of talk with a friend knows that he is sacrificing a reality for something which does not exist (friends being friends but in that sweet folly we have at the outset of life to which we lend ourselves but, in the depths of our minds, know to be the error of a madman who believed the furniture was alive and conversing with him.)"

—Proust.

"I want nothing of the world except that it may leave me rest for works that some day shall belong to it ; therefore let it also judge me charitably."

—Wagner.

CHAPTER ELEVEN

LONDON

I

LORD BEAVERBROOK TURNS HIS SEARCHLIGHTS ON ME

WHEN a powerful newspaper proprietor, whom you had imagined to be an arch lowbrow who would dislike you, and whose name you accordingly pooh-poohed whenever it cropped up, writes of his own accord inviting you to come and see him and then says : " Look here, you're enormously brilliant and haven't had the success which you deserve. We must do something about it," you melt, you shed tears of self-reproach, and you begin to love him.

I was immediately fascinated by the man. Lord Beaverbrook, like Mr. Lloyd George, has the air of being enormously privileged in meeting someone whom no one else has ever met, or even heard of. He made me feel as if I had indeed heard of myself. He looked a sort of new specimen from Mars, inhuman, at the same time afflicted with glands of prodigious lacrimosity, so that if you inquired about his health he hovered on the brink of tears.

Posterity would not excuse me if, living in the age of Lloyd George, Beaverbrook, Wells, Lawrence, Kingsmill, Bernard Shaw, I did not transcribe my impressions of them. Lord Beaverbrook, then, struck me as a potential great man without a mission. Already a little megalomaniacal, but possessed of something very like genius. I liked his forceful, youthful personality, that of a man who had come up by his own acumen and was bossing all these glittering old fogies about, and sided with the young and the new.

Now when I meet a captain of industry, particularly a king of the Press, my first impulse is to say to him: "It's untrue! I mean all the hard things that the ignorant say about you—lies, calumnies. Untrue! Untrue! And anything that you may do to help me refute the wicked legend associated with you—publicity on behalf of my works, a contract for articles over a number of years at a reasonable figure—all will go towards proving that the hard things they say of you are untrue."

I realized that Lord Beaverbrook was prepared to do a great deal for me had I elected a career in Fleet Street, but nothing was further removed from my mind. As well might Mozart have been offered to write popular scores. It will be recalled that when Mozart's father advised him to write music for the popular ear, Mozart replied that he wrote music for any sort of ear except long ones. But because Lord Beaverbrook's achievements were of an order foreign to me, his attention flattered me. The man at once attracted me irresistibly. He was irresistible. His force and charm were irresistible. Realize the situation. Here was I—and there was he. I don't know if I make myself clear. What I mean is that here was I, on the one hand, and there was he, on the other. I cannot put it more succinctly. I said to him: "I am an artist. Probably a great artist. It pleases me when you treat me as an artist. If you treat me as a journalist it pleases me less."

He treated me as an artist. He treated me well, grandly, tenderly, with affection. I arrived, wearing my ill-fitting Vienna black suit, which caused H. V. Morton, who, at the suggestion of Lord Beaverbrook, was writing an article about me, to say, "Mr. Gerhardi is a poor judge of clothes." I mentioned, as a point of interest, the low exchange prevailing in Austria, as a result of which my father, my mother and I had been able to live at the Innsbruck *pension* at the rate of 7s. 6d. a day. H. V. Morton's article about me contained a headline: "Novelist lives on 2s. 6d. a day." D. H. Lawrence told me his father, a miner in Nottingham, had

sent him an article cut out of the *Daily Express*, about a
novelist called Gerhardi who lived on 2s. 6d. a day, compared
with whom his son David Lawrence was not doing at all
badly. And Evelyn FitzGerald, Beaverbrook's brother-in-
law, every time he saw me, thought it his duty to tell me how
as a boy he ran off to Russia and lived on a small sum. An
American editor in London, who saw the reference alleging
that I had lived on 2s. 6d. a day, invited me to write an article
to the effect that I considered doing so a salutary way of
living. " You believe in it, don't you ? " he prompted.

" Yes," I said.

" It is a principle with you, isn't it ? " he asked.

" Yes, a sort of religion."

Lord Beaverbrook endeavoured to get up a sale of " The
Polyglots," which, though only out a few months, was
bringing in something equivalent, in terms of royalties, to
nothing. I was tremendously buoyed up. The same
evening I dined with my publisher, Mr. R. Cobden-Sanderson,
whom I assured that we were as good as made. Lord Beaverbrook's efforts, however, were but scantily rewarded, and
my faith in the sovereign powers of newspaper proprietors
was proportionately reduced. They were not, I learnt,
almighty. Lord Rothermere, whom I asked whether he
thought a newspaper could turn a novel into a best-seller,
replied, with characteristic moderation, " Yes, when a book's
sales are already on the increase ; no, when a book has not
yet got to its feet." Newspaper proprietors, I soon saw,
were less powerful than generally imagined. A newspaper
proprietor may begin a crusade. But a crusade, to succeed,
must be continued over a longer period than a paper is able
to harp on one subject without boring its readers.

My publisher, moreover, was a Baldwin type of Englishman, and Lord Beaverbrook's enthusiasm for this type is
intermittent. Finally, Lord Beaverbrook offered to buy
" The Polyglots " from Mr. Cobden-Sanderson, and to give
it to one of the mass-production publishers—" factories "
as they call them. Armed with powers of negotiation, I

arrived at Mr. Sanderson's office, only to find him out. Conscious of the momentous consequences of my negotiations, I waited for him two hours. When he arrived and saw me he waved a hasty greeting and shouted as he passed from one room into the next, " Can't stop, haven't a minute ! Good-bye ! " I ran after him and blurted out the nature of my mission. Mr. Sanderson repulsed the proposal with indignation. I gradually increased my offer, rising to the sum of £75—after which it was clear to me that money could not tempt him.

Unfortunately Lord Beaverbrook did not put the same thought and energy into increasing the sale of my " Polyglots," as, for example, into the Empire Crusade. My Baldwinine publisher had damped his initial enthusiasm. The book sold about a hundred more copies by virtue of his publicity. I thanked him prodigiously, hoping that this would release generous tears from his all-too-human glands, and increase his publicity efforts. But he merely said, modestly : " I tried to get up a sale for your book. But I have failed."

II

FLATTERY IS NOT ENOUGH

My knowledge of newspaper proprietors till then had been confined to a reading of Tchehov's relations with Suvorin, the Russian Beaverbrook. When I mentioned this to Beaverbrook one night at the Kit Kat Club, all he said was : " Was Tchehov grateful ? " I was surprised by this and tried to draw him out, but he only varied his question, in wondering did Suvorin not have reason to regret his kindness to Tchehov. My private idea was that Lord Beaverbrook was benefiting in the eyes of posterity, as indeed Suvorin had done. But he said, rather wistfully : " You know, many young men would have given anything for the chance you've had." I told Lord Beaverbrook, as a point of interest, that Lord Balfour did for young Wells very much what he was doing for me; and Lord Beaverbrook said: "Was Wells grateful?" "Definitely not!" I replied. I did not tell Beaverbrook Napoleon's remark that men were rather more grateful by nature than ungrateful, and that if one complained about them it was because one was apt to count on thanks disproportionate to the service rendered. When, on the contrary, I deplored that gratitude should be the most evanescent of emotions, he said: "Not at all. I've done nothing. You would have got there all the same, with or without me."

He discussed willingly his work in the world and somehow invited you to share the glamour of it. In this lay the secret of his great charm. I would go to see him almost daily, and then he would take me to dine at his house, or his office at the top of the *Daily Express*, or some night club. He would say: "I will provide the champagne, and you the conversation." I would reply: "You will provide both." One day I found him sitting on the floor, examining *Sunday Express* advertising posters. I said: "I've thought of a good sub-title for the *Daily Express*." "What is it?" he asked. I told him. Instantly he jumped up and going over to his table, made a note, without a word. Next day he showed me a copy of the *Daily Express* with the sub-title: "The Organ of Imperial Democratic Opinion."

The man, in his variety of moods, fascinated me. If you asked him whether "Max" was not an abbreviation of Maximilian, he would say: "Maximultimillion." One thought of his pious father, the New Brunswick rector, and wondered however he had produced this worldling of genius. His mother, like Napoleon's, had brought several sons into the world; but, unlike Mrs. Harmsworth, only one Napoleon. But when someone had said to her, "I so admire your son, Mrs. Aitken," she inquired: "Which one?"

Of course what pleased me was the prodigality with which he showered the description "genius" upon me. I could never have enough of it, after being regarded for eighteen years as the fool of the family. Liking to be called a "genius" is an acquired taste. At that time everyone called me a

genius ; and as I danced with Lady Beaverbrook one night
I said to her : " What a charming man your husband "—
just to get her to say " He says you're a genius."

" Yes," she replied, " he's a genius."

" How ? What ? Yes, of course," I agreed.

III

MAN OF THOUGHT AND MAN OF ACTION

One day I asked Lord Beaverbrook whether he considered
the man of thought or the man of action deserving of first
place in the esteem of men. " The man of action, undoubtedly ! " said Lord Beaverbrook.

Sir James Dunn grunted assent.

Thereby they proved they were not yet men of thought.

There is, if we scan history, an immemorial attraction
between the man of action and the man of thought : Periander
of Corinth and Thales of Miletus ; Pericles and Anaxagoras ;
Solon and Cyrus ; Cromwell and Milton ; Frederick and
Voltaire ; Napoleon and Goethe ; Mussolini and D'Annunzio.
" Man of thought and man of action," says Mr. Wells, " are
mutually necessary—or, at any rate, the co-operation seems
to be necessary to the man of thought." And we accordingly
find Plato writing to Dionysius, tyrant of Syracuse : " Note
too that any marks of respect you show me, if you take the
lead, will be evidence that you think highly of philosophy ;
and the very fact that you have examined other teachers
of philosophy besides me will cause many to honour you as
a true philosopher. On the other hand any marks of respect
that I show you, unless you return them, will be interpreted
as evidence of my admiration of and desire for wealth —
and such a name, we know, is nowhere an honest one. To
put it in a nutshell, if you do homage to me, we both rise in
men's esteem ; if I do homage to you, we both sink. So
much for this subject."

We have no record as to whether Plato received a reply

to his letter.   I strongly doubt it.   Why indeed should Plato
have expected the tyrant Dionysius to think himself in need
of Plato's wisdom ?   Did he suppose a tyrant deems he has
acquired his power through imbecility ?   In an interview,
Lord Beaverbrook confesses that when he received an autograph copy of H. G. Wells's " William Clissold," with the
inscription : " To Max for the good of his soul from H. G.,"
he deliberately declined to read the work, deeming his soul
no concern of H. G. Wells.

The fascination, supposed to be that of thought, exercised
by the man of thought on the man of action, ends invariably
in a discovery by the thinker that what the man of action
really requires him for is to vent on him his own thoughts.
A man of action, having tasted of the illusion of power, is
conscious of a certain sense of injustice, in that the oracles
of a mind which has conceived and created a business like
Selfridge's or the Ford car factories, should not be listened to
with the same high respect as the oracles of men who have
apparently done nothing more than set pen to paper.   The
kings and captains have weighed the sayings of poets and
dreamers and, by the test of their own illusions, have found
them wanting.   And so Mr. Henry Ford and Mr. Edison
come out with sayings of their own about God and the
universe which Mr. Gilbert Chesterton is later called upon
to characterize as " painfully futile."

But when I questioned Lord Beaverbrook as to his views
on immortality, he said something which enhanced my
opinion of him.   He replied he had neither studied the
question nor given it any sustained thought ; that one had
either to be in possession of a philosophical mind if one
wished to probe this subject, or if one were not so endowed,
leave it alone.

Lord Beaverbrook has eyes like Ivan the Terrible's, a
beautiful voice with a scale which rises from the low burr
of a *basso profundo* to the highest pitch of a tenor, a register
appropriate to all moods, and a symbol of a charm which,
in my experience, is unique.   He has the faculty of giving

everybody he meets his "individual" attention. The impression is assisted by his habit of conducting his business by telephone while entertaining his guests, as if his friends were his real preoccupation, and business an agreeable irrelevance. There is something irresistible when, behind all this solid success, behind the solemn outposts of editors, you penetrate to the signal-box and find the man who pulls the strings a youngish little man with the face of a mischievous urchin. You cannot resist the fascination of being there with him in the signal-box. By not going out and so being accessible only in his own house, Lord Beaverbrook has created an impression of something socially and intellectually special going on there. Town dwellers with nowhere to go for the week-end may envy those of whom they read in the *Sunday Express* as spending the week-end at the country house of so-and-so ; and their surprise would be great if they knew that most of the guests were passing the afternoon on their beds lazily reading, in the same *Sunday Express*, news of their friends spending week-ends in similar country houses. Lord Beaverbrook's social strength lies in his habit of never stepping out of the signal-box.

He is fully aware of his advantage, and even tends to restrict the possibility of seeing you alone, inviting you to unburden yourself at a moment when his other guests are in full strength, and taking a mischievous delight in your attempts to put an essentially intimate communication in popular form. I once rang him up to ask his advice on a romantic impasse in which I found myself. He at once asked me to come along at half-past ten in the evening, when I presumed I would find him alone. When I arrived he invited me to tell my troubles to a party of guests which included Mr. Lloyd George.

His friends would prepare stories which would be received in silence, or for which he would award his commendations : " That is a fine story." " That is a good story." " You're in good form, Phyllis. It's a first-rate story." " It's poor stuff, Charles ! " Sometimes he will exasperate you by

taking a subtle thought, delicately, if fumblingly put, out of
your mouth and restating it bluntly—and inaccurately. I
have known only Arnold Bennett, whom he loved, to shake
him, so to speak, by the collar. I have never met a public
man who less resented any scrutiny, however intimate. Most
leading novelists have written of him without restraint. His
reply has invariably been : " Say what you like, I don't care
a damn." He has shown me, with amusement, the most
abusive of anonymous pasquinades, both in verse and in
prose ; and on one occasion when a friend of mine wrote him
an insulting letter, he in return offered her a job on his newspapers, " if that's what she's after," he said.

I know, of course, that successful business men like Mr.
Gordon Selfridge, Sir Thomas Lipton, and the late Lord
Leverhulme, have their devotees who rank them as great
men ; and I am aware of the risk of exaggeration in writing
of a man for whom I have a great affection. But, discounting
my enthusiasm (for, as Lord Balfour said, when we are
most enthusiastic we are least accurate), I still think Lord
Beaverbrook is incomparable. He cannot be shocked, he
is uncontaminated by moral indignation, and is open to
argument at any hour of the day or night on any subject
in the world. I have myself, at two o'clock in the morning,
when everyone was fagged out and longed to go home,
opened a conversation concerning the illusory nature of time,
and Lord Beaverbrook, who was helping himself to a
whisky and soda in the corner of the room, swiftly turned
round, took up the question and argued ably till half-past
three.

What then is the secret of his admittedly irresistible attraction for women of the world, and men seasoned in action
and thought ? One often hears people draw a distinction
between liking a person for himself and liking him for his
position. The question is full of pitfalls. Whether Lord
Beaverbrook would be as sought after if he were suddenly
stripped of his wealth and power is a question to be answered
in the negative. It would not become him to be poor. He

would not be himself. For when we like a man for "himself," we do so for that individuality, that style of his which he and life together have made out of him. And the nucleus of Lord Beaverbrook's charm is a combination of seemingly irresponsible gaiety and an attitude of appealing confidingness, the whole encased in an armour of power and wealth.

This legendary millionaire has a way with him, as charming as it is disarming, of dealing with downright people or hostile commentary. When we were dining with Rex Ingram and Alice Terry at Nice, a struggling artist anxious to show that he was not going to be browbeaten by a newspaper proprietor, took up the attitude of " Not at all—on the contrary," hoping to get Lord Beaverbrook to lose his temper. Lord Beaverbrook, however, cunningly allowed the young artist's wrath to spend itself on itself, and when the artist had run completely dry, acquiesced : " Yes, that disposes of the argument. I agree there is nothing further to say." Or again, during that very funny South Paddington Election, when accused by rival interlocutors, with that credulity of suspicion which always believes the incredible, of furthering Empire Free Trade so as, in the ensuing prosperity of trade, to increase the circulation of his own newspapers, he replied : " Yes, I hope it will. But if you think this the real motive behind my policy, I have nothing to say," thereby throwing the imbecility of the suggestion back on the man who had made it. Or again, when charged with contradictory ideas in the *Daily Express:* " I read that paper. But I do not write it all myself." Or he would answer some other unpleasant insinuation with a simple " You say so," thereby again associating the heckler with the odium of the insinuation, leaving the audience with the impression that the fellow is a man who deals in such things. Lord Beaverbrook owes much of his language to the Bible. He has the fervent look of a prophet with a high mission. His creed is the imposition of taxes on foreign foodstuffs.

IV

THE BISMARCK OF THE BRITISH EMPIRE

In politics—and an artist's politics is to get away from politics—my inclination, running contrariwise to my affection, would be to vote not for Lord Beaverbrook (who hides as much " old gang " behind him as Mr. Baldwin), but for some sociologically-minded young leader like Sir Oswald Moseley. But it is on the cards that if there is to be a Fiscal British Empire, Lord Beaverbrook is to be its Bismarck. Whether Empire Free Trade is good for Britain is beside the point : it is good for Lord Beaverbrook. It is not that the conditions have produced the man. It is rather that here is a man in need of a vocation to complete his personality, and so Empire Free Trade had, like Voltaire's god, to be invented. This is, of course, the spectacular view of history. And there is something to be said for it. After all, here is the British race, England, a fine old country about to sink to the destiny of Spain, etc., etc. And there is an indomitable character, a new product, a being who requires self-expression, etc., etc. You might say : let Mr. Baldwin, the trusted English gentleman, remain at the helm of the State. I see no reason why Baldwin of Messrs. Baldwin, Ltd., should continue to command Conservative confidence in preference to Max Aitken of the *Daily Express*, already steeped in tradition. When it comes to a leader for Tories, no politician can be upstart enough if he serves their interests. Even the Jew Disraeli, largely because he is dead, is the model imperialist with diehard generals.

When I first met Lord Beaverbrook he was in a period of surprising modesty, and he told me that I was fortunate to meet him while he was still open to other people's opinions. Sooner or later, he avowed, he would become, like Northcliffe, a megalomaniac. And indeed I was surprised, when I went to stay with him in Cherkeley two years later, how he had altered. There was a sort of absent gleam in his eye—

not as if he was not there, but as if his guests were mere shadows—coupled with an extraordinary volubility. Beaverbrook now usurped more than the lion's, more than three lions' share of the conversation; which to those of us who believed in give and take, seemed a little excessive. He no longer said " I'll provide the champagne and you the conversation." Nor did I need to say " You'll provide both." I merely observed to myself, wistfully, that that was so; and felt that without the champagne he would be taking it out of one unduly. Why shouldn't the man talk in his own house? I suppose there was no reason why he shouldn't. But there was an air of " What I say, goes " about his utterances which robbed them of their former charm.

These Mussolinis and Napoleons, rising to the summit of mundane glory, feel the need of commenting on what lies beyond it. But their comprehensions of philosophic propositions and artistic processes is imperfect and their utterances are not happy. Their intelligence, though quick to disengage a point, is not one to perceive the finer shades of " The Critique of Pure Reason." Consider the piteous report of Napoleon's interview with Goethe—the Emperor's laying down the law : " *It would be necessary* to show how Cæsar could have made the happiness of mankind and how his assassination prevented his carrying out his vast projects. . . . This (a Cæsar drama) could become your life work. Come to Paris ! I require it of you."—" Tut-tut ! " one is tempted to say.—" Tragedy is to be a school for kings." " Tut-tut ! All you know of imaginative creation is your own propaganda."

My admiration of Lenin has always been temperate, and I was surprised to find Lord Beaverbrook and Mrs. Richard Norton speaking of him with veneration. I should have thought that a fellow like Mussolini would be more nearly their hero. I was wrong. From the heights of wealth or fashion, and at a proper distance, political or social enmity vanishes like a cloud; nothing remains but a blue sky of appreciation, a sunny serenity. I was attacked for my tepid attitude to Lenin's greatness. Lord Castlerosse was enjoined to write a life of Lenin.

I said, no books written with a political bias were literature. At once I was pounced upon by a number of women. Mrs. Edwin Montague said—I knew it would come—" Swift." The truth, however, is that Swift in "Gulliver's Travels" was not exposing contemporary politics, but only expressing, artistically, his general dissatisfaction with life. And it was worth incurring the disagreement of everyone else in the room just to get Lady Weymouth alone to agree with me.

Lord Beaverbrook has shown himself capable in other fields—Empire Free Trade, for example—of sustained application. Not so in my case. After " The Polyglots " showed no visible sign of increased sales Lord Beaverbrook slackened.

I saw the incomparable Max again at the Paddington Baths, where he was speaking in support of Admiral Taylor, the Empire Crusade candidate. Growing cheers conveyed his approach to my ears, and there he was with a strange mystic look in his eye, raising his arm now and again as he walked up to the platform. The hall was filled with hysterical women. Lord Beaverbrook, after shaking hands with the personages on the platform, immediately began to rage and weep and implore, looking at a distance like a sublime frog. A hysterical woman, who shook her fist at the least sign of opposition in the audience, wept and sighed, as if in a delirium of voluptuous ecstasy, at every reference to king and country, and the greatness of the Empire: " Good . . . good," in a paroxysm of emotion unspent elsewhere. His voice rose and sank, rose and sank, his gestures went out in appeal, in defiance. He staggered back, and, spent, sank into his chair. With eyes that did not see, the eyes of a sleep-walker, he left the platform. Up sprang the Admiral, a huge, burly fellow—looking at a distance like a sublime ape—and bawled at the audience as if he were on deck his old battleship. " I love a fight," he began, and finished his speech with an appeal for peace and goodwill.

Was it a dream?

And now enough of that lovable peer, who has inspired all the novelists of his day to create newspaper proprietors in his image. Who can forget that urchin's wink in his eye from the other end of the table surrounded by brilliant guests, beautiful women, phosphorescent conversation? At one time, all newspaper proprietors resembled Lord Northcliffe. Now it is Lord Beaverbrook who is the standard type of British newspaper proprietor. Lord Beaverbrook has stamped himself on the imagination of half a dozen contemporary novelists. Yet I fail to find his grey searchlights turned on me when I visit the galleries of Madame Tussaud's. Why this omission? Why are we so deprived?

V

D. H. LAWRENCE IS DIM ABOUT SHAW

While my people clamoured for my immediate return to Paris to collect the urn from the station cloakroom, I was in the middle of meeting people. At a literary tea party, where the most strenuously besieged person was Margaret Kennedy, just then resting on the laurels she had won with "The Constant Nymph," a curiously untidy person in a morning-coat, which bore evidence that he had put it on under protest, came up to me, with a very fetching grin on his face and a curiously girlish, hysterical voice. I guessed immediately that he was D. H. Lawrence. He at once conveyed to me his disapproval of nearly everybody else in the room, and this, coupled with his jolly sort of approval of my "Polyglots" and a lot of advice as to what I should avoid as a writer, all proffered in the most cheerful way, surprised me agreeably, since I had imagined Lawrence to be a disgruntled individual. He told me I had an absolutely original humour; that I should eschew sentimentality like poison; and that he thought I displayed an uncalled-for fear of death. Though feeling that nothing could be more baleful for the natural development of my own talent than the influence of that great rough force contorted

into soured rhetoric, I nevertheless said to him at once,
feeling that the occasion demanded it : " You're the only
one we younger men can now look up to." He lapped it
up, grinning with an air which suggested that he agreed with
me, and later remarked to someone else how pleasant it was
at last to have met an intelligent man.

Lawrence took me across the room to introduce me to
his wife, who, interrupting her conversation with another
woman, beamed at me very largely and said : " What do
you make of life ? "

" Come, come," said her husband.

Mrs. Lawrence told me how intensely her husband admired
my books. Lawrence qualified this. " I liked the humour,"
he said. He scribbled down his address on the back of a
cigarette box. I was to come to tea the next day.

When I called, Lawrence himself opened the door. His
satanic look was absent. In the sunlight his red-bearded
face looked harrowed and full of suffering, almost Christ-
like. There were a couple of women at tea who seemed to
resent a little our man-to-man conversation. One woman
even went so far as to show impatience at the dryness, to her,
of our subject, when finally she rose to leave. This roused
Lawrence's fury. He imitated her inflexions. " The in-
solence of the bitch ! " he said when she was gone.
" Imagining we're here to entertain her ! " And he once
more imitated her unmercifully ; after which he relapsed
again into a serene tone of voice appropriate to our subject-
matter—immortality. I mentioned Tolstoy saying life was
a dream, death the awakening. Lawrence shook his head.
" No," he said, " I don't see it like that." And he explained,
very gently, looking at me very kindly with a sort of
Christ-like expression. " You see," he said, " it's like
this : in your inside . . ." And I looked very attentive,
very coy.

Our discussion continued for several hours. Lawrence's
idea of immortal life was not something which would start
after death, but a living reality within us going on even now,

all the time, though intermittently clouded over by the illusion of time. He grew enthusiastic. Anything true to its own nature, he declared, was immortal. And his eyes expressed a gleam of self-satisfaction, certainly not immortal. A cat bristling his fur, a tiger in his fierceness . . . He stopped, a little troubled. I nodded comprehendingly.

We talked of Katherine Mansfield and Middleton Murry, whom, Mrs. Lawrence told me, they regarded as children to be helped out of their troubles. I regretted that Middleton Murry, so sensitive and understanding a critic, should be himself devoid of any talent whatever; and D. H. Lawrence sneered : " I should have thought it was the only thing he had."

It was now dinner time, and Lawrence asked me to stay. Mrs. D. H. Lawrence, when you first set eyes on her, is the type of woman to gladden your heart. A real German Hausfrau, you say to yourself, suits him down to the ground, the intellectual, incompetent husband ! The reality, however, is the reverse of this. Mrs. Lawrence dislikes housework ; her husband excels in it. Lawrence, a beam on his face, which was like a halo, brought in the dishes out of the kitchen, with the pride of a first-class chef in his unrivalled creations : no, as if cooking and serving your guests were a sacrament, a holy rite. When I told Lawrence of my friendship with Beaverbrook, he astonished me by the intensity of his deprecation. Why should I allow myself to be patronized ? Why should I, a messenger of the spirit, acknowledge Cæsar ? I, on the other hand, urged that the Holy Ghost in me prompted me to treat Cæsar with that extra grace which the spirit can so easily lavish on the flesh—providing always that Cæsar does not take unto himself that which is not Cæsar's. But Lawrence demurred. If I wanted money, why not write articles for the magazines ? He sat down and there and then wrote me a letter of introduction to Lengel of the *Cosmopolitan*. Authors, he implied, had been known to get on without the boosting of newspaper proprietors. " And even with it," I said. " But why see any harm in the genuine interest in me of a charming newspaper proprietor, himself half a genius, who obviously cannot cherish an ulterior motive in regard to me ? "

" Because," Lawrence insisted, " he hates you."

" Come, come," I said.

" I don't say he hates you personally," Lawrence contended. " But these men, they're like vampires. When they see an immortal soul they hate it instinctively." His eyes gleamed. " With a terrible black hatred, and instinctively try to annihilate what is immortal in you."

At which remark Mrs. Lawrence trembled with rage and expressed her agreement with some violence, which seemed to me a waste of effort, since if she had met Lord Beaverbrook she would undoubtedly have bowed to the man's extraordinary charm. D. H. Lawrence, wincing at this display of superfluous emotion, said quietly : " Not so much intensity, Frieda."

Mrs. Lawrence, perhaps living up to the elemental naturalness of her husband's heroines, replied : " If I want to be intense I'll be intense, and you go to hell ! "

" I'm ashamed of you, Frieda," he said. Whereupon Frieda's hatred for Lord Beaverbrook transformed itself into hatred for her husband, and was soon a spent cartridge.

I told Lawrence of some scientific difficulty I had about my plot for " Jazz and Jasper." I wanted a handful of people left on a mountain top with the rest of the world disintegrated to nothing. The problem had defeated H. G. Wells, who told me that the only plausible thing I could do was to make it a dream. D. H. Lawrence brushed aside the suggestion as unworthy and mapped the whole thing out for me in five minutes, breaking into ripples of girlish giggles at the ingenuity of his solution.

Lawrence said that the cells of Tchehov's writing were disintegrating cells, emitting, as they burst, a doleful twang which remained with us. Tolstoy's, on the contrary, were reintegrating cells, which gladdened the heart and tightened the nerves. When I told this to Middleton Murry, he sighed and said Lawrence never understood Tchehov. And I would add that, in my experience, I had never known anywhere, Russia not excepted, two souls more sensitively appreciative of Tchehov's work than Katherine Mansfield and Middleton Murry, though both could read him only in translation.

There was something so genuine and attractive about Lawrence, in spite of his curiously adolescent habit of derisive generalities, deploring the trend of his time, and other ballast of this kind, which he could have chucked overboard with advantage. Pointing to a crowd in the street, "These London girls," he said to me. "I would as soon sleep with them as with a water closet." And I pictured a number of attractive young girls, for no crowd is without them, mortified at the refusal of a sickly, red-bearded, untidy individual of middle-age to meet their advances, which in fact had not been forthcoming. "I am fleeing again from my native country," in a letter. Sad, bad stuff! His being capable of it explains perhaps his readiness to surround himself with the most inconceivable mutts, patient listeners, haggard women, towards whom he no doubt conceived it his duty, at great effort—no wonder—to inculcate in himself a feeling of sex. And though he preached the gospel of the " complete man," harmoniously attuned, Lawrence wore his red hair brushed down over the forehead, as if to conceal it—possibly to identify himself with the lowbrow primitive, whose centre of gravity is below the belt.

There was in Lawrence a real passion, a real longing to adjust his feeling about things to the enduring, the immortal side of life, intimated to us in fitful glimpses of Nature. Lawrence's revelation of animal life, his landscapes, and his human portraits are nearly always beautiful, original, powerful and moving. They are spoilt sometimes by needless reiteration prompted, one suspects, by a sort of gauche adolescent vanity—"I'll do it again, I will, if only to annoy you." He is like a man who wants to show off his strength with a great big hammer and proceeds to drive the nails too far, and spoils the woodwork somewhat. Then testing it : " It's strong," he says, and walks away swinging the hammer. Lawrence told me he liked his books while he wrote them, but hated them the moment he saw them in print. I am not surprised. His bitterness is the reaction of a proud spirit subjected from an early age to social and bodily humiliations. His inauspicious birth caused him to exert his strength fully as a rebel with little humour left to dispose of as a free man. Hence his hatreds, his insistence on his need of " blood contact " with the lower classes, as if it were not the inadequacy of all human contacts which throws one back on oneself, and makes the artist. Social self-consciousness, when it becomes articulate and tries to explain and justify itself, is a nuisance.

Everything I told Lawrence about the writers I had met seemed to provoke a kind of savage satisfaction in him, a grunt confirming his worst suspicions about the man. But when I mentioned Shaw, the passion and indignation which inspired his remarks evaporated completely. He said, with a disdain which did not pay Mr. Shaw the compliment of being positive, a mere absence of interest, a mere negative : " Are you interested in sociology ? I'm not ! "

With all his cheerful simplicity, his strength, his instinctive preoccupation with the real meaning of life (which is to " evade," as Tchehov says, " to circumvent, the unreal, the shallow, gratuitous, phantom-like which prevents us from being happy ") there was withal something superfluous, something gawky and left-handed about Lawrence. His humour was defective. Yet, like so many people whose humour is poor, he prided himself on his tremendous sense of fun. " I wish," he wrote to me, " *we* created a *Monthly Express*, out of our various anatomies, to laugh at it all. Just a little magazine to laugh a few things to death. ' The Big Toe Points out the Point or Points in Point Counter Point '—and so on. Let's make a little magazine, where even the liver can laugh." Hardly first-rate.

It is not perhaps what a writer sees that matters in the end, but the " smell " he exudes. Zola also thought he

saw the truth and that it needed saying. Where is Zola's
" truth " to-day? Where Lawrence's " truth " will be to-
morrow. One writer's " truth " is in the end as problematic
as another's. It's the taste, the smell of his writing, which
matter. And I cannot help thinking that D. H. Lawrence
has a " smell " about him which is unsatisfactory.

I heard of Lawrence's death, one morning, as I happened
to look in at the office of a New York publisher. " Is that
true ? " I asked, and I was thinking that at last he had severed
the tortuous cord of his thoughts, which now went on and
on, coiling and winding on their own; while the publisher,
note-book and pencil in hand, addressed in insistent whispers
the deceased author's agent : " Is there anything ? A
completed book ? No ? Any unfinished manuscript that
could be issued as a novel ? "

VI

I EVADE MR. WELLS'S BALL-GAME

When I read a few flattering sentences about " Futility,"
in *The Adelphi*, under the signature of H. G. Wells, I spent,
like Hannibal after his victories, a whole week in satisfied self-
contemplation. But I had not yet met Mr. Wells in person.

I was dining with Lord Beaverbrook at Stornoway House.
The Aga Khan, Lord Beatty, and Mr. Reginald McKenna
had been announced in turn; and then the butler came in
once more and said : " Mr. and Mrs. ' H.' —— ' G.' ——
' Wells.' "

Had the butler let drop a small bomb which, in the ensuing
explosion, produced clouds of fire and smoke out of which
pyrotechnic display eventually emerged Mr. Charles Dickens,
my incredulity could not have been greater.

Nevertheless, Mr. Wells appeared on the threshold, with
Mrs. Wells. For many years I had silently communed with
him through a long series of books; and now the man,
rotund and on the small side, with humorously sad eyes
under brows that were almost naïve, came towards us. Lord

Beaverbrook introduced me to Wells as he might have
introduced me to Julius Cæsar, Count Leo Tolstoy, or Martin
Luther.   Mr. Wells inclined his head and, shaking hands with
a cordiality essentially impersonal, passed on to the person
beside me, thus testifying to the nullity of his impression.

It was not till Mrs. Wells had drawn her husband's attention to my name, which had evidently escaped him, that he
came back with that little air of geniality of his : " What
do I hear ? It's you ? " and took me by the arm.   It was
as if a man had long called to a saint, and the saint had taken
him at his word and descended.   And the tall great men
in the room suddenly dwindled in stature and seemed dwarfs.
" M-m-m," H. G. Wells murmured with a sort of sad compre-
hensiveness.   " How old are you ? "—" Twenty-eight "—
" You're very young to have written such books.   You must
come over this week-end to Easton Glebe.   There are so
many things we must talk over together, m'm.   That lady
on the sofa wants to meet you.   M-m-m.   She's read all
your books.   M-m-m, she has.   It is my business to please
her, as she happens to be my wife, m'm."   Half of what he
said I couldn't hear—but I laughed all the same, out of
complaisance.

As we all trooped down the stairs to dinner, and I deferred
to Mr. Wells at the door, H. G., still in a mood of beatitude,
protested : " No, you go first : you're To-morrow, I'm
Yesterday."

But possibly these things, compliments uttered out of
politeness or kindness of heart, may startle their authors
when they see them in print, as it would amaze me if some
man who had called on me and to whom I had said : " Please
sit down," later wrote in his memoirs : " Mr. Gerhardi
displayed the greatest solicitude for my personal comfort,
while disregarding his own. Perhaps unconsciously he
recognized in me, I will not say his better, but at least his
successor, and this was the outward sign of his inward conviction."   However this may be, Wells's gesture was
dramatically right, in that Lord Beaverbrook's intuition in

singling out my books was endorsed by the premier novelist of England.

After dinner, when the men drew together over port, I noticed that Wells had a very clever way of contributing to a conversation which, at that stage, was purely hearty in quality and did not call for any worth-while remark. He merely, without really listening, but while appearing to do so, punctuated the narrative with a periodical acquiescent " M'm ! " and so was one with them without being of them.

At the end of the evening H. G. repeated his invitation for the week-end.

" Next week-end, dear," Mrs. Wells whispered, since no doubt her forthcoming party was already complete.

" Bother ! This week-end," H. G. said irritably. " I will call for you myself in my car."

" Next week-end," Mrs. Wells insinuated to me, with a smile.

When, the week after, I set out to spend the week-end with the H. G. Wells's, I missed the train, upset their lunch hour, threw Mrs. Wells and her son who had motored up to the station to meet me into jeopardy ; and when H. G. came out of his room, he greeted me with a pungent : " Damn you ! " During lunch he said I was " not yet in grace." Then he became very jolly. There was no " side " at all about H. G. Wells. His occasional irritability is not the least human side of him.

After lunch, Bertrand Russell arrived with his wife. Sensitive intelligence shone in his large dark eyes. His mind was alert and ready to spot instantly some intellectual inaccuracy and obligingly put it right for you. H. G. Wells seemed in a restful Saturday afternoon mood, tired of God and all the scaffolding he had in his day put up and pulled down for that " invisible king," and told me, who was trying to ferret him out of his burrow with Middleton Murry, to tell Murry he could have all his scrap iron, all the spare parts, yes, and the nails and screws as well, of God, the lot delivered to him in a sack. But I still clutched Wells's pants, trying to hoist him up on to the High Horse of Philosophy. Considering me critically, he suddenly asked : "How old are you ? " "Twenty-eight." "A child," he replied. "When I was your age I also thought of the earth and the sky above it, the stars and the sun, and wondered what was beyond it. I don't think of it that way now." To me, who had never thought of it that way, Wells's earlier conception denoted a lower standard of approach than my own, and I did not see why he should saddle me with a discarded, discredited, attitude of his own. I implied, with the barely concealed arrogance of youth, that what could interest me was, of course, not what he could solve, but what he couldn't, and that so far from haughtily dismissing the question as unworthy of thought, all the great writers of their day had always been moved to account for the universe as a whole by making what they could of the fraction.

"You cannot," said Bertrand Russell, quietly from his corner, "account for a whole when you are a part of it."

"Say it again," from Wells.

"Mathematically, you cannot," Bertrand Russell explained more largely, "account for the whole universe because, to do so, you would have to stand outside it. Being ourselves a part of the universe, we cannot circumscribe the whole."

Wells thought hard, and said : "Yes."

I then returned to the subject from another angle, quoting Tolstoy as saying that conscience was the only proof we had of divinity. Wells said that conscience was merely an acquired thing, a growth of habit and usage and prejudice. To reassure him, I told him that if it saddened him to see me side with Tolstoy against him, he might comfort himself with the thought that Goethe would have sided with him against Tolstoy : that when Eckermann similarly invested conscience with divinity, old Goethe cried vehemently : "Who requires you to have a conscience ! " But Wells, instead of being comforted, unearthed a remark about Goethe, dating back to his war-time book "Boon." "Goethe," he said, "was the German contribution to that myth 'The Great

Man.' They felt it was time they had their great man ; so they dressed up a poet called Goethe for the part."

I had heard that H. G. Wells insisted on all his guests joining, before lunch, in some obscure ball game of his own invention, and this news disquieted me. I had not emerged sane from compulsory school, compulsory drill, compulsory chapel, etc., to go mad in the garden of H. G. Wells, who had upset all oligarchies and systems of convention, even at one time advocated military service in preference to the mental disease of sport erupting over the land, only, it seems, to establish a horrible game of his own. I recoiled from such tyranny, nor would all my respect for the man make me play it. I investigated the report, and was told by Bertrand Russell, with a sad smile of submission, that it was indeed true. You either played or H. G. Wells had no use for you. Then, bringing out of my dormant soul all the reserves of ammunition I could dispose of, I went up to H. G. and, suppressing a fury that must needs destroy us both, yet keeping my mind's eye on the railway station, I asked him if it were true that I was expected to play games. "Not if you don't want to," he said with rather a pained expression at this slur on his game, so airy, so witty, so well-devised.

"Good," I thought, my wrath evaporating. But to make certain my escape from the coils of the devil of compulsion, I went up to my room and wrote letters till I heard voices of strained and unconvincing heartiness, as the athletes, headed by Mr. Bertrand Russell, came in for their well-earned luncheon.

Next day, a Sunday, wearing a leather coat, a cap, and Russian boots, and looking like a militant Bolshevist leader in charge of an armoured car, H. G. drove some of us, very precariously, into the village and showed us round the village church. On our way there we picked up two fervent lady disciples who seemed to regard the novelist primarily as a revolutionary leader about to engineer a long awaited coup d'état. H. G. Wells talked to them freely on left-wing matters, every now and then lifting a hand from the steering gear, when the car would zigzag violently, skirting the ditch by an inch or so.

Bertrand Russell remained behind with a book which, on our return, I was glad to recognize as my " Polyglots," a copy of which was on view on the drawing-room table. When I saw Bertrand Russell's latest by its side, I was struck by the double coincidence, and my sense of the riddle of things deepened. Bertrand Russell, who had taken no notice of me on the Saturday, came beaming up to me on Sunday morning, explaining that he had not been told till now that I was the man who had written " Futility " ; after which we two went for a long walk in the morning sunshine, and Bertrand Russell, whose eyes gleamed with loving-kindness, answered my discreet inquiries into the realm of the Mind with the utmost willingness and lucidity. Only when I mentioned D. H. Lawrence's theories did the look of serenity fade in his large wise eyes, and a note of intellectual fastidiousness crept into his voice, and he said " Lawrence has no mind." He referred to the letters Lawrence wrote to him during the war, and how, of course, he, Bertrand Russell, was not going to be instructed in wisdom by D. H. Lawrence. A week later, meeting Lawrence, I told him how enchanted I had been by the lucidity, the suppleness and pliability of Bertrand Russell's mind. He sniffed. " Have you seen him in a bathing-dress ? " he asked. " Poor Bertie Russell ! He is all Disembodied Mind."

Bertrand Russell expressed himself delighted with " The Polyglots." I was delighted with Bertrand Russell. I was not sure whether I did not prefer him as a companion to H. G. Wells who, because he was so human, was also a more irritable and irritating being. Bertrand Russell's sunny, even demeanour suggested that he had never left the soft elysian glades and streams of Cambridge where meditation shelters and thought ripples gently on.

I found I had left behind my black tie, and H. G. took me up to his bedroom and asked me to select one from his wardrobe. I wish I had kept it. For dinner, Wells, with sadly humorous eyes, donned a dark-blue velvet jacket, which suited him uncommonly well, giving him that appearance of the " cher maître " he lacked in his Russian boots. Lady Warwick arrived to dinner, and the Guedallas, likewise close neighbours. Philip Guedalla, with great facial contortions, rather like an ancient clock which scrapes and wheezes before it strikes the hour, delivered himself of a few brilliant, brilliantined, remarks. Suddenly I felt so mortally tired that I could not open my mouth. Wells was very genial. Mention was made of " Hamlet " in Modern Dress. Wells said that it was a poor play, anyhow, in plain clothes or period. Then, looking teasingly at me : " Fishhooks . . . fishhooks . . ." he said. Talking of Uncle Emmanuel in my " Polyglots," " There," he declared he had said to himself, when perusing the amorous adventures of that knight of the bedchamber, " there, but for the grace of God, goes H. G. Wells ! " When I doubted whether he had really read my novel through, he replied : " I have wept over it."

Next morning when I came down to breakfast I saw Mrs. Wells and her son Frank, arm in arm, exercising their legs up and down before the portico. Monday morning breakfast is a cheerful affair for the host : in an hour, he knows, he will have the house to himself. I pondered the indignity of the contrast between the reception of the guests at the station on Saturday, and their dismissal at the door of the house on Monday. I remembered how Wells had said to me : " Come to Eaton Glebe : there are so many things we must talk over," and how, when I arrived, he had shown me over a village church. I related, without stressing the moral unduly, how Goethe as a young man had undertaken a long voyage to Hamburg to meet Lessing, whom he admired enormously, and with whom he proposed to discuss all the problems of life, art, criticism and philosophy, and how Lessing had talked to him of horse-racing. " I suppose," Wells laughed ribaldly, " Lessing should have talked to him of the Absolute, what ! "

On the railway platform Bertrand Russell bought himself

a detective novel to read in the train. When I expressed mild amazement that he should not want to read anything better, he said : " You, a novelist, read popular science. I, a scientist, read popular fiction."

VII

THE FOREMAN OF BRITISH FICTION

When Beaverbrook had asked me whom I should like to meet I had said : " H. G. Wells." When H. G. Wells, in his turn, made a similar offer, I said : " Bernard Shaw and Arnold Bennett." Accordingly, when I lunched with Mr. and Mrs. Wells on the following Wednesday, there by my side was Enoch Arnold Bennett ; and when I lunched with them, on Friday, there was George Bernard Shaw. It seemed simple.

Arnold Bennett's appearance astonished me. I had imagined him as a gay dog about town with smooth heavily brilliantined black hair—the psychological adviser of Lady Diana Cooper. I saw a grey-haired, morose man who one moment looked as if he had been struck by a fit of apoplexy and would not recover ; the next moment came to life with a twinkle. There was about that face with the sad, languorous brown eyes under the half-closed lids an air of intolerable tedium, as if he were slowly dying of agonized boredom, had endured you, but could endure no longer.

Arnold Bennett resented oral invitations to dinner, marvelling at the meanness of prospective hostesses who stooped to such tactics. It was taking an unfair advantage of him. Invitations to authors, he held, should be sent through the post ; and a considerate excuse conveyed through the same channel.

At first you were disagreeably intimidated by the pompous seriousness with which he seemed to insist on what he said. But the smile which flickered at the end of every such utterance conveyed that Mr. Bennett was laughing at the sort of man who would talk like Mr. Bennett ; and you were charmed. Moreover, Arnold Bennett, cleverly turning a hesitating speech to both dramatic and comedic advantage, had to say very little indeed for everyone present to see a great deal in it. " What do you think of X. Y. ? " he might be asked. " She is . . ." and then a high falsetto : " a cat." Loud laughter. Deadly apt ! What an epigram ! you involuntarily felt. Yet the same sentence said by a man who was not Arnold Bennett—said by an Arnold Bennett deprived of hesitation and a tendency to rise into a high falsetto—would have passed unnoticed.

There he was, however, eating at my side in silence. When Commander Kenworthy passed him some petition for his signature, with a note : " Your opinion is worth more than H. G.'s," Arnold Bennett as, with silent seriousness, he drew my attention to these words suddenly twinkled into that smile which revealed all the warm humour latent in the man and playing through all his pages. Instead of discussing with me the new situation created in literature by my advent, he contented himself by putting a few questions relative to my education—which college I was at at Oxford, what did I read for, etc.—questions of a formal rather than genuine interest. Once in the drawing-room, however, and near to his departure, he gravely produced a pencil and notebook and inquired for my address. I had said nothing, he less. But when, a few days later, Beaverbrook, whom I had told about my meeting with Bennett, rang him up to inquire what he thought of me, Bennett's reply was : " Excellent talker ! "

After a dinner at his house, A. B. took us aside and gravely showed us the original manuscript of " The Old Wives Tale." There was scarcely a correction in it. I questioned whether this could be the original manuscript. I did not understand how a man could have written a novel straight out in this neat hand, or why he should want to, why he should pause unnecessarily, strain his memory, sacrifice a better version of a phrase to an inferior one, which had occurred to him first. I again questioned A. B. " Surely," I said, " it isn't, it *cannot* be the first attempt."

Without speaking, A. B. opened the manuscript at the title page and pointed again to the words : " First and last writing."

" But how, and above all, why ? " I asked. " You can't write always at the same rate of speed. You may get excited. . . ."

At this Mr. Bennett's upper lip stiffened. " No first-class artist," he said, " gets excited."

Taking a passage, which came back to me from his own published diary, I threw at him : " I have written to-day ten thousand words without stop. I finished my novel in exultation, in excitement."

He smiled divinely and lifted a hand. " Hit ! "

I asked Arnold Bennett whether he thought he or Wells was the greater writer. At this my host's protruding upper lip seemed to stiffen and lengthen. " Look here," he said, " you are dining here at my house for the first time to-night, and you put me to the ordeal of answering such a question." Then his eyes twinkled with warm humour. " As a matter of fact," he said, " the answer is perfectly simple. Wells has by far, by far the greater mind, but I——" Here Arnold Bennett got stuck ; his mouth worked convulsively. We all looked at him wishing, but not daring, to help him out. He put his hand to his mouth, as if to stop the loose play of the joints and hinges. " But I," he presently said, " I'm the better n-n-n-n-novelist. Wells doesn't know how to write a novel," he concluded quite effortlessly.

As we left, Bennett insisted on coming down with us and making sure that a separate taxi was called for everyone. Very courteous, I thought, but awkward for anyone who can't afford to pay for the taxi at the other end. As I took leave of him, he said to me : " I am pleased with you." I thought, Why ? Because I had behaved at table ? Not spoiled the carpet, not smashed the furniture ?

On another occasion the manuscript of " The Old Wives Tale " again went round and I no longer questioned its authenticity as a first and last draft. Having by luck alighted on

a passage I liked and noted the page, I closed the book
and then, expressing enthusiasm for a certain passage which
I insisted should be read aloud forthwith, I turned it up on
the instant, as one who knew his way perfectly in the book,
and enlisting public opinion on my side compelled Osbert
Sitwell to read it aloud. It was the passage which showed
the wife looking at her dead husband, " who had once been
young, had grown old, and now was dead," thinking of him
without bitterness. But Osbert Sitwell, thinking of me,
read in a surprised, resentful, almost accusing voice. Arnold
Bennett sat there, quiet and demure, the " cher maître " surrounded by disciples of his art.

I commended a passage in Hugh Kingsmill's " Dawn's
Delay " which I thought got the salient points of Arnold
Bennett's personality. Arnold Bennett, priding himself on
the efficiency of his library, went out and came back with
the book. I was enjoined to read the passage aloud to an
audience which included Osbert Sitwell, Margaret Kennedy
and Cynthia Noble. " An attempt," I read, " in the manner
of Max Beerbohm. The gentleman examining the menu
is Arnold Bennett. He is exuding a delight, naïve and
profound, in the complex apparatus of a decadent and luxurious
civilization, and in his own ability to handle that apparatus
like a master. Note the head waiter's mixture of deference
and affectionate esteem. The face in the background rising
out of a mist, hair on end, eyes dilated with wonder, or
horror, is the face of William Blake. I call it ' Astonishment
of William Blake, who has been informed that Arnold Bennett
is also a creative artist.' "

The last words fell on a constrained silence. Then Arnold
Bennett said, wearily : " Well——yes——"

A year later I was surprised by the change in Arnold
Bennett's appearance. It was as if after having pumped
himself up as befits the undisputed foreman of British fiction,
some jovial foe to pomposity had stuck a pin into him, and
A. B. had fizzled out like a penny balloon. He was emaciated,
even his shirt front was soft—all the starch had gone out of

him. But his head still went to one side a little stiffly, like
that of a doll which you adjust as you please.

Arnold Bennett did not consider Galsworthy as in a class
with himself, but understood why the practical uninspired
Germans should regard him as significant, since he gave
them all the handbook information about the English, which
their Teutonic thirst for detail craved. Wells, on the other
hand, referred to Galsworthy twice in my presence as a
fastidious artist, while modestly describing himself as a mere
journalist !

At another dinner, Bennett told a story about Sir Hall
Caine who, priding himself on his resemblance to Christ,
was exhilarated to discover a striking resemblance to himself
in an ikon displayed in a shop window in St. Petersburg.
Approaching it, he saw, however, that it was a portrait of
Hall Caine in an English bookshop.

Another evening, when H. G. Wells was dining with
Bennett, the merits of Conrad came up for discussion over
the port, and both novelists puffed out smoke over the quickly
vanishing reputation of a writer once deemed too fastidious
for the common, now puzzling to us with his solemn retiring
charlatanism—surely a new type in literature. The discussion moved between Arnold Bennett, H. G. Wells, and,
if I remember rightly, Desmond MacCarthy. Then Wells,
with his faith in the regenerative contribution of youth,
turned to me and said : " What do *you* think of it, Gerhardi ? "
Forgetting at the moment the perfection of " Typhoon," I
replied that Conrad was cheap wood, poor in grain, but
with an expensive varnish. A cloying melodiousness, which
seems imposed on the theme from outside and not arising
naturally out of the subject. Wells looked baffled, while
Bennett nodded approvingly. " Yes," he said, " first-rate
stuff is not like that—more simple," and we rose to join
the ladies.

Upstairs in the drawing-room I observed Bennett insisting
on his esteemed colleague, H. G. Wells, occupying a more
comfortable chair, and himself sitting down on a plain one

beside him. Arnold Bennett was now quite thin, H. G. Wells gaining in rotundity ; and there they sat, side by side, the two foremost novelists of England.

When Arnold Bennett lay dying in his luxury flat at Chiltern Court, with the straw spread lavishly across all the width of Marylebone Road, I reflected, as sadly I stood and looked up at his windows, that the astute A. B., were he conscious, would have been the first to point out how obsolete in our day of pneumatic tyres and smooth roads, with no sound but the hooting of horns and the changing of gear, is a custom designed to deaden the noise of wooden wheel and iron hoof on cobble-stones. Presently, I hoped, he would come to and expose the archaism in an article in the *Evening Standard*. When I passed again the straw had been removed, and Arnold Bennett was dead.

VIII

AT THE MOVIES WITH SHAW AND WELLS

Authors should not expose themselves in public. Their mystery is their capital. Once seen, nobody wants to see them again. If they must show themselves, let it be at a distance—at the end of a long corridor, at the top of the stairs. The Prince Consort, Mr. Lytton Strachey tells us, always kept out of reach. Even the Ministers of State could only catch a glimpse of his tall, erect figure flitting across the far end of a stateroom. A stiff bow—no more. Authors should emulate the Prince Consort's example. " Who's that fellow ? " people would ask. And the name would be divulged. A close scrutiny of a poet is unrewarding. People, calling on Byron and expecting to find him as beautiful as his portrait, noted : " Short, fat, podgy hands, grey hair, unhealthy complexion." A romantic young girl who met Goethe said he looked like a Frankfort wine merchant ; another woman who saw him on the same occasion reported he looked like a god. From which statement one might infer that a Frankfort wine merchant looks like a god. Unless one inclined to the alternative conclusion that a god may look not unlike a Frankfort wine merchant.

However that may be, when we were all gathered in Mr. and Mrs. Wells's drawing-room in the Whitehall Court flat the butler came in and said in a loud clear voice :

" Mr. Bernard Shaw."

If the butler had announced : " His Holy Apostolic Majesty," the effect could not have been bettered.   There is perhaps nothing to touch, in point of social effect, an illustrious " Mr."   The simplicity of it seems to throw the fame into relief, adding dignity to both, as with the O. M., whose prime distinction is that, notwithstanding the merit which goes with it, it disdains the used-to-death " Sir " which goes with other honours of this kind.

Shaw had a red nose which belied a little the good things we hear said about his diet.   He beamed at me and came up to me, very like D. H. Lawrence, and took me aside to the mantelpiece.   There was the same look of felicity in Shaw as in Lawrence.   Shaw asked me whether I was English.   I qualified my English nationality by explaining that I was brought up in Russia, because I always feel that to ask anyone to swallow at one go my name, intonation, and place of birth, none of which is English, is to overstrain their credulity.   Shaw, however, did not give me a chance to lay myself out autobiographically.   " If you're English," he said, " you're a genius, but if you're Russian . . . well, then, of course . . ."

" I am English," I interjected, not wishing him to take away the award.

" Well, then——" he said, and did not continue, the conversation not lending itself to a successful paradox. Shaw expressed himself as dissatisfied with my " Futility," but singled out the weakest passage in " The Polyglots " for warm praise.   Mrs. Shaw had read it to him.   My hero's monologue on the unknown soldier's opinion of the ceno-taph, Shaw declared, " real writing, classical stuff.   I said to my wife . . ."

I reciprocated with a complimentary reference to "Saint Joan," and Bernard Shaw said, deprecatingly, "Oh, well, it's good melodrama." But I would not hear this. "It's drama," I said, ". . . that scene where the chaplain staggers in from the burning."

"Oh, well," said Shaw, "if you can't make drama out of burning a woman alive . . ." and he laughed deprecatingly. He then drew my attention to John Knox, whose life, he said, offered material for drama hardly less rich than Saint Joan's. I asked Shaw if he had ever come across a reference in Tchehov's letters to the publisher and newspaper proprietor Suvorin, who was enjoying a fishing holiday : "For the sake of all the pike you are going to catch on your holiday, do be sure to translate and publish the English humorist Bernard Shaw."

"It was very kind of Tchehov," was Mr. Shaw's comment. A deprecating smile showed on his face. He had, he said, recently come across one of those marvellous long words that the German language seems to specialize in—*Weltverbesserungswahn*. Tolstoy's son said his father suffered from a *Weltverbesserungswahn*. "And I think I suffer from it too," concluded Bernard Shaw.

No sooner had I taken my seat at the side of Mrs. Bernard Shaw than she said : "Are you American ? We thought so from your book."

"If you think I should be, I am," I replied bitterly.

The wives of great men oppose serious obstacles to one's intellectual enjoyment. When you sit next to one and hope she may be quiet to enable you to hear what her illustrious husband is saying, she engages you in small talk and drowns your attention. I told Mrs. Shaw that I was going out to night clubs a good deal with Lord Beaverbrook. Shaw looked up and said that night clubs were the dullest things in the world, and Wells said : "Shall we, you and I, Shaw, make a night of it together ? "

Lunch over, H. G. Wells took us up in the lift to the roof of the building, from which we got a fine view of the river and a comprehensive view of London, and H. G. even pointed out the church at which his father and mother were married. Shaw, straight as an arrow, looked wonderful with his beard flying in the wind.

Then we descended to the ground floor. Ivor Montague remarked on the oddity of my wearing a bowler hat, and Shaw said that bowler hats were the best, but that the sensible hats to wear were top hats. We got into two taxis. I with H. G., Montague, and H. G.'s younger son Frank into one; Mrs. Wells, Mrs. Shaw, a German guest and Bernard Shaw into the other. And when we alighted, there was Bernard Shaw paying out of "Candida," "How he Lied to her Husband," "Back to Methuselah" and "Saint Joan," for one vehicle, while H. G. Wells paid for the other out of "The Wife of Sir Isaac Harman," "Tono-Bungay," "Mr. Britling" and "Joan and Peter." The German guest was the producer of some neo-realistic films, the private production of which we were about to witness. I settled myself, between Mr. Wells and Mr. Shaw, to enjoy the spectacle. The first film showed a young literary aspirant down on his luck, and Wells said in a loud voice, which echoed through the darkness: "This is Gerhardi hawking his 'Futility' about." The next film presented Ivan the Terrible in his most extravagantly cruel moods, and Bernard Shaw said: "Why, instead of presenting all this bunkum that nobody believes in anyhow, don't they give us a Russian drama based on the depreciation of the currency?" The last film was of an advanced kind, dispensing altogether with pictures and human faces and merely expressing itself in a quick series of dots and dashes, triangular symbols and splashes which hurt the eyes. "Mr. Shaw," said the German producer, as the film came to a finish, "I will now explain to you the meaning of this picture."

Shaw looked at him blankly. "You *couldn't*," he said. Suddenly he rose to his feet, said he had work to do, and rushed away.

When we came out of the darkness into the afternoon

light of the street, Wells turned to me and said : " Well, you expressed the wish to see Arnold Bennett and we've shown you Arnold Bennett ; you expressed the wish to see Bernard Shaw and we've produced Bernard Shaw for you. Now for the next month or so the family will disperse, and Gerhardi will be pushed back into the cold world."

IX

THE BIG THREE

I have heard it said that Wells was not a patch on Shaw ; and I have heard it said that Shaw was not a patch on Wells ; and I have heard it said that Bennett was not a patch on either.

May I bring order into this chaos ?

Of the three Mr. Shaw has, to look at, the most genius, to read, the least ; Mr. Wells, to look at, the least genius, to read, the most ; and Arnold Bennett more of what the others have less, and less of what the others have more. What is so trying about the admirers of Bernard Shaw is that they are the stodgy backward folk who once, in Shaw's fresh and stimulating prime, were shocked by his revolutionary spirit, and now that the doors at which he hammered are wide open, admire him for his " prose style." Now Mr. Shaw is a great fighter : his style is a great fighting style. It is not adapted to other uses. He is thin, metallic in sound, and like mineral water to the taste—in fact, the champagne of table-waters. He has a curiously narrow range of experience. A grass-eating animal, who, however, looks as if he fed not on grass but on such things as insects and spiders. His judgment of literary values is based on whether a pantomime production did or did not knock over some old superstition. In a word, *ein guter Mensch aber schlechter Musikant*. The Germans use the word *Dichter* to distinguish a writer of prose whose imagination is of a quality to engage the forces of the soul, and who is thereby lifted to the rank of poet—a term formerly confined to writers of verse. I wish somebody—Mr. Bennett understood this best—would popularize the use of the word "poet" to designate the poetic quality in English prose writers, as a substitute for the unpalatable "creative writer," "literary artist," and so forth. It would help to distinguish authentic literature from that which is merely controversial and intellectual. Now the curious, to us irritating, anomaly about Mr. Shaw is that while he is not a poet, he is, owing to the befuddling effect of translations, regarded as such abroad, as well as by people in England who are not themselves poets and do not quite know what real poetry is. Shaw's flights into emotion are pitiable; pure tinsel. And he writes in one dimension, by intellect alone, which, on his own confession, when not determined by the soul, is a stick to beat anyone with. There was a novelty, a brightness, and withal a moral compulsion, about Bernard Shaw. The world is better and freer for his having lived. One admires the integrity of his character. One respects him as a master of witty, indignation. One reveres him as a great social reformer. No one would begrudge him the place he has attained, and the position he adorns so becomingly. But one is bewildered by the *literary* praises bestowed on him by statesmen like Mr. Churchill, as we should be if a man whom we admired as a lion tamer were declared the greatest dancer since Nijinsky because of the graceful economy with which he handled his whip, and who, encouraged by such praise, pronounced himself a super-dancer of the post-Diagelev school, explaining that no dancing was real or serious unless it had for its object the taming of wild animals. But by the time Shaw has mastered the lioness and all her cubs, Mr. Churchill and his kind, in sympathy with lions, the British lion especially, exclaim: "True, he had no business to enter that cage. Infernal cheek, disturbing a gallant old lion who is resting. But what a great dancer!"

Close on Mr. Shaw's heels came Mr. Wells, the most richly endowed of that generation but intimidated by the utilitarian example of the other, bitten by the same *Weltverbesserungswahn*. This, in Mr. Wells, is double the pity. It was natural for Mr. Shaw to disdain art for art's sake, since his art was a whip which he could not reasonably flourish for its own sake. Mr. Wells was different. Here was a rich, human, essentially poetic nature, simple, profound. But he chose to force his nature, harness it for social service. With paradoxical results. His hasty temper would get away with him while he was proving his point and, by exposing his bias, defeat his own end and all but ruin the general artistic effect of a novel. " We think," says somebody in Mr. Hugh Kingsmill's " The Return of William Shakespeare," " that if Mr. Wells were indefinitely protracted through the ages, the world would eventually consist of a collection of Utopias, each embodying a different idea of Mr. Wells's, and all on such bad terms with each other, that the ensuing Armageddon would come as a pleasant relief." On the other hand, such felicities, beauties and profundities as emerged inadvertently, while Mr. Wells was not looking, not only save his books but are of greater sociological value than his more conscious attempts in that direction.

And this is the double justification of authentic literature : that while giving pleasure it cures. Gogol and Dickens at their artistic best accomplished more for social reform than all the social reformers of their time put together. Genuine literature resents conscious intimidation. The great poet is concerned with one thing and one thing alone : the mystery which envelops the human soul into whose caverns he descends unconsciously, noting the strange things he finds there. " And," says Proust, " around such truths reached in oneself there will always float an atmosphere of poetry, the softness of a mystery which is but the vestige of the penumbra we must have traversed, an indication, marked exactly as by an altimeter, of the profundity of a work."

Mr. Wells flowered at a bad time, being caught in the reaction against what then was mistakenly believed to be " Art for art's sake." Now for any normal healthy artist, devoid of political ambition, it would be difficult to conceive for what other sake but that of the art in which he finds his happiest expression he should write, paint, build, sculpture, and compose. But the men who took the name of art in vain—Stevenson and Wilde and Pater and George Moore—indulged in something so superficial that there would have been no art in their performances had they not taken a proper pride in polishing their surfaces, since they had no depths to descend to. This strenuous floor polishing, an infinite capacity for taking pains to make their surfaces as shiny and slippery as possible, they called " style." And since one kind of varnish is so like another and will suit any floor surface, they would take a side glance, learn the trick from a neighbour, imitate, compare—which they called " playing the sedulous ape." Had there been any depth about them, any real value, they would have known that there is but one thing an original artist has in common with another—originality. They would have known that style is the leaves of the tree. No tree, no leaves. A writer's style is the measure of his personality, and cannot be acquired consciously. It shows unmistakably what you are : gives you away for what you are. Mr. Churchill's style, for example, full of bombast and " Armageddon," is a good platform style which, when you read it in a book, makes you smile. Lord Birkenhead's style, so agreeable and effective when listened to at a public meeting, shows the stuff he is made of when examined in an article. Only a great comprehensive spirit will produce a great comprehensive style. No ornament from outside will hide a man's nakedness. After Tolstoy, Tchehov, Proust this is obvious. But it must have been less obvious when Mr. Wells, who wanted to shake up England, stir up the world, was requested to lower his voice in the temple of art so as not to disturb the floor polishers ; and he gazed down on them, a little awed, a little amazed, on the men who would not look up because their devotion to art was so great that they must remain on their knees, polishing, polishing, till the style of their particular parquet outshone that of other competitors. And that astute, competent man, Arnold Bennett, also looked, and I daresay it was one of the many " things that had interested him." To such early intimidation from the stylists, we must ascribe Mr. Bennett's exaggerated admiration for Mr. Shaw's " English prose style " as a thing-in-itself, and Mr. Bennett's frequent assertions that so-and-so either can or cannot " write English "—as if there were a certain way of writing English. Mr. Wells, who more often than not is inclined to praise a novel on sociological grounds for the " waste " or " incompetence " in certain quarters which the author (all but unaware of it himself) is assumed to be exposing, nevertheless has his queer literary moments, as when, in the course of attacking Mr. Shaw's irresponsibility in the columns of the *Sunday Express*, he has a word of praise for the beauty of Mr. Shaw's English prose style : " I know enough of it to know how well Shaw does it " (or similar words), as if there were a certain special way of doing it suited to everyone. This from the most gifted writer of the day ! Mr. Bennett, who has a rich nature of nicely balanced qualities, reflects a smiling style flexible with tolerance, tenderness and gentle humour, only spoilt by a sort of perky knowingness, but redeemed again to some extent by the kind of irony which insists on the dire seriousness of these worldly-wise remarks, while also laughing at himself or any man who would speak thus seriously. The more facets a writer has to his personality, the more facets there will be to his style. Whereas Mr. Shaw's nature expresses itself in more or less good-humoured invective confined to showing up persons who are more fools than knaves ; his style, limited to this purpose, is a cold, rigid, colourless, strait-laced, though insidious, long-armed style that reaches out and gets the culprit by the throat.

This is the man who has knocked down more moral barricades than any other ; and who recommends us so to order our lives that when we die God shall be in our debt. It seems incredible that he is still with us.

The second time I saw Shaw was at Lord Swaythling's party for Ernst Toller. Shaw was talking to me when a hush fell on the room, and Toller began to read his poem about a man, probably himself, looking through the prison

bars at a swarm of swallows in the sky. "Die Schwalben!
die Schwalben! die Schwalben!" resounded his voice, while
Shaw and I tiptoed to the nearest sofa. There we sat, the
rest of the company spread in a semicircle before us. Shaw
whispered to me something I could not hear. I nodded
comprehendingly. And I thought : there, they are all
looking now at me and Shaw.

The cessation of Toller's reading marked the beginning
of a flank attack on Shaw. He was in the midst of a group
of young women, who laughed before Shaw had said anything.
"Mr. Shaw," piped one maiden, "I've just been over to
Ireland." "Did you get married ?" asked Shaw. Excru-
ciating laughter greeted the remark. A foreign London
correspondent, attracted by the merriment and told what
Shaw had said, took out pencil and notebook.

Elderly ladies were closing in on Shaw. "Mr. Shaw,"
said an Ambassador's wife, "I want you to read my novel
in manuscript and write to me *frankly exactly* what you think
of it. I don't mind what you say." "I am too old," Shaw
defended himself, "I don't read anything but Walter Scott."
Then Mrs. Shaw came and took her husband away.

Shaw and I—I was dreaming—were, owing to scarcity
of accommodation in some remote country sanatorium,
confined within one bed. The war was in full swing, men
were sunk in the mud of trenches only a few yards away, so
we deemed our accommodation ample. Shaw was very
benevolent and smiling, and admitted me into his bed with
the courtesy of a true socialist who saw nothing private in
it, but regarded it as a national institution. Any scruples
that I might have had on account of being confined under
the same blanket with an octogenarian vanished when I
remembered that he was also a vegetarian—and so scrupulously clean. We each had our pillow at opposite ends of
the bed, and Shaw's feet hardly ever got in the way. The
whole thing was so civilized—Shaw so benignant. I told
him a long story which I thought might interest him. But

Shaw, I realized, was a very old man ; his attention, though he knitted his brows, tended to relax, he wearied of the story, missed the point, yet received it with courtesy. We lay like this in the dark, and at last I asked Shaw how old he was. He said he was ninety-seven, and as he said it he realized he couldn't have much longer to live, three years at most ; but it was all right and he was prepared for it, still it rather tended to distort one's sense of values, make one throw one's whole weight into the remaining three years ; and when, to take off his thoughts from his impending death, I came out with another story, he said he could not listen, he had only three years left to himself, but he lay quite still with the same expression of benevolence on his aged face, passing the brief balance of his life in gentle courtesy.

X

LORD BIRKENHEAD FORGETS

I met the Smith of His Own Fortune, who, like Disraeli, has not disdained the appellation of adventurer, after having listened to him at the Oxford Union. Lord Birkenhead, by diverting his activity from the Bar to Westminster, depleted his coffers of potential gold ; and so the second earl, true to the device engraved on the shield of his father, will likewise have to prove himself a Smith of His Own Fortune. " This is," said our host, " Lord Birkenhead. You've said something about him in your book. What was it ? " Lord Birkenhead put his podgy palm into my hand, leaving it to me to exert the customary pressure. However, M. de Charlus only tendered young Proust his middle finger. My remark about Birkenhead—" To take the Churchills and Birkenheads seriously is not to know how to be serious "—was not of a nature to be removed from the context with advantage to the author, and I confined myself to the statement that it had been airy. " I have not read your book," said Lord Birkenhead, in suave sonorous periods, more suitable to a court of law than to informal conversation, " but I shall certainly take an early opportunity of perusing it; and if what you say is correct I shall take it to heart, and if it is uninformed I shall despise it." During dinner he said that all Jews were sadists and all Bolsheviks Jews, hence the cruelty in Russia. I was saddened by this indifferent reasoning in a Cabinet Minister; my heart sank and I felt I must render him first aid. When I had finished, Birkenhead looked at me cloudily, as if asking: "Who is this youth who dares heckle me?" When, however, I added that I had spent two-thirds of my life in Russia, he said: "In that case I shall certainly take an early opportunity of re-examining my facts." After dinner my mistrust of Lord Birkenhead evaporated completely as he began to address himself more and more to me. We often feel for certain public men, when we read their speeches and articles, an acute dislike, which, after meeting them personally, changes to an exaggerated liking, since we feel ashamed of our unworthy feelings and are anxious to justify our recantation, perhaps with unduly generous zeal. Let this be a warning to any readers who may be forming an unfavourable judgment of the author of the present book. If there is anything in my book you don't like, let us meet, let us discuss it, let us thrash it out together.

Birkenhead told how, when he was an athletic young man at Oxford, Oscar Wilde joined them at lunch and indulged in his famous talk, which on this occasion was all—"I will tell you a fairy tale . . ." while the young man, who was later to assist in placing the story-teller in prison, gathered more and more of the bottles around himself. Lord Birkenhead, who, at a later trial, referred to Wilde as "that unhappy child of genius," endeared himself to me by expressing his admiration for the creative literary gift. With unconvincing humility, he deprecated his own "first-class brains" when, in an endeavour to return the compliment, I drew allusion to them. He had, he said, a "certain facility for dealing with a great mass of legal material." But he was completely devoid of the artistic gift. Music meant nothing to him. As a writer, he said, he was nothing but a journalist.

I disputed this warmly. I remembered a flattering reference, in a review of a book of his, to a paper on Kitchener; and though I had not read this paper I now defended it as a piece of writing coming very near to what is known as creative writing.

"How nice of you to say so!" exclaimed Lord Birkenhead, with genuine pleasure. "Michael Arlen said the same thing to me; and indeed I myself think that in that essay I have perhaps come nearer to the kind of imaginative writing which, had I but the gift, I would have so willingly pursued as a vocation." After that Lord Birkenhead suggested that if I "did him the honour" of sending him my book he would be "proud" to send me one of his own. He again placed the palm of his hand in mine, on which, however, I this time declined to exert any pressure, and asked me if he could give me a lift in his car.

Disarmed by his unexpected charm and modesty, I at once sent him a copy of "The Polyglots," with an inscription designed to please him. But by the time, a few days later, I met him again, at a large party at the Savoy Hotel, no book of his had found its way to my flat. He sat there, in a state of extreme lassitude, caressing his dog. I reminded him that I had not had his book. He looked up at me. It was obvious that he did not recognize me. His voice was tired and querulous. "*Which* book?" he kept asking. "I've written many books. D'you see that man over there? He is my secretary. Ask him, he'll send you my book. Any book you like. Send it to-morrow. I can't think of these things. I'm a busy man. I'm a Cabinet Minister. I've got to think of all kinds of things. Can't think of books."

Affairs of State must have exhausted his vitality, his eyes were half closed.

His book had ceased to interest me, and his secretary had not begun to. After a while Lord Birkenhead turned his head and saw that I still stood behind him. There was a pause. "Th . . . thank you," he said, "for your book."

XI

MR. LLOYD GEORGE CONTEMPLATES THE CARPET

A blissful ignorance is perhaps the best basis for meeting eminent men. You are introduced to Mr. Lloyd George. You smile a smile of semi-recognition and extend your hand : " Mr. Lloyd George—in politics, I think ? " The Prince of Wales—" Oh, yes, related, I understand, to the reigning house ? "

Mr. Lloyd George looked tricky in the extreme. As he sat there slowly wagging his leonine head with the fine snow-white hair, he looked as if he were up to some awful political mischief.

Lord Beaverbrook, with his usual air of being able to produce any rabbit you liked out of his hat, said : " This is Mr. Lloyd George." To make Lloyd George interested, he asked me, had I written about him—no ; had I mentioned him in my books—no ; had I reflected upon him profoundly —no ; had I—no. Mr. Lloyd George looked down on the floor and said, sepulchrally : " That's done it ! "

When I turned away to another group, I was aware that Beaverbrook was telling Lloyd George something about me. A moment later Mr. Lloyd George came up to say good-bye. " I enjoyed a book of yours," he said, " about Vladivostok. I can't remember the title."

" ' Futility,' wasn't it ? " I suggested not uneagerly.

But Mr. Lloyd George either did not hear or deemed he had said enough. " Good-bye," he said, " good-bye," and he went.

XII

LORD ROTHERMERE'S EAR-ACHE

They fascinate me, these great men of action, newspaper magnates, captains of industry, kings of the mart. Wealth, like kingship, has its distinction. A millionaire, like a king, is a symbol. How much finer if kings were to sign themselves, as referred to in Shakespeare, " France," " England," etc. In the same way a millionaire who represents numerous companies, banks, enterprises, becomes, whatever he looks like, the symbol of hidden power and wealth. A millionaire, it has been said, rarely looks his part. But he does. For, if he does not, the very insignificance of his looks, contrasting with the idea of his might, enhances our impression of the man. " Just fancy," we say to ourselves, " that little man controlling such vast power ! " And we gain the impression that all great men must be little. I have seen tall, portly millionaires whose bulk suggested weight in gold. I have seen dapper little men whose smallness emphasized that they were yet the masters of men twice their size. And I have seen shabbily dressed millionaires whose clothes suggested that they could afford not to dress well. And in each of these cases they looked peculiarly representative, in their own way, of the idea they stood for.

They are a queer race. You delight in telling them, because they delight in hearing, of your modest way of living, your small, laughable items of expenditure, the absurd rent you pay for your accommodation, and you feel as it were that in the mere fact of such narration, and their amused astonishment, these things must have receded into the past. And you are surprised that at the end of this delightful talk none of these smiling millionaires has grasped the chance of settling a sufficient sum of money on you to make your tale indeed a legend of the past.

Yet their attentions are enchanting. To hear flattering references to my " brains " from financiers, men of affairs, after being regarded for twenty years as a congenital idiot by my father and brother, was very comforting. Had Thomas Hardy praised me it would have only meant praise of one doleful soul by another. But " I am pumping his brains "— this from Lord Beaverbrook was agreeable. " In England we have plenty of everything except brains. Let me have your address "—this from Lord Rothermere was no less so. May the Recording Angel set this down against their faults !

Very strangely there seems to have been a line of demarcation in my intelligence : from the day I left Russia I ceased to be stupid and great lords of action conceived me to be brilliant. It pleased me that here was a man even richer than Lord Beaverbrook, and one presumably with an even firmer hold on the realities of life as expressed by the stock market, and that he should immediately point to my " brains " as worthy of cultivation. This at once stirred a response in my mind. " That man," I said to myself, " must have brains to have discovered my own without having read a line of my writing. He is a thousand times more successful than ever was my father, who considered me a fool. He is the real financial genius, the mechanism behind Lord Northcliffe, who, perhaps, was just the façade."

I met Lord Rothermere for the first time when discussing the Immaculate Conception with Lord Beaverbrook. We were in the thick of the discussion when Lord Rothermere was announced. Beaverbrook was so engrossed in the subject, so excited over it, that he had forgotten to dress, although he had asked Lord Rothermere to dinner. Lord Beaverbrook has a disconcerting habit of asking two people he is introducing what they think of each other—a method of introduction more agreeable to the introducer than to the introduced, who find it difficult to think of something profound or amusing to say on the spur of the moment. Lord Beaverbrook, introducing me, asked what I thought of Lord Rothermere, and while I giggled foolishly, ferreted an opinion out of me that didn't sound happy. Lord Rothermere produced on me an impression surprisingly sympathetic. He gurgled bashfully, like a girl, and tempered his uneasiness with manly grunts of resentment. Meanwhile I could say nothing significant. Then Lord Rothermere was dragged into the debate on the Immaculate Conception. I think he had arrived on business, and would have been well content to leave the Immaculate Conception alone. But Lord

Beaverbrook would not have it so and ferreted an opinion out of Lord Rothermere.

The next time I saw Lord Rothermere was at Monte Carlo, at a dinner party. He recognized me and came up to me and all through dinner he was particularly genial. " Say what you like," I thought to myself, " these great newspaper kings and captains of industry are a much maligned race of men, sorely misjudged individuals with golden hearts." Two of Lord Rothermere's nieces or cousins, pretty girls, were there and added zest to life. I suggested to Lord Rothermere that Lord Beaverbrook was a man of wide sympathies. " He's a live wire," was his reply. Next, we all went to the Casino and I sat between Lords Rothermere and Beaverbrook on a sofa, discussing religion, while the croupier cried : " Metez vos mises, messieurs. Faites vos jeux, messieurs. Ils sont faits ? Rien ne va plus ! "

A night or two later I again sat facing Lord Rothermere at a dinner party at the "Negresco." We talked of Byron, Sheridan and Thomas Hardy. The blue-eyed Mrs. Richard Norton sat next to me. She said she had recently seen Tchehov's " Sea Gull " and had wept over it. At any statement denoting too much emotion or enthusiasm Lord Rothermere made a slightly deprecatory *moue*. He seemed suspicious of overpraise. When I praised Hardy, Lord Rothermere made the same *moue*. I asked him if he did not think highly of Hardy. He said that he was much praised ; this made him suspicious. I urged that his brother, Lord Northcliffe, had thought highly of Hardy. Lord Rothermere looked at me. He was not keen on contemporary English novelists. But he was enthusiastic over Sheridan and extolled the " School for Scandal." Byron's Letters appealed to him also, and he said he would send me a copy of them. Byron, he said, was every inch a poet, was a poet in appearance, in attitude, in renown. Lord Rothermere approved of my secluded and modest existence. He deprecated the desire on the part of a certain novelist to own a yacht. He commended me for living in the South of France all the year round and hinted, obscurely, that I would make all the more money in the end.

The next day he asked me over to his place on Cap Martin. I was astonished at the modest size of the house. It was a villa which once belonged to Mrs. Williamson, who wrote those innumerable motor-car novels and knew her geography. There was a lovely terrace overlooking the bay, but viewed from behind, the villa might have been some suburban house in the north of London. Lord Rothermere, moreover, had ear-ache. And he was anxious to get back to England but could not secure a berth in the train, since they were all booked up for several weeks ahead. His garden was cut off from direct access to the sea, and Lord Rothermere was cut off from immediate access to London. With all his money he could not avoid the ear-ache. With all his money he could not get back to London, for his own sense of the ridiculous prevented him from buying a train. A sudden feeling of the futility of wealth came over me. A business associate was staying with Lord Rothermere, and he and Lord Rothermere's brother, St. John Harmsworth, gave me much pious encouragement, and the three of them gave me lunch and tea and a wealth of good wishes.

I drove away with St. John Harmsworth, who, though incapacitated in a motor accident some years ago, had founded a flourishing business, the table-water Perrier. He told me that his brother Rothermere had this little rough air because he had a soft heart, as soft fish have a shell to protect themselves from the world ; or like a dog at the gate who only barks out of a sense of canine propriety, wagging his tail timidly. His garden had no fence but was open to the public. He had that very day given a gift of a great London park to the nation. And now he had ear-ache.

Arrived back at my little Toulon cottage with the well and its rusty chain off the wheel, I did not resent my poverty. I had no ear-ache. I had not to wait for a berth in the train, and there was no business calling me to London : and I had direct access to the sea.

CHAPTER TWELVE

THE COTTAGE AT TOULON

I

MRS. WHARTON OBJECTS

LORD BEAVERBROOK'S hospitality proved so absorbing that Mr. Curtis Brown feared I would not be able to write a new novel unless I retired abroad. I joined my mother and sister at Marseilles, and after making inquiries went on to Toulon, where I rented, against my mother's advice, a cottage, which called itself a villa, in an orchard, more picturesque than comfortable. One glance at it was sufficient to convince my mother that the house was uninhabitable, but my eye insisted on seeing " possibilities " in it. Whenever now I see " possibilities " in any line of accommodation, my mother knows at once what to expect. Nevertheless, the little house had the first roof which I could call my own, and though it leaked and the furniture made for me by a village carpenter was of the scrappiest, I was not displeased with the abode, which, including vines, an orchard and stables, cost me in rent £18 per annum.

There were extensive grounds descending to the sea in terraces, but they were very wet. Indeed, so wet that if one ventured beyond the gravel path which led up to the gate, one sank ankle deep in the red soil of southern France. Below was a fence, and beyond it a narrow railway track along which people threw their empty tins and other rubbish. But every couple of hours in twenty-four, a tiny tea-kettle of a locomotive puffed along, trailing in its wake a string of undersized coaches, and gave a piercing whistle each time it passed the house at the bend, lurching perilously over the curve on its way to Hyères.

At Hyères lived Mrs. Wharton, a journey of some forty minutes by car. To be able to visit her frequently I purchased a horse and trap. The tribulations following this enterprise have been recorded in " Pending Heaven." Mrs. Wharton was very much in favour of my getting a little Citroën instead. When I said, reproachfully, " You don't seem to encourage my coming to see you on horseback," she answered : " I don't at all want to seem inhospitable ; but I admit one would scarcely enjoy seeing your horse nibbling one's favourite pear tree."

Mrs. Wharton's garden is famous, and her fastidiousness accordingly not unjustified. I had not been in Toulon a day before she had caused her friend, Mme. de Préveaux, to call on me to take me to the Governor's ball in Toulon. The Governor, an admiral, inquired of another lady, who was with us, what I had written ; and she answered out of her ignorance : " Ah ! des belles choses," after which I was accorded all the honours which an educated Navy like the French pays to literature. The French Navy, I may add, is literary at heart. While we call our battleships *Vindictive*, if not *Malignant*, they call theirs *Voltaire*, *Pascal* and, if I may anticipate, *Marcel Proust*.

Toulon is the Portsmouth of France, and Naval families are socially in the ascendant ; and writers are looked up to by French Naval officers. When Paul Valèry came down to Toulon he was fêted by the quarter-deck. Imagine Mr. T. S. Eliot being received with the same enthusiasm at Portsmouth, Naval ratings lining up for his autograph ! The Commander of a French battleship at Toulon cultivated a romantic Alfred de Musset melancholia and played Chopin with exquisite sensibility. Another wrote novels of the misunderstood, anti-gregarian, enemy-of-the-people variety, and hated "good fellows." He went about in a two-seater with a chauffeur, and frequently called on me and took me to his windy house on the cliff ; and one day he confided to me

the theme of his novel and asked my advice. Was he justified
in writing a full-length novel to expose a friend who had
turned truant? His friend had borrowed money from him
in order to start a magazine in which he promised he would
boom his work; but had failed to boom him, failed to found
the magazine, but had kept the money. Hence his violent
hatred, which demanded expression in a work of fiction.
Was he justified in proceeding with the writing? I said that
it would do him a world of good to let off steam, but that
such a course, though morally unimpeachable, was perhaps
not to be recommended on artistic grounds. But before
expressing a definite opinion, I should like to see something
of the manuscript. This, shown to me, confirmed my opinion
that hate was a bad conductor of art. For already in the opening chapters the novelist was flaying his hero in these terms:
" This incredible villain was born in a squalid Paris slum, of
undesirable parents, and already in early childhood revealed,
though in a latent form, that degradation of character which
I am about to unfold." " Goethe," I said, " counselled
against hate, which, he said, was a phantom of one's own
imagination. It left the object of one's hate untouched,
while making a slave of oneself to the person hated. But
love, I submit, is more rewarding: it renews the man continually. So, please, do not grow bitter; that way lies ruin.
I once knew a journalist who was bitter. He wrote with
clenched teeth, muttering: 'There, eat it! Choke yourself
over it!' Closely written, impenetrable stuff. His book
was a failure. I knew," I added, " another man. He was
insulted by his employer, but was afraid of losing his job.
So he wrote an insulting book about his employer. But
the book was not accepted. He then wrote and insulted the
publishers." He listened to me attentively, but later we
became estranged, then quarrelled, and eventually separated,
my friend engaging to ventilate his grievance against me in
an early work of literature.

As I only had a young Italian girl, who chared for me in
the morning, and I neither could nor would be bothered to

cook myself, I lived almost entirely on fruit and milk.   One
day a party of French Naval officers with their wives, who
wore large picture hats, descended on me unexpectedly.   I
offered them milk by way of drinks, as I did not indulge in
other beverages, which they interpreted as " originality "
on my part.   I later overheard fragments of a conversation.
" A wonderful, original man," said a young woman.   " You go
there, and he offers you milk.   Delightfully unconventional."

At Carqueiranne, about forty minutes from Toulon and an
equal distance from Hyères, lived Mme. de Béarn, a sort of
combined Mrs. Guinness-Lady Cunard, and between her and
Mrs. Wharton flitted all that has distinguished itself in literature, in the arts, or has failed to distinguish itself as the issue
of illustrious parents.   At Mrs. Wharton's I met Paul Valéry,
who told us of the extravagant way he had been received by
D'Annunzio.   Edith Wharton shook her head at the end of
the recital, and said : " Yes, but think of the simplicity, the
modesty of someone like Bach.   No, great souls aren't made
of such stuff."

Another day Princess Bibesco, whose personality might
have been borrowed from the prodigious world of Rabelais,
submerged all in an ocean of brilliant talk.   Neither Edith
Wharton, nor I, nor anyone else could open our mouths,
but I thoroughly enjoyed that part of her talk which dealt
with her father, Lord Oxford's, enjoyment of my " Futility."

On the peak of the tallest hill of Hyères, the ultra-modern
Comte Charles de Noailles with his attractive wife had built
himself a sort of futuristic fortress.   Across the bay, on the
isthmus of Tamaris, Edouard Bourdet and his wife entrenched
themselves in a white house on a cliff.   At the far end of
Hyères a French family, flying the flag of Citroën, were greatly
admired by virtue of two exquisite daughters who graced
and exhilarated bathing by moonlight.   At the foot of Mrs.
Wharton's hill, the gifted and charming Comtesse de Lévis-
Mirepoix, authoress, gave small literary parties.   With these
points of attraction within a radius conveniently to be covered
in my trap, life was more than bearable.

At the other extreme, I indulged the joys to be procured from contact with simple people. One morning on my way to lunch at Hyères, I passed a lovely blonde peasant girl, who was working the pump in the road. I forgot my lunch with Paul Valèry, invited the blonde and her little sister into my trap, and took them for a drive. I made her sit next to me in the narrow trap so that I could feel her hips against mine ; and as we approached La Garde suddenly I kissed her. She was to me the virgin, sun-warmed soil of southern France ; I tried to penetrate into the dream of her life. But next time I met her, the village boys jeered, and her position in the village, if she were seen with me, a foreigner, not a village boy, would, I understood, become untenable.

Another day I passed a girl on the road who was pushing a bread cart. I stopped my horse, attached her cart to mine, invited her into my trap and we drove off, not too quickly, for the cart rattled precariously. But we delivered all the bread. I made an appointment with her for the next day. But she appeared with her friend, a girl of such astounding proportions that we could scarcely squeeze ourselves into the trap. My horse, too, found it an uphill task, and finally stood still on the tramlines and refused to budge, attracting a crowd, and a policeman who made unkind comments. I had to unload my passengers and water the horse, who, recovering a little, went on of his own accord. Unlike the other girl, this one had no reputation to lose, and from each trap we passed she was hailed by a man, who had at one time or another failed to make an honest woman of her, and every time I kissed her she hinted she would like a gold wrist-watch. And when she came to my house she resented bitterly that I had only milk to offer her, which, unlike the Naval society guests, she did not regard as the quaint and imponderable originality of an artist, but the beverage of a milksop. She was venal ; and we men quickly tire of impurity.

There was a third, the daughter of an Admiral yet the bosom friend of the milkmaid, who introduced her to me.

She was a nurse in a Paris hospital, and had won *le premier prix de courage*, having successfully passed the test of sleeping in the same bed with a male skeleton, nicknamed " Anatole," one who perhaps in life had longed in vain for a girl as beautiful as her. Fresh from this experience, she would cycle to my cottage early in the morning while I was still asleep, and jump into my room through the unshuttered window. One morning while her brother was riding my horse, we gave a swift expression to the passion in us, but disengaged ourselves in the nick of time, for the brother, instead of coming back through the door, as we expected, climbed up the balcony and entered through my window. It was a hot morning. These things, since they persist in the memory, are the contrary of the fleeting impressions they are deemed to be.

II

THE GIRL FROM VIENNA

At the end of the winter my mother returned to England, and I, finding the maidens of France not all that they are deemed to be, invited the watchmaker's daughter of Vienna to come and share the summer with me. She could only talk German, and the French, who had not yet got over the war, threw baleful glances at us, which made me feel we were jarring on their nerves ; but she scorned them for their stupidity in not understanding a language which offered no difficulties to her, and their inability to understand her provoked indignant exclamations : " Aber, das ist ja unerhört ! " As the months passed she grew more and more serious, talked more and more of " reactions," " her real ' I '," and so forth, till even the things of the senses annoyed me by the false poetry she imported into them. With an eye to effect she would say, " My sister always talks to me of married love. To me it is too sacred a subject for words." Trudl was always seeking her real " I," and was always being seduced anew, and got into trouble, and always told every fresh lover :

" You will never be like Hans." Sometimes an air of complete forgetfulness would descend on her, and she would say, " I thought you were Hans." There is a limit to my powers of impersonating a dead man. And when at last her stay came to an end, and returning from the station after seeing her off to Vienna, I chanced to come across a packet of her letters to me, I was amazed at their unmeaning import. " Surely," I thought, " I can burn them now. I will never want them."

But when, later, no news came from her, I began to perceive a unifying beauty in the chaos and confusion of our days. I re-read her letters about the " unforgettable hours we had known together." And it was true. Her poems which at one time nauseated me now touched me by their naïve emotion. Her uncertainty itself which I once thought ludicrous now charmed me. I remembered how when I had asked her whether a poem of hers was good she had merely shrugged her shoulders.

" Don't you know ? " I had asked irritably. " Have you no idea yourself ? "

" How do I know ? I'm too objective."

" You mean subjective."

" Yes—subjective. Too subjective."

Now her ignorance touched me to the heart. The little details of her girlhood, to which I had listened cursorily during our walks together, rose up and filled my thoughts. Too late ! Too late !

When my mother came back she took a little house of her own, so that whenever we quarrelled we could each retire dramatically to our own house, which we would do, only to come back again in the morning. For the most part we lived together ; either in her house or in mine.

What a winter ! What miseries to endure ! We were, it is true, on the *New* Riviera. But was it near Nice or Monte Carlo ? Near enough, one had thought, at the time of settling at Toulon. But for all the difference it made we might have stayed in England. My mother's life consisted in going to the *épicerie* two or three times a day, buying an eighth of a kilo of ham, half a kilo of cheese, and some nondescript stuff to throw into the soup. Eggs, thank God, we bought from a peasant neighbour, who, to save us trouble, as a rule sent her son with them, who delivered them unwillingly. Milk was brought to the house by a grimy milkmaid at unforeseen hours, and if we were not on the spot to pay her, she took it away again, so that we had to go a mile to fetch it, or, if we preferred a short cut, we climbed over barbed-wire fences in the slush and the dark, while dogs barked ferociously at us and even snapped at our heels. Nor did the weather favour us. It rained for weeks on end. Our little servant girl was exhausted. The roof leaked. The chimney would not draw. The proprietor's boasted drainage proved ineffective. The walls were so wet that my boots got all green and mouldy inside within a week of arrival. Apart from the proprietor, who came at week-ends and ruined two days of the week for us, and our peasant neighbour, whom we tried to avoid, and a pious family who practised Adventist rites assiduously, we had no company but our own ; and an exchange of opinion invariably ended by dusk in our withdrawing into ourselves, I to my cubicle, my mother to hers.

If my mother and I differ occasionally, it is no reflection on either of us. To my father I only said what I deemed agreeable ; to my mother I tell the truth. I have no thought, no feeling that I cannot share with my mother ; and she is like a second conscience to me, her eyes like a mirror reflecting my own image. My irritation is that of Hannibal seeing in the mirror the image of him seen by his mother. She has passed on, with her blue eyes and fair complexion, her sense of humour and reality to all but the youngest of her children, my youngest sister having retained the brown eyes together with an unhumorous nobility of nature, essentially my father's. Under my tuition my mother has developed an amazing understanding of literature, a blow having been dealt by me at the prestige of cotton-spinning. Had my father lived longer even he might have begun to write books.

III

THE CHOICER SPIRITS

I have heard the integrity of my oft-expressed admiration
for Hugh Kingsmill as a writer questioned by friends of
mine; and Mr. Humbert Woolfe has even suggested that
Hugh Kingsmill is another name for myself. Others think
that my literary enthusiasm for his writings is biased by
friendship. The truth is my literary enthusiasm for him
has inveigled me into a precarious friendship. I feel in
regard to Hugh Kingsmill the satisfaction of a man who
backs an outsider knowing him to be a " dead cert." It is,
of course, possible that Mr. Kingsmill has, unconsciously
perhaps, forecast his future in the lines :

> " I heard men crying in the streets
> That the horse my shirt was on,
> The great horse Sprig o' Rosemary,
> Had finished last but one.

" Last but one ! To me that is even bitterer than last, more
humiliating. The great horse Sprig o' Rosemary ! And
victory had seemed so sure. The pity of it ! Oh life, oh
life ! "

About this time Alec Waugh sent me a copy of " Georgian
Stories for 1925," with an invitation to contribute to the
1926 series. The volume contained a story which gave
me such extraordinary pleasure that I could not conceal it
in my reply to his letter. Alec Waugh sent my letter on to
the author of the story, Hugh Kingsmill, who promptly
responded by sending me the book, " The Dawn's Delay,"
which included this story. This was the beginning of a
friendship which has been not uneventful. It has survived
two storms, which so dislocated our lives that each of us
remains to this day to the other's mother a sinister influence
in the career of her son. Kingsmill's habit, I regret to say,

is to abscond and set up house with somebody in whom I have invested a good deal of emotion, and then to defend the purity of their hearth against my visits, though indulgent enough to consent to meet me outside his new home. His personality helped to provide me with a hero for " Pending Heaven." In return, I may claim to have provided him with the main idea of his book " The Return of William Shakespeare." He is still the greatest stimulant, the most congenial spirit I have yet met. But at that time I had not yet met him, and the stimulation was provided by correspondence. A person in his " Dawn's Delay " called Polmont, was, I thought, a prototype of the author; and I was not wrong. And as I read about Polmont, how I wished he had already arrived and we were going on a walking tour in Touraine, and talking together as one can only talk with a kindred spirit.

" Polmont glowed as they left the inn. A spring day in Touraine ! He felt akin to Balzac and Rabelais, and strode capaciously. He felt akin to du Bellay, and drifted, drifted, conceiting himself a pensive shade.

" ' Azay-le-Rideau ! ' he murmured, ' Azay-le-Rideau ! ' The sweet name of the little village enchanted him. His heart yearned over its inhabitants. A stout woman was standing in a doorway, and he waved his hand to her; and when she smiled back placidly he could have wept for joy over the excellence of human nature. His companion sighed.

" ' What, sagging, man ? ' boomed Polmont. ' Look round you ! Pluck up your heart ! Rich prose, Glayde, rich prose —these cobbled streets, snug houses, plentiful food, good wine, and love and love ! Exuberance and strength ! And the gently-flowing Indre, Glayde—there's poetry; and the bright sky beyond the line of that slope. There lies the South—blue hills and tiny horses bearing tiny cavaliers past toy castles. Isn't there a memory that includes all memories ? Is it mere years and facts we recall ? Do we not remember centuries and the dreams of dead men ? Ah ! The château !

How it all comes back to me ! Out into the world beyond these trees, Glayde ! High politics, bloody slaughter : then home again, white clasping arms, rest after a long war. Oh, Glayde ! Glayde ! Glayde !'

" ' Polmont,' Glayde quavered suddenly, ' don't you think that they at any rate must have been happy, those old kings and their mistresses, in this charming place ? It's as beautiful as a dream, these turrets and spires, this stream wandering here and there, the grass, the trees. Perhaps after all it's been worth while, I mean this world, life generally, simply because these wonderful creatures once lived here, and were happy, happy.'

" ' And yet,' he added, after a pause, ' I dare say this notion of their happiness is merely another illusion, due perhaps to my having drunk somewhat freely, that is for me. I dare say they were as miserable as the rest of us. It's a poor world, Polmont. Why should we funk death and destruction ? Man ! ' he yelled, ' why the devil should we ? ' ' "

I was reading " The Dawn's Delay " when Rebecca West, who had heard I was in the South of France, wrote to me in these pleasing terms :

" I have been told," she wrote, " that you have spoken of me without active repugnance," and she suggested my meeting her at Antibes. I went. Miss West offered me tea in the garden, but she had a strange worried look in her eye. She seemed distracted by something, and failed to make the most of my stay. She is, however, a witty woman and has a beautiful cooing voice. She also has, as I was careful to point out to her, a " weitverbreiteter Name," which Goethe said was undeniably one of the good things in this world. I urged on Miss West how singularly she had been endowed with this gift—singularly, I explained, since usually it is accompanied by another.

Lloyd Morris, an American critic, or, as his mother who was with him put it, *the* American critic, was staying with us at the same hotel. And there was a story about him that nobody could tell, least of all Morris himself, what his books were called. Once, under pressure, he consented to give the titles of his books on condition that his questioner went bathing with him. Having swum out a mile, the exhausted companion said to him, " Now, Morris, tell me ! What are the titles of your books ? "

" Help ! " he cried. " I am drowning."

Hugh Kingsmill did not arrive at once. He sent a herald in the shape of a gaunt, red-bearded young man called John Holms, who had never published a book but accepted the description of him as a genius without a wink or smile. He said that when a man had a great deal in him it took a long time to boil. Starved of intellectual companionship, I was delighted to listen to him. His literary judgment enchanted me. I had been asked to contribute to T. P.'s, which I had been told was looking for new writers, and in the purity of my joy at meeting again a cultured spirit, I suggested to Holms that I should introduce him to the paper. But he looked at me with great pity. " T. P.'s ! " he murmured with infinite sadness, " T. P.'s ! "

We dined in town, and on the way back we bought a bottle of wine and talked and talked till late into the morning. I provided him with a room for the night ; and in the morning for breakfast he went out into the orchard and ate grapes. Then he took up his hat and cane and rucksack and was gone.

Holms, like Lloyd Morris, was reluctant to tell you what he had written, but I discovered he carried with him an old copy of *The Calendar of Modern Letters*, which contained his one and only story. I borrowed it, and promised to send it back without fail, but was unable to finish the story, Holms's wife telegraphing that they required it immediately as proof that Holms was a writer to enable him to secure a *carte d'identité*.

Two years later, Holms visited me in London. He arrived in a grand Rolls-Royce lent to him by a friend ; but he wore a very old mackintosh. We went for a long drive together, and the immaculate chauffeur regarded us with faint distaste.

IV

MR. HUGH KINGSMILL ARRIVES

I have consecrated the opening chapter of " Pending
Heaven " to the arrival of Hugh Kingsmill in Toulon and
the extraordinary day we spent together. He did not disappoint my expectations. He was indeed exactly like
Polmont. " Come on, old man," he exclaimed as he took
me by the arm and marched me on as though he and not I
were the resident. He strode capaciously, his arms swinging
to and fro ; he walked thus with a sudden burst of initiative
as who might say : " Come on now, old man, we'll show 'em
what we can do ! "

We boarded an open tram, the clanking familiarity of
which palled on me. But I noticed that Kingsmill sat beside
me with a wondrous smile ; and when an Italian peasant
passed us in his donkey-cart Hugh murmured beatifically,
and when, screeching, we curved into Toulon past a slatternly
old woman who was hanging out her washing, Hugh, like
Polmont, waved his hand to her, and when she smiled he
said these folk of the Midi were hard to beat for sheer
excellence of human nature.

Hugh Kingsmill, I saw at once, was made for open spaces.
His voice would carry well across a prairie. He would do
well as Wotan summoning his vassals to his side in a loud,
persistent war cry. All the Lunns have resonant voices,
said to be the result of rounding up tourists. For Hugh
Kingsmill Lunn (to give him his full name) is the second son
of Sir Henry Lunn, while George Lunn is his uncle. In
their movements, in their affection for each other, the brothers
Lunn are bulky. When Brian Lunn was getting married, his
brother Hugh consigned his wedding present, two dozen
volumes of the " Encyclopædia Britannica," to the registry
office. After the ceremony the young couple departed
hurriedly by Underground to catch their train at Victoria,
their witnesses at the ceremony each carrying six loose

volumes of the "Encyclopædia," which they flung into the train after the bridal pair, who set off with them on their honeymoon to Oberammergau.

A brother officer in the war gives this picture of Hugh Kingsmill. "He has a very sympathetic nature, but at times, through thoughtlessness, gives the impression of being selfish . . . he is one of those people whom nature never intended to live in a confined space. . . . If he does not knock over the candle, he upsets the table and scatters the food all over the floor. Failing either of these little acts he kicks the brazier over, or looks for a stud he has not lost, carefully holding a dripping candle over your tunic all the time. He has other little ways such as dropping jam on the petrol can which we use for sitting on, or snatching away the only light just as one is negotiating a difficult corner, in the desire to find his fountain pen which he is holding all the time in his left hand. . . ." It is not unusual for subtle and delicate artists to express themselves clumsily in real life. In this Hugh Kingsmill was not unlike Beethoven, who, according to Ries, was very awkward and maladroit in his behaviour. "There was a total lack of grace about his clumsy movements. He could rarely take anything in his hands without letting it fall cr smashing it. He would often knock his inkstand into his piano, which stood by his writing-desk. No furniture was safe when he was near it— least of all if it was valuable ; everything was knocked over, soiled and broken. It is a mystery how he managed to shave himself, so many were the cuts on his face. He could never learn to dance in time."

Hugh Kingsmill usually broke something or set something on fire in mere inadvertency, and when I proffered the mildest objection would exclaim in the voice of a man outraged in his deepest feelings, " Damn it all, you're the host ! " identifying the vocation of a host with that of a martyr. But this did not prevent him from being as sensitive as Beethoven on the artistic side, and he had the same look of human suffering in his eyes. It was clear to me at once that here was a man who understood exactly what forces, what interests were implicated in life or, as the Germans would say, *worauf es eigentlich ankommt*, and which nearly all other writers miss. It was a feeling that the reality in life and in literature was hidden behind symbols, resided in " a unique relation which," as Proust puts it, " the writer must recapture, enchaining for ever the two different terms in his brain. The relation may be of little interest, the objects mediocre, the style bad ; but so long as there has not been that there has not been anything." Goethe meant exactly this when he told Eckermann : " I will confide to you something : my things can never be popular. They are only for the few who want and seek something similar, and who are launched in similar directions." Hugh Kingsmill and I stimulated each other to such a pitch that after the first meeting he had a brain storm and I lay sleepless all night and in the morning was on the brink of a nervous breakdown.

There was about him, I noticed at once, a certain ebullient naturalness, a glint about the eyes which I also noticed, the moment I first saw them, in Bernard Shaw and D. H. Lawrence—yes, and Beaverbrook, too ; which denotes a kind of gaiety of spirit, the real name for which must be genius, and which intoxicates one.

Although I had had school friends in my time, and in the Army and at Oxford, Hugh Kingsmill, I realized, was the first man whose mind exhilarated my mind and exercised it to the full ; that is, a being to merit the term " friend."

V

DIGRESSION ON LOVE

Twice in my life to date, I have come across women with some of Hugh Kingsmill's inherent poetry, simplicity, high spirits, and deep-rooted humour ; women with whom I think I could have been lastingly happy. One was Katherine Mansfield, with whom I only carried on a correspondence, and who died before I could have met her. The other woman was a German, daughter of a colleague of Einstein, who visited Innsbruck and stayed at my *pension*. She was unhappily married. Her mind was as genuine as a man's and so congenial to my own that, during the long walks we took together through the hill-side pinewoods, we stimulated each other so happily that she mistook the common ecstasy we felt in literature and in nature for love and all that love between a man and a woman implies. But she was fifteen years older than I was, and I was fascinated only by her mind. Yet even perfectly intelligent women seem not to understand that, for physiological reasons, a man's impotence to satisfy the passion of a woman who loves him, but whose body does not excite him, is not a sign of ill-will or lack of affection, or proof of his emasculation, or a slur on her sex attraction, any more than the fact that a particular pair of spectacles handed to him by an optician prevented him from seeing with them would imply (a) pig-headedness on his part ; (b) personal animosity towards the optician ; (c) conclusive proof of his blindness ; and (d) wholesale condemnation of the lenses. When I said somewhere that a woman's aversion to sex may, no man should ever forget, be confined to himself, my statement was readily understood, was indeed applauded by women. But when I define an impotent man as one deemed unable to seduce a woman who, lacking attraction to him, has really failed to seduce him, the applause I hear, if any, is unmistakably male. And certainly it is the woman's demand in such cases which is the more unreasonable of the two, for while she reproaches him with a temporary disability due only to herself, of her, in reverse circumstances, no more is demanded than that she submit herself passively to a will not her own.

We parted and for some time wrote letters. She wrote a very large hand and covered numerous pages with exquisite humorous German not unlike Katherine Mansfield's English. Her little son, she wrote, had died and her husband who, when the boy was alive, grudged him a new suit, now

ordered an enormous wreath and fussed over the funeral.
She would send me her German short stories, little gems
which no German paper would print, and I translated them
and tried them in England, with similar success. Then
replies on each side became overdue; the letters grew fewer,
and finally, in the way of all written human relations, ceased
altogether.

VI

ALGERIAN INTERLUDE

When I called at his hotel next morning, I was informed
Hugh Kingsmill had gone on a walking tour across France,
without leaving an address. And a little later I left Toulon
for Algeria.

I can add nothing to the emotion I expressed in "Pending
Heaven" on approaching Algiers from the sea. As we
talked the coast had projected forward to meet us, the landscape had crystallized itself, the streets and houses had come
into focus; and as the afternoon wore on we saw the town,
like a Christmas-tree lit up in daylight, prepare itself for the
falling dusk. Still the engines throbbed impassively and
still the coast came nearer to meet us, and then grew blue
with dusk, and there were all the lights of Algiers, aglow,
quivering. "Look! Look!" this or that experienced
traveller would say, and he would point out Mustapha
Supérieur, the Casbah, the Jardin d'Essai, the Great Mosque.
Then there were hoots, a tug at work like a small sheep-dog
propelling a stray, brainless lout of a sheep into righteous
ways. The clumsy thing we were on was alongside a floating
pier, at last. We came down the gang-plank and at once
found ourselves in the midst of a gibbering, gesticulating
Oriental canaille.

Another memory remains with me. Early one morning
I started by motor coach for Bou-Saada. It was cool, but
the sun rose, and we began to ascend the steep rosy gorges.
As the day lengthened the gorges were left far behind, and

we were traversing vast plains which gradually turned into
dunes, the vegetation becoming more bitter and desolate till
all was sand, at first hard and uniform, then more rebellious,
the wind having grafted waves like those of the sea. And,
to think of it, this dreary desolation we were now traversing
once had been the ocean floor! And athwart and across
stooped and staggered camels laden with wares. When,
after hours of travel, dusk was falling around us, we perceived, south-west, a cluster of lights—the oasis of Bou-
Saada. Another hour brought us to the gates of the stronghold. Guides and menials of all kinds, jibbering and
clamouring, had jumped on the side-boards and clung to
them for dear life, claiming precedence over one another.
The motor coach drove down the chief street, depositing its
passengers at the various hotels. It was dark, mild, and
peaceful. Here we were, then, in this oasis, walled in from
the desert without, steeped in palm-trees which swayed,
whispering in the breeze.

It is experiences like these which remain with us, and that
we later incorporate in a work of fiction, making some character
who has never left Putney fly to India or cross the Gobi.

A scrupulous autobiographer feels he must not leave out an
account of the places he has lived in. Yet he cannot afford
to deal adequately with all the countries he has lived in
without causing his book to swell to an unportable size.
I am tempted to dismiss certain countries, such as Algeria
and Tunisia, with the first of which I have dealt at length in
my novel, " Pending Heaven," and confine myself to a section
containing the names of the places I lived in, and having for
its text merely the words : " I been there." Tunisia : " I
been there." Paris : " Also been there : Hôtel Chambord."
Venice : " Hotel Bauer," and so forth. I beg to remind
the reader that I have been twice round the world. My
autobiography accordingly could be rewritten, were this
desirable, on a geographical basis. But would this exhaust
the thoroughness of one's treatment, unless, writing of the
places I had visited and reluctant to remain superficial in

my reports of their scenic aspect, I probed everywhere down to the earth's core, rearranging my material and viewing the whole life from a geological standpoint?

Of Algiers I will only say that during the carnival, while we sat in the stands and watched, an aeroplane flying from the direction of France appeared over us, as the festivities were at their height, and dropped flowers, as a greeting from sister France across the sea. It was the kind of thing to move me to tears, and I groped for my handkerchief.

CHAPTER THIRTEEN

THE ARTIST AND THE WORLD

I

BACK IN ENGLAND

AFTER two years abroad I left Algeria, left Toulon, and Lord Beaverbrook's yacht conveyed me back to England. There were on board all the "old gang." Yes, he was there, and she was there, and they were there. When the yacht lay-to in Harwich Harbour it was a Monday morning. Lord Beaverbrook lay in his cabin, morose, remote, plunged in his own thoughts, and all the guests filed to his bedside and said, "Good-bye, Max." "Thank you so much, Max," and he lay there brooding and unhearing. When I, in my turn, entered to take leave of him, he groaned in the accents of a dying man: "*You're* not going to desert me, are you?" I vowed I would not. Lord Beaverbrook lay on in bed for one hour, for two hours, maybe three, while I paced the decks and surveyed the hen-pens of Harwich called "houses," and reflected that here, after two years, I was back again in England. Towards midday Lord Beaverbrook suddenly bestirred himself. He jumped out of bed, called for his secretary, told him to hire a motor car and said we would race the others up to London.

We failed to overtake them, however, and at some small junction boarded a train; and so I steamed into Waterloo along with Lord Beaverbrook. On the steps of the *Daily Express* office Lord Beaverbrook said, "Good-bye to you," and when I reminded him that he had not solved the problem of the serial publication of my novel, which he was going to

307

do on the yacht, he turned on the step and said : " Come yachting with me the day after to-morrow."

Again we bounced about in the Channel, again I was sick, and again by the time we returned to Harwich Lord Beaverbrook had not opened his mouth on the subject of my serial. Nor would he give the slightest idea whether he was conveying us back to London or setting off on a cruise to the Mediterranean. This secrecy in my host irritated me a little, and I gave expression to it. My host, with the utmost amiability, agreed that we were going back to London if this was what we wished. But all the way in the train he read a book, and did not open his mouth. When at Waterloo the compartment pulled up opposite his Rolls-Royce, and the two doors opened simultaneously, Lord Beaverbrook said : " Good-bye to you," and drove off in his car while we dispersed at different tangents in taxis.

I repaired to a little furnished flat at the top of a house in Dean Street which I rented from Clifford Allen, very meticulous in going over the inventory with me, so that, after a while, even his wife said to him : " Clifford, aren't you overdoing it ? " But he proved an excellent landlord, and in the end even paid my electric light bill for all the time I was there. The flat had at one time been occupied by Karl Marx, and Keir Hardie's picture looked down on me while I wrote. As my father's workmen had at one time spared his life, believing him to be the English Socialist Keir Hardie, the veteran's picture was an appropriate ikon.

Later I moved to a West Kensington flat with Hugh Kingsmill. After our quarrel, to avoid complicating our joint accounts which would have involved us in discussion, we decided not to have meals in the flat. Our jointly-paid cook procured for her midday meal an enormous steak, which she garnished with greens and potatoes, and the smell and sizzling of the gravy drove me mad with hunger, and I slunk down the steps to the nearest Lyons ; while Kingsmill hurried along the opposite pavement, to the nearest A. B. C.

From the West Kensington flat I moved into another,

near Baker Street, and on my return from India, America and Tunisia finally established myself in an abode once occupied by another English man of letters, Dante Gabriel Rossetti.

II

THE " SOCIETY " MYTH—I INTRODUCE PROUST INTO THE " GRAND MONDE " OF LONDON

And now let me write of society—that " Society " which seems to exist only in the newspapers and to which everybody denies belonging—rightly so, since " society " only exists in relation to our own self-consciousness. Society, the antithesis of his natural state of being alone with his thoughts, intrigues the artist as an occasional means of bringing him out of himself. As a recreation, he may delight in testing his prowess in handling dexterously the apparatus of the world of appearances, of concealing under an air of geniality his revulsion from the continual cross-fire of deceit, steadying his nerves, telling himself " one must not lose the habit of going among people," flattering himself : " I am a potential man of the world—yes, capable of bringing more wit and grace to the vocation than any of them—if I really cared enough for the game."

A writer like myself, who in his natural state spends, as a sort of exercise of the spirit, a minimum of six hours a day by himself, mostly pacing at considerable speed the London parks, finds himself lunching, let us say, at Lady (Ian) Hamilton's. " Hello, Hugh. Hello, Reggie. Hello, George." And he finds that Hugh is Lord Hugh Cecil, and George perhaps the Lord Chancellor of England, and Reggie an Ex-Chancellor of the Exchequer, and the square-built man in a morning coat the German Ambassador ; and then he lines himself up, as a young man, at the end of the queue, to sit next to the youngest of the women present, half intimidated, half flattered at finding himself with the engine-drivers of the world, over their pot of beer.

Or, let us say, you find yourself at a gathering like Mrs. Somerset Maugham's. You ask yourself, how would you answer that arch-snob of genius, Marcel Proust—the young Proust who asked M. de Charlus who exactly was Mme. de Vileparisis and what exactly was her *salon* and was told : "*Rien !*" —how would you answer young Proust if he made discreet inquiries regarding the *salon* of Mrs. Somerset Maugham —or, let us say, Lady Lavery ? You recognize a former Foreign Secretary, no other than Sir Austen Chamberlain, conversing with Lady Londonderry. You catch a glimpse of Lady Oxford and Asquith who, too kind to withdraw the boon of her attention from the woman with whom she is in conversation, but reluctant to prolong your suspense, proffers you, still talking with averted face, her left hand. May you reassure Proust that he has penetrated into the veritable *grand monde*, or may you not ? There is Lady Diana Cooper to lend strength to the illusion. There is Lady Milbanke, and that charmingly intelligent, likewise blue-eyed, Mrs. Richard Norton who, when confronted with pretentiousness in others, affects a witheringly disarming modesty herself. Well, do the presence of these fashionable luminaries entitle you to tell Marcel Proust, who is eager to be informed on this point with precision, whether the gathering is one to make him feel that he is mixing with the English aristocracy ? ". . . whoever the aristocracy may be (says Mr. Kingsmill). It is difficult to be precise on this important point since it has become the general practice in our heterogeneous society to refer to everyone as middle-class. A, in conversation with B, refers to C, whom B has hitherto placed among the upper classes, as ' of course hopelessly middle-class.' B, a moral coward, assents mournfully, and shuddering at his own gross lack of discrimination, determines henceforth to assume and assert that everyone is middle-class. And so the rot spreads, B practising on D, as A previously practised on him."

But Proust at your side is not satisfied with your explanation and persists : " *Is* this the *grand monde*, or is it *not* the *grand monde?*" You look round and you see the "smart young set" in full strength. You see the Beatons and the Jungman sisters and perhaps Stephen Tennant, and the rest of the "younger set," whose spirit has been faithfully reproduced by "Beachcomber" in the diary of a *soi-disant* society girl. "I do so wish," she writes, "you could have seen us last night at the Mixed Vermouth. We *were* such a happy party—just 'Sloppy' Oldcraft, the Duchess, Babs, Bulger, Lady G., Soapy, the Fudge girl, and I. We all went on to Dibby's afterwards, and sat on the oilcloth and ate cold spinach. I have never laughed so much as when Sybil hit Bulger on the jaw with a piece of coal. After that we all went on to 'Sloppy's' and sat on clothes-horses and ate *éclairs*." But Proust waves your discursion aside as irrelevant. Is he, or is he not, in Society? And you delight in getting back at him with something of his own subjectivity. The answer, you tell him, depends on himself. If the gathering intimidates him, then assuredly he is in Society. If it does not, he has only looked in to be with his friends. Objectively, there is no reality in the conception. The presence of a number of fashionable peeresses might lead you to suppose that they are luminaries into whose orbit men and women of achievement have been drawn, to make one brilliant gathering called "Society." On the other hand, it may be said that the luminaries you see there to-night are but the tail ends of comets who naturally gravitate towards another solar system and consider their presence here as an excursion into Bohemia, an irresponsible side of them called Côté Chelsea. There can be no objectivity about a heterogeneous gathering of individuals whose reality resides in their subjectivity. You may innocently imagine you have brought your snobbish friend Proust into a gathering of unrivalled distinction, while some others in the party may regard your presence there as a tribute to your hostess' talent for mixing successfully heterogeneous elements. Such criticism seems to you without worth, when the most brilliant peeress in the gathering picks on you and begs you to make

sure to come to her party. But a fastidious friend, who has
not been asked, assures you that she is completely *déclassée*.
This opinion is refuted by another friend of yours who acknow-
ledges the illustrious brilliance of your prospective hostess,
but suggests that your invitation must be explained by
the fact that the particular party to which you are going
is one of her more uncritical gatherings, not to be confused
with the smaller dinners she gives for the King of Spain and
people of their own set. You might become the intimate
friend of every fashionable man and woman in London :
there will always be someone who will maintain that the
real aristocracy has eluded you, having entrenched themselves
against you in Shropshire. They alone are the aloof impreg-
nable stronghold meriting the much abused designation
" society." Them you will never know, he suggests, at
the same time claiming by his very ability to speak of them
with knowledge a certain connection with them. They
alone, to our fastidious friend, are " society." But he forgets
that if they are " society " to him, it is because he does not
belong to them. To them these gatherings, which he self-
consciously describes as " society," are again just a means of
seeing their friends. They are no more conscious of being
" society " or " the upper classes " than he who can read is
conscious of being a member of the literate class—a difference
of which he is reminded, with a certain surprise, only when
brought into contact with someone who puts a cross instead
of writing his name. Conceive of a person who has just
learned to write his name referring to himself as " we, the
literate classes," and you will understand why any mention
of the word " society " at once arouses suspicion mingled
with irritation in the people who, for others, seem to compose
that illusory body.

But, conversely, if some provincials, having settled in a
London suburb, begin to frequent a family who seems to
them in touch with a few noteworthy people, the provincial
family, if they are at all self-conscious about it, will feel
they are already moving in London society. Their provincial

friends paying them a brief visit in the suburbs, and returning to their small town, will feel that they too have had their season of London society.

The social aspirant is subjected to the continual strain of awe before a social set in which he does not yet feel himself completely familiar. Familiarity with one set necessarily making him feel worthy of another. Could he, however, have envisaged simultaneously these feelings of awe for all the different stages of human society which it was to be his Golgotha to climb, they would have assuredly neutralized one another. The highest peak having been reached he might well ask himself : " How has it furthered me ? " All his anxiety in the past may now seem vain, now that he is no longer in the vice of self-consciousness, now that he is half out of the world, and he might well reach up to that altruistic, Christian, attitude, which necessarily is the next step on the ladder of human perfection.

III

KINDNESS AND MR. BEATON

It was, no doubt, with an eye on these heights of human perfection, that Mr. Cecil Beaton once, in a discussion with Mrs. Henry McLaren, emphasized so exclusively the virtue of kindness : " She's *so* kind," or " I thought it *so* unkind of her," as if kindness were the sole quality he valued in the world. And I was almost tempted to take him at his word and inflict on him an assorted lot of people whose only claim to distinction was their kindness : some big, fat market-woman, breathing benevolence ; a taxi-driver with a melting eye ; a lavatory attendant with a golden heart. " Cecil, my dear, I've brought along a woman and two men, perfect darlings, the souls of human kindness." Picture the expression on Cecil's face—an expression which may well imply that you were " *so* unkind ! " or, alternatively, " *so* unfunny ! "

Mr. Cecil Beaton has an uncanny fascination for me.

Sometimes a queer, humorous light comes into his eyes when you tell him something quite ordinary, such as that you have missed your train, and he throws back that graceful head of his and says : " *Oh*, I think this is *so* funny ! I think it is the *funniest* thing I have ever heard," and you wonder whether he has some strange sub-lunar sense of humour that you cannot follow. He has, however, a sense of line, and he has trained his sisters to a pitch of exquisite insincerity. When I arrived at his exhibition, Nancy Beaton welcomed me eagerly : " *So* nice," she said, " to see a familiar face among all this crowd of unknown people." But as I turned to greet another friend I heard her say to a stranger, " *So* nice among all this crowd of . . ." She already possesses that unassuming kindliness of manner of a dowager duchess who wants to put you at your ease. It is all her brother's doing. She has much of her own, too—and her hands which are poems.

At Cecil Beaton's private show I renewed my friendship with Mrs. Richard Guinness. I said to her : " You know, you are more beautiful than your daughters, the celebrated Jungman sisters." " You know," she said, with an air of imparting a secret she had treasured too long and was now glad to reveal to me, " I always knew it."

IV

LITERARY LONDON

Count Keyserling — Michael Arlen — The Welsh Maupassant — Somerset Maugham — Hugh Walpole — W. B. Yeats — Katherine Mansfield — Middleton Murry

The late Mrs. Benjamin Guinness arranged a few literary parties for Count Keyserling, who, after his triumphant tour of the United States, was staying with her in Carlton House Terrace. I do not think that any of the much-boomed Germans—Ludwig, Zweig, Feuchtwanger, Remarque, different though they are, are prophets. But Keyserling is not the shallow fool some people think him. He has indeed looked into the depths—and fallen into a pit. If he did not splutter in his animation the stimulus of his conversation would be less blurred. Lady Astor, who was next him at table, turned, in self-defence, to me, and asked me why I chose to write about Lord Beaverbrook, when Josephine Butler, the great Victorian champion of fallen women, offered a theme so much richer in human interest. I replied, that certainly both were Crusaders, but that for my part I regarded the protection of wheat as preferable to the protection of virtue.

Count Keyserling is one of those humourless persons who refer to their tremendous sense of humour as ensuring their sanity in a mad world, and then make you wonder what they had done with it. "Nowadays," he said, "I only laugh." Despite Lady Astor and Sir Denison Ross and the Grand Duchess Maria Pavlovna, Count Keyserling held the fort, assigning the future to Soviet Russia and the United States, to the uneasy alarm of several opulent financiers. Sir Denison Ross and myself tried to wedge in a word, but in vain. I, however, succeeded in inveigling Keyserling into a subject I was interested in and, with Sir Denison Ross, we were the last to leave the dining-room. I deferred to Count Keyserling at the door of the lavatory, but when I suggested to him that we might wait for Sir Denison before we went upstairs, he said : "I never wait for any man, especially a man in a lavatory."

Indeed, Count Keyserling never waits. At a sign from the hostess to go in to dinner, Count Keyserling casts one short glance round the room and then strides in first, though grey-haired senators may be present, as Lord Haldane for example on one occasion, very silent and ponderous and half-dead, in his black waistcoat which senior politicians assume together with waiters. I met him again at Sir Ian Hamilton's, who was delighted by Keyserling's appearance, describing him as "utterly legendary—a sort of Flying Dutchman." I met him for the third time at a small luncheon given by Mrs. Benjamin Guinness. Only four men were present: Bernard Shaw, Keyserling, Mr. Benjamin Guinness and I. Keyserling cast one short glance at us and marched in first to lunch. I sat between Countess Keyserling and the then Tanis Guinness, with the adorable blue eyes. Conversation between Keyserling and Bernard Shaw did not flow very freely, though when you ask Keyserling about Shaw, he replies, with an acid lack of enthusiasm: "Yes, I know Shaw. He's a great friend of mine." Bernard Shaw tended to monopolize the conversation with reminiscences. He talked sonorously about what his father in Ireland had said to him when he asked him: "'Papa,' I said," and what Papa had replied, while Keyserling laughed independently and with ribaldry, apparently at his own remarks, to which no one paid much attention, since we were all anxious to listen to Bernard Shaw. Then at last Keyserling said something which gained Shaw's assent, and Keyserling spluttered off at incredible speed into a discourse of his own and suddenly, by way of emphasis, brought his fist down on the table with ribald laughter. Everybody jumped, and the glasses jingled resentfully, and the hostess looked as if she was all right again—only a little shock. Then Shaw recaptured the conversation and held it to the end of lunch. In the drawing-room Keyserling retired to one end of the room, where he was delivering a discourse before his wife, while we all gravitated to the other end around Shaw, who was trying to amuse us by imitating his voice on the gramophone as appearing in different pitches according to different speeds.

This is necessarily a subdued account of my literary contemporaries. Were I to say all I think, the matter would not end with this book.

Michael Arlen, then, is—oh, ever so much better than his books! But since an author's interests are not served by praise of the man at the expense of his work, let me hasten to say that Michael Arlen's charm does not gain on further acquaintance. He and I had just left Arnold Bennett's party in the same taxi-cab, when Michael Arlen, possessed of that sense of the truly fitting on every occasion which is Goethe's definition of virtue, discerned that the man with the lantern who summons cabs at a crowded party was not a servant of the house but a specially hired menial and consequently entitled to a tip. My own view was that Arnold Bennett, while not being John Galsworthy, was yet quite capable of balancing the scales of justice, and would see to it that the man with the lantern was remunerated for his work. But Michael Arlen said it would never do, and instructed the taxi-cab driver to back to the door, causing considerable inconvenience to on-coming vehicles. In the circumstances, I felt that if one of us was to disgorge it was not going to be myself, whose poverty was an indictment of contemporary literary taste only equalled perhaps by Michael Arlen's prosperity. The author of " May Fair " searched a long time in his waistcoat pockets and finally produced a sixpence, after which we departed in peace.

Michael Arlen, if he wished, could make a fortune on the films. He has an uncanny facial expression, and is not unlike Menjou in appearance. I remember his solo dance at this party. A moustached smile ; eyes like buttons, fixed, unmoving. And just a twitch of the moustache.

One evening, when I was with Caradoc Evans, the Welsh Maupassant, he became increasingly gloomy, and repeated to me several times that life was awful. But he would not give in, would not abandon the struggle ; and when I urged him into a taxi he resisted with energy : " I," he said, "Caradoc Evans, pay for a taxi ? Not on your life ! " Whereupon we went by Tube. The journey deepened the gloom of Caradoc Evans. We reached Hammersmith, the terminus of that line, but the Welsh Maupassant sat still, wrapped in thought. " Life is awful," he said. " Don't you think it's awful ? "

" Awful. We get out here. This is Hammersmith."

" I *hate* Hammersmith ! " he exclaimed.

" You've got to get out here," I said.

" Why should I ? " he cried. There was in that cry all

the protest of a free spirit against the shackles of civilized life, and the inadequate recognition of talent. "Man!" he yelled, "why should I?"

"Very well," I said. We rolled back to the City.

As we rolled back, doubt and a general dissatisfaction with the state of the world pervaded my mood. Why should I, a poet, have to write articles? Why should I? I grasped Caradoc by the elbow. "Man!" I yelled, "why should I?"

"Steady," he said. "Don't shout; you're not at home."

Somerset Maugham I met only once, on the steps of the Opera. He looked exceedingly wicked. "Cakes and Ale" proves him a richly endowed novelist. Two fundamental failings rob him of greatness. His works do not suggest those "mysteries" which, as Proust puts it, "have their explanation probably only in other worlds and a presentiment of which is precisely what moves us most in life and in art." His other fault is the fear of appearing old-fashioned. Who but an emotional coward would have dragged out the story of "Cakes and Ale" to its inartistic ending, for the sake of getting the heroine to say in old age that she loved her loud and vulgar lover "because he had always been such a perfect gentleman," when the book, every sensitive reader must feel, called for an emotional ending—at the point where the second, so perfect but unsympathetic Mrs. Driffield, indicts the first Mrs. Driffield, so imperfect but lovable and now vanished, and the man who had truly known her champions her sensitively before her bland and insensitive accusers. But Mr. Maugham, who always has one ear to the ground to know what "the young" are doing, felt that Mr. Evelyn Waugh might call him sentimental, and spoiled the end of his book.

Then we have Mr. Hugh Walpole, whose career is more interesting than his subject-matter—which latter is interesting for sheer toughness of matter. For there is not a gleam of spirit about the gratuitously *invented* psychology of his characters. "You can invent anything you like, but you cannot invent psychology," said Tolstoy.   Human psychology is so subtle, so unaccountable that, given a real person, we can't hope always to foretell his behaviour.   Why, then, go to the gratuitous trouble of inventing characters ; and, moreover, pretend that you can invent a completely real character by deducing how he will react to circumstances and the behaviour of others ?   And of Mr. Walpole it may be truly said that all there is in his books is his own : no divine spark has assisted him.   On the other hand, there is nothing like advances on royalties, serial rights, and so on, to engage the united interest of authors ; and of these discussions Mr. Walpole's career is invariably the centre.   For, barring royalties, what has any original artist, if we come to think of it, in common with another ?   Originality, that is all.

At a P. E. N. Club dinner I heard W. B. Yeats second a speech to welcome Ernst Toller.   Yeats, tossing back his forlorn locks, dismissed Toller's plea for world peace and universal brotherhood as moonshine and pursued some private image of his own.   I recalled Katherine Mansfield's story about Yeats who had dreamed his head was circled with a flaming sun, went to sleep and dreamed of a woman whose hair was afire, woke up, lighted a candle, and by and by discovered " by the odour " that he had set his own hair ablaze.   " I think it's wondrous apt.   It's just as far as he and his crew can get to set their hair afire—to set their lank forlorn locks a-frizzle.   God knows there's nothing else about them that a cartload of sparks could put a light to."

Katherine Mansfield adored Tchehov.   Despite her "Little Me " mannerism, which spoils her writing here and there, there was a good deal of natural simplicity in her and a miraculous faculty for transmuting her memories into an acquisition for all souls.   Arnold Bennett, however, when I asked him what he thought of Katherine Mansfield, said he didn't think very much of her work.   " Why ? " I questioned.

" It's all Tchehov," he said.

Lord Beaverbrook : " She's justified, isn't she ? "

Arnold Bennett : " *Of course* she is ! "

Middleton Murry, for whom I, in pure devilry, reproduced this dialogue, fixed the floor with his usual mystical look, and said sombrely : " She is a test."

Middleton Murry has a faculty of estranging you by a manner which suggests that you are in a stage of development from which he has just emerged, and that he is watching your progress with hope from a point further along the road. Thus he once described a poet, Palmer, who contributed to the *Adelphi*, as having the makings of a popular poet, only to call from Mr. Palmer a poem which depicted himself achieving God's point of view, and looking back on the tortuous journey with benign extra-human comprehension. I do not suggest that Middleton Murry, in seeking God, is not sincere.   But I don't see why two writers, both of whom have failed to find God, should be on terms of excessive mutual deference.   But, as a critic, he is serious, honest, persevering.   Step by step, he has built up a vast critical system, and by filing them a little here and a little there he has fitted in Shakespeare and Hardy, Tchehov and Keats, and has erected a critical tower, The Tower of Acceptance (by omitting from it all that Shakespeare and Hardy, Tchehov and Keats did not accept).   Still, there you are : it is a tall, lofty edifice.   But do not blow on it.

V

WOMEN OF MOMENT—AND OF THE MOMENT

When, from time to time, I take up my pen to suggest in the Press that women have no position to speak of in literature, female writers spring at me like hyenas, and tear me with their claws.   I, however, survive.

Never yet have I committed the error of looking on women writers as serious fellow artists.   I enjoy them rather as spiritual helpers who, endowed with a sensitive capacity for appreciation, may help the few of us afflicted with genius to bear our cross with good grace.   Their true rôle, therefore, is rather to hold out the sponge to us, cool our brow, while we bleed. If their sympathetic understanding may indeed be put to a more romantic use, how we cherish them for it !

It was therefore with a degree of surprise that I read in Ethel Mannin's book of confessions a rather ungrateful account of my demands on her time. She accuses me in truth of cherishing unliterary designs on her during her brief visit to my flat. Miss Mannin was clad in a heavy overcoat. All I said indeed, with a grave old-world courtesy, was : " Madam, I have a few minutes which it pleases me to place at your disposal. Pray divest yourself of your overcoat." Miss Mannin, however, failed lamentably to rise to the occasion. I may say she behaved most extraordinarily— she refused. But she has had her punishment. The offer was not repeated.

Yet authors are human ; they like to meet women authors to discuss literary scandal, love, royalties, etc. From women writers one sometimes turns to painters and musicians. Harriet Cohen palpably regarded her own playing as a " thing-in-itself " rather than a contribution to the amenities of life ; she would not adopt the pleasing attitude of women in the ancient world and old-time Turkey, playing the lyre and cymbals to divert their lords and distract the weary poet. So back to literature I went.

But here all the women seemed absorbed in their own work—Rose Macaulay so much so that, despite her humorous kink, she has a face like a martyr tortured by the Inquisition. Stella Benson, who understands me, is away in China.

For Margaret Kennedy I have a warm regard. But her hair is coiled so tightly round her ears that it tends to deafen her. Her contribution, therefore, to a spiritual conversation is a series of " What ? " Once she said to me : " When I am ill I read your ' Futility.' " " And I ' The Constant Nymph,' " I replied.

How much better we would like it, were it, let us say, " Red Sky at Morning " and " Jazz and Jasper," respectively.

Most of the other women, however, like Sheila Kaye-Smith

and her school, who find my novels too imponderable for
their grasp, turn out fiction like pudding which I, for one,
don't attempt to read for fear it might cramp my digestion.

A work of art must " rise " like a *soufflé*, not flop like a
damp pancake, as, I am afraid, in most novels, especially
those written by women.

This I will say, and then no more. When the literary
history of our time is written future historians will note
with regret that, in the 'thirties, rather than keep up our
spirits by weeping with us and laughing at our jokes, our
women contemporaries preferred to scribble books of their
own. So unwomanly !

VI

MR. ALDOUS HUXLEY'S LOUDSPEAKER

As we were waiting for dinner at the St. John Hutchinsons,
Mr. and Mrs. Aldous Huxley were announced. Effect
somewhat sinister, nightmarish. You imagine a sort of
undertaker on stilts. Your involuntary wish is to retire,
slink away quietly. Aldous Huxley sits there and without
looking at you, or at anyone else in particular, emits streams
of impersonal sound, like a sort of loudspeaker, about the
habits of bees and ants, the excretions of elephants, and
sexual intercourse among whales. By a kind of studied
fastidiousness avoiding reticent language : For aren't we
the unashamed Intelligentsia ? And as he speaks a look of
anxiety comes on the faces of the women present as though
they would be unspeakably shocked if anyone thought they
could possibly be shocked by anything. Biology is his
stronghold. The information he imparts is absorbingly
interesting. To me the ways of insects appear to throw
light on human beings, indeed on life itself. To Goethe
and the older scientists science meant just that : that it took
them from the particular to the whole, revealing something
of the ways of God and the laws of the universe. To Aldous

Huxley, who not for nothing is the brother of Professor Julian, the antics of the insects shed light on the ways of the insects. Every time I suggested we could deduce something human or universal from what he said about them, he grew cold, drew back into himself, and the loudspeaker ceased to function.

Aldous Huxley has a voice which booms like Big Ben. I met him again dining with the Arnold Bennetts, when, arriving late for dinner, I explained that, to avoid being late, I had specially gone to set my watch by Selfridge's chronometer, which operation deflected my journey so that if indeed I was late it was in the good cause of being on time. Aldous Huxley laughed deeply. "Next time you had better set it by Big Ben." And as he laughed I thought I could hear Big Ben striking sonorously.

I spent a whole day and night reading Aldous Huxley's "Point Counter Point," until four o'clock in the morning, and again all the morning. It isn't really good, though for a number of reasons it is so interesting, so readable, that one can't put it down. Aldous Huxley is diluted, over-intellectualized, not really creative or original—a younger modernized Galsworthy. Many people, I know, will disagree. To them I can but reply in the positive words of the late Lord Birkenhead: "I know, and you don't know." May they find comfort in these words. The only characters that are really good are Burlap and Sidney Quarles. Rampion, though very faithfully drawn, is not good because Huxley's admiration for him is too transparent. Aldous Huxley has laughed at Middleton Murry for his prostration before D. H. Lawrence, but his own books, of late, are distorted by the same overcharged fealty to the same left-handed suzerain. Lawrence seems to ravage Huxley's purest emotions, as if by exercising a statutory "Droit de Seigneur." The novel is full of redundancies. For instance, there is this sort of thing, which is inexcusable: "I am feeling very tired," a character might say. And the author adds, gratuitously: "In fact, she felt greatly fatigued." Then the characters don't stand out somehow. They are not embossed, like Wells's or Tchehov's. There is no warmth, no tenderness, no suppleness here. It is all flat, described; the characters can't reveal themselves. They don't breathe. And it is mostly a collection of contemporary opinions, the sort of thing a novelist should reserve for articles.

There is a fashion which persists in literature and is (unjustifiably, according to musicians) carried by literary critics into music—a fashion of conceding a superiority to reconciliation over the attitude of, let us say, rebellion and despair. This fashion, if we examine it more closely, springs from a sort of literary inferiority complex which vents itself in priggishness. It is generally assumed that the universe, though veiled to our mortal sight, is a harmonious entity. Hence writers who end their work on a note of reconciliation are credited with a vision which perceives all there is to perceive, the entire universe, by a sort of intuition, while others who rebel and despair are assumed to do so because their shorter sight enables them to see but a portion of the whole. No writer wants to lag behind another in sensibility and perception. Hence the tendency in Matthew Arnold, for example, to force reconciliation into his poetry, which does not ring true to his nature. The real modern genius of reconciliation is Tchehov. This fragment jotted down in his note-book gives expression to a feeling latent in all his writing : " Essentially all this is crude and meaningless, and romantic love appears as meaningless as an avalanche which involuntarily rolls down a mountain and overwhelms people. But when one listens to music, all this is, that some people lie in their graves and sleep, and that one woman is alive and, grey-haired, is now sitting in a box in the theatre, seems quiet and majestic, and the avalanche no longer meaningless, since in nature everything has a meaning. And everything is forgiven, and it would be strange not to forgive."

Here we have to do with a warm, living feeling which found effective expression in, for example, the reconciliatory scene in "The Duel." Goethe, wisest of critics, believed that literature at its best, when touching poetry, was invariably the outcome of a naïve, sub-conscious state of mind which dealt in terms of the things of this world, behind which the Absolute lay concealed. Demands from above, he held, destroyed this naïve productive state of mind and passed off for literature something which was not literature but self-conscious rhetoric. Nevertheless, he imposed a reconciliatory ending on "Faust," which is more forced and formal than spontaneous—a "demand from above." Still, what was he to do? What is a man to do in the face of life and death? Is he to rebel stupidly? Submit meekly? Submit gladly, with a smile insinuating as it were (like Mr. Middleton Murry) that he is "in the know," that nothing of the hidden machinery of omnipotence is really hidden from him? Or singing psalms, hoping inertly? Or turn into a sort of Mr. Aldous Huxley, who, having received uncharitable treatment at the hands of a mystical critic, sighed bitterly: "Of such is the Kingdom of Heaven," and attacked the mystic with a brutality not of the other world. But anxious lest he be thought insensible to the mystic qualities of Heaven, anxious to prove that "I have understanding as well as you. I am not inferior to you. Yea, who knoweth not such things as these?" but unable to work the miracle himself, Mr. Huxley very wisely harnessed Beethoven to his rusty chariot, in the last chapter of "Point Counter Point." Paying ten-and-six for Mr. Huxley's volume does not initiate us into Heaven; we have for that to buy a record of Beethoven and turn on the gramophone. His language does not throb. It is Perrier water, decanted into a jug overnight. It is a tired old horse who jogs along a familiar route on loose reins. Nevertheless he is readable, and that is much; and he is the most well-read and the best-informed of living novelists. The May-bug he has wings of gold, the June-bug wings of flame, the bed-bug hasn't any wings, but he gets there all the same.

VII

AND, OF COURSE, THE SITWELLS

Osbert Sitwell and I, on the rare occasions when we meet, always hail each other with a shy, fastidious benevolence, only to find, as we stand there face to face, that we can think of nothing helpful to say. We come out with some complimentary but unconvincing remark and pass on—a situation which bears out Dr. Johnson's words that the mutual civilities of authors are among the most risible spectacles in the farce of life. Osbert Sitwell's good opinion of himself is justified by at least sixty per cent., for he has a sensitive, lyrical nature. But forty per cent. of his soul is congested and the execution laboured.

Edith Sitwell is not without talent. But she shrinks back when you talk to her, as if your voice were too loud and your presence too actual. She shrinks from telephones and such things, and is as fragile as if she came from a waxworks. You need have no compunction in writing freely about the Sitwells, for they are capable of standing up for themselves. Edith Sitwell's articles in the *Daily Mail*, in one of which she suggested that a woman who did not appreciate her poetry should emigrate to the Colonies and lessen the gravity of unemployment in this country, a scheme by which she hoped to win the approval of the Home Government, contain touches which gladden my heart.

Sacheverell Sitwell's " All Summer in a Day " has an exquisite passage here and there, and a few irritating mannerisms, as when he writes, " As I have said," " As I have explained," having stated nothing meriting reiteration. He has good thoughts beautifully expressed ; good thoughts incoherently expressed ; and thoughts so incoherent that one is not surprised they have remained the other side of expression. Great writers, like Shakespeare and Goethe, Tchehov and Proust, contrive to express the subtlest, the profoundest thoughts lucidly and beautifully. With a man like Sacheverell

Sitwell, you feel you are in the presence of a potential poet who, for the time being, is emotionally congested. When you see him, his bleak, somnolent face, mute, dreaming, you feel that there is something very good, very precious, fluttering imprisoned in that breast.

The three Sitwells, one feels, are capable of a beautiful page, a beautiful paragraph, at least (no one will dispute) a beautiful line. How good, how exquisite, is the ending of Osbert Sitwell's " Charles and Charlemagne."

" My readers know the rest. Arrived at the ocean-gardens of the Southern Seas, the cradle, which, like a submarine, manufactured its own air, was let down by steel cables. A terrible storm, unexpected by the Weather Bureau, and of an unequalled severity, blew up without warning. Something, we know not what, occurred to break the metal ropes. And so, deep-down, turning over and over, bumping on every current, the steel and crystal cage, devoid of any decoration, essentially stark in outline, now floats along with its two skeletons. She is still dressed in the fashions of 1932, and wears eight rows of pearls ; a grotesque exhibit for the fishes that peer and point their cruel, sneering or sworded beaks at it, or lash at it in fury with their tails. Or, again, as though in mockery of an idyll that is over and yet is thus forced for ever to parade its continuance, the cradle settles for a while in some leafy, spring-like glade of the ocean bed, some watery glade that resembles a grove in England, with little flowers blowing from the rocks, and small highly-coloured fishes moving through the foliage, as birds move through the branches of the trees on land, and over all the refracted light plays in an illusional splendour of sunrise, patches falling here and there : and, sometimes, the light hits the glass of the cabin, and reveals within it the terrible white-fingered figures, knocked together by the rolling, until, as it were embracing, their mouths meet in a double, lipless grin. Then the swell comes, and the figures fall apart : and so for countless ages, these figures, in their barnacled hut, moving and tumbling on every tide, will dwell in a semi-eternity of endless green water, alone, and now forgotten."

We other authors cannot be expected to be entirely dispassionate judges. Though it is true that great artists, by virtue of the fact that their heart is in their work, are more prejudiced judges than intellectually leisured consumers and tasters, it is nevertheless true that the opinions of those who can themselves do something are alone interesting. What Goethe said about Byron; Tolstoy about Tchehov; Byron about Wordsworth or Keats is, in the enlightened opinion of posterity, more than a little unsound. But it is interesting. It is more interesting that what a first-rate critic like Mr. Desmond MacCarthy, for instance, might say, though Mr. MacCarthy's estimate is likely to be nearer the future's, when, unfortunately, to discover Mr. MacCarthy's writings among a pile of forgotten criticism will be one of those obscure curiosities indulged in by students incurious of contemporary realities. What happens is this: the opinions of critics like Mr. Desmond MacCarthy may survive as they converge with the opinions of another thousand Desmond MacCarthys, none of whose names survive their opinions. But Tolstoy's absurd opinion of Shakespeare would have perished but for Tolstoy, who survives to perpetuate an opinion in itself not immortal.

Each strives for something different, and no one can tell who will win the race, because the winning-post shifts about all over the course and the judges have all their own rules of judging and are liable even to a change of opinion.

VIII

TRUE LOVE

Nature has seen fit to torment the genuine artist with a hunger for the love of women, beyond the capacity of a single woman to satisfy. If the vivid artist tends to love woman in her utmost variety, it is because she fails to satisfy the idealist in him in her singleness. True love in this differs from gold or clay, Shelley says, that to divide is not to take away. The great artists of vivid powers, the Shakespeares and Tolstoys and Dickens, were not to be sated by a single passion. Their lust for life dragged them out of their shell of contentment into fields which they would otherwise have left unvisited. It is the casual love, I suggest, of the miller's daughter which sheds an immortal light over Chaucer's picture of the miller and the mill, so different from the fastidious essayings of the weaker-sexed artists, whose solitary, intellectual love for a congenial woman robs them of unrest and makes their work exchange vitality for placidity.

It is generally considered that real love lasts a long time. But time is relative and, in the opinion of scientists, inextricably mixed up with matter. Not for nothing has the " moment " been called " eternal." Each individual, each woman, is a curved lens which lets the light of God through at a different angle. Yet each woman I have loved had something in common with the other. Were I to write my actual love story, it is this composite woman, this chameleon, who would be my real heroine, to whom I have remained true, whom alone I have loved. Like Proust, I have learnt the austere lesson that it is not to beings we must attach ourselves, that it is not beings who exist in reality and are consequently susceptible to expression, but ideas. It is ideas which are real in this phenomenal world, not persons—ideas which are but the coin, the currency, the intellectual assignations, the promissory notes, the spiritual equivalents of some other existence. Salutary, if painful, the discovery we make teaches us not to cling too much to the phantom-like pageant of life, and reveals to us the stuff we are made of.

There is an essential similarity in the effect certain types of women produce on us ; and by reacting to each type more or less in the same way we seem to invite in each case the same treatment. There is the girl who at first implicates my happiness by her loving attitude to me, and then, when she is conscious of my love, begins to exploit my pain by eluding me. There is another, either older than myself (when I was very young) or in some way momentarily inaccessible, whose attitude to me is intimately sensitive but who responds to my love benignantly : " Have another cup of tea," " How is your sister ? "—never very much more. There is a third, whose incomprehension of intellectual processes places a chasm between me and her beauty ; a woman, however, so situated in life that though she possesses no natural inclination for art, literature, music, or philosophy, she nevertheless cannot ignore these things, or, in the circumstances, myself. When we artists have ceased to love her, her hitherto unsuspected zeal for art and literature irritates us. Then there is the type I might have loved happily, the type who adores the things I adore, but some outward circumstance, such as that I live in London and she in Detroit or Shanghai, keeps us apart, for better or worse, at any rate for ever. Then there is the girl who, whether intellectual or not, has tended to give me more pleasure than pain. Then the self-absorbed artist girl who begins by sitting at your feet gobbling down everything you have to say, who exhorts you, the superior man that you are, not to sink to mere animal passion but to treat her as an intelligent being interested in the things of the mind, and who, as you branch out into Schopenhauer or Proust, Goethe or Nietzsche, nestles close up to you on the sofa, interferes with the fluency of your discourse by punctuating it with kisses, and presses her limbs impatiently against yours. There are the musicians whose interest in your literary work takes the form of advising you to use them as heroines, and whose interest in your career takes the form of exhortations to attend their concerts.

The rhythm of our life has a way of repeating itself. Several of the women who had eluded me when I wanted them returned to me years later, as if I had sat still in the intervening years, apparently sure I would be ready to shoulder their burdens at a time when the state of my love and my purse were both low.

It does not follow that an indulgent acceptance of one's own frailties necessarily impairs one's censoriousness in respect of others. A pretty chorus girl, who told me she had seven contemporaneous lovers in London and enjoyed physical love quite frankly, took away my " Pending Heaven," and next day said : " Why don't you write clean books ? "

" But what is wrong with this one ? "

" You have a girl there who first carries on with one man, then another, and a third. Now what kind of a girl is that ? "

If I hinted that, as a result of being jilted by the one woman I ever loved, I had vowed to repay all women by seducing, in a state of dark melancholia, every woman who came my way, my book would command the sympathy of the feminine world. What a chapter I could then write on how different women react differently to a man's demands on them. The woman who hates physical love, and concedes it grudgingly. The woman who doesn't care for it, but yields out of comradeship. The woman who does it out of fun. The woman who thinks she is being unconventional. The woman who likes it. The woman who makes demands on you. And so on.

O women who are the path we tread between desire and realization ! The heart-sinking fear : " Dare I speak to her ? " It is done. She leans against you intimately, you take her slender hand—just think of it !—the hand of another being making her adventure through life. Your desire is realized. Why then that sigh ?

" Doubtless," says Proust, " in those perfect coincidences, when reality suddenly turns round and adapts itself to that which we had yearned for so long, it hides itself for us entirely and merges with it, like two equal figures posed against each other and making but one, whereas, on the contrary, to give our happiness its full significance, we should like to keep in view all the edges of our desire in the very moment we cover it, and, to be certain that it is verily it, the prestige of its intangibility." I only once achieved the miracle, when my desire was overtaken by a surprising and almost simultaneous fulfilment.

It happened at a dance in England. I met a girl who so answered to my inmost dreams that I was torn between longing and apprehension, timidity and resignation. Dare I speak to her? Dare I ask her to dance with me? She, however, not only spoke to me, not only danced with me, but the moment we were alone in the garden, where sounds of music reached us from the ballroom, we, as if by some mutual signal, forgot everything, ourselves and our separateness. This act was as beautiful as the first with the peroxide-haired woman, when I was nineteen, was ignoble. It was realization, which at the same time had not lost sight of the contours of desire. It had begun to drizzle, and our clothes were ruined. Thereafter, for the rest of the evening, we walked mournfully in our overcoats, looking rather like wet birds, but birds of a feather. These " moments," criticized on the score of their shortness, are remembered when all our days are forgotten.

PART V

EAST AND WEST

' Why do people describe only the weak and complaining as misfits ? And everyone who advises you to write only of the strong and significant means himself.''

—Tchehov.

CHAPTER FOURTEEN

THE ADVENTURE OF FAUST

I

THE FLIGHT TO INDIA

THERE are many ways of writing an autobiography. One of the less agreeable ways would be to write it in the form of question and answer, replying very unwillingly, having your confessions, so to speak, extracted from you with a pair of tongs :

" And what happened then ? "

" Then . . . oh, well—then—then I went to Paris."

" And then ? "

" Then—oh, well—then I came back to London. But that will do, respect a fellow's privacy."

" But, my dear fellow, think of the publishers ! The cover of the book bears the word ' autobiography.' Come, man, give us something to put between the covers. What happened next ? "

" Next—oh, well—next I flew to India. But not a word more."

I was on my way to Algeria, for which I felt a sudden nostalgia, when my journey was interrupted in Paris by Lord Castlerosse, who had conceived for me the plan of flying to India with the Maharani of Cooch Behar. From his description I visualized the project as being an experiment to ascertain how much good fortune a given individual could endure. I was to be taken by the hand and led into a new world—still in Time—where wishes were realities. The old problem of Faust was being put to the test again, and Lord Castlerosse, who hinted darkly : " Nothing, so far as earthly pleasures go, is to be denied you," was the modern Mephistopheles.

I met the Maharani at dinner with the Fairbanks in Paris. When we behold a world-famous film star, our wonder is not like that we might experience in beholding Richard Wagner and saying to ourselves, with incredulity: that is the man, in flesh and blood, who brought all that rapturous music out of himself. In beholding Mary Pickford or Rudolph Valentino we rather feel as we might feel beholding the city clerk who won the Calcutta sweepstake, marvelling at the dramatic wonder of those fortuitous circumstances which lift one man or woman out of a million others, all as like each other as peas.

After a pleasant evening spent in the company of the American Montparnassian, Mr. Edward W. Titus, I left Paris for Rome. At Naples news reached us of the homeward bound flying-boat, *City of Rome*, whose crew and passengers had been drowned like rats in a trap. Our pilot, who had been vainly searching the night through for the missing plane, which he used to pilot, took us off before dawn in the *City of Alexandria*, and soon we were crossing the instep of Italy, making straight for her heel, away, away across the sea, and presently flying quite low over the rapturous bays and islets of Greece. From a height these things look like a map: the waves dead, sullenly apathetic, as if utterly bored with themselves: indeed, curiously like a slow-motion picture of their natural state.

From Corfu over Missolonghi, where poor Byron died, to Athens. An enormous black eagle passed us, propelling his way like an aeroplane. Thence to the now god-forsaken island of Crete, where we alighted, in Suda Bay, in very troubled waters on a rocking launch which heaved against our bouncing sea-plane: so that when the pilot called out: "Will two gentlemen go first?" a would-be hero among us sprang to his feet and "volunteered" to do so at once, till his wife asked what the hell he meant by leaving her behind, and the pilot said that, anyhow, there was no danger whatever: which sobered him. The gale prevented our refuelling and we did not set out till early next morning, flying in the direction of Egypt. At Mersa Matruh we came down for petrol, and taking off all but missed an awkward buoy which bobbed out of the water and ripped off one of the struts of the machine. And our flying-boat which had carried us so gallantly over wave and mountain was temporarily incapacitated. The pilot wirelessed for a relief plane from Alexandria, while boats came and took us ashore, where the Governor provided us with luncheon. Then we trooped down to the sea, and presently another sea-plane, *City of Athens*, appeared in the sky and alighted gracefully over the masts of the moored schooners on the green-blue surface of the lagoon. No time was wasted in transferring our baggage. The new pilot, a ginger-haired young man, waved a cheery hand to his colleague: "Good-bye, old man! You'll be here a few days yet, I can see!" wishing him joy of the place—and off we went, gaily skimming the water. I leaned back in my seat. Flying was so simple, so sure, so delightful, I thought to myself, henceforth I should always be flying; when suddenly the boat, which had striven to rise in the air, came down with an ominous bump, then another. "Nothing unusual," I thought. "These fellows know what they are up to." Either for technical, individual, or mystical reasons—the passengers are inclined to differ on this point—the boat did not take to the air as promptly as is customary. And now we were heading straight for the breakwaters. They were of natural rock. It was a matter of seconds, and in these few seconds the pilot made up his mind. He could neither stop the plane, nor dodge the rocks: he decided to jump it. He stopped his engines: the boat dived and leapt into the air, to land with a crash on the rock, which ripped open the bottom of the machine like a tin of sardines. Water gushed in. "Ah! So this can happen to oneself also. Good God, how strange!" When the water flooded the seats and the passengers jumped to their feet, I begged to remind

fate: " This aeroplane trip was only a lark, you know:
you really can't think of killing me for that. It isn't fair."
This was the private thought which passed through my mind
when, for a moment, it looked as if we would be drowned
like rats in a trap. Before we could realize what had happened
the boat was flooded and we were to the hips in water. Somebody shouted: " Open the hatches." With commendable
promptness the two hatches were thrown open. A passenger
among us, who had been itching to take a hand in this en-
thralling business of aeronautics, now found that his chance
had come and shouted: " Ladies first ! " which lent the
incident a sombre air of gravity, not to say gallantry. It
became clear to me that it was most important that *I* should
not perish. But sheer good manners kept me in check:
I stood still and deferred, through no love of my fellow
creatures, but dislike of panic and the fear of showing fear,
to several passengers. I climbed on top of the machine,
quietly, the excitement in me subduing my movements. I
felt as you do when praised, that you would like to excel
yourself. Nobody praised me; they were preoccupied with
themselves. But I had merited my own approbation for
behaving with composure. At the slightest encouragement
I might have sacrificed my life ; for of such emotion heroes
are made. Or my nerves might have betrayed me. I don't
know. Clearly, it would have been touch and go. It is
fitting therefore that the deeds of heroes be immortalized in
the memory of men, for their own exaltation lasts but a
moment at the price of a lifetime.

To prevent us capsizing, the pilot again put on his engines
and got the plane into comparatively shallow water. As we
huddled on the slippery roof of the plane, the three propellers
were still kept resolutely going, to prevent us capsizing.
Around us was shark-infested water. As I sat down, and
crossed my legs, the central propeller, now slowing down,
struck my right heel and split it to the bone in two places, while
only denting the shoe. All our baggage was soaked through
and through. One passenger, an engineer by profession,

would not get out till he had found his portfolio which contained, he was at pains to explain, his "life work"—without which life to him seemed purposeless. And, among other manuscripts, the manuscript of this autobiography, already in an advanced stage of composition, was considerably decomposed. Our former pilot had been watching us take off with what, in fiction, is called "suspense," resigned to see us crash straight into the breakwater, and thus to bits; and, even before the impending crash, was already hurrying to us in a boat. Had our pilot not attempted the jump, little more than fragments would have been left of us.

Boats took us ashore, where already stood the Governor and his assistant. His Excellency at once dispatched me to the local hospital, where my heel was dressed and stitched with horse-hair, while the Maharani, soaking wet, sat on a bench, puffing at a cigarette, and smiling to herself at the thrills which life provides, unasked.

The heel is among the least interesting parts of the body; nevertheless, it secured me considerable sympathy and precedence at the expense of the other wet survivors, and ministered to my self-pity.

It was dark, damp. Most of us expressed the desire not to fly on after the accident. But the pilot of *City of Alexandria* kept on repeating, as if to put us on our mettle: "I must say, a cheerier, more sporting crowd I've never met."

Next morning a land-plane, *City of Bagdad*, came out from Alexandria to take us on, and so serene was our passage, so unruffled the taking-off and graceful the landing, that we all resolved to continue by air to India. Some ladies of Alexandria, beholding my bandaged heel, brought me flowers.

II

ELEPHANTS AND THE VICEROY

When I arrived in India there were lots of little green mosquitoes who, of an evening when the lights were lit in the palace, fell scorched on your face, down your neck,

into the soup : there was no end to them.   This depressed
me exceedingly and I wished I had not come to India.

A personal valet had been engaged for me.   When I
arrived at Calcutta, and was escorted to my apartment, there
he was already squatting on the floor—a bearded, barefoot
man of about forty-five, waiting hand and foot on me and
never out of earshot.   He looked very like our old Russian
coachman, Alexei.   But as I have not described Alexei, the
comparison is not illuminating.   Another enormous man
with a hell of a turban on his head was also in attendance,
and now and then asked me if I required anything.   When
I wanted a drink he brought it with great pomp and solemnity,
and mixed a lime-juice soda for me.   A damp, moist heat
attacked insidiously my vitality, made me feel I was not the
man I was in London or Paris or Petrograd.   I realized I
was in India.

My apartment was spacious—a vault of a place, consisting
of a great bedroom, sitting-room and bathroom.   And I
had a car and chauffeur at my disposal.   When I strolled
into a drawing-room, to essay the piano, one of the attendants
dashed forward to switch on the light, and fused the whole
electric system by putting the big chandelier on at one go !
The palace was in darkness.   I sat down to the piano and
played my poor one and only Tristan !

One of the Maharani's A.D.C.s asked me what I thought
of the food.   When I said it was excellent, he smiled happily.
" I am in charge of the kitchen," he said.   " I know all
about food.   I studied digestics."

" What is that ? " I inquired.

" Don't you know ? " he said, astonished.   " It is the
science of foodery."

I found India neither here nor there.   The eastern side
of it was, on the whole, as unpalatable as the western social
life was dull.   My purpose in going to India was to give the
potentialities of an eastern monarch latent in me, and which
balance so nicely my very western intellect, full play.   I
expected on arrival at the palace to find that a wing of it

had already been prepared for me and equipped with a reasonably sized harem. I may at once say that my Indian paradise fell short of the harem, and erred grievously on the side of monogamy; to be exact, my one romance during the whole month was with a Parisian lady not of the first youth, and necessarily brief, since I met her on her arrival in India as we crossed roads on my hurried dash home on my way to America.

Even on its theoretical side, my knowledge of love was not amplified by my Eastern visit. The Maharani introduced me to the Yuvaraja of Mysore as a connoisseur in these matters, and invited me to compare views with him. We found ourselves sitting side by side. Suddenly I discovered the subject did not exist. I was silent. The Yuvaraja, out of politeness, suggested that women in one country were different from women in another. I agreed. "Women in Paris," I found myself saying, "are attractive." "Ah?" queried the Yuvaraja. "And in Vienna, too," I proceeded. "Ah, and in Vienna, too?" queried the Yuvaraja. "Yes, in Vienna, too," I replied. This rounded off our contribution to sex-lore.

When you are a novelist people think that there are things, aspects, countries, people, which it is salutary for you to see. I did not sleep for two nights in the same bed because all the time we were on the move, so that I might see more of India, and when my curiosity was exhausted and it was time for me to depart, to keep my lecture engagement in America, my Indian servant who accompanied me to Bombay had instructions to draw my attention to as many stipulated places of interest en route as possible, and tugged incessantly at my sleeve.

Scarcely had we reached the Maharani's Calcutta home, when we all started off, by way of Madras, to the state of Mysore—two days and nights in the train. The Viceroy and Lady Irwin and the Commander-in-Chief, as well as several maharajas with their retinues, had just arrived to watch the wild elephant-catching, and the capital looked

W

festive. A model camp, to accommodate no less than ten thousand people, and looking like a small city of canvas by night, had sprung up in the midst of thick jungle. From across the river Kapini came the tapping sound and distant yelling of the beaters rounding up a herd of wild elephants to drive them across the river into a large and cunningly concealed enclosure. But the elephants, unconscious of the feelings of the Maharaja who had provided this rare and costly spectacle to entertain his august visitor, the Viceroy, broke loose time after time. The Maharaja and his brother, the Yuvaraja, who looked like twins, displayed such vivid hospitality, contrasting with their charming, gentle natures, quiet voices and sad eyes, that we all felt the elephants had been very unkind to disappoint them.

On the third day some forty wild elephants, captured the previous week, were being roped in a stockade with the aid of tame elephants. The struggle put up by the big tusker, leader of the herd, and his subsequent humiliation as he rolled in the mud and sobbed with anger before his own cows, till his spirit was broken and he was dragged along by four tame elephants, exhausted and looking a little ashamed, and tied to a tree, henceforth a prisoner, perhaps for a hundred years to come, reversed our feelings. And we felt sorry for him and angry with man and disgusted with the tame elephants who, at the bidding of man, turn on one of their own kin and betray him to their common enemy.

The party lasted nearly ten days. When the Viceroy and Lady Irwin appeared for dinner, the guests, assembled in a semicircle, bowed, the ladies curtseyed gravely. Blame me if you must. But there you are : humiliating as it is for a messenger of the spirit to prostrate himself before a representative of the temporal power, I had to do it. It was the Viceroy's holiday ; speech-making was reduced to a minimum. " It is my privilege to drink to the health of our very hospitable host," from the Viceroy. " The King-Emperor ! " the Yuvaraja said, almost inaudibly. And a number of dusky men repeated : " The King-Emperor ! " Proof of India's loyalty to the throne? I reflected that those who would have rather drunk the health of Ghandi would not be here.

One morning, while we sat there waiting for the elephants, I watched Lord Irwin's face, interested to see the man who had to mingle so much coaxing with rebuking; who combines the type of the young pioneer, when he is wearing his topee, with the sedate, scholarly type of face when he is uncovered. Presently Lord Irwin fell asleep, and his mouth opened. I had a vision, now that the titular head was in the realm of dreams, of all activity throughout India being suspended, waiting for the Viceroy to awake. The sight of Lord Irwin walking amicably arm in arm with the Commander-in-Chief, Sir William Birdwood, suggested another image, that of Lord Curzon and Lord Kitchener, who, I fancy, did not walk arm in arm. Lord Curzon's influence, however, is at once apparent when you visit any of the great monuments of Indian architecture. Here it is a lamp that he had hung and paid for out of his private funds. There, a cornice or a pillar he had caused to be repaired. Lord Irwin, however, was the most popular Viceroy of the last fifty years. And I am not surprised. He combines personality with a modesty which appeals to the Indians, and he goes through the farce of it all in a manner which appeals to everyone. Rather than invite idolators to worship his own graven image, he quotes, with reference to a bridge named after himself, from Tennyson's poem about the brook—implying that viceroys may come and viceroys may go, but the brook goes on for ever. "Fortunately," he adds, "bridges are more permanent than viceroys," and he expresses the hope that the water will still flow under that bridge when we are all forgotten. A graceful, moving sentiment, and not without literary merit.

III

HIGHNESSING INDIA

A strange mixture of inferiority and superiority is a prevailing condition with the princes of India. Inferiority, because of the colour prejudice which operates against them.

Superiority, because they deem themselves little kings and queens, while really being the equivalent of feudal barons. India is so rigidly caste-conscious within her own social structure that she might accept European condescension with better grace and understanding. But just because of this excessive caste-consciousness, which while despising an inferior caste is sensitive to being snubbed by a more complex civilization, the educated classes are morbidly self-conscious of the colour prejudice to which they find themselves exposed. The princes in particular find themselves baffled by the social paradox of their position. On the one hand, a maharaja is all but a monarch, and on arrival at an Indian port is greeted (always provided he is prepared to foot the bill) with a salute from British warships of as many " guns " as his eminence entitles him to hear. If he has a palace in any town in British India he becomes a leading social figure among the European community, who would consider it a privilege to be invited by him. On the other hand, his colour disqualifies him from joining a European club. The poor man could not plunge into the cool swimming bath without getting into hot water. " From the sublime to the ridiculous," said Napoleon, " is but one step." Is it then not natural that, snubbed by a white population, who may have nothing more than their fair skins to recommend them, men and women often of inferior education, the maharajas recoup themselves by an excessive interest in the privileges to which they are entitled. Hear one maharaja discuss with another a third and the " guns " to which he is, or is not, entitled. Listen to one maharaja addressing another as " Your Highness " across the tennis court—" thirty-fifteen to Your Highness." The word flies back and forth with such rapidity, it might be the tennis ball. The " Highnessing " that goes on in India is comic opera. I first pricked up my ears when Lord Beaverbrook referred to the Aga Khan as " His Highness." I felt I was witnessing a stage play. Later in India my palate— like that of a man once fond of ice-cream, which has become odious through over-eating—my palate winced at the mention of His Highness—Your Highness—Their Highness. Enough of a good thing. Enough now! Don't do it again.

Mysore competes with Baroda for the second place among the Indian states in order of wealth, area and general importance, the first being Hyderabad. Mysore is about the size of Scotland; a modern state run on constitutional lines. The Maharaja is a very orthodox, devout, retiring man, who leads a quiet life in the old palace of his capital, which looks a little like a pleasure resort in the South of France. Spacious gardens; well planned roads; palatial guest-houses.

Mysore is a constitutional monarchy of sorts; whereas in the North the maharajas are apt to be more monarchical than constitutional. If you ask any Indian whether a maharaja has the power of life and death over his subjects, he will say: "Absolutely." In reality, a maharaja has a little more power than the Home Secretary. By that I mean that if the Home Secretary cannot, whatever his ingenuity, hang a man on the ground of personal antipathy, it would require considerable ingenuity on the part of a maharaja to do so.

India is a curious combination of splendour and shabbiness. You behold, from a distance, a palace which looks as if it were out of the Arabian nights. You inspect the interior, and find a really ghastly combination of colours, and furniture which may have come from the Tottenham Court Road. Or there is a floor of Italian marble shipped all the way from Venice—under a whitewashed arcade. Our European civilization they do indeed wear; but the suit is a little ill-fitting.

IV

DEATH OF THE LEOPARD

The Maharani of Cooch Behar, who is a woman of great natural taste, and thoroughly at home in Europe, bridges the gulf with charming grace. The more orthodox maharajas affect to deprecate her europeanization; but in actual fact consult her in their affairs and invite her to smarten up their wives, mentally and socially, by her example. To the womanhood of India she stands for social progress. She is, in their eyes, a heroine. The only daughter of the Gaikwar of Baroda, her parents had intended her to marry the ruler of one of the leading states, only to discover that their daughter had preferred to trust her own choice and married the late Maharaja of Cooch Behar in a registry office in London, on the eve of her projected wedding. She hunts, rides, and flies, and since her husband's death rules over her subjects. Her palace in Cooch Behar is surrounded by the jungle, and at night one can hear a savage kind of music—cries of jackals who, unless you shut your doors, are apt to come into your bedroom and nibble at your toes. One such miscreant actually carried away a guest's slipper.

Leopards and tigers abound, and I had the privilege of assisting at the death of a leopard. We set out on the backs of howda elephants, with their feminine waddle, while another party on elephants scoured the jungle and advanced towards us in extended order, the elephants breaking the trees with their trunks and stamping the ground before them. It was not till the third day that the culprit, who had killed several cows in the neighbourhood, was tracked and surrounded. She (for it was a lady) showed no fight at all but hid herself under a bush, and only her eyes glared and she growled diffidently, as if not sure of herself. Then came several shots. She died quietly. One of the elephants was invited to kneel down. The leopard was hauled up by the tail and flung across the elephant's back, a big, spotted cat with eyes closed, asleep for ever; and back we went, the elephants trudging heavily, brushing past branches, as the sun set on the jungle.

V

THE PARADOX OF INDIA

" Where there is vision," says Mr. Kingsmill, " the people perish. I admit," he hastens to add, " they perish also where there is no vision. Either way, in fact, their situation appears to be damnably awkward."

I am in no wise a politician and I would deprecate any attempt (if such were made) to call me a prophet. Nevertheless, what struck me during my brief but extensive tour of India is the political enthusiasm of the Indians over questions of national and social franchise, so tediously familiar and threadbare to us Europeans that Indian grievances inspire in us a sympathetic yawn. India may have been treated a little unkindly in the past, but her way of complaining is cruelly boring. In India (like Queen Victoria who came across many Highlanders in the Highlands) I met many Indians—among them one man of outstanding intellect, but such amazing vanity that it was a pity he was not king, for he carried the solution of India, of the world, of the universe, in his pocket. It was a pity, I said to him, he was not God. Sir Hari Singh Gour himself seemed to share my regret. Sir Hari, besides being a politician, is an eminent barrister, a scholar, and a philosopher of note, and I found his book, " The Spirit of Buddhism " edifying reading. But the other politicians who surrounded me in Bombay emitted such sad, bad stuff on me that I felt ill-used. What had I done to deserve such mental punishment ?

I will contribute my quota to the view which already prevails about the situation in India by adding that it is a question " so beset with difficulties." It may be, however (since brevity is reported to be a virtue), summarized in two sentences.

The British attitude to the Indians resolves into :

" We can do nothing till you show signs that you can contain yourselves in patience."

And the Indian repartee :

" Your showing little sign of wanting to do anything makes it difficult for us to contain ourselves in patience."

Round this impasse, speeches are spun and the phrase " in the fullness of time " is mentioned with a certain relish which causes one to correct one's initial impression of the dire humourlessness of the speaker and to believe that he must indeed be a finished ironist.

Throughout my tour I was reminded of the feeling which

prevailed in Russia on the eve of the revolution : inarticulate, unfocussed dissatisfaction with the present state of things and no very workable alternative to take its place.

What distinguishes India from other continents is that there are in India to-day more sections of people suffering from dissimilar grievances, imaginary and real, than anywhere else in the world. What adds to the confusion which arises out of such multiplicity of motives is an all-round hesitation. There is, for one, the hesitation of the far-sighted Indian to let the British go. This hesitation would grow into a real anxiety that the English should stay—were it not that the English hesitated going.

What strikes one at once in India is the morbid feeling of inferiority in the educated Indians towards the ruling English race—a feeling which in varying degrees embraces (though far from uniting) the whole population of India, irrespective of race, class, or religion.

Another feature of the Indian situation is a grievance latent in the Moslem minority, who grudge the English a place once occupied by themselves and who would like to occupy it again. They criticize the morality of British rule on the ground that, unlike themselves, who have become Indians, the British resident in India has not allowed himself to be assimilated and has but one idea—to make money and to clear out of India as soon as possible. Which, considering the desirability of money and the comparative undesirability of becoming an Indian, is understandable. Equally so is the resentment of the Indian Moslem—but so, also, is the resentment of the British trader in India, who finds it more and more difficult to make money, in unrewarding exile.

Another interesting phenomenon is the growing democratic resentment against the princes, only merged in the common resentment against foreign rule, which, for the moment, permeates all classes ; and the consequent effort of the princes to reconcile their hurt pride (a circumstance inseparable from vassalage) with their real interests, which, as they know only too well, are furthered by British rule, with its protection from the growing democratization and indeed probable bolshevization of India.

But they are a polite people, and shrewd. Politeness and a candid admission that we are in India for our own gain will win any Indian's heart. Rudeness, high-handedness, calling them " natives," and at the same time impressing on them that the British Empire is the greatest agency for good, irritates them into questioning—Whose good? The intellectual lucidity (though I should hesitate to call it vigour) of the Indians is insulted by the incurable hypocrisy of a certain English type (ridiculed by Bernard Shaw) who must needs identify his own interests with the supposed good of others. Our claim, moreover, that we have the interests of the downtrodden at heart is only partly valid, because were we to withdraw from India, the downtrodden would themselves overthrow their oppressors.

But, on the other hand, the reluctance of British pioneer-imperialists who, in a trying climate, amidst dust, heat, dirt, smell and disease, have sunk an amazing amount of productive energy, not to say money (Indian though it be), to clear out of a country which, uninviting as it is, they have nevertheless licked into shape, introduced law, order, roads, railways, is equally human and understandable.

India's attitude towards England is like that of an adolescent daughter who can live neither with nor without her mother. And the position of the Viceroy is not unlike that of a mother of a young girl on board my homeward boat who complained to me that, whenever she corrected her daughter, the daughter did not answer back but withdrew into herself or walked away—the attitude, I suppose, which old Tolstoy termed " non-resistance to evil." What, asked the conscientious mother, could she do with a daughter who met well-intentioned criticism with " no-cooperation " tactics ? " Give her a good hiding," advised a passenger. "What! For no apparent cause! the whole ship looking on! Never! Besides, don't forget, she is now seventeen. And if I hurt her she would dislike me more than ever."

The Viceroy is in the position of that unfortunate mother. I may add that India is in the position of the perhaps more unfortunate daughter. Things being what they are, the situation is what it is, and the Government is doing what it can ; and accepting existing factors, if you incline towards prophecy, you must, as in a game of chess, arrive at whatever conclusion you may. You may agitate in Parliament for a " firm hand in India " ; or you may counsel a " statesman-like compromise." Either will do equally well—if you are fond of the sound of your own voice. Or if you hold another opinion, by all means retain it, since it gives you pleasure. But my own particular prophecy, based on my combined powers of observation and divination (such as they are), is this : whether Dominion status or Home Rule or nothing whatever is granted to India to-day or to-morrow, the result will be substantially the same—and, in the main, painful. One thing emerges clearly. There is nothing to be done—and we are the very men to do it. That is, to " hang on " to India, tentatively, complaisantly, almost absent-mindedly, while the Indians, a nation of barristers, exhaust themselves in garrulousness—hang on to India till the time comes when England will feel, without undue sentimental regret, that it is just as well, all things considered, to be rid of India. Since one day, " in the fullness of time," there will be neither gratitude nor material advantage to be got from staying there any longer. But we who believe in the recuperative, adaptive, improvising genius of the British race, view the future with—yes, equanimity. To face realities, to deaden the shock, to bridge precipices is, after all, the essence of statecraft.

VI

DEPARTURE

On my way home a route was mapped out for me to enable me to see Agra and Delhi, and visit Baroda. At Agra a gentle-man waited for me in the middle of the street, approached me several times, asking me to come into his shop, and, when I resolutely walked away, that man, and another who had come across the street, eyed me suspiciously. On the veranda a bearded man with some rubbishy pieces of skin again and again asked me if I wished to buy them. And when next morning I set out in a tonga to the Taj Mahal, two eager men on bicycles blowing whistles, like policemen, pursued and overtook me and turned out to be guides offering their services. As I said, wherever you go in India, you hear that this pillar has been restored by Lord Curzon, here a chip of marble has been inserted by him, there a cornice propped up. In the Taj he has, out of his private funds, hung a lamp. When I asked Robert Byron, who toured India with an eye to its architecture, what the Taj Mahal was like, he said, "I don't know. Probably awful." Nevertheless, I visited the Taj by moonlight. Moonlight being what it is, I felt the Taj was indeed a mystery of loveliness. The Taj Mahal, when finished, was so perfect that the Hindu king who had erected it to the adoring memory of his wife, ordered that the architect's eyes be put out, lest he build such another for a rival king. The Taj Mahal is described as "a labour of love."

The Maharani of Baroda, whom I had met in Paris with her daughter, received me in a way which made me think of her as a very kind Queen Victoria. I was shown everything worth seeing in the palace and outside, including the famous jewels and the performing elephants. In the afternoon the Maharani played tennis, which she does regularly despite her considerable age, with three Generals of the Baroda army. Then I stepped into the train and rolled on to Bombay.

On the boat for Europe the passengers—a medley of Anglo-Indian Colonels and tolerably good-looking virgins—depressed me. At table I was silent. Nobody knew who I was. I had not told them. Because if I had, they still wouldn't have known. So silence, in the circumstances, was, I judged, the more dignified course.

There was an Indian on board who was a little nervous of the colour prejudice, but being a proud man was ready to defend his human dignity. He complained to me bitterly of the humiliations to which Indians are invariably exposed at the hands of English passengers. But, as it happened, the English army officers who shared a table with him were quite nice to him; thus encouraged he finished by calling them by their pet names. When, on Christmas night, speeches were made, and the Captain was cheered by the passengers, the Indian got up on to the table and cheered louder than any. One thing he, however, dared not do, and that was ask a white girl to dance with him. This bothered him, and on the last day of the voyage he risked it. The girl could not refuse, but did not look happy. She was, however, a well-brought-up girl and when, at Pisa, she took leave of the passengers, all of whom she treated alike, she shook him by the hand and expressed the hope that they would meet. " Of course ! " he cried, " we'll meet. And when you come to Calcutta look me up, and we will go dancing together." There was a boy on board who had fallen in love with her, and as they parted she gave him a kiss. The Indian, by now the stage manager of the parting scene, said to me : " What a nice girl ! Didn't you kiss her ? " " No," I said. " Why should I ? " " I nearly did," he replied.

And when we came to Venice, which I had never seen before, the beauty of it took my breath away, and the three or four days I stayed there wiped out my memory of India so completely that I did not give a thought to it for months to come.

Arrived in London, I went to a hotel, and the next morning came upon two housemaids sniggering over a book of mine, digging each other in the ribs. I wondered what was amusing them, and saw it was a picture of the Taj Mahal, entitled " A Sigh of Love in Marble."

CHAPTER FIFTEEN

HOW TO LECTURE IN AMERICA

I

THE LADY OF RICHMOND

I ACCEPTED a lecture engagement in America as being in the tradition of a novelist's career. My lecture agent, rightly uncertain of my potentialities, did not transport me too lavishly. Whereas in the war I travelled, at Government expense, in a stateroom of the *Aquitania*, I was now conveyed in one of the smaller Cunarders, which had in the library innumerable photographs of ladies of title, including Russian non-royal princesses at two a penny, one and all described as Their Imperial Highnesses; which added to my irritation. There was also a photograph of Rosita Forbes dressed as a sheikh, with her hand to her brow scanning the horizon. This also irritated me.

The moment I reached New York I was subjected to a system of publicity interviews, which, until then, I had always believed to be exaggerated. I was advised by my publishers to have some witty answers regarding what I thought of the American woman, etc., up my sleeve. I wearily tried to remember what I had said of women at one time and another in old articles and recalled a tag about women generally being all different, though alike on one essential point, namely, in their desire to be different. I had used this remark more than once without anybody ever commenting on it. Now when the girl interviewer, pencil and note-book in hand, said to me, " And what do you think of the American women, Mr. Gerhardi ? " I paused as if for thought, and then said : " It is my considered opinion that the American women are all different ; but there is one point in which they're all alike ; " (I paused) " and that is in their uniform desire to be different." No sooner had this been given to the world than I was rung up by editors with the request to enlarge this epigram in an article. All through the country this tag, which I had used in England, presumably with reference to the English or any other blooming woman, without arousing the slightest comment, was now reported in large headlines : " British Novelist says of American Women ——." " Gerhardi says American Women all Different while all Alike." There were hints that I had sized up the American woman ; also hints that I had already overstayed my welcome, having come to extract what money I could out of the sheepish American lecture-goers, while flinging mud at their womanhood.

My first lecture was at Richmond, Virginia, and a very effusive lady with earnest eyes behind spectacles took charge of me from an early hour, insisting that I must see as much as I could of the sights before my lecture in the afternoon. She drove a two-seater, all the while telling me with great expense of emotion of her love for a certain young Russian Englishman ; and as she reached the crisis of her narration, ran at right angles into a street car standing peacefully in the bright noon in the deserted main street. We were all but killed ; but my hostess seemed quite unruffled, and as we got out of the car proceeded to show me snapshots of the man in question : " Look, here is Voldimar, taken in Switzerland last year," and only then noticed that the front wheels of her vehicle were all twisted and the street car had a large dent in its side.

I had never before lectured in my life. I had not even made as much as an after-dinner speech. And here I was being ushered into a hall as large as the Marble Arch Pavilion, crammed with humanity, and not a man among them, the audience casting curious glances at me as I walked between the rows, not unlike a vicar through his congregation. I travelled with a bottle of port in my bag and before each lecture I would take a pull, after which life seemed kinder and my lectures more profound and meritorious. Nevertheless, the President's statement that she would cut short her laudatory remarks, since she was convinced everyone was impatient to hear what I had to say, was not the sort of remark to put me at ease. I fumbled my notes and consoled myself that at any rate I had memorized my opening sentence, whatever might happen after. She ends; she calls on me; she sits down. I realize that there is nothing for it: that there are moments in life when one has to stand up and face the music. I stand up, blinking. Applause. I bow, thinking: "Don't applaud; wait till I've done, you fools, then you may feel differently about it." But I have already uttered the words: "Madam Chairman, Ladies and Gentlemen," surprised at the firmness of my voice, but a sickly feeling stealing over me that having said so much I must go on. A blur of expectant faces behind glittering glasses.

Years ago I had read that Mr. G. K. Chesterton in opening a lecture in Stockholm complained of the height of the platform from which he was to speak, expressing his anxiety that were he to fall from the platform he would create a deeper impression by his fall than by his lecture. This struck me as a very good opening. By preceding it: "As Mr. Chesterton once said," I could turn it to my own account. After a time I found that the qualification "as Mr. Chesterton once said" robbed the statement of a certain spontaneity, and in the throes of my ordeal I felt that Mr. Chesterton would not begrudge it me if I left him out of the business. So, in every fresh town, I would say to the representatives who met me at the station: "Has Mr. Chesterton ever visited your city or spoken here?" "Mr. Chesterton? No, he hasn't." "Good; that satisfies me."

"Madam Chairman, my Lord Bishop, Ladies and Gentlemen," I would begin, "I could wish that the platform from which I am addressing you to-night were not quite so high." A few looks of consternation; looks implying tactlessness in a speaker and offended pride in their hall. General expectancy. " I am aware that your hall is among the finest in the country. I am only a little afraid that were I to fall off this platform on to the floor I might create a deeper impression by my fall than by my lecture." Loud laughter.

These openings were all very well till I came to a place where, after first making sure that Mr. Chesterton had not lectured there, I discovered at the last moment that neither was there a platform to lend force to my opening words. It was too late to jeopardize my opening, and I said how glad I was there was no platform, for were there a platform, and were I to fall off it, I might create a deeper impression by my fall than by my lecture. There was no laughter. But worst of all were those places where the platform was no higher than four inches. My opening sentence did not carry conviction on these occasions. It was not so' much the fall of my body as that of the joke itself which the audience seemed to see before them. I had a small stock of other anecdotes up my sleeve, which I would produce in succession. But I felt that the audience, while mildly amused, expected me to keep up the supply of fun at the same rate. Here would come a little cough and a pause, and the prosaic part of the lecture would succeed the more brilliant opening with a certain amount of shuffling and hesitation on my part. I had two lecture subjects. American audiences had chosen " The ' Message ' of the New Generation," while Canada had declared itself whole-heartedly for " Love and Literature."

Much of my " message " was concerned with the essence of Proust. My attitude was really this : Here is this man Proust. I am interested : it seems to me he is about to make a difference to our attitude to life : let us now examine him together and see what we can draw from him for our own ends.

I have often heard it said even by the French (which shows that a knowledge of one's own language is, in the absence of other qualities, no passport to understanding) that Proust's style is not good because his sentences are too long. Now his sentences, I suggested, are long because, dissecting as he does life at a different angle from his predecessors, his mind illustrates to him several truths at one go, and he wishes the reader to get them at one go, because if cut into several sentences, they would pretend to a significance in themselves they only possess as illustrations. To a reader with a mind as advanced and cogent as Proust's, such reading is as easy and enjoyable as the reading of an orchestral score to a practised conductor, who would be impatient if the musical score of each instrument were offered to him on separate pages, accustomed as he is to take it all in at a glance. Such mental glances some men have and others have not; and to those who have them it is painful to see their peers criticized on false grounds, when the explanation should be sought rather in the incapacity of the cavillers.

I felt that I was falling between two stools. My audience had neither the subtlety for the spiritual equations of Proust nor the higher gaiety to appreciate the frivolities of a Max Beerbohm. At Providence, R. I., I struck the audience I could most have wished to avoid, one assembled for a drinkless collation on the occasion of Lincoln's birthday. The speaker preceding me, a local man, spoke without remuneration on the boy scout movement in America, fluently, like a man who has learnt his speach by heart, and importing a good deal of false emotion. I suddenly realized that my subject would not fit the occasion. The meal continued till ten o'clock and I felt heavy, distressingly sober. I thought, " Now I've got to get up. My God ! " But the chairman gave a tremendous bang on the table with a big wooden hammer and said : " We shall sandwich the two speeches with a piece of music in between. Miss Smith will give us a vocal rendering of ' Come into the Garden, Maud.' " She was the only woman in a sea of red faces and boiled shirts. I felt it was very wicked to expose me to such an ordeal. " And now Mr. Gerhardi, the principal speaker to-night, will, etc., etc." The President leaned back, and as I came up with my prepared jokes, smiled contentedly. My jokes and his smile vanished simultaneously. I heard myself talking, something about India, something incoherent and not to any point. I got very bored with India, very bored with my listeners, some of whom were getting up and leaving the room for a drink. Why was I given no drink? Why all this heavy, tasteless food? I finished on a note of some emphasis. I looked at the President. He smiled and said: "That was all right."

But next morning he wrote to my agent and asked for the money back.

Beverley Nichols, I heard, lectured successfully to the citizens of Providence a year before. I am not surprised. It was a ladies' night. Beverley Nichols is a brilliant speaker, he has a beautiful voice, and the platform enhances his stature.

II

LORD WILLINGDON RELAXES

By the time I reached Canada, I was so disgusted with lecturing that I only thought of the great day when it would all be over, and I would never have to lecture again. Lecturing was not the same as writing. If a reader does not laugh at your joke it's his affair. If a listener abstains from laughing at your joke, it becomes very much *your* affair. Leaving the Hotel Laurier, I walked disconsolately in a thin coat down the frozen snow-covered streets of Ottawa, where I did not know a soul. It was Saturday evening, and my lecture at the Little Theatre was not till Monday night. I saw a crowd, smoke, fire-engines, and I was told that a theatre was burning. A wild hope rose in my breast that it was my theatre, that I would be able forthwith to step into the train and roll back to New York.

No such luck. It was a cinema theatre that was burning. Let everything burn! As I walked, I saw in a bookshop a huge portrait of a young man. I gave it a sick glance. It was myself, young, happy, taken before I had ever heard of the ordeal of lecturing. Round the portrait, which bore a description of myself as a brilliant Englishman whom to hear was sheer delight, were grouped numerous copies of "Pending Heaven." I hurried back to the hotel, and buried myself in my room. The "brilliant Englishman" got on my nerves. I have always felt self-conscious in talking, as if by the slightest slip in intonation I might expose myself to the charge of trading under false pretences. You cannot spend your first eighteen years in Russia without getting the habit of keeping the chin down, which stifles the windpipe, whereas the English habit of holding the head back gives a high, sustained outlet of melody. Added to this was the family habit of talking at incredible speed. In the circumstances it embarrassed me to be described in America as a typical Englishman, to be introduced as an *English* author, an *English* lecturer, as if the English side of me were the most, rather than, as it was, the least important part of me, to be asked questions about the English countryside, as if I were a product of Sussex. I like to be described as an Englishman without stress, with the lightest of touch. I would try to explain to my hostesses what kind of a bird I was. I would stress that my early background was Russian, that I went to school in Russia, and that it was the first language I learnt to speak, only to get them on the wrong track again in introducing me to the audience, and have people surround me after the lecture and ask me whether I knew a man in Sevastopol called Popoff. It is not that I regard being English as a first-rate investment; it is rather that I do not see why I should be put to the trouble of inventing a nationality for myself. Once I found myself sitting by the side of Osbert Sitwell, who said, after a time : "William, are you English ?" I affirmed the fact, and, in accents more reminiscent of the Neva than the Thames side, began to support my statement by some details from my autobiography. These, for the sake of clarity, I divided into three sections dealing, first, with the Italian barons and the German Ritter ; secondly, with the eventual landing in England, viâ Belgium, of my great-grandfather Henry, including a short, hypothetical account of the gold-stick whose granddaughter he married ; and thirdly, with the vicissitudes of William Alexander, and, on my mother's side, of Grandpa Wadsworth, whose corporal father put it across Napoleon at Waterloo. I was already well into the period when my father's father, on landing in Russia, travelled with his family in sleighs from Riga to St. Petersburg, wolves pursuing them, when I noticed that Osbert had, probably some time ago, turned to the other side and was conversing with a middle-aged lady of mournful mien.

Early next morning a very English voice inquired over the telephone in rather acerb tones why I had not replied to the invitation of their Excellencies to luncheon, and the voice seemed disinclined to believe that I had not received the invitation. I hired a car and was conveyed to Government House, on the steps of which I was received by a bespurred and aiguilletted aide-de-camp, who still found it difficult to reconcile my statement I had not received the invitation with the fact of his having sent it. Upstairs in the drawing-room we were arranged in a semicircle and every guest who arrived was made to run the gauntlet of introduction. Every new arrival I took to be the Governor-General, and bowed tentatively in shaking hands, only to realize that it was now the Vicar, now a visiting politician, now a mayor. The Canadian insistence on repeating a name when introduced struck me as excessive. A clergyman was being presented by the aide-de-camp to the other guests in rotation : " Mr. Smith, Mrs. Jones, Mr. Ferguson." And he shook hands and said : " How d'you do, Mr. Smith ? " " How d'you do, Mrs. Jones ? " " How d'you do, Mr. Ferguson ? " Then the bespurred A.D.C. vanished, leaving behind his incredibly tall colleague in a morning-coat. Suddenly the double doors into the drawing-room were flung open and the A.D.C. called in a clear, clarion-like voice, which contained a note of alarm, as if warning us to get out of the way : " Their Excellencies ! " In his wake, with a spring-like gait and a smile of amiability contrasting with the formidability of the announcement, flitted in the graciously charming Lady Willingdon, followed by her husband, like a playful old leopard in sober morning-coat and the universal affability of a man who had done everything, from captaining his team at Eton to representing the King in his distant dominions. Lady Willingdon charmingly, and with that youthful informality one might expect from lovely Tanis Guinness, assumed that she had met me in London and that I was an old friend, and how much rather, her perfect manner implied, she would talk to me than anyone else; and I sat at her side during luncheon and she told everyone to come to my lecture and that she was going herself and bringing her husband as well. When I asked her what sort of a lecture she thought I ought to give, Lady Willingdon was in favour of wit, daring, and above all brevity. It was clear she could not endure more than half an hour of my lecturing. I resolved to please her alone, and prepared a light, scintillating lecture which might have secured the approval of an Oscar Wilde heroine, a Lady Windermere, a shining, exquisite creature.

When, duly dressed and very nervous, I rang up the local manager an hour or so before the lecture to ask whether he would provide me with a drink to lessen the perils of lecturing, he advised me to go to a chemist myself, first obtaining a medical certificate which might entitle me to a bottle of invalid port. He was sorry, there was no other way he could think of to provide me with a drink. Could he, I then asked, provide me with a stand for my notes which would make me feel less of an ass than if I stood unsupported in the middle of the stage. As to this, he was very doubtful. He would try, he said, but he was not sure where a stand was to be obtained in Ottawa. He would inquire at a second-hand furniture store, but could promise nothing, nothing at all. On his side, he had a piece of news: the literary gent, a rare thing in Ottawa, who was going to introduce me to-night, would not be able to come. Did I mind walking on to the stage alone and plunging forthwith into my discourse?

Of course, there would be a band who would welcome the arrival of their Excellencies with "God Save the King," after which I might come on and say what I had to say on Love and Literature. I then inquired if the booking had been hot, and whether the theatre was by any chance sold out. What about the galleries ? I distrusted galleries. Well, no, he said. The booking so far had been very poor ; only forty seats had been sold. Enough, I gathered, to fill the first row and half of the next.

With a joy that was almost insane in its intensity, I leapt into the air and asked him whether he did not think it an insult to their Excellencies to carry on with a ridiculous solo performance in an all but empty house ; and the agent said that these were exactly his own feelings, but he did not like to offend me by suggesting that we might call the lecture off. " My dear fellow, my dear fellow ! " I cried, " you could not have done me a greater service, or afforded me a keener joy." I asked him to telephone to the Governor-General, who, no doubt pleased at being released from an irksome engagement, nevertheless with the obliging charm that characterises highly placed personages, replied that he left the decision to me. If I wished to go on with the lecture, he and his staff would attend ; if I chose to cancel the lecture, he would be pleased if I would dine with them at Government House at 8.45.

I was all in favour of dining with the Governor-General. Lord Willingdon, resplendent in medals, with his staff dressed up to the nines, treated me with a peculiarly satisfying blend of flattery, coming from one who could talk of " my Cabinet " and at the same time assume that your free pen may influence that public opinion at home of which he is but the paid obedient servant in Canada. After dinner Lord Willingdon relapsed into that informality which is so much more pleasing in a Governor-General than in a near relation. He talked a great deal, and with real love, of India, for whose people, I could feel, he had a genuine affection. He spoke of his days as Governor of Bombay and later Madras, of the

Willingdon Club he had founded, the unique social meeting ground for Indians and Europeans. He referred, in an adorable way, to " that rather marvel of a wife of mine," who during the war suddenly brought into being a relief organization as large as the Army and Navy Stores. Warmed with reminiscences, he went out and brought back an album of snapshots taken during his governorship in India. I asked him, diffidently, if he who so loved India would not please consider going back there as Viceroy. He laughingly brushed aside the suggestion in a way which showed that the idea, as such, did not displease him. But he had been away from home so long in the service of Empire; it was time, he felt, he settled down in the home counties. And when I read that he was appointed Viceroy of India I felt absurdly as if my suggestion had borne fruit. Earlier in the evening, an A.D.C. had handed me a note from Lady Willingdon who hoped I " would be very brilliant and shocking at the lecture and that her husband would come home and tell her all about it ; " and I felt happy that fate had spared me the ignominy of making a fool of myself. Descending the staircase of Government House, flattered by the way I had been received by his Excellency and gladdened by his champagne, I felt like Proust, who in similar circumstances taking leave of the Guermantes, could not help murmuring to himself : " Ce sont tout de même des êtres exquis avec qui il serait doux de passer la vie."

III

THE LAST AGONY

Early next morning I departed for Montreal, where I was met by the local agent who had brought a young Russian prince with him to the station to impress me, and also by the second-in-command of my New York Lecture Manager who, owing to some disagreement with the local agent, told me to call off my lecture. I met some Canadian friends

I had known years before in Algeria and we spent the afternoon together merrily ; and great was my distress when, some half-hour before the time originally fixed for my lecture, in strode my New York friend, and informed me that, the point in dispute having been settled, I could now go ahead.

I jumped into my clothes, and swallowed an omelette, while rapidly revising my lecture notes, since I had been informed that the Montreal audience, mostly elderly, would not tolerate a light, cynical lecture such as I had prepared the day before for Lady Willingdon, a revision interrupted by an interviewer and a photographer. I jumped into a taxi and drove to the Ritz-Carlton Hotel. I was exhausted mentally and physically, and it seemed odd to me that taxis and private cars should be pulling up at the entrance of the hotel, and men and women in evening clothes emerging and repairing to the cloakroom, evidently come specially for my lecture, while I was too tired to think of what I was going to say. The ballroom was packed, and programmes describing me as " England's remarkable literary genius and most brilliant lecturer " were being sold at 25 cents a piece. I divested myself of my coat and hat in the cloak-room, and crumbling my much-travelled notes went up to the lady, the local agent's wife, who was selling the tickets and said : " Do you know, I'm so tired that I can't connect one thought with the next." She looked at me hardly, without a trace of sympathy, as if thinking to herself, " This is our last chance of making any money ; it's bad enough without your not being able to think." I then asked if I could not have a drink to buck me up a little ; and her husband presently got hold of a waiter, who brought me half a bottle of champagne. I gulped it all down, and suddenly I felt revived and absurdly pleased with myself. I walked past the audience and on to the platform with a sprightly step. The chairman introduced me briefly and sensibly, without any extravagant praise, so jarring to a nerve-racked performer, who fears it will not be borne out by his subsequent discourse. I rose, and, in a voice which did not sound my own, began to deliver myself of a string of sentences, which no longer represented my present thoughts but those conceived long ago, and which, as I delivered them, seemed to me now open to criticism. I was so sure of myself, on the top of the champagne, so idiotically pleased with myself, that even when I knocked over the lamp from my stand my countenance remained unruffled. I picked up the lamp, which had not broken nor even extinguished itself, with an air as if I knew it could not have done such a thing, and continued my lecture. Having forgotten to consult my watch I stopped before the prescribed time, and the audience looked a little as if I had dragged them out of their houses on insufficient pretext. I then suggested that I might be asked questions, and the president very charmingly rose and said that I had very charmingly offered to answer questions. There was a short pause and then a very nice man said, very helpfully : " Will Mr. Gerhardi tell us about various famous writers he has met ? " The champagne was still working wonders. Finished sentences from old articles rose to the surface of my brain and I told them what I thought of, and in what circumstances I had met, Aldous Huxley and D. H. Lawrence, Edith Wharton and the Sitwells. More questions were asked. A plump, complacent elderly lady asked me whether I agreed with Bertrand Russell's nefarious opinions on marriage and divorce ; and when I said that if any of Bertrand Russell's ideas were unsound I had yet to see an intelligent disproof of them, the questioner grunted a sour " H'm ! " When I said that Stendhal's mistress, Mme. Dembovsky, who professed to love him, was very wrong in refusing to yield herself to him, two old ladies in the back row rose and left the hall. The lecture over, a number of youths and young women surrounded me with autograph books, and all of them I asked in turn whether they wrote books, and why not, since they looked so intelligent, which did not seem to displease them.

Thank God my lectures were over, and I could return to New York. There had been a few agreeable by-pleasures, as in Richmond, when, after the lecture, a band of pretty young girls came up to me and murmured in low, soft, purring, southern accents : " We are the new generation of Richmond," and took me for a delicious ride in a car. I enjoyed meeting the local manager in Montreal, who had known Lord Beaverbrook as a young man and showed me the cement works and the Windsor Hotel, which were among his first flotations. But, on the whole, there was nothing but fatigue and self-disgust in it. Nor, most important, had I made a cent of profit out of lecturing.

IV

CEMENTING WITH MR. OTTO KAHN

New York was a different matter. New York exhilarated me. In New York I spoke on the wireless. But whereas, at Savoy Hill, I read a short story, reclining comfortably in a soft chair in a little room all to myself, in New York I was crowded into a cubicle which contained a lady, who introduced me into her weekly twenty minutes' literary talk, and a pianist ready to take over, and an announcer, who begged me to keep my feet away from the coils of wire lying all around, and not lean on this, or touch that, if I didn't want the lot of them to be blown into the air, and three operators grinning at one through a glass window while one spoke. As it happened, my speech fell a few minutes short and the literary lady jumped in with : " Thank you, Mr. Gerhardi, we have enjoyed your speech very much," and, herself falling short by a few minutes, the pianist leapt into the breach with an intermezzo.

Next I mingled in Greenwich Village with the American intelligentsia. A fascinating Jewish girl, lying like a lioness on a couch, read aloud from Schopenhauer and later put some of his theories into practice. New York women reporters, calling on me to inquire as to my views on love and sex, would sometimes allow me to cut short the theory by a practical illustration. I was questioned about my rumoured engagement to a beautiful young widow of New York. "Do you intend to discontinue your love affairs after marriage?" "I repudiate your suggestion with contempt."

And I was fortunate to meet Mr. Horace Liveright and go to his parties, which, as Mr. Horace Liveright knows, are unique. I was well placed between Carmen Barnes, the youthful author of the successful "Schoolgirl," and admired her thin hands. On my left was a girl, who turned to me more and more, while Maurice Hanline's face grew increasingly sombre. "What's the matter, Maurice?" I said at last.

"I love the bitch," he replied, and a tear glistened in his eye.

Altogether, Maurice Hanline, who is Liveright's right hand man, is of a lugubrious nature. I remember how he and I went together to the second performance of "Journey's End" in London and how when I looked at him I saw he was in tears. He cabled, with my support, to Liveright, recommending him to buy the American rights of the play. Liveright disregarded our advice and, as he said, has never since ceased to kick himself for it.

That day I met at Miss Hoyt-Wiborg's a lady, whose name I did not catch, but who informed me that I was going to meet her husband at Mr. Liveright's party that night. And now her husband, none other than Mr. Otto Kahn, cape on, very debonair, and a nice grey moustache, looked in as I was turning to the "Schoolgirl." The other guests, determined to show that a millionaire could not intimidate them, took no notice of Mr. Kahn, while I, anxious to cement my acquaintance with him, invited him to share my admiration for the hands of the author of "Schoolgirl."

Mr. Otto Kahn promised to give a party for me, but later forgot about it; whereas I was anxious to cement my acquaintance with him in some useful way which might lead him to produce a play of mine, which so far nobody else had seen fit to produce. I did indeed once give it to Robert

Loraine, and as there were no male parts in it worthy of his virility, suggested that he take the part of an old woman. He did not reply.

One morning I was rung up on the telephone, but cut off before I had time to speak. I thought it might be Mr. Otto Kahn ringing me up. I inquired from the telephone operator who the gentleman was. He had not left a name. All she could say was that he had a foreign accent.

It turned out to be Mr. Cecil Beaton, who was laid up at his hotel with a cold, while I was similarly entrenched in mine ; and we rang each other daily to sustain each other's spirits. When I told Cecil Beaton that he had been described to me as having a foreign accent, he said : "I know. In Chicago they always ask me whether I am French. It is *so* funny !" I sympathized with his being ill. He agreed that it was "*so* unfunny !"

Mr. Otto Kahn, nevertheless, seemed to have forgotten about the party which was to cement my acquaintance with him. The next night at dinner I found myself sitting beside a very good-looking young woman, whose name I was trying to wheedle out of her, while she was trying to find out who I was. When I at last disclosed my identity she expressed genuine delight, having read with real pleasure my earlier books and, as is the tradition of readers, being proportionately hard on my latter ones. When, in return, I insisted on a disclosure of her identity, she told me that her married name would not convey anything, but that I might have heard of her father, a man called Otto Kahn. At once visions of cementing my acquaintance with Otto Kahn, with a view to the eventual production of my play, flooded my brain. I had been discomfited earlier in the evening, for as I was hurriedly dressing for dinner I discovered that my patent leather shoes had disappeared. I had scant comfort from the hotel detective, who held out hopes of ultimately finding my shoes, for in a few minutes I was due to dine, and at Mrs. Vanderbilt's of all places (and if you ask *which* Mrs. Vanderbilt, I reply, with the King of Spain, " There is

only one Mrs. Vanderbilt, Mrs. Cornelius Vanderbilt ").
I accordingly drove off in plain black shoes, and felt rather
ashamed of them and tried to hide them under the sofa,
though I was repeatedly asked to sit down. But it is significant of the great world that nobody there minds how you are
dressed, and your apologies appear uncalled for, since they
seem to emphasize an interest in your clothes not shared by
anyone else. Mrs. Vanderbilt's drawing-room contained
an armchair with the cover ripped and the stuffing coming
out of it ; and there is, if the drawing-room is Mrs. Vanderbilt's, a distinction in that, too.

But the moment I felt I was once more in a fair way to cement
an acquaintance with Mr. Otto Kahn I could heed nothing
else. Lady Louis Mountbatten was radiantly there, who
stirs a sense of brilliant well-being in everyone around her.
I had not seen her since a Whitsun morning in the country,
in the loveliest of hats, itself a creation of spring, when she
motored me at great peril to her Hispano, whose brakes began
to smoke by the time we reached London, to keep what that
day for me was a life-and-death appointment. It made no
difference. My one preoccupation was Mr. Otto Kahn.
His daughter, at my side, had quoted Rheinhardt to me : " Der
Champagner hebt die Hemmungen auf." I pretended that the
phrase had endeared itself to me, and rang her up next morning so that she might ask me round to tea. Once in her
house, I stayed. Tea was long over, dinner was near. Otto
Kahn must arrive at any moment, and then I could at last
cement my acquaintance with him. There came a time
when Mrs. Ryan, born Miss Kahn, began to look as if I might
soon decide to go. But I knew how sick Otto Kahn would
feel afterwards at the lost opportunity, and sat resolutely on.
My hostess informed me that she and her husband were
dining with her father and mother on the floor below (for
Otto Kahn's mansion in Fifth Avenue is of a size to accommodate a dozen families). It was to be a family gathering to
discuss her husband's new venture in journalism. I felt it
would suit me perfectly to assist at such a gathering ; and

after a while Miss Kahn shyly decided she would go and tell her mother I was here, so that I might dine with them.

Mrs. Kahn did indeed, with unexpected enthusiasm, though I now protested that I was not dressed, ask me to stay to dinner; and a moment after Otto Kahn himself came in, and beholding me said: "This is indeed a pleasant surprise!"

I shook him long and passionately by the hand. Here was I; there was he. It could have happened so easily that our roads had diverged and that Otto Kahn would never have had the opportunity to produce my play. What use then remorse? If we had missed each other no posthumous regrets would have availed. But it had been ordered otherwise.

At dinner Otto Kahn talked at length and with animation of the state of the theatre, of the poor class of plays which were being produced; and I tried to make him feel how right he was. Here was my own play, for example, and with nobody in sight to produce it. And Otto Kahn said that this was precisely what always happened. When I was dead and buried, someone would arise and produce it.

After dinner, as we moved into the Italian room, I was just about to expand this point of his, leading up to the conclusion that Otto Kahn himself was the man to avert this posthumous tragedy, when, suddenly, he gave an eerie laugh and vanished into another room with his son-in-law to continue the family conversation in private.

I never saw him again.

V

I ADVISE ON A CAREER

When I left New York, sleet was falling. The leaden waves splashed a cold, indifferent farewell. Liberty pointed her hand round, turning her back on me.

On board was a family from Providence, R.I.—father, mother and daughter. We sat talking and they told me about themselves; there were two boys, an elder boy, good at sports, mechanics, etc., and the younger boy, apparently good at nothing. My interest was at once aroused on behalf of the younger boy. I warned them not to be too sure in forming their judgment; since I had known a case where the fault, as it turned out later, lay not with the boy, but with the judgment. I told them of a boy of twelve in the South of France. His father was a motor-car agent, and this boy, because he had no interest either in motor-cars (just the sort of thing, I said, to attract a shallow brain), or in school, was dismissed by his parents, brother and sisters as a complete dunce. I had questioned the boy, and, by placing myself in the position of a man ignorant and anxious for enlightenment, had drawn from him an ebullient stream of information regarding the cinema world, which was the one thing that interested him and on which subject there was nothing he seemed not to know. To-day this boy is a film director. His elder brother, the pride of the family, is an inconspicuously successful motor-car salesman, in his father's business at that.

That was different, they said: that boy did have some interest, if only the movies; their young boy had none whatever in anything. "An ass!" said the father.

Were they quite sure? I persisted. Was there nothing at all? How did he spend his leisure? What did he do alone?

"Oh, well—poetry," said the mother. "He writes poems," echoed the sister.

"And what is *that*?" capped the father.

Then I told them of my own case—of my own family who were no great shakes at things literary. "And to-day," I said, proudly. "To-day!" (as my thoughts whirled back to my lecture at their home town where the audience, after my attempt to hold them, had written to demand their money back), "To-day I can fill any hall in America if I choose as much as to open my mouth!"

New York had faded out. It began to roll. Striding up and down the deck, I reflected that "success" and "failure" and all the other fetishes which this complacent

Anglo-Saxon world of Test Matches, trade depressions, trade revivals, cherishes, was about as true to the essential richness of existence as a father and mother's disapproval of a schoolboy who has failed to " make good " at school bears any relation to their real affection for him. I understood that success and failure, pain, pleasure, sorrow and happiness were not realities to be attained or avoided, but the necessary ingredients of the nourishment we need. The body feeds on joy, the soul on sorrow, and they make bad dinner companions. Not the least of life's troubles is that in addition to reasonable grievances we suffer, oh, quite as much! from grievances which are unreasonable ; that little things can pain as much as big things : and we are tempted to ask whether suffering is not the indispensable aliment which the soul at all hazard must have to keep alive, so that, failing to find that fertile green vale irrigated with tears, it must, like cattle in arid lands, extract its fill from any sparse growth in the waste and sandy soil of indifference.

When I disembarked at Liverpool it was raining. The train rushed through fields and marshes sodden with fog and damp. My perfect though very youthful secretary, Miss Patricia E. E. E. Rosenstiehl, such a wise, sweet-tempered girl, met me at Euston. When we were driving home in the taxi I asked at once about the press-cuttings of " Pending Heaven," which had been out a month. " Tell me quickly. Are they very good ? " But she wrinkled her nose and said : " No-o. Rotten. But Arnold Bennett," she added, " has written a jolly nice review."

" Good old chap, Arnold Bennett ! "

The letters, accumulated during my absence, were a source neither of profit nor of pleasure. There were returns, over-due, from H.M. Inspector of Taxes, telephone bills, and other accounts ; press-cuttings I had seen before and in-vitations long out-of-date. I did not trouble to unpack, and on the whole felt as little pleased to be back in England as I had been glad to leave America.

Reverses, except in love, do not seem to have the effect

of lowering my spirits ; nor do I feel the need to give the unforgiving minute its sixty seconds worth of distance run, contenting myself, even in a crisis, with about thirty. Why must we, in the western world, dramatize everything, that is, make it unreal ? Can't we see that any "message"— even if it be "the quiet courage of the human soul "—is little more than grandiloquence, out of focus with our ever-changing, ever-deepening feeling of things ? If we artists write or paint, sometimes in the teeth of adversity, it is not "courage" which prompts us, nor is it the craving for glory or money, but because our nature impels us ; and that is the end of it.

For the artist beauty is inherent ·in everything, though the realization of it depends on the distance, the angle, the vantage point, from which we view it. So childhood, though it was to me the saddest portion of my life, the one least desirable to live over again, yet holds some precious feelings which, when tapped, release springs of happiness, and seem typical of that elusive life of ours whose "permanency" resides more in casual images caught on an impromptu journey than in the profession and activities we seriously pursue from day to day. And I am glad I have stepped out of the bog of childhood, the morass of youth. I thought of the unhappy American boy enmeshed in the tortuous years, which his parents, on the contrary, will later deem his happiest time, because it will have synchronized with their own happiest period when, having shed the shackles of parental discipline, they are just entered upon their own independent married life. But I am happier now, at thirty-five, than I have ever previously been. My interests in life are widening. My simultaneous work on several books suits my nature. I cannot push ahead with one book at a time because my method of slow collation of fragments from real life, and leaving them to seethe for months in the slow oven of memory, till I can see them more dispassionately, favours a simultaneous concentration on several works, with precedence for one in particular. My various interests and memories enrich my happiness. At the moment I am engaged on three novels and collaborating in a play, as well as on an extensive historical work, the reading for which and the human contacts it involves are affording me considerable happiness. I go out among my friends neither too often nor too seldom. I enjoy domesticity in my bachelor home. I think it is financial independence based on your own efforts, a balance of interests and passions, and the enjoyment of one's ripening judgment, as the shackles of youth are cast aside, which work for happiness; and not for anything in the world would I exchange the slowly advancing years for the pink miseries of youth or my unhappy childhood.

I like sometimes to tease my mother by saying that I have decided to give up writing and take up dirt-track racing, conjuring, or psycho-analysis as a profession; that they are sure to prove uphill, impecunious work at first, but in the long run—who knows?—perhaps more rewarding. My mother, who apparently can never be sure of the extent of my sanity, takes me seriously and dissuades me from these sudden whims in favour of the writing of fiction, since I have, she remarks, made some little start in that direction. And she thinks my friendship with Lord Beaverbrook may prove useful, and regrets that Lord Rothermere's interest in my "brains"—so surprising in view of my believed dullness as a child—should after all have proved of a transitory nature.

But *I* say that "failure" has let no man down. Lack of success with women did not prevent a man like Stendhal from writing the most successful romances. Nor indeed has my failure as a lecturer apparently prevented me from publishing my autobiography. And, for my own part, I would welcome a work in three volumes by an unknown man explaining why he has failed in his examination. Such a book, intensely human, ought to reveal a few things; at worst, is bound to be unconsciously humorous, and, at the very worst, cannot but explain why the author has failed in his examination.

But recognition in life comes sooner or later. On the 6th of August, 1930, I drove triumphantly through the streets of London, densely lined with cheering crowds. As my vehicle plied slowly between cordons of police holding back the eager mob, shouts of welcome rang through the air. It was the lunch hour. Office girls and shop girls pressed forward eagerly, and mothers with small children in their arms were conspicuous. The windows overlooking the route teemed with faces, and boys were perched on the house roofs. Louder and louder grew the cheering, like a wild fire carried from branch to branch. " Amy ! Amy ! " the people shouted, as I preceded Amy Johnson, who was in a car just behind me, while I was in a taxi just in front, on my way to assist at the famous *Daily Mail* banquet, holding my fare in my fist, and mentally adjusting the fare and tip in conformity with the leaping meter.

VI

SPRING IN TUNISIA

To " get away," to " get away " from wherever you are, is the strongest of human impulses. This half desolate shore of Tunisia harmonizes so well with my mood, with the joy of being subjective, throwing my inveterate practice of objectivity overboard, for once. As yet this shore is desolate, and the brave little hotel is but a lonely outpost between the desert and the sea. When I alighted here a week ago, from a tiny train with doll-like carriages, I was enchanted. No porters. No cabs. A little Arab boy hauled down my suitcases, and set them in a ditch—then on his donkey cart. As we set off it began to rain ; then a storm burst. Half way to the hotel we met a female donkey and our own took a good deal of persuading to part from her, and afterwards hardly budged—" parce-que maintenant il est triste," the little boy explained. Now it began to hail, and the visitors at the hotel, who had taken shelter under the roofed veranda, beheld with curiosity the arrival of a drenched stranger sitting on his bags in the donkey cart, pulled by a meditative donkey who was " triste."

It had stopped raining, and I walked in solitude, between dripping lilac bushes, to the sea. The star-lit road extends indefinitely, as do my thoughts. And I do not believe this is the end of us, for at certain times, as now, we reach the essences of things which float above our mortal tangles and are more truly us.

In the morning the sun was up, the little white Arab town with its turrets and wall rising on yellow sand out of the blue bay, like a fairy tale. The rolling surges dragged wearily to the shore. They had rocked liners, and now— ugh ! they were tired. The stuffing was out of them. And suddenly there came a whistle, as I stood there, and a train went past. Where ? To Sousse, to Gabès . . . to the desert. Why was I so happy ? I knew. It brought back my childhood ; the railway whistle recalled another blown by the train that I longed to carry me away from school, from drudgery, from town, from Petersburg to the sea-shore.

INDEX

DUCKWORTH

3 Henrietta Street, London

1931